Organized Crime and International Criminal Law

Organized Crime and International Criminal Law

History, *Lex Lata* and Developments *De Lege Ferenda*

By

Kathrin Strobel

BRILL
NIJHOFF

LEIDEN | BOSTON

Library of Congress Cataloging-in-Publication Data

Names: Strobel, Kathrin, author.
Title: Organized crime and international criminal law : history, lex lata, and developments de lege ferenda / by Kathrin Strobel.
Description: Leiden ; Boston : Brill/Nijhoff, 2021. | Includes bibliographical references and index. | Summary: "This book presents the first comprehensive study of international criminal jurisdiction over organized crime. Taking into account a broad range of profit-generating crimes, including human trafficking, migrant smuggling, drug trafficking, and illicit trade in arms and ammunition, Strobel draws a concise picture of who can be prosecuted for what under which circumstances by analysing the current legal framework as defined by the Rome Statute, and by discussing future developments that could further facilitate such prosecutions. Whereas international criminal law in the strict sense has long been considered not to apply to organized crime, Strobel convincingly demonstrates that international criminal prosecutions hold underexploited potential to bring leaders of cartels and trafficking rings to justice"– Provided by publisher.
Identifiers: LCCN 2021016929 (print) | LCCN 2021016930 (ebook) | ISBN 9789004462571 (hardback) | ISBN 9789004462588 (ebook)
Subjects: LCSH: Organized crime–Law and legislation. | International criminal law. | Rome Statute of the International Criminal Court (1998 July 17) | International criminal courts. | Criminal procedure (International law)
Classification: LCC K5240 .S77 2021 (print) | LCC K5240 (ebook) | DDC 345/.02–dc23
LC record available at https://lccn.loc.gov/2021016929
LC ebook record available at https://lccn.loc.gov/2021016930

Typeface for the Latin, Greek, and Cyrillic scripts: "Brill". See and download: brill.com/brill-typeface.

ISBN 978-90-04-46257-1 (hardback)
ISBN 978-90-04-46258-8 (e-book)

This book is printed on acid-free paper and produced in a sustainable manner.

Contents

Abbreviations

AFRC	Armed Forces Revolutionary Council
ASP	Assembly of States Parties
ATT	United Nations Arms Trade Treaty
AU	African Union
BiH	Bosnia and Herzegovina
CIFTA	Inter-American Convention against the Illicit Manufacturing of and Trafficking in Firearms, Ammunition, Explosives, and Other Related Materials
CITES	Convention on International Trade in Endangered Species of Wild Fauna and Flora
CND	Commission of Narcotic Drugs
COP	Conference of the Parties to the Convention
DRC	Democratic Republic of the Congo
ECOSOC	United Nations Economic and Social Council
ECtHR	European Court of Human Rights
ELN	*Ejército de Liberación Nacional*
EU	European Union
Europol	European Police Office
FARC	*Fuerzas Armadas Revolucionarias de Colombia*
FATF	Financial Action Task Force
ICC	International Criminal Court
ICCPR	International Covenant on Civil and Political Rights
ICESCR	International Covenant on Economic, Social and Cultural Rights
ICJ	International Court of Justice
ICL	International Criminal Law
ICTR	International Criminal Tribunal for Rwanda
ICTY	International Criminal Tribunal for the former Yugoslavia
IHL	International Humanitarian Law
ILC	International Law Commission
ILO	International Labor Organization
IMO	International Maritime Organization
IMT(s)	International Military Tribunal(s)
INCB	International Narcotics Control Board
INTERPOL	International Criminal Police Organization
KSC	Kosovo Specialist Chambers and Specialist Prosecutor's Office
MONUSCO	United Nations Organization Stabilization Mission in the Democratic Republic of the Congo

NATO	North Atlantic Treaty Organization
NGO	Non-governmental organization
OAS	Organization of American States
OECD	Organization for Economic Cooperation and Development
OSESG	Office of the Special Envoy of the Secretary-General
OTP	Office of the Prosecutor
PKK	*Partiya Karkerên Kurdistanê*
PrepCom	Preparatory Committee
RUF	Revolutionary United Front
SCSL	Special Court for Sierra Leone
SIPRI	Stockholm International Peace Research Institute
TDG	Thiodiglycol
UN	United Nations
UNEP	United Nations Environment Program
UNESCO	United Nations Educational, Scientific and Cultural Organization
UNGA	United Nations General Assembly
UNIDROIT	International Institute for the Unification of Private Law
UNODC	United Nations Office on Drugs and Crime
UNSC	United Nations Security Council
UNTAET	United Nations Transitional Administration in East Timor
UNWCC	United Nations War Crimes Commission
USA	United States of America

Table of Treaties, Resolutions and Other Legal Documents

I League of Nations

Convention to Suppress the Slave Trade and Slavery, 60 LNTS 253, Registered No. 1414, 25 September 1926.

Convention for the Suppression of the Illicit Traffic in Dangerous Drugs, 198 LNTS 301, Registered No. 4648, 26 June 1936.

II United Nations

Statute of the International Court of Justice, 24 October 1945.

UN General Assembly Resolution, A/RES/177 (II), Formulation of the principles recognized in the Charter of the Nürnberg Tribunal and in the judgment of the Tribunal, 21 November 1947.

UN General Assembly Resolution 217 A (III), Universal Declaration of Human Rights, 10 December 1948.

Convention for the Protection of Cultural Property in the Event of Armed Conflict, 14 May 1954.

First Protocol to the Convention for the Protection of Cultural Property in the Event of Armed Conflict, 14 May 1954.

Constitution of the International Criminal Police Organization—INTERPOL, I/CONS/GA/1956 (2017), 13 June 1956.

Supplementary Convention on the Abolition of Slavery, the Slave Trade, and Institutions and Practices Similar to Slavery, 266 UNTS 3, 7 September 1956.

Single Convention on Narcotic Drugs, 520 UNTS 151, 30 March 1961.

UN Security Council Resolution, S/RES/217, 20 November 1965.

UN General Assembly, Resolution 2200 A (XXI), International Covenant on Civil and Political Rights, 999 UNTS 171, 16 December 1966.

UN General Assembly, Resolution 2200 A (XXI), International Covenant on Economic, Social and Cultural Rights, 993 UNTS 3, 16 December 1966.

Vienna Convention on the Law of Treaties (Vienna Convention), 1155 UNTS 331, 23 May 1969.

UNESCO Convention on the Means of Prohibiting and Preventing the Illicit Import, Export and Transfer of Ownership of Cultural Property, 14 November 1970.

Convention for the Suppression of Unlawful Seizure of Aircraft, 860 UNTS 105, 16 December 1970.

Convention on Psychotropic Substances, 1019 UNTS, 175, 21 February 1971.

Protocol Amending the Single Convention on Narcotic Drugs, 976 UNTS 3, 25 March 1972.

UNESCO Convention Concerning the Protection of the World Cultural and Natural Heritage, 16 November 1972.

UN Security Council Resolution, S/RES/418, 4 November 1977.

Convention on the Physical Protection of Nuclear Material, No. 24631, 26 October 1979.

UN Economic and Social Council, Resolution 1981/40, Combating the traffic in persons and the exploitation or the prostitution of others, 8 May 1981.

UN General Assembly Resolution, A/RES/36/106, Draft Code of Offences against the Peace and Security of Mankind, 10 December 1981.

Convention on the Law of the Sea, 1833 UNTS 3, 10 December 1982.

Montreal Protocol on Substances that Deplete the Ozone Layer amending the Convention for the Protection of the Ozone Layer, 1522 UNTS 3, 16 September 1987.

Convention Against Illicit Traffic in Narcotic Drugs and Psychotropic Substances (Drug Trafficking Convention), 1582 UNTS 95, 19 December 1988.

Basel Convention on the Control of Transboundary Movements of Hazardous Wastes and their Disposal, 22 March 1989.

UN General Assembly Resolution, A/RES/ 44/39, International criminal responsibility of individuals and entities engaged in illicit trafficking in narcotic drugs across national frontiers and other transnational criminal activities: establishment of an international criminal court with jurisdiction over such crimes, 4 December 1989.

UN Security Council Resolution, S/RES/713, 25 September 1991.

UN Security Council Resolution, S/RES/731, 21 January 1992.

UN Security Council Resolution, S/RES/827, Statute of the International Criminal Tribunal for the former Yugoslavia, 25 May 1993.

UN Security Council Resolution, S/RES/918, 17 May 1994.

UN Security Council Resolution, S/RES/955, Statute of the International Criminal Tribunal for Rwanda, 8 November 1994.

UN General Assembly Resolution, A/RES/49/60, Measures to eliminate international terrorism, 9 December 1994.

UNIDROIT Convention on Stolen or Illegally Exported Cultural Objects, 2421 UNTS 457, 24 June 1995.

UN General Assembly Resolution, A/RES/50/46, Establishment of an international criminal court, 11 December 1995.

UN General Assembly Resolution, A/RES/50/167, Traffic in women and girls, 22 December 1995.

UN General Assembly Resolution, A/RES/51/207, Establishment of an international criminal court, 17 December 1996.

UN Security Council Resolution, S/RES/1132, 8 October 1997.

International Convention for the Suppression of Terrorist Bombings, 2149 UNTS 284, 15 December 1997.

UN General Assembly Resolution, A/RES/S-20/2, Political Declaration, 10 June 1998.

Rome Statute of the International Criminal Court, A/CONF.183/9, 17 July 1998.

UN Security Council Resolution, S/RES/1189, 13 August 1998.

Rotterdam Convention on the Prior Informed Consent Procedure for Certain Hazardous Chemicals and Pesticides in International Trade, 2244 UNTS 337, 10 September 1998.

Second Protocol to the Hague Convention of 1954 for the Protection of Cultural Property in the Event of Armed Conflict, 26 March 1999.

International Convention for the Suppression of the Financing of Terrorism, 2178 UNTS 197, 9 December 1999.

UNTAET Regulation on the Establishment of Panels with Exclusive Jurisdiction over Serious Criminal Offenses, Regulation No. 2000/15, UNTAET/REG/2000/15, 6 June 2000.

UN Security Council, S/RES/1296, 19 April 2000.

UN General Assembly Resolution, A/RES/55/25, Palermo Convention, 15 November 2000.

Convention against Transnational Organized Crime (Palermo Convention), 2225 UNTS 209, 15 November 2000.

Protocol to Prevent, Suppress and Punish Trafficking in Persons, Especially Women and Children, Supplementing the United Nations Convention against Transnational Organized Crime (protocol on Human Trafficking), 2237 UNTS 319, 15 November 2000.

Protocol against the Smuggling of Migrants by Land, Sea and Air, Supplementing the United Nations Convention against Transnational Organized Crime, 2241 UNTS 507, 15 November 2000.

Stockholm Convention on Persistent Organic Pollutants, 2256 UNTS 119, 22 May 2001.

Protocol against the Illicit Manufacturing of and Trafficking in Firearms, their Parts and Components and Ammunition, Supplementing the UN Convention against Transnational Organized Crime, 2336 UNTS 208, 31 May 2001.

UN General Assembly Resolution, A/RES/56/83, Responsibility of States for Internationally Wrongful Acts, 12 December 2001.

UN Security Council Resolution, S/RES/1446, 4 December 2002.

UN Security Council Resolution, S/RES/1483, 22 May 2003.

UN General Assembly Resolution, A/RES/58/4, United Nations Convention against Corruption, 21 November 2003.

UN Security Council Resolution, S/RES/1540, 28 April 2004.

Negotiated Relationship Agreement Between the International Criminal Court and the United Nations, ICC-ASP/3/Res.1, 4 October 2004.

UN Security Council Resolution, S/RES/1566, 8 October 2004.

UN Security Council Resolution, S/RES/1593, 31 March 2005.

International Convention for the Suppression of Acts of Nuclear Terrorism, adopted by A/59/766, 13 April 2005.

UN Security Council Resolution, S/RES/1718, 14 October 2006.

UN Security Council Resolution, S/RES/1903, 17 December 2009.

UNODC, Model Law against the Smuggling of Migrants, 2010.

UN Security Council Resolution, S/RES/1925, 28 May 2010.

UN Security Council Resolution, S/RES/1970, 26 February 2011.

UN Security Council Resolution, S/RES/1977, 20 April 2011.

UN Security Council Resolution, S/RES/1989, 17 June 2011.

Arms Trade Treaty, 3012 UNTS, 2 April 2013.

UN Security Council Resolution, S/RES/2194, 18 December 2014.

UN Security Council Resolution, S/RES/2195, 19 December 2014.

UN Security Council Resolution, S/RES/2199, 12 February 2015.

UN General Assembly Resolution, A/RES/69/281, Saving the cultural heritage of Iraq, 28 May 2015.

UN Security Council Resolution, S/RES/2388, 21 November 2017.

UN General Assembly Resolution, A/RES/74/276, 2 June 2020.

UN Security Council Resolution, S/RES/2554, 4 December 2020.

III Other International Treaties, Resolutions and Legal Documents

International Civil Aviation Organization, Convention on Offences and Certain Acts Committed on Board Aircraft, 14 September 1963.

Project of an International Declaration concerning the Laws and Customs of War (Brussels Declaration), 27 August 1874.

Institute of International Law, The Laws of War on Land (Oxford Manual), 9 September 1880.

Hague Convention (IV) Respecting the Laws and Customs of War on Land and Its Annex: Regulations Concerning the Laws and Customs of War on Land, 18 October 1907.

Charter of the International Military Tribunal—Annex to the Agreement for the prosecution and punishment of the major war criminals of the European Axis ("London Agreement"), 8 August 1945.

Control Council for Germany, Law No. 10, Punishment of Persons Guilty of War Crimes, Crimes Against Peace and Against Humanity, 20 December 1945.

Geneva Convention for the Amelioration of the Condition of the Wounded and Sick in Armed Forces in the Field (First Geneva Convention), 75 UNTS 31, 12 August 1949.

Geneva Convention for the Amelioration of the Condition of Wounded, Sick and Shipwrecked Members of Armed Forces at Sea (Second Geneva Convention), 75 UNTS 85, 12 August 1949.

Geneva Convention Relative to the Treatment of Prisoners of War (Third Geneva Convention), 75 UNTS 135, 12 August 1949.

Geneva Convention Relative to the Protection of Civilian Persons in Time of War (Fourth Geneva Convention), 75 UNTS 287, 12 August 1949.

International Civil Aviation Organization, Convention for the Suppression of Unlawful Acts Against the Safety of Civil Aviation, 974 UNTS 177, 23 September 1971.

Convention on International Trade in Endangered Species of Wild Fauna and Flora (CITES), 3 March 1973.

Protocol Additional to the Geneva Conventions of 12 August 1949, and relating to the Protection of Victims of International Armed Conflicts (Protocol I), 1125 UNTS 3, 8 June 1977.

Protocol Additional to the Geneva Conventions of 12 August 1949, and relating to the Protection of Victims of Non-International Armed Conflicts (Protocol II), 1125 UNTS 609, 8 June 1977.

Agreement between the International Criminal Police Organization and the Government of the French Republic regarding INTERPOL's headquarters in France (INTERPOL Headquarters Agreement), 3 November 1982.

Basel Committee on Banking Supervision, Prevention of Criminal Use of the Banking System for the Purpose of Money-Laundering (Basel Accord), December 1988.

IMO Proposed Multilateral Convention to Combat Illegal Migration by Sea, LEG 76/11/1, 1 August 1997.

OECD Convention on Combating Bribery of Foreign Public Officials in International Business Transactions, 21 November 1997.

Statute of the Special Court for Sierra Leone, 16 January 2002.

Rules of Procedure and Evidence of the Special Court for Sierra Leone, 16 January 2002.

International Criminal Court, Regulations of the Court, ICC-BD/01-01-04, 2004.

Resolution of the Review Conference of the Rome Statute, RC/Res.5, Amendments to article 8 of the Rome Statute, 10 June 2010.

Resolution of the Review Conference of the Rome Statute, RC/Res.6, The Crime of Aggression, 11 June 2010.

Elements of Crimes of the International Criminal Court, ICC-PIDS-LT-03-002/11_Eng, 2011.

Resolution of the Assembly of States Parties, ICC-ASP/16/Res.5, Activation of the jurisdiction of the Court over the crime of aggression, 14 December 2017.

IV Regional Legislation

IV.1 African Union

African Union Convention on Preventing and Combating Corruption, 11 July 2003.

IV.2 Council of Europe

European Convention on Extradition, ETS No. 24, 13 December 1957.

European Convention on Mutual Assistance in Criminal Matters, ETS No. 30, 20 April 1959.

European Convention on the International Validity of Criminal Judgments, ETS No. 70, 28 May 1970.

European Convention on the Transfer of Proceedings in Criminal Matters, ETS No. 73, 15 May 1972.

Convention on Laundering, Search, Seizure and Confiscation of the Proceeds from Crime, ETS No. 141, 8 November 1990.

Criminal Law Convention on Corruption, ETS No. 173, 27 January 1999.

Civil Law Convention on Corruption, ETS No. 174, 4 November 1999.

Council of Europe Convention on Laundering, Search, Seizure and Confiscation of the Proceeds from Crime and on the Financing of Terrorism, CETS No. 198, 16 May 2005.

IV.3 European Union

Convention based on Article K.3 of the Treaty on European Union, on the establishment of a European Police Office (Europol Convention), OJ C 316, 27 November 1995.

Joint action of 21 December 1998 adopted by the Council on the basis of Article K.3 of the Treaty on European Union, on making it a criminal offence to participate in a criminal organisation in the Member States of the European Union, 98/733/JHA, OJ L 351, 21 December 1998.

Convention of 29 May 2000 on Mutual Assistance in Criminal Matters between the Member States of the European Union, OJ C 197, 29 May 2000.

European Council Framework Decision 2008/841/JHA on the fight against organized crime, OJ L 300/42, 24 October 2008.

Directive 2008/99/EC of the European Parliament and of the Council on the protection of the environment through criminal law, OJ L 328/28, 19 November 2008.

IV.4 Organization of American States (and Other Inter-American Treaties)

Inter-American Convention on Extradition, 49 Stat. 3111, Treaty Series 882, 26 December 1933.

Inter-American Convention on Extradition (B-47), OAS TS No. 60, 25 February 1981.

Inter-American Convention on Mutual Assistance in Criminal Matters (A-55), OAS TS No. 75, 23 May 1992.

Inter-American Convention against Corruption (B-58), 29 March 1996.

Inter-American Convention Against the Illicit Manufacturing of and Trafficking in Firearms, Ammunition, Explosives, and Other Related Materials (A-63), 14 November 1997.

Hemispheric Plan of Action Against Transnational Organized Crime, CP/RES. 908 (1567/06), 25 October 2006.

IV.5 League of Arab States

Riyadh Arab Agreement for Judicial Cooperation, 6 April 1983.

V National Legislation, Agreements and Orders

V.1 Australia

Criminal Code Act, Act No. 12, 15 May 1995.

V.2 Bosnia and Herzegovina

Criminal Code, consolidated as of February 2010, 27 June 2003.

Law of the Court of Bosnia and Herzegovina (Consolidated version), 49/09, 18 May 2009.

Law on Specialist Chambers and Specialist Prosecutor's Office, 05/L-053, 3 August 2015.

V.3 *Germany*

German Narcotic Drugs Acts (*Betäubungsmittelgesetz*), BGBl. I p. 358, 1 March 1994 (as amended by BGBl. I p. 1078, 2 July 2018).

V.4 *Iraq*

Statute of the Iraqi Special Tribunal, 10 December 2003.

V.5 *Kosovo*

Amendment of the Constitution of the Republic of Kosovo, Article 162: The Specialist Chambers and Specialist Prosecutor's Office, Amendment No. 24, Law No. 05-D-139, 3 August 2015.

Law on Specialist Chambers and Specialist Prosecutor's Office, Law No. 05/L-053, 3 August 2015.

V.6 *Rwanda*

Code Pénal du Rwanda, 18 August 1977.

V.7 *Sierra Leone*

Peace Agreement between the Government of Sierra Leone and the Revolutionary United Front of Sierra Leone (Lomé Peace Agreement), 7 July 1999.

V.8 *South Africa*

Prevention of Organised Crime Act 121, 24 November 1998.

V.9 *United States of America*

Instructions for the government of armies of the United States in the Field (Lieber Code), General Orders No. 100, 14 April 1863.

Table of Cases

I Post-World War II International Criminal Tribunals

International Military Tribunal, *Prosecutor v Martin Bormann et al.*
Final arguments by the prosecution, 215th day, 30 August 1946.
Judgment, 1 October 1946.

International Military Tribunal, *Prosecutor v Alfred Rosenberg*, Judgment, 1 October 1946.

International Military Tribunal, *Prosecutor v Baldur von Schirach*, Judgment, 1 October 1946.

International Military Tribunal, *Prosecutor v Julius Streicher*, Judgment, 1 October 1946.

British Military Court, *Prosecutor v Drohsin, Tesch and Weinbacher* (Zyklon B Case), No. 9, Judgment, 8 March 1946.

International Military Tribunal, Trial of the Major War Criminals before the International Military Tribunal, Nuremberg 14 November 1945—1 October 1946, 1947.

Military Court for the Trial of War Criminals, *Prosecutor v Toda Mitsugu et al.* (Kinkaseki Mine Case), Hong Kong War Crimes Trial Collection, WO235/1028, Judgment, 28 May 1947.

U.S. Military Court, *United States of America v Josef Altstoetter et al.* (Justice Case), No. 3, Opinion and Judgment, 4 December 1947.

U.S. Military Court, *United States of America v Flick et al.* (Flick Case), No. 5, Judgment, 22 December 1947.

UN War Crimes Commission, Case No. 7150 (Polish Forestry Case), 1948.

U.S. Military Court, *United States of America v Otto Ohlendorf et al.* (Einsatzgruppen Case), No. 9, Opinion and Judgment, 9 April 1948.

U.S. Military Court, *United States of America v Carl Krauch et al.* (IG Farben Case), No. 6, Judgment, 30 July 1948.

U.S. Military Court, *United States of America v Alfried Krupp et al.* (Krupp Case), No. 10, Judgment, 31 July 1948.

Entscheidungen des Obersten Gerichtshofes für die Britische Zone in Strafsachen, Volume I, 1949.

II International Court of Justice

Nottebohm Case (Liechtenstein v Guatemala); Judgment, ICJ Reports 1955, p. 4, 6 April 1955.

North Sea Continental Shelf Cases (Germany v Denmark; Germany v Netherlands); Judgment, ICJ Reports 1969, p. 3, 20 February 1969.

Barcelona Traction, Light and Power Company, Limited (Belgium v Spain) (New Application: 1962); Judgment, ICJ Reports 1970, p. 3, 5 February 1970.

Case Concerning Military and Paramilitary Activities In and Against Nicaragua (Nicaragua v United States of America); Decision on the Merits, ICJ Reports 1986, p. 14, General List No. 70, 27 June 1986.

Case Concerning Application of the Convention on the Prevention and Punishment and Punishment of the Crime of Genocide (Bosnia and Herzegovina v Serbia and Montenegro); Further requests for the indication of provisional measures, Order of the 13 September 1993, Separate Opinion of Judge *ad hoc* Lauterpacht, ICJ Reports 1993, p. 407, 13 September 1993.

Case Concerning Application of the Convention on the Prevention and Punishment and Punishment of the Crime of Genocide (Bosnia and Herzegovina v Serbia and Montenegro); Judgment, ICJ Reports 2007, p. 43, 26 February 2007.

Case Concerning Armed Activities on the Territory of the Congo (Democratic Republic of the Congo v Rwanda); Judgment, ICJ Reports 2005, p. 168, 18 September 2002.

III International Criminal Tribunal for the Former Yugoslavia

Prosecutor v Duško Tadić, IT-94-1, Decision on the Defense Motion on Jurisdiction, 10 August 1995.

Prosecutor v Duško Tadić, IT-94-1, Decision on the Defense Motion for Interlocutory Appeal on Jurisdiction, 2 October 1995.

Prosecutor v Dragan Nikolić, IT-94-2, Review of Indictment pursuant to Rule 61 of the Rules of Procedure and Evidence, 20 October 1995.

Prosecutor v Duško Tadić, IT-94-1, Opinion and Judgment, 7 May 1997.

Prosecutor v Zejnil Delalić et al., IT-96-21, Judgment, 16 November 1998.

Prosecutor v Anto Furundžija, IT-95-17/1, Judgment, 10 December 1998.

Prosecutor v Zlatko Aleksovski, IT-95-14/1, Judgment, 25 June 1999.

Prosecutor v Duško Tadić, IT-94-1, Appeals Judgment, 15 July 1999.

Prosecutor v Goran Jelisić, IT-95-10, Judgment, 14 December 1999.

Prosecutor v Zoran Kupreškić et al., IT-95-16, Judgment, 14 January 2000.

Prosecutor v Tihomir Blaškić, IT-95-14, Judgment, 3 March 2000.

Prosecutor v Anto Furundžija, IT-95-17/1, Appeals Judgment, 21 July 2000.

Prosecutor v Zejnil Delalić et al., IT-96-21, Appeals Judgment, 20 February 2001.

Prosecutor v Dragoljub Kunarac, Radomir Kovač and Zoran Vuković, IT-96-23 & IT-96-23/1, Judgment, 22 February 2001.
Prosecutor v Dario Kordić and Mario Čerkez, IT-95-14/2, Judgment, 26 February 2001.
Prosecutor v Radislav Krstić, IT-98-33, Judgment, 2 August 2001.
Prosecutor v Milorad Krnojelac et al., IT-97-25, Judgment, 15 March 2002.
Prosecutor v Dragoljub Kunarac, IT-96-23 & IT-96-23/1, Appeals Judgment, 12 June 2002.
Prosecutor v Mitar Vasiljević, IT-98-32, Judgment, 29 November 2002.
Prosecutor v Mladen Naletilić and Vinko Martinović, IT-98-34, Judgment, 31 March 2003.
Prosecutor v Milomir Stakić, IT-97-24, Judgment, 31 July 2003.
Prosecutor v Milorad Krnojelac, IT-97-25, Appeals Judgment, 17 September 2003.
Prosecutor v Blagoje Simić et al., IT-95-9, Judgment, 17 October 2003.
Prosecutor v Miodrag Jokić, IT-01-42/1, Judgment, 18 March 2004.
Prosecutor v Radoslav Brđanin, IT-99-36, Decision on Interlocutory Appeal, 19 March 2004.
Prosecutor v Radislav Krstić, IT-98-33, Appeals Judgment, 19 April 2004.
Prosecutor v Tihomir Blaškić, Appeals Judgment, 29 July 2004.
Prosecutor v Dario Kordić, IT-95-14/2, Appeals Judgment, 17 December 2004.
Prosecutor v Vidoje Blagojević and Dragan Jokić, IT-02-60, Judgment, 17 January 2005.
Prosecutor v Pavle Strugar, IT-01-42, Judgment, 31 January 2005.
Prosecutor v Fatmir Limaj et al., IT-03-66, Judgment, 30 November 2005.
Prosecutor v Nikola Šainović et al., IT-05-87, Decision on Ojdanić's motion challenging jurisdiction: indirect co-perpetration, 22 March 2006.
Prosecutor v Milomir Stakić, IT-97-24, Appeals Judgment, 22 March 2006.
Prosecutor v Sefer Halilović, IT-01-48, Judgment, 16 October 2007.
Prosecutor v Ramush Haradinaj et al., IT-04-84, Judgment, 3 April 2008.
Prosecutor v Pavle Strugar, IT-01-42, Appeals Judgment, 17 June 2008.
Prosecutor v Ljube Boškoski and Johan Tarčulovski, IT-04-82, Judgment, 10 July 2008.
Prosecutor v Milan Milutinović et al., IT-05-87, Judgment, 26 February 2009.
Prosecutor v Vujadin Popović et al., IT-05-88, Judgment, 10 June 2010.
Prosecutor v Jadranko Prlić et al., IT-04-74, Valentin Ćorić's final trial brief, 28 March 2011.
Prosecutor v Ante Gotovina et al., IT-06-90, Judgment, 15 April 2011.
Prosecutor v Zdravko Tolimir, IT-05-88/2, Appeal Judgment, 8 April 2015.
Prosecutor v Ratko Mladić, IT-09-92, Judgment, 22 November 2017.

IV International Criminal Tribunal for Rwanda

Prosecutor v Jean-Paul Akayesu, ICTR-96-4, Judgment, 2 September 1998.
Prosecutor v Clément Kayishema and Obed Ruzindana, ICTR-95-1, Judgment, 21 May 1999.
Prosecutor v George Anderson Nderubumwe Rutaganda, ICTR-96-3, Judgment, 6 December 1999.
Prosecutor v Alfred Musema, ICTR-96-13, Judgment, 27 January 2000.
Prosecutor v Jean-Paul Akayesu, ICTR-96-4, Appeals Judgment, 1 June 2001.
Prosecutor v Ignace Bagilishema, ICTR-95-1A, Judgment, 7 June 2001.
Prosecutor v Juvénal Kajelijeli, ICTR-98-44A, Judgment and Sentence, 1 December 2003.
Prosecutor v André Ntagerura, ICTR-99-46, Judgment, 25 February 2004.
Prosecutor v Sylvestre Gacumbitsi, ICTR-01-64, Judgment, Separate Opinion of Judge Schomburg, 17 June 2004.
Prosecutor v Eliézer Niyitegaka, ICTR-96-14, Appeals Judgment, 9 July 2004.
Prosecutor v Andre Rwamakuba, ICTR-98-44C, Decision on Defense Motion for Stay of Proceedings, 3 June 2005.
Prosecutor v Tharcisse Muvunyi, ICTR-00-55A, Judgment and Sentence, 12 September 2006.
Prosecutor v Emmanuel Rukundo, ICTR-2001-70, Judgment, 27 February 2009.

V Special Court for Sierra Leone

Prosecutor v Brima et al. (AFRC Case), SCSL-04-16, Judgment, 20 June 2007.
Prosecutor v Brima et al. (AFRC Case), SCSL-04-16, Appeals Judgment, 22 February 2008.
Prosecutor v Sam Hinga Norman et al., SCSL-04-14, Appeals Judgment, 28 May 2008.
Prosecutor v Sesay et al. (RUF Case), SCSL-04-15, Judgment, 25 February 2009.

VI International Criminal Court

Prosecutor v Joseph Kony, ICC-02/04-01/05, Warrant of Arrest for Joseph Kony Issued on 8 July 2005 as Amended on 27 September 2005, 27 September 2005.
Prosecutor v Thomas Lubanga Dyilo, ICC-01/04-01/06, Decision on the Prosecutor's Application for a Warrant of Arrest, 10 February 2006.
Situation in the Democratic Republic of Congo, ICC-01/04, Judgment on the Prosecutor's appeal against the decision of Pre-Trial Chamber I entitled

'Decision on the Prosecutor's Application for Warrants of Arrest, Article 58', 13 July 2006.

Prosecutor v Thomas Lubanga Dyilo, ICC-01/04-01/06, Decision on the confirmation of charges, 29 January 2007.

Prosecutor v Ahmad Muhammad Harun and Ali Muhammad Ali Abd-Al-Rahman, ICC-02/05/01/07, Decision on the Prosecution Application under Article 58(7) of the Statute, 27 April 2007.

Prosecutor v Jean-Pierre Bemba Gombo, ICC-01/05-01/08, Decision on the Prosecutor's Application for a Warrant of Arrest Against Jean-Pierre Bemba Gombo, 10 June 2008.

Prosecutor v Germain Katanga and Mathieu Ngudjolo Chui, ICC-01/04-01/07, Decision on the confirmation of charges, 30 September 2008.

Situation in Darfur, Sudan, ICC-02/05, Summary of the Prosecutor's Application under Article 58, 20 November 2008.

Prosecutor v Omar Hassan Ahmad Al Bashir, ICC-02/05-01/09, Decision on the Prosecution's Application for a Warrant of Arrest against Omar Hassan Ahmad Al Bashir, 4 March 2009.

Prosecutor v Omar Hassan Ahmad Al Bashir, ICC-02/05-01/09, Decision on the Prosecution's Application for a Warrant of Arrest against Omar Hassan Ahmad Al Bashir, Separate and Partly Dissenting Opinion of Judge Anita Usacka, 4 March 2009.

Prosecutor v Jean-Pierre Bemba Gombo, ICC-01/05-01/08, Decision Pursuant to Article 61(7)(a) and (b) of the Rome Statute on the Charges of the Prosecutor Against Jean-Pierre Bemba Gombo, 15 June 2009.

Situation in the Republic of Kenya, ICC-01/09, Decision Pursuant to Article 15 of the Rome Statute on the Authorization of an Investigation into the Situation in the Republic of Kenya, 31 March 2010.

Situation in the Republic of Kenya, ICC-01/09, Decision Pursuant to Article 15 of the Rome Statute on the Authorization of an Investigation into the Situation in the Republic of Kenya, Dissenting Opinion of Judge Hans-Peter Kaul, 31 March 2010.

Prosecutor v Callixte Mbarushimana, ICC-01/04-01/10, Decision on the confirmation of charges, 16 December 2011.

Prosecutor v Francis Kirimi Muthaura et al., ICC-01/09-02/11, Decision on the Confirmation of Charges Pursuant to Article 61(7)(a) and (b) of the Rome Statute, 23 January 2012.

Prosecutor v Wlliam Samoei Ruto, Henry Kiprono Kosgey and Joshua Arap Sang, ICC-01/09-01/11, Decision on the Confirmation of Charges Pursuant to Article 61(7)(a) and (b) of the Rome Statute, 23 January 2012.

Prosecutor v Thomas Lubanga Dyilo, ICC-01/04-01/06, Judgment, 14 March 2012.

Prosecutor v Callixte Mbarushimana, ICC-01/04-01/10, Judgment on the appeal of the Prosecutor against the decision of Pre-Trial Chamber I of 16 December 2011 entitled 'Decision on the confirmation of charges', Separate Opinion of Judge Silvia Fernández de Gurmendi, 30 May 2012.

Prosecutor v Mathieu Ngudjolo Chui, ICC-01/04-02/12, Judgment pursuant to Article 74 of the Statute, Concurring Opinion of Judge Christine Van den Wyngaert, 18 December 2012.

Situation on the Registered Vessels of the Union of Comoros, the Hellenic Republic and the Kingdom of Cambodia, ICC-01/13, Referral of the "Union of the Comoros" with respect to the 31 May 2010 Israeli raid on the Humanitarian Aid Flotilla bound for Gaza Strip, requesting the Prosecutor of the International Criminal Court pursuant to Articles 12,13 and 14 of the Rome Statute to initiate an investigation into the crimes committed within the Court's jurisdiction, arising from this raid, 14 May 2013.

Prosecutor v Germain Katanga, ICC-01/04-01/07, Judgment on the appeal of Mr Germain Katanga against the decision of Trial Chamber II of 21 November 2012 entitled "Decision on the implementation of regulation 55 of the Regulations of the Court and severing the charges against the accused persons", Dissenting Opinion of Judge Cuno Tarfusser, 27 March 2013.

Prosecutor v Germain Katanga, ICC-01/04-01/07, Decision transmitting additional legal and factual material (regulation 55(2) and 55(3) of the Regulations of the Court), 15 May 2013.

Prosecutor v Saif Al-Islam Gadaffi and Abdullah Al-Senussi, ICC-01/11-01/11, Decision on the Admissibility of the Case against Saif Al-Islam Gaddafi, 31 May 2013.

Prosecutor v Saif Al-Islam Gadaffi and Abdullah Al-Senussi, ICC-01/11-01/11, Decision on the Admissibility of the Case against Abdullah Al-Senussi, 11 October 2013.

Prosecutor v Germain Katanga, ICC-01/04-01/07, Judgment pursuant to article 74 of the Statute, 7 March 2014.

Prosecutor v Bosco Ntaganda, ICC-01/04-02/06, Decision Pursuant to Article 61(7)(a) and (b) of the Rome Statute on the Charges of the Prosecutor Against Bosco Ntaganda, 9 June 2014.

Prosecutor v Laurent Gbagbo, ICC-02/11-01/11, Decision on the confirmation of charges against Laurent Gbagbo, 12 June 2014.

Prosecutor v Saif Al-Islam Gadaffi and Abdullah Al-Senussi, ICC-01/11-01/11, Judgment on the appeal of Mr Abdullah Al-Senussi against the decision of Pre-Trial Chamber I of 11 October 2013 entitled 'Decision on the admissibility of the case against Abdullah Al-Senussi', 24 July 2014.

Prosecutor v Thomas Lubanga Dyilo, ICC-01/04-01/06, Appeals Judgment, 1 December 2014.
Prosecutor v Charles Blé Goudé, ICC-02/11-02/11, Decision on the confirmation of charges, 11 December 2014.
Situation on the Registered Vessels of the Union of Comoros, the Hellenic Republic and the Kingdom of Cambodia, ICC-01/13, Decision on the request of the Union of Comoros to review the Prosecutor's decision not to initiate an investigation, 16 July 2015.
Prosecutor v Ahmad Al Faqi Al Mahdi, ICC-01/12-01/15, Judgment and Sentence, 27 September 2016.
Prosecutor v Bosco Ntaganda, ICC-01/04-02/06, Second decision on the Defense's challenge to the jurisdiction of the Court in respect to Counts 6 and 9, 4 January 2017.
Situation on Bangladesh/Myanmar, ICC-RoC46(3)-01/18, Decision on the "Prosecution's Request for a Ruling on Jurisdiction under Article19(3) of the Statute", 6 September 2018.

VII Regional Courts

VII.1 *European Court of Human Rights*

König v Germany, Application No. 6232/73, Judgment (Merits), 28 June 1978.
Piersack v Belgium, Application No. 8692/79, Judgment (Merits), 1 October 1982.
Timurtaş v Turkey, Application No. 23531/94, Judgment, 13 June 2000.
Nachova and Others v Bulgaria, Applications Nos. 43577/98 and 43579/98, Judgment, 6 July 2005.
Sergey Kuznetsov v Russia, Application No. 10877/04, Judgment, 23 October 2008.

VII.2 *Inter-American Court of Human Rights*

Myrna Mack Chang v Guatemala, IACtHR (Ser. C) No. 101 (2003), Judgment, 25 November 2003.

VIII National Courts

VIII.1 *Bosnia and Herzegovina*

Prosecutor v Samardžic, Judgment, X-KR-05/49, 7 April 2006.
Prosecutor v Gojko Janković, Verdict, X-KR-05/161, 16 February 2007.
Prosecutor v Bašić et al., First instance verdict, X-K-07/486, 26 December 2008.

Prosecutor v Miralem Mustafagić, Judgment, S1 2 K 005325 11 KO, 14 September 2011.

VIII.2 The Netherlands

District Court of The Hague, *Public Prosecutor v Frans Cornelis Adrianus van Anraat*, Judgment, 09/751003-04, 23 December 2005.

Den Bosch Court of Appeals, *Public Prosecutor v Guus Kouwenhooven*, Appeals Judgment, 21 April 2017.

VIII.3 Venezuela

Supreme Court of Venezuela, Criminal Chamber (speaker Cabrera Romero), No. 1712, Decision, 12 September 2001.

Supreme Court of Venezuela, Criminal Chamber (speaker Aponte Aponte), No. 568, Decision, 18 December 2006.

CHAPTER 1

Introduction

Just like legal economies, illicit markets have been internationalized over the last three decades because of political changes, technological advances as well as new modes of transport and communication. As a consequence, organized crime has flourished, becoming one of the most pressing issues of international cooperation. International criminal law, however, is currently not applied to organized crime. Thus, this book aims to analyze the pertinence of international criminal law *stricto sensu* to organized crime from legal, empirical, and historical perspectives; furthermore, it examines the potential of prosecutions of organized crime *de lege lata* as well as *de lege ferenda.*

Several observations lay the basis for the analyses in this book. First, organized crime is well established as a subject addressed by international law, in particular transnational criminal law. Numerous international and regional conventions cover various forms of organized crime, many of which have been signed by a large majority of States. Hence, wide support exists for fighting organized crime through international law as does a broad legal basis in terms of definitions and provisions to build upon.

Second, current efforts to contain organized crime—and thus reduce its repercussions—remain unsuccessful. Organized crime causes serious economic losses, has detrimental effects on peace and human security, hampers economic and social development, hurts the legitimacy of state institutions, and negatively impacts the well-being of affected populations.[1] However, neither national nor international law enforcement and the corresponding legal regime are currently effective at curtailing organized criminal activities.

Third, prosecutions of organized crime would both be in line with the purpose of international criminal law and account for the empirical interconnection between core crimes and organized crime. International criminal law *stricto sensu* was established to prosecute the "most serious crimes of concern to the international community as a whole"[2] that currently remain unpunished. Because of its numerous detrimental effects and the ineffectiveness of current efforts, organized crime constitutes one of these most serious crimes. Attesting to this is the crucial role of organized crime in the development of the Rome Statute. Moreover, organized criminal and armed groups, many of whose crimes

1 Kofi A. Annan in: Palermo Convention 2000, Foreword; van Dijk 2007; see section 2.1.5.

2 Rome Statute 1998, Preamble, para 4.

 | DOI:10.1163/9789004462588_002

already fall under the jurisdiction of the International Criminal Court (ICC), converge increasingly often, thereby blurring the lines between organized crime and international crimes. In this regard, the Office of the Prosecutor (OTP) of the ICC noted in its Strategic Plan for the years 2016 to 2018 that, "a lack of coordination of efforts from all actors makes it difficult to close the impunity gap for ICC crimes and *related crimes, including transnational and organized crime.*"[3]

Based on these observations, the absence of a discussion as to the value and potential of international criminal law *stricto sensu* in the fight against organized crime is surprising. The scant legal literature on the applicability of the *lex lata* to organized crime either focuses on specific activities and criminal groups, leaving aside many of the complex questions in this regard, or makes general claims but lacks detailed analysis.[4] The aim of this book was to fill the gap by conducting an in-depth study of the legal relevance of international criminal law to organized crime, of empirical and historical connections, of international criminal jurisdiction *de lege lata*, and developments that might facilitate the use of international justice in the context of organized crime *de lege ferenda*.[5]

To this end, Chapter 2 lays the basis for a legal analysis of international criminal jurisdiction over organized crime. It derives a legal definition of organized crime as the commission of one or more crimes by a "structured group of three or more persons, existing for a period of time and acting in concert […] to obtain, directly or indirectly, a financial or other material benefit."[6] The chapter legally defines and describes from a criminological perspective different categories of organized crime in terms of activities, organization, and geographic spread as well as its impact on individuals, society, the economy, and the State. Different activities constituting organized crime are categorized based on a market approach; that is, crimes are defined and distinguished based on the illicit product or service a profit is derived from.[7]

3 Office of the Prosecutor of the International Criminal Court 2015, 6. Emphasis added. In its Strategic Plan 2019–2021, the OTP sees improvements regarding its goal of closer cooperation of all actors "while still early in implementation": Office of the Prosecutor of the International Criminal Court 2019a, para 5d.

4 E.g., Smith 2009; Hauck 2016.

5 This book focuses on aspects of particular relevance for prosecutions in the context of organized crime. Analyses of justification and excuse, for example, have been conducted comprehensively in the literature and are not repeated in this book.

6 Palermo Convention 2000, Article 2(a); see section 2.1.1.

7 As a consequence, piracy is not included in the discussion of this book as it distinguishes itself from other organized criminal activities based on the location of the crime, i.e. the sea. Nevertheless, depending on the goods stolen and their subsequent use, crimes committed in the context of piracy are covered by analyses relating to different types of illicit trade and organized crime-related violence.

This book examines both profit-generating activities of organized criminal groups, such as drug trafficking and illicit trade, and activities that frequently accompany illegal market operations, such as corruption and money laundering.[8] Furthermore, Chapter 2 discusses the existing body of international law related to organized crime, including transnational suppression conventions and other relevant international treaties, regional conventions, and the international enforcement regime. Subsequently, it examines the relevance of international criminal law *stricto sensu* to organized crime from a teleological as well as empirical perspective, and studies the historical role of organized crime in international tribunals as well as in the drafting process leading to the establishment of the ICC.

The third chapter presents a detailed analysis of international criminal jurisdiction over organized crime *de lege lata*, namely under the Rome Statute of the ICC. First, it discusses questions arising in relation to procedural requirements for jurisdiction, in particular with regards to trigger mechanisms and the requirements of the Charter of the United Nations (UN) for a referral by the UN Security Council (UNSC); to preconditions to the exercise of jurisdiction and establishment of a personal or territorial nexus in case of organized crime that is spread over numerous state territories; and to the principle of complementarity and issue of corruption. Second, an in-depth study of the jurisdiction *ratione materiae* under the Rome Statute follows. With regards to three core crimes—genocide, crimes against humanity, and war crimes—the overall contextual elements and their applicability to organized crime are discussed. Moreover, the applicability of the individual acts enumerated in the different crime definitions to specific offenses of organized crime are examined. Among others, these analyses relate human trafficking, which includes forced prostitution and labor and organ trafficking, to individual acts constituting genocide; migrant smuggling and drug trafficking to acts constituting crimes against humanity; and the illicit trade in natural resources and cultural goods to acts constituting war crimes. Third, the Rome Statute's rules relating to the attribution of a crime are examined regarding the individual criminal responsibility of members of organized criminal groups. Different forms of perpetration and participation (e.g., of indirect and co-perpetration as well as of aiding, abetting, assisting, and contributing to the commission of a crime in any other manner) are analyzed along with superior responsibility.

8 See sections 2.1.2.1–7. In order to provide a comprehensive picture of the applicability of international criminal law to organized crime, the author bases her analyses on changing examples and facts.

The fourth chapter examines international criminal jurisdiction over organized crime *de lege ferenda*, discussing possible developments within the current legal framework, an expansion of the ICC's jurisdiction *ratione materiae*, and the establishment of a new specialized international tribunal. Regarding developments within the current legal framework, the analysis includes both material and mental elements as currently interpreted. Regarding the inclusion of new crimes in the Rome Statute's jurisdiction *ratione materiae*, criteria for new crimes are established and discussed along with material elements regarding drug trafficking; the illicit trade in arms and ammunition, natural resources, and cultural goods; migrant smuggling; corruption; and money laundering. Finally, the possibility of a new specialized tribunal is studied with regard to procedural requirements for jurisdiction, jurisdiction *ratione materiae*, and organizational setup.

CHAPTER 2

The Status Quo of Organized Crime in International Criminal Law

Organized crime has long been a subject of international law, transnational criminal law in particular, and numerous international conventions exist regarding various organized crime offenses. However, organized crime has never been prosecuted as an international crime before an international tribunal. Because the aim of this book is to analyze the potential of international criminal law in the fight against organized crime, the present chapter lays the basis for a legal discussion of *lex lata* and *lex ferenda* by answering the questions of organized crime's legal definitions, the effectiveness of current legal regimes, and the teleological and historical relevance of organized crime in international criminal law.

Setting the stage, this chapter first develops a legal definition of organized crime for the purpose of this book. It then proceeds to derive definitions for the most relevant offenses perpetrated by organized criminal groups. In addition to legal analyses, this chapter aims to provide the reader with an overview of organized crime from an empirical and criminological perspective. Thus, it describes the prevalence of the most relevant organized criminal activities, the most well-known organized criminal groups, and the types of organizations in organized crime as well as their geographic operation. Furthermore, this chapter discusses the impact of organized crime on various aspects of society. Furthermore, the existing body of international law addressing offenses of organized crime is examined with regard to its content and effectiveness. In the following sections, the pertinence of international criminal law to organized crime as well as the interconnection between organized crime and crimes conventionally addressed by international courts are demonstrated. Lastly, the role of organized crime in international tribunals as well as in the drafting history of the ICC's Rome Statute are examined.

2.1 Organized Crime

2.1.1 *Legal Definition of Organized Crime*

From a political science perspective, organized crime is first and foremost a social construct, influenced by its use in varying political contexts and with

 | DOI:10.1163/9789004462588_003

different ideological aims, which—at best—provides an "umbrella concept [...] for a broad range of people, structures and events in varying degrees and combinations."[1] With growing mobility and advanced technology and methods of communication, organized crime has become a "hot topic, [...] a catch-phrase to express the growing anxieties of national and supranational public institutions and private citizens."[2] One scholar argued that as a result of the elusiveness of the concept and a persistent lack of empirical evidence, stereotypes threaten to drive public perceptions, policies, practices, and research.[3] Thus, for the purpose of this book, developing a clear legal definition of organized crime is of paramount importance, and even more so because the concept of organized crime is to be analyzed in the context of international criminal law. The principle of *nullum crimen sine lege* requires a precise legal definition of prohibited acts before anyone can be prosecuted or punished for their commission.

Today, no consensus definition of the term "organized crime" exists. Nevertheless, existing legal definitions share two fundamental concepts, namely the activity constituting the crime and a set of persons constituting a type of organization.[4] Regarding the activity, organized criminal activities are an illegal enterprise of some sort supplying goods and services in illegal markets.[5] Regarding the organization, requirements differ regarding the degree of organization, its structure, and the minimum number of persons that must be involved.[6] Moreover, to further differentiate organized crime and "crime that is organized,"[7] a variety of elements are used in existing legal definitions, including in text books. In several comparisons of legal definitions, up to 18 different elements were found to be used in different combinations.[8] Nevertheless, a large majority of definitions include: a continuous or self-perpetuating

1 von Lampe 2002, 191.
2 Paoli 2002, 51.
3 Finckenauer 2005, 73.
4 Papachristos and Zhao 2015, 170.
5 Obokata 2010, 19.
6 Mitsilegas, European Parliament 2011, 8–9.
7 Finckenauer 2005, 76.
8 Hagan 1983, 53. The characteristics were non-ideological, continuing organized hierarchy, violence (force or threat of force), restricted membership, rational profit through illegal activities, public demand, corruption (immunity), monopoly, specialization, code of secrecy, extensive planning; Hagan 2006, 130. The characteristics were recognizable, monopolistic, self-perpetuating, hierarchical, violence/threats, corruption of officials, vice/illegal activities, criminal enterprise, ritual, rules/secrecy, organizational tithing, infiltrate legitimate business, planned activities, profit, adapt to supply/demand, non-ideological, exclusive membership, division of labor; Albanese 2011, 3.

organized hierarchy, the primary goal of profit from illegal activities, the use of violence and threats, and attempted immunity from law enforcement (e.g., through corruption).[9]

To arrive at a definition for this book, turning to definitions in international law is instructive. The UN Convention against Transnational Organized Crime (also called the Palermo Convention) and its Protocols are the most comprehensive and recent legal texts in this regard.[10] During the *travaux préparatoire,* several draft definitions of organized crime were presented. In a first proposal by the Polish government, organized crime was defined as

> group activities of three or more persons, with hierarchical links or personal relationships, which permit their leaders to earn profits or control territories or markets, internal or foreign, by means of violence, intimidation and corruption, both in furtherance of criminal activity and to infiltrate the legitimate economy, in particular by [...],[11]

before adding a list of specific criminal activities, including the illicit trafficking of drugs, humans, cultural objects, and arms. The definition was simplified later; for example, a proposal by the United States of America (USA) defined organized crime as "[the commission of] serious crime involving a group of [three] or more persons, [either for its own sake or] for any purpose relating, directly or indirectly, to the obtaining of a financial or other material benefit."[12] It then added a definition of serious crime: " 'Serious crime' means conduct constituting a criminal offence punishable by a maximum deprivation of liberty of at least [] years, or more serious penalty."[13] Over the course of the negotiations, the view emerged that an organized criminal group and the specific crimes covered should be defined separately. As a consequence, the Palermo Convention defines an organized criminal group as

> a structured group of three or more persons, existing for a period of time and acting in concert with the aim of committing one or more serious crimes or offences established in accordance with this Convention,

9 Hagan 2006, 128 and 133.

10 See section 2.2.2.1.

11 UN General Assembly Third Committee 1996, A/C.3/51/7, Article 1(1).

12 UN General Assembly Ad Hoc Committee on the Elaboration of a Convention against Transnational Organized Crime 1998, A/AC.254/5, 18 (brackets were not added by the author); see also McClean (Commentary) 2007, 38–39.

13 *ibid.*

> in order to obtain, directly or indirectly, a financial or other material benefit.[14]

This definition includes a number of elements. First, there must be a "group of three or more persons."[15]

Second, the group must be "structured,"[16] which is defined as "a group that is not randomly formed for the immediate commission of an offence and that does not need to have formally defined roles for its members, continuity of its membership or a developed structure."[17] While some organizations (e.g., the mafia) are highly structured and hierarchical, the drafters deliberately included other, more fluid organized criminal groups in the definition.[18]

Third, the group must exist "for a period of time,"[19] interpreted broadly as some degree of continued existence.[20]

Fourth, the group must "act in concert,"[21] excluding simultaneous acts by several members of the group that each act independently.[22]

Fifth, the group must act "with the aim of committing one or more serious crimes or offenses established in accordance with [...] [the] Convention."[23] A serious crime is defined in Article 2(b) of the Palermo Convention in line with the proposal by the USA cited above as "conduct constituting an offence punishable by a maximum deprivation of liberty of at least four years or a more serious penalty." Offenses established in accordance with the Convention include participation in an organized criminal group, money laundering, corruption, and obstruction of justice, as well as the offenses established in additional Protocols, namely human trafficking, migrant smuggling, and illicit trade in arms and ammunition.[24]

Lastly, the group must act with the aim of obtaining, "directly or indirectly, a financial or other material benefit."[25] The interpretative notes indicate that this motivational requirement

14 Palermo Convention 2000, Article 2(a).
15 *ibid.*
16 *ibid.*
17 *ibid.*, Article 2(c).
18 McClean (Commentary) 2007, 43; see section 2.1.3.
19 Palermo Convention 2000, Article 2(a).
20 McClean (Commentary) 2007, 41.
21 Palermo Convention 2000, Article 2(a).
22 McClean (Commentary) 2007, 41.
23 Palermo Convention 2000, Article 2(a).
24 *ibid.*, Articles 5,6, 8 and 23 respectively as well as Article 37 regarding the relation of the Convention with the protocols, and the three Protocols to the Convention.
25 *ibid.*, Article 2(a).

> should be understood broadly, to include, for example, crimes in which the predominant motivation may be sexual gratification, such as the receipt or trade of materials by members of child pornography rings, the trading of children by members of paedophile rings or cost-sharing among ring members.[26]

Furthermore, the Palermo Convention is limited to organized crime of a transnational nature.[27] However, this limitation is not a definitional element of organized crime but a question of scope of the particular convention.

The definitions of an organized criminal group and of a structured group of the Palermo Convention have been adopted, though not *verbatim,* in the 2008 Framework Decision on the fight against organized crime of the Council of the European Union (EU).[28] The Framework Decision, however, only requires two or more persons instead of a minimum of three.

For the purpose of this book, organized crime is defined in a manner consistent with the cited definitions in international law as well as with relevant provisions in international criminal law. Thus, organized crime is understood as the commission of one or more crimes by a "structured group of three or more persons, existing for a period of time and acting in concert [...] to obtain, directly or indirectly, a financial or other material benefit."[29]

The elements of a structured group, its existence for a period of time, its members acting in concert, and their aim of obtaining a financial or material benefit ought to be interpreted according to the corresponding elements in the Palermo Convention outlined above. The understanding of a group consisting of at least three persons, in line with the Palermo Convention but contrary to the EU Framework Decision, is consistent with interpretations in international criminal law; for example, the term group in Article 25(3)(d) of the Rome Statute concerning complicity in group crimes.[30] With regard to the crimes committed, the definition used in this book does not require them to have a threshold of seriousness. Therefore, the proposed definition incorporates organized crime in its entirety, including less serious offenses such as the sale of drugs to the end consumer. Depending on the exact circumstances, a sentence can vary in Germany, for example, between

26 UN General Assembly 2000, A/55//383/Add.1, Note 3; McClean (Commentary) 2007,40.

27 Palermo Convention 2000, Article 3.

28 EU Council Framework Decision 2008, Article 1; see also Mitsilegas, European Parliament 2011, 11–13.

29 Palermo Convention 2000, Article 2(a).

30 Eser (Commentary edited by Cassese, Gaeta and Jones) 2002, 802.

1 and 15 years of imprisonment, thereby falling short of the requirement of 4 years in the Palermo Convention.[31] Nevertheless, the offense constitutes an integral part of drug trafficking, a prime example of organized crime. Furthermore, with regard to possible prosecutions of organized crime under international criminal law, the relevant treaties—especially the Rome Statute—already contain gravity thresholds, such as in the contextual elements of the defined crimes and as a criterion to consider when applying prosecutorial discretion.[32]

These definitional elements not only allow a distinction between organized crime and other types of crime but also exclude crimes committed by groups that do not lay their focus on material gain, especially terrorist groups and organized armed groups.[33] Regarding terrorism, the international community has struggled for decades to find a general definition of the term.[34] Based on a sectoral approach, numerous international conventions have been developed that address and define specific types of terroristic acts, such as those on aircrafts, terrorist bombings, and nuclear terrorism.[35] The UN General Assembly (UNGA) described terrorism as

> [c]riminal acts intended or calculated to provoke a state of terror in the general public, a group of persons or particular persons for political purposes [...], whatever the considerations of a political, philosophical, ideological, racial, ethnic, religious or any other nature that may be invoked to justify them.[36]

31 German Narcotic Drugs Act 1994, §§30 and 30a.

32 Rome Statute 1998, Preamble, para 4, and Articles 6 to 8; see sections 2.3.2.1, 3.2.1.1, 3.2.2.1, 3.2.3.1, and 4.2.2.

33 An example of a less stringent definition can be found in, e.g., Bundeskriminalamt 2009, 8–9, which defines organized crime as "the planned commission of criminal offenses determined by the pursuit of profit *and power*". Emphasis added. See also the definition in EU Council 1998 Joint Action on Criminal Organisations (no longer in force), stating "whether such offenses are an aim in themselves or a means of obtaining material benefits, and, where appropriate, of improperly influencing the operation of public authorities".

34 E.g. Bassiouni 1988, xv–xvi.

35 For example, Convention on Offences and Certain Other Acts Committed On Board Aircraft 1963; Convention for the Suppression of Unlawful Seizure of Aircraft 1970; Convention for the Suppression of Unlawful Acts against the Safety of Civil Aviation 1971; International Convention for the Suppression of Terrorist Bombings 1997; International Convention for the Suppression of Acts of Nuclear Terrorism 2005.

36 A/RES/49/60 1994, Annex, para 3.

The UNSC built on this definition, adding the motivation of "compel[ling] a government or an international organization to do or to abstain from doing any act" but omitted the requirement of a political purpose and limited the criminal acts to those defined in international treaties relating to terrorism.[37] Both UN bodies recognize, however, that only publicly oriented violence constitutes terrorism: A public motive, aim or objective—political, ideological, religious, ethnic or philosophical in nature—distinguishes terrorism from private violence, such as blackmail or extortion.[38] This is also the essential feature for distinguishing terrorism from organized crime and organized crime-related violence, which are motivated by financial or material gain and have no public orientation.

In Article 43(1) of the First Protocol Additional to the Geneva Conventions, organized armed groups participating in an international armed conflict are defined as being "under a command responsible to [...] [a] Party [to the conflict] for the conduct of its subordinates" and as "subject to an internal disciplinary system." This has become a norm in international customary law.[39] Furthermore, the existence of a non-international armed conflict requires the involvement of organized armed groups, although the appropriate level of organization remains unclear.[40] In any case, organized armed groups act with the purpose of fighting an adverse party in an armed conflict; for example, to win power or territory. They are not motivated by material gain like organized criminal groups, but pursue military, political, or ideological goals.

Nevertheless, the distinctions between both organized criminal groups and terrorist groups as well as organized criminal groups and organized armed groups are becoming increasingly difficult in many conflicts. Terrorists benefit from transnational organized crime, such as Daesh from royalties charged to organized criminal groups, and some organized armed or terrorist groups continually engage in organized crime and become hybrid in nature, such as the Colombian *Fuerzas Armadas Revolucionarias de Colombia* (FARC).[41] Some organized criminal groups have a paramilitary wing and compete with governmental or other armed groups for territorial control. Although these settings are analyzed in this book, the focus always remains on groups that satisfy the definition of organized crime set out above, even if they may, in some cases, also qualify as organized armed or terrorist groups.

37 S/RES/1566 2004, para 3.

38 Saul 2008, 9.

39 International Committee of the Red Cross 2019, Rule 4.

40 ICTY Tadić 1995, para 70; for a detailed discussion see section 3.2.3.1.1.

41 S/RES/2195 2014; see sections 2.3.2.2 and 3.2.3.2.2.2.

2.1.2 *Relevant Crimes*

The definition of organized crime set out above focuses on organized criminal organizations and their motives; it merely stipulates that the profit-generating activity performed by such a group must be a crime. Although, theoretically, any crime can satisfy this definition, it is instructive to more closely examine the illegal activities performed by organized criminal groups.

While the market in which organized criminal groups operate is always illegal (even if its illegal status is not necessarily known to all market participants), the traded goods or services do not necessarily need to be illegal in and of themselves; they can be regulated in such a way that the illegality is grounded in the evasion of these regulations.[42] The following sections provide an overview of the illegal markets that are most relevant to the context of international criminal law, and thus are treated in the analyses of history, *lex lata* and *lex ferenda,* in this book. Relevance is determined based on the historic role of a crime in the development of international criminal law; on the status of a crime in international law in general, especially with regard to its legal definition and universal jurisdiction; on the potential of a crime to fall under international criminal jurisdiction as it stands today (i.e., under Article 5 of the Rome Statute); and on the negative impacts and persistent impunity of a crime that make it relevant in the context of "the most serious crimes of concern to the international community as a whole [that] must not go unpunished".[43] Drug trafficking, human trafficking, migrant smuggling, and different types of illicit trade satisfy these criteria. Each crime will first be legally defined in connection with the general definition of organized crime. Subsequently, the following sections will provide the reader with some criminological facts, such as those regarding the size and characteristics of the illegal market. This information is instructive, first, to show that the particular crime is indeed committed in the context of organized crime as defined above; second, to evaluate the relevance and potential impact of international prosecutions of organized crime; and third, to understand the specificities and challenges of prosecutions of organized crime from a legal perspective.

In addition to profit-generating crimes, organized crime frequently encompasses illegal activities that are required because of the illegal status of the market in which they operate, namely corruption and money laundering: "The enormous financial profits from organized crime explain some of [its] most striking features [:] [...] the egregiously corruptive power and [...] the pressing

42 E.g., von Lampe 2016, 83.

43 Rome Statute 1998, Preamble, para 4.

need to launder these profits."[44] Furthermore, organized criminal groups often engage in violence to consolidate their power, intimidate competitors, or pressure public authorities. These crimes will also be defined and criminologically described in the following subsections.

2.1.2.1 Drug Trafficking

Drug trafficking is defined in detail in the international drug control conventions, and encompasses:

- the production, manufacture, extraction, preparation, offering, distribution, sale, delivery, brokerage, dispatch, transport, importation or exportation, possession, or purchase of certain drugs;
- the cultivation of certain plants for the purpose of the production of drugs;
- the manufacture, transport, or distribution of equipment, materials, or substances to be used in or for the illicit cultivation, production, or manufacture of certain drugs; and
- the organization, management, or financing of any of the offenses enumerated above.[45]

The illegality of the market originates from the drugs involved. In international law, the Single Convention on Narcotic Drugs of 1961, the Single Convention as amended by the 1972 Protocol, and the Convention on Psychotropic Substances of 1971 define the narcotic drugs or psychotropic substances for which the abovementioned activities are illegal.[46] Moreover, domestic systems usually contain specific regulations. Drug trafficking can thus be illegal because of the illegality of the products traded or because of the evasion of existing regulations regarding the products traded. In both cases, drug trafficking constitutes a crime in the sense of the definition of organized crime and is conducted with the aim of financial or other material gain.

From an empirical perspective, the trade in illicit drugs is the most widespread and lucrative activity of organized criminal groups. In 2005, the global retail market was estimated at $320 billion.[47] Large parts of the markets are

44 Stessens 2000, 8.

45 Drug Trafficking Convention 1988, Article 3(1)(a); see section 2.2.2.2 for a more detailed discussion of the conventions.

46 *ibid.*, Article 3(1)(a)(i) and (ii).

47 UNODC 2005, World Drug Report. More recent estimates of the global market from UNODC are not available due to the methodological difficulties involved. However, the volumes of specific markets, e.g. cocaine, opioids and cannabis, are included in UNODC's annual reports. See UNODC 2018c, World Drug Report.

controlled by highly organized cartels, such as the Sinaloa cartel in Mexico, which yield significant power and possess an extraordinary capacity to cause harm; for example, through corruption or violence. Many cartels are heavily armed or have their own paramilitary wing. Local or regional groups (that often expand their scope of operation as they grow) play a critical role in drug trafficking and have been shown to display " 'corporate' " organizational features.[48] However, research suggests that parts of the value chain of drug trafficking—especially smuggling the products across borders—are intentionally left out of the tight control of organized criminal groups to strengthen network security and minimize the risk of detection and law enforcement to the detriment of efficiency.[49] Social, ethnic, or other bonds that are often critical to the composition of these organized criminal groups, as well as their capacity and organization, can be relevant in the context of both organizational or intensity requirements in international criminal law and regarding protected groups.[50] Moreover, the degree of control of the value chain can be decisive for establishing individual criminal responsibility, especially superior responsibility of group leaders.[51]

2.1.2.2 Trafficking in Persons and Subsequent Exploitation

Trafficking in persons, or human trafficking, is defined in international law as the

> recruitment, transportation, transfer, harbouring or receipt of persons, by means of the threat or use of force or other forms of coercion, of abduction, of fraud, of deception, of the abuse of power or of a position of vulnerability or of the giving or receiving of payments or benefits to achieve the consent of a person having control over another person, for the purpose of exploitation.[52]

Most trafficked persons are victims of labor or sexual exploitation.[53] However, the definition also encompasses illegal adoption and marriage markets as well

48 Natarajan 2000, 273.

49 Benson and Decker 2010, 130.

50 E.g. with regard to an organizational policy as part of crimes against humanity or the intensity threshold for the existence of a noninternational armed conflict and groups defined as the subject of persecution. See, e.g., sections 3.2.2.1.1, 3.2.2.2.5, and 3.2.3.1.1.

51 See section 3.3.

52 Protocol on Human Trafficking 2000, Article 3(a) first sentence.

53 Feingold 2005, 26; UNODC 2012, Global report on trafficking in persons. Sources differ on relative magnitudes.

as trafficking in persons with the aim of removing and trading their organs, or for begging.[54] Although the profit for organized criminal groups is often derived from the subsequent exploitation of victims, the definition of human trafficking implies that the victims are trafficked for the purpose of exploitation. Thus, human trafficking satisfies the motivational element of organized crime. Both the act of trafficking and the crimes committed in the course of the exploitation, such as sexual violence, rape, or forced prostitution, can constitute organized crime in the sense of its definition.[55]

The size of the global market in trafficked persons is estimated at $32 billion p.a. for forced labor only.[56] Although trafficking in persons has become globalized and professionalized, not all parts of the supply chain are controlled by organized criminal groups. Rather, crucial steps, especially when victims are first recruited, are often "disorganized, [...] linked on an *ad hoc* basis."[57] Nevertheless, especially the exploitation of trafficking victims often remains in the hands of well-organized criminal groups, such as the Japanese Yakuza, and thus it displays all elements of the definition of organized crime.

2.1.2.3 Migrant Smuggling

Migrant smuggling is defined as the "procurement, in order to obtain, directly or indirectly, a financial or other material benefit, of the illegal entry of a person into a [State] of which the person is not a national or a permanent resident."[58] Migrant smuggling should be clearly differentiated from trafficking in persons, because the traded good in this case is not the human being but the service of illicit border crossing. The definition overlaps with the general definition of organized crime with regard to the *mens rea* or motivation of the perpetrator.

Empirically, two of the main smuggling routes alone that lead from East, North, and West Africa to Europe and from South America to North America were estimated to have generated a profit of $6.75 billion in 2010.[59] Evidence exists of both smaller and larger more organized criminal groups involved in smuggling, although the degree of organization is growing as professional

54 E.g., Protocol on Human Trafficking 2000, Article 3(a) second sentence.

55 The crimes of forced labour, different sexual crimes and the crimes committed for illicit organ trade are defined and analyzed in light of the relevant provisions in the Rome Statute in sections 3.2.1.2.2.1, 3.2.2.2.1 and 3.2.3.2.2.3.

56 ILO 2005, 55.

57 Feingold 2005, 28.

58 Protocol on Migrant Smuggling 2000, Article 3.

59 UNODC 2010, 59 and 67. It must be noted that migration between Africa and Europe has increased significantly since the estimation was made.

cross-border criminal networks emerge.[60] With an increase of migration flows as well as the implementation of stricter border-control measures in many regions of the world, the market has seen significant growth in recent years.[61]

2.1.2.4 Illicit Trade in Arms and Ammunition, Natural Resources, and Cultural Goods

While trade in drugs and human trafficking constitute the largest illicit markets today, organized crime can also encompass trade in numerous other goods and services.

International trade is defined (e.g., in the Arms Trade Treaty [ATT]), as "export, import, transit, trans-shipment, and brokering."[62] From the abovementioned definition of drug trafficking, the following can be added: "offering, offering for sale, distribution, sale, delivery on any terms whatsoever, brokerage, dispatch, dispatch in transit, [and] transport,"[63] as well as the "organization, management or financing"[64] of any of the activities enumerated above.

To qualify as organized crime, however, the trade must be illegal. Three possible types of illegality of a traded product exist: the first is absolute contraband, meaning prohibited goods, such as humans, contract murders, or counterfeit currency; the second is relative contraband, meaning goods that are regulated with regard to their production and sale, such as medical drugs but also counterfeit brand products, nuclear material, or protected wildlife; and third is fiscal contraband, meaning goods and services that become illegal because taxes or other fiscal duties imposed on them are evaded.[65] Cigarettes, alcohol, or gasoline could be examples of this last category.

Illicit trade that will be relevant to this book is that in arms and ammunition, natural resources, and cultural goods, which fall under the category of relative contraband.[66]

Definitions for firearms, ammunition, and conventional arms can be found in the Protocol on Arms Trafficking supplementing the Palermo Convention

60 UNODC 2011b, 1 *et seq.*

61 *ibid.*, 6.

62 Arms Trade Treaty 2013, Article 2(2); Article 1(c) of CITES defines trade as "export, re-export, import and introduction from the sea"; Article 3 of the UNESCO Convention on the Means of Prohibiting and Preventing the Illicit Import, Export and Transfer of Ownership of Cultural Property defines trade as "import, export or transfer of ownership."

63 Drug Trafficking Convention 1988, Article 3(1)(a)(i); see section 2.1.2.1.

64 *ibid.*, Article 3(1)(a)(v).

65 Naylor 2003b, 86.

66 See sections 3.2.2.2.4, 3.2.3.2.2.1, 3.2.3.2.2.2, 3.3.2 and 4.2.3.2.

as well as in the ATT.[67] Natural resources are not clearly defined in international law except for specimens and species whose trade is prohibited under the Convention on International Trade in Endangered Species of Wild Fauna and Flora (CITES). Natural resources are defined in the Cambridge Dictionary as "things such as minerals, forests, coal, etc. that exist in a place and can be used by people."[68] They include, among others, wildlife, oil, coal, gas, and minerals. Cultural goods are defined in the *chapeau* of Article 1 of the UN Educational, Scientific and Cultural Organization's (UNESCO) Convention on the Means of Prohibiting and Preventing the Illicit Import, Export and Transfer of Ownership of Cultural Property as "property which, on religious or secular grounds, is specifically designated by each State as being of importance for archaeology, prehistory, history, literature, art or science." The Convention then adds a list of specific categories.

From an empirical perspective, the illicit markets for arms and ammunition, natural resources, and cultural goods are all significant. Regarding weapons, it is estimated that every year, small arms and light weapons are manufactured and traded globally at a value of $4 to $7 billion.[69] Regarding natural resources, crimes such as the illicit trade in iconic wildlife, rare wood, gold and minerals, illegal fisheries and activities in the forestry sector, and trafficking of hazardous waste and chemicals are estimated to grow.[70] Concerning wildlife only, 2013 revenues from trade were estimated to be comparable to revenues from drug trafficking.[71] Revenues from environmental crime were more broadly estimated at a value between $91 and $258 billion annually.[72] The illicit trade in nonrenewable natural resources, especially minerals, is valued in the Democratic Republic of Congo (DRC) alone at $1.25 billion p.a.[73] Regarding cultural property, the extent of illegal trade is largely unclear because of a lack of reliable data. However, the example of Daesh reportedly having installed a system for plundering historic and cultural sites after their capture on an industrial scale by giving out licenses to organized criminal groups that paid 20% of their revenues in return for the license show the high level of organization and relevance of the trade in the context of organized crime.[74]

67 Protocol on Arms Trafficking 2001, Article 3(a) and (c); Arms Trade Treaty 2013, Article 2(1).
68 Cambridge Dictionary 2019b.
69 Fellmeth 2016, 197.
70 UNEP and INTERPOL 2016, 7.
71 Ratchford, Allgood and Todd 2013.
72 UNEP and INTERPOL 2016, 7.
73 UNEP, MONUSCO and OSESG 2015.
74 von Schorlemer 2016, 72–73.

2.1.2.5 Corruption

The term corruption encompasses several activities that are usually described as separate criminal conduct. Corruption can generally be described as the abuse of power for private gain and encompasses bribery, embezzlement, misappropriation or other diversion of property, trading in influence, abuse of functions, illicit enrichment, and obstruction of justice, which are individually defined in the UN Convention against Corruption.[75] Crucially, both offering and accepting a bribe or an undue advantage of any type constitute a crime. Organized criminal groups are usually on the offering side. Moreover, corruption can entail the abuse of power to avert negative personal consequences, such as in case of threats. Extortion in this sense is also frequently used by organized criminal groups and can in some cases becomes their source of income.[76] However, corruption usually accompanies other crimes that are at the core of the profit-generating business of an organized criminal group. Still, corruption is used by such groups to facilitate their illicit business, thereby satisfying the definitional elements of organized crime.[77]

From an empirical standpoint, it is highly difficult to assess the exact scope of corruption. However, it is argued that corruption has grown in scope because of the growth of international trade and business to economic changes, particularly in transition countries, as well as to more important government involvement.[78]

2.1.2.6 Money Laundering

Money laundering describes the method used to disguise the illegal origins of assets from law enforcement.[79] It is defined in international law as

> [t]he conversion or transfer of property, knowing that such property is the proceeds of crime, for the purpose of concealing or disguising the illicit origin of the property or of helping any person who is involved in the commission of the predicate offence to evade the legal consequences of his or her action; [and] [...] the concealment or disguise of the true nature, source, location, disposition, movement or ownership of or rights with respect to property, knowing that such property is the proceeds of crime.[80]

75 UN Convention against Corruption 2003, Articles 15–22, 25.
76 Abadinsky 2016, 246 *et seq.*
77 See section 4.2.3.4.
78 Tanzi 1998, 6–7.
79 See section 4.2.3.5.
80 E.g., UN Convention against Corruption 2003, Article 23.

Money laundering broadly encompasses three phases: the placement of funds, the layering of funds by funneling them through many different institutions and jurisdictions, and the reintegration of the funds into the legitimate economy.[81] The details of these steps can be highly complex, and contrary to the crimes that generated the proceeds, the individual acts of money laundering are innocent in and of themselves.[82] Like corruption, organized criminal groups do not derive their profits from money laundering. However, the crime is conducted for financial or material gain, and thus also falls under the set-out definition of organized crime. Indeed, many States have implemented anti-money laundering legislation and indeed prosecuted organized crime based on charges of money laundering rather than of the original crime.[83]

Estimates of the worldwide volume of money laundering range from $400 billion to $2.85 trillion per year.[84]

2.1.2.7 Organized Crime-Related Violence

Violence or threats of violence are used by organized criminal groups to accomplish different goals: to weaken competitors to increase revenues, to weaken public institutions to avoid law enforcement or shape policies, to frighten debtors or extortion victims to force payment, as well as to intimidate the general public to ensure their support.[85] For some criminal organizations, violence constitutes "the backbone of power."[86]

Such violence can be characterized as organized crime-related violence. As opposed to (for example) sexual violence in the context of human trafficking, organized crime-related violence has no direct link to a profit-generating activity. It can encompass numerous criminal acts, such as murder, execution, mutilation, and sexual violence. Such violence is intended to facilitate the illicit business of an organized criminal group, and thus falls under the definition of organized crime.

The most notorious empirical examples of organized crime-related violence are the so-called "drug war" in Mexico and the situation in Colombia prior to the 2016 peace agreement. They are used throughout this book to illustrate analyses relating to organized crime-related violence.[87]

---

81 Reuter and Truman 2004, 3.

82 Naylor 2003a, 276.

83 *ibid.*, 277.

84 Schneider and Windischbauer 2008, 392.

85 Finckenauer 2005, 66.

86 Paoli 2002, 73.

87 See sections 3.2.1.2.2.2, 3.2.2.2.5, and 3.2.3.2.2.5.

2.1.3 *Types of Organizations*

Discussions on organized criminal groups have historically been "mafia-centered."[88] Ideas of large, highly organized organizations connected through some type of kinship or family relationships or with exclusive membership shape public opinion on organized crime to this day. However, the focus on large hierarchical structures only accounts for a small part of the complex organization of organized crime today. In fact, "the illegal status of the products [...] tends to prevent the consolidation of large-scale, durable criminal enterprises" so that their provision is largely conducted in a "disorganized way."[89] Different types of groups are apparent depending on the geographic location and level of the criminal hierarchy within a business system.

Since wrong perceptions of the type of organization conducting organized crime can potentially distort the legal analysis of the phenomenon, the following subsections briefly describe some archetypes of existing organized criminal organizations. Well-known or typical organized criminal groups are briefly presented as well as used later in the book as illustrative examples.

2.1.3.1 Hierarchical Organized Criminal Groups

The first archetype of organized crime is a highly structured, hierarchical organization; the "mafia type." It displays characteristics that are essential for efficient large-scale operations, such as division of labor, extensive internal rules and regulations, and a chain of command.[90] Because of the inherent threats of this type of organization to criminal groups, namely a high level of traceability of crime and responsibility, loyalty is chosen over competence among its members.[91] Although sometimes associated with the term "mafia," the archetype developed here does not (necessarily) entail the exercise of quasi-governmental power.[92]

In 2014, Fortune estimated the annual revenues of several organized criminal groups and identified the five largest players. Although all of them represent the mafia archetype of organized criminal groups because of their size and historic origins, the following descriptions illustrate the breadth of possible internal structures and activities. The first is Solntsevskaya Bratva ($8.5 billion), also known as the Russian mafia, which consists of 10 quasi-autonomous subgroups whose operations and finances are overseen by a 12-person council.

88 Paoli and Vander Beken 2014, 16.

89 Paoli 2002, 63.

90 Abadinsky 2016, 5.

91 *ibid.*

92 Finckenauer 2005, 74.

Bratva is mainly involved in drug trade and human trafficking.[93] The second is Yamaguchi Gumi ($6.6 billion), one of the groups forming the highly centralized Japanese Yakuza with elaborate hierarchies constructed over centuries. Their main business is drug trafficking, with human trafficking, illegal gambling, and extortion as additional sources of revenue. Camorra ($4.9 billion) and 'Ndrangheta ($4.5 billion) are the most successful Italian mafia groups with large parts of their operations in the USA and Europe and, for 'Ndrangheta, with close ties to South American drug dealers. They hold a diversified portfolio that ranges from sexual exploitation to firearms and drugs.[94] Mexico's largest drug cartel, the Sinaloa Cartel ($3.0 billion), ranks fifth and is estimated to hold 60% of the market share of the illegal drug trade from Mexico. It links drug producers in South America with the large North American market and has been responsible for heavy violence against the Mexican civilian population, other cartels and state representatives.[95]

Other well-known organized criminal groups are the Colombian Medellín and Cali drug cartels that were based on coordination agreements between single manufacturers regarding the transport of cocaine into the USA. While these cartels were also well-organized and hierarchical, the composition of partnerships frequently changed.[96] With regard to the traditional Italian mafia, "status and fraternization contracts [forming the basis of] territorial control and political power" hindered groups such as the Sicilian Cosa Nostra from adapting to "fluid transnational market conditions."[97]

2.1.3.2 Criminal Networks

The second archetype of an organized criminal group is a criminal network that is not run from an authority center but rather consists of a number of local or regional actors with different roles in the system.[98] The resulting "cross-border crime trade"[99] is driven by "normal, rational, profit-oriented entrepreneurs [and] […] the rules of supply and demand."[100] This archetype of

93 Matthews 2014; for a detailed account see Finckenauer and Voronin 2001.

94 *ibid.*

95 *ibid*; evidence regarding heavy violence has also be presented at the trial of Joaquin "El Chapo" Guzman, former leader of the Sinaloa Cartel; see U.S. Attorney's Office Eastern District of New York 2019. Court documents of the trial, including the verdict, have not been released to the public by the time of writing.

96 Paoli 2002, 68.

97 Kleemans 2014, 46.

98 van Duyne 1996, 373.

99 *ibid.*

100 Kleemans 2014, 35.

organized crime has "more amorphous, free floating and flatter"[101] structures. While a network generally consists of a "collection of connected points or junctures," criminal networks typically operate within a certain subculture—the "underworld."[102] Although within the subculture there are often "points of convergence,"[103] such as bars, restaurants, or cyber hangouts that provide a space for socialization and business conversations, information gaps still arise frequently. These are filled by brokers whose role it is to connect loose ends in the network and sometimes to act as a guarantor of the agreements they facilitate.[104] "[S]ocial systems of organized crime" are formed that transcend culture, time, and space.[105]

Chinese triads are a prominent example of organized criminal networks. Triads are criminal associations of mainly Chinese members with highly ritualized rules of behavior.[106] While triads have a strong international presence, no one network or centralized control exists over cross-border activities.[107] Nevertheless, the structure of triads is continuous and self-perpetuating, thereby satisfying the organizational and temporal requirements of the definition of organized crime. The distinction between a criminal network that constitutes an organized criminal group in the sense of the aforementioned definition and a criminal network that does not can be drawn based on the following criteria:

> [U]nless the members of [a] network go beyond [a] single or limited criminal opportunity and actually organize themselves to continue to commit crimes; unless they actually view themselves as a criminal organization; unless they have or develop durability and reputation; and unless they have continuity both over time and over crimes, they are not a true criminal organization. [...] Criminal organizations can have more or fewer of these characteristics, but criminal networks that are totally or even substantially lacking in them should not be considered true criminal organizations.[108]

101 Finckenauer 2005, 66.

102 Abadinsky 2016, 8.

103 *ibid.*

104 *ibid.*, 8–9.

105 McIllwain 1999, 319–20.

106 Abadinsky 2016, 203.

107 *ibid.*, 194.

108 Finckenauer 2005, 75–76. For example, gangs have been analyzed regarding their qualification as a criminal organization. Their degree of structure and organization, gang activities and relationships with other groups vary widely, but some gangs indeed qualify as an organized criminal group: Decker, Bynum and Weisel 1998, 401.

Many organized criminal groups exhibit characteristics of both archetypes depending on the geography or specific activity in the value chain. For example, the Russian mafia primarily consists of small, democratic, and highly specialized groups operating locally; secondarily of mid-sized, more sophisticated groups with ties to higher government officials; and finally of highly organized criminal organizations run by leading figures of the crime world. The latter organizations correspond to the mafia archetype but base their business on the criminal networks of small and mid-sized groups below them.[109]

2.1.4 *Geographic Scope*

The geographic scope of illegal markets varies from local to national, national to regional, and regional to global. Based on the definition of organized crime, the analyses in this book encompass all forms of geographic operations and are not limited to transnational criminal activities.[110] Nevertheless, the short discussion of the geographic scope of organized crime in this section should enable readers to better understand legal analyses, with regard to (for example) territorial jurisdiction and the *forum conveniens,* the origins of the challenges experienced in domestic prosecutions, as well as the development of corresponding international and regional treaties, such as for the purpose of judicial cooperation.[111]

Today, the vast majority of organized crime is of a transnational nature, meaning illegal activities by organized criminal groups that "exploit differences between countries to further their objectives, enriching their organization, expanding its power, and/or avoiding detection or apprehension."[112] In short, organized criminal groups operate in and benefit from activities in multiple jurisdictions. Organized crime has "diversified, gone global and reached macro-economic proportions"[113]: criminal networks in different geographies have become more closely connected and show greater flexibility, sophistication, and global reach.

Much of this development can be explained by the effects of globalization: trade liberalization, technological change, and the global expansion of transportation networks have facilitated both legal and illegal business while complicating the tasks of customs and law enforcement.[114]

109 Shelley 2006, 100.

110 See section 2.1.1. The Palermo Convention, for example, is limited to transnational organized crime in order to ensure an interest of the international community.

111 See sections 2.2.1., 2.2.2., 2.2.4, 2.2.5 and 3.1.2.

112 Abadinsky 2016, 10.

113 UNODC 2010, ii.

114 Serrano 2002, 25.

For most illegally traded goods today, the country of origin differs from the country of destination, creating "solid international relations between all of the most dangerous criminal organizations."[115] As a consequence, "groups are now so multinational that no State can be fully responsible for their control."[116] Among other reasons, this is why international criminal law may be a conceivable addition to the toolbox in the fight against organized crime.

2.1.5 *Impact of Organized Crime*

Studying the impact of organized crime is essential, not only to understand the need for and challenges in its prosecution but also to effectively evaluate (legal) measures to fight it. Organized crime differs from conventional crime in the breadth of societal interests it threatens. Organized crime "threatens peace and human security, violates human rights and undermines economic, social, cultural, political and civil development of societies worldwide."[117] While conventional crime conflicts with legally protected interests, such as those of security, individual safety, and human rights, organized crime has the capacity to undermine an economic system or democratic or State institutions as a whole. This section focuses on these effects.

However, before analyzing the impact of organized crime on the legitimate economy and public institutions, it is important to note that the immediate effect of organized crime is, of course, on its direct victims; for example, trafficked persons, victims of violence, or people experiencing economic losses. Individuals suffering, for example, from increased insecurity and violence in their environment as a result of the activities of or competition between organized criminal groups are also direct victims of organized crime in a broader sense. The individual harm caused by organized crime is in many ways comparable to the detrimental effects of conventional crime. However, the greater the sophistication, structure, self-identification, and reputation of an organized criminal group, the greater its capacity to cause harm, especially compared with an individual committing a crime.[118]

Regarding the effect of organized crime on the legitimate economy, the exact value of the resulting economic losses is difficult to estimate. However, a few figures on specific illegal markets illustrate the magnitude of the issue. For example, the annual value of drugs sold on the darknet are estimated by

115 Violante 2000, ix.
116 Shelley 1995, 78.
117 Council of Europe 2014, 49.
118 Finckenauer 2005, 78.

European authorities to amount to up to $300 million per year.[119] The profits from human trafficking for forced labor are estimated at $32 billion p.a.[120] Economic harm is also inflicted by illegal manipulation of market competition or increased entry barriers, such as through business extortion. Furthermore, an empirical study based on an organized crime index showed that the prevalence of organized crime and GDP per capita have an inverse relationship, as well as that organized crime weakens the rule of law, leading to increased levels of corruption and reduced national wealth.[121]

Regarding State institutions, high revenues from organized crime can benefit a State or economy in the short run. Still, study results showed that tolerating organized crime "implies letting the Trojan horse [...] into the walls of government," resulting in the deterioration of law enforcement and judicial and political institutions.[122] In particular, the corruption of politicians and law enforcement officers that often accompanies organized crime undermines political processes, public trust in a democratic system, and long-term sustainable development. "These effects are not of a kind likely to be caused by individual criminals [...]. They are, instead, among the most negative of the impacts of true organized crime."[123]

Organized crime has complex reciprocal relationships with weak State institutions as well as violence, conflict, and poverty, not only causing these conditions but also exploiting and prolonging them.[124] In Mali, for example, expanding drug traffic and the collaboration of State institutions with organized criminal groups were at least partly responsible for the emergence of conflict in 2012. This in turn attracted additional organized criminal activities and aggravated direct or indirect State involvement in illicit activities, thereby weakening both the State and the economy.[125] The close connections between organized crime and organized armed groups and terrorists have been addressed, among others, in UNSC Resolution 2195 "emphasizing that the combined presence of terrorism, violent extremism, and transnational organized crime may exacerbate conflicts in affected regions [...] and noting that terrorist

119 UNODC 2018c, World Drug Report, Executive Summary: Conclusions and Policy Implications, 13.

120 ILO 2005, 55.

121 van Dijk 2007, figures 4 and 5, 51 *et seq.*

122 *ibid.*, 54.

123 Finckenauer 2005, 79.

124 See section 2.3.2.2.

125 Lacher 2012, 9 *et seq.*

groups benefiting from transnational organized crime can, in some cases and in some regions, complicate conflict prevention and resolution efforts."[126]

2.2 Organized Crime in Transnational Criminal Law

In international criminal law, a distinction is made between transnational criminal law or so-called suppression regimes and international criminal law *stricto sensu*.

Transnational criminal law prescribes criminal provisions to be adopted in domestic legal systems by way of customary international law or treaty. In addition to provisions on the domestic criminalization of certain offenses, suppression treaties often provide for extra-territorial jurisdiction, harmonized severe penalties, and harmonized cooperation procedures.[127]

International criminal law *stricto sensu*, on the other hand, establishes criminal responsibility directly under international law for international crimes which, since World War II, have been prosecuted by international tribunals.[128] Thus, while transnational crimes, or so-called treaty crimes, are subject to domestic jurisdiction, international crimes are subject to international jurisdiction.[129] Hence, international criminal law in the strict sense is built on the principle of universality.[130]

In this book, the term international criminal law is synonymous with international criminal law *stricto sensu*.

Different forms of organized crime are currently addressed in transnational criminal law. This section provides an overview of the existing legal regimes: of international and regional transnational criminal conventions on organized crime, of other international conventions potentially relevant to organized crime, and of the international enforcement regime. After a short overall discussion of the role of international law in combating organized crime, an overview of the established material and procedural norms and review mechanisms is provided for each treaty, as well as an evaluation of its role in increasing the effectiveness of domestic prosecutions of organized crime. The question of

---

126 S/RES/2195 2014; see section 2.1.1.

127 Boister 2003, 955.

128 van Schaack and Slye 2007, 7; Werle and Jessberger 2014, 45.

129 Madsen 2016, 17.

130 Nevertheless, there are crimes subjected to the universality principle by way of customary international law which are not prosecuted before international criminal tribunals, e.g. piracy; see section 2.3.2.1.2.

effectiveness of the existing legal regimes is central to the consideration of a potential need to apply international criminal law to organized crime.

2.2.1 *The Current Role of International Law in Combating Organized Crime*

Until today, organized crime has largely been considered a domestic issue and addressed focusing on domestic institutions. Although piracy and certain forms of privateering were already dealt with on an international level several hundred years ago, applied mechanisms were focused on domestic institutions, whose rights over foreign nationals were expanded for defined criminal conduct.[131] Bilateral agreements such as extradition and mutual legal assistance treaties that still govern much of the international cooperation regarding organized crime today substantially follow the same logic.

However, with the facilitating effects of globalization on organized crime becoming increasingly apparent, international efforts were envisaged to "fortify the world against the threat of international organized crime."[132] Still, the distrust among States during the Cold War impeded cooperation in criminal matters that often involves the exchange of sensitive information and requires a common goal.[133] Therefore, most international conventions dealing with organized crime have only entered into force in the last few decades.

The relevant international conventions establish so-called suppression regimes and are considered part of transnational criminal law. Existing legislation can be subdivided into different categories according to their geographic scope (i.e., regional versus international treaties) as well as based on their approach to combating organized crime. While some focus on the criminal business activity itself (e.g., drug control treaties), others address activities that often accompany organized crime, such as money laundering.[134] The most recent international convention is the UN Convention against Transnational Crime and the protocols thereto, which complement the pre-existing legal framework. Given that organized crime can also touch upon originally unrelated legal regimes, such as human rights or humanitarian law, a complex legal patchwork relating to organized crime has developed.

As the following sections show, despite the efforts to combat organized crime by way of transnational criminal law, they have not been able to curtail

131 Madsen 2016, 4 *et seq.*

132 Guymon 2000, 55.

133 Hauck and Peterke 2010, 417.

134 Parashiv 2013, 176.

the organized criminal activities addressed. Many illicit markets, such as drug trafficking, human trafficking, and migrant smuggling, have been flourishing.[135] Not only corruption but also procedural difficulties, especially across jurisdictions, hamper effective law enforcement.[136] As a consequence, organized crime often remains unpunished. The resulting impunity gap is an integral part of the discussion in this book of the potential role of international criminal law *stricto sensu* regarding the prosecution of organized crime: Because the ICC follows the principle of complementarity, international prosecutions require that domestic law enforcement fails.[137] This topic will be discussed in more detail with regard to the *telos* of international criminal law and its implications for organized crime.[138]

2.2.2 *Transnational Criminal Law Conventions*

2.2.2.1 The UN Convention against Transnational Organized Crime and the Protocols Thereto

The UN Convention against Transnational Organized Crime, also called the Palermo Convention, was adopted by UNGA Resolution 55/25 in November 2000 along with the Protocol to Prevent, Suppress and Punish Trafficking in Persons, Especially Women and Children and the Protocol against the Smuggling of Migrants by Land, Sea and Air supplementing the Convention.[139] The third supplementing Protocol against the Illicit Manufacturing of and Trafficking in Firearms, their Parts and Components and Ammunition was adopted by UNGA Resolution 55/255 six months later in May 2001.[140] During the signing conference in Palermo, 124 States signed the Convention, which entered into force in September 2003, followed by the Protocol on Trafficking in Persons in December 2003, the Protocol on Migrant Smuggling in January 2004, and the Protocol on Firearms in July 2005.[141] Drafted over multiple years by a special committee comprised of 120 UN Member States, the Convention was supposed to "satisf[y] a worldwide yearning for an international response

135 See sections 2.1.2.1—2.1.2.3.
136 Marcus 1998, see section 2.1.2.5.
137 See sections 2.3.2.1.1, 3.1.3, and 4.2.1.
138 See section 2.3.2.1.
139 Palermo Convention 2000; Protocol on Human Trafficking 2000; Protocol on Migrant Smuggling 2000.
140 Protocol on Arms Trafficking 2001.
141 Enck 2003, 375; United Nations Treaty Collection 2019, Chapter XVIII: Penal Matters.

to transnational criminal activity" by providing a "common toolkit of criminal law techniques."[142]

The Palermo Convention contains several novel features. First, it does not define transnational organized crime directly but rather describes the concept by defining the terms "organized criminal group" and "structured group."[143] The resulting scope is broad: the structural requirements for an organized criminal group are not to be "randomly formed for the immediate commission of an offence" but not necessarily possessing "formally defined roles for its members, continuity of its membership or a developed structure."[144] The *travaux préparatoires* confirm the scope as encompassing "both groups with hierarchical or other elaborate structure and non-hierarchical groups where the roles of the members of the group need not be formally defined."[145] With regard to the crimes, the Convention stipulates the aim of committing "*one* or more serious crimes,"[146] leaving it open to debate whether the commission of a single crime can constitute organized crime. Finally, the intention to obtain "financial *or other material benefit*"[147] also leaves room for interpretation.[148]

Second, the Palermo Convention does not directly refer to criminal activities constituting organized crime. Instead, it defines "serious crimes" as "an offence punishable by a maximum deprivation of liberty of at least four years," tolerating that this definition can lead to significant differences in different national jurisdictions.[149] The Convention goes on to prescribe the criminalization of acts associated with organized crime, namely participation in an organized criminal group, money laundering (backed by a requirement for regulatory and supervisory mechanisms for financial and other relevant institutions), and corruption.[150] The criminalization of core activities of organized criminal groups (that is, the activities that generate their profit) is left to the Protocols.

Furthermore, the Palermo Convention contains several provisions on procedure and international cooperation. According to Keith Morrill, chief

142 Enck 2003, 370; Elisabeth Verville (Head of the US delegation), cited in *ibid.*, 376. For a detailed discussion in favor of a comprehensive international convention see Guymon 2000.

143 See section 2.1.1.

144 Palermo Convention 2000, Article 2(c).

145 UN General Assembly. 2000, A/55//383/Add.1.

146 Palermo Convention 2000, Article 2(a). Emphasis added.

147 *ibid.* Emphasis added.

148 A detailed discussion of the definition can be found in Orlova and Moore 2005.

149 Palermo Convention 2000, Article 2(b).

150 *ibid.*, Articles 5–9.

Canadian negotiator of the Palermo Convention, the cooperation provisions, namely extradition, mutual legal assistance, and police cooperation, were the main focus of the negotiations.[151] Regarding jurisdiction, the Convention contains an interesting combination of the territorial or flag principle (a crime committed on a State's territory or on a vessel under a State's flag), the active and passive personality principle (the offender or victim is a State's citizen), and a modified effect principle (a crime impacts a State), in which a crime committed outside a State's territory but "with a view to the commission […] within its territory" can also be tried by that State.[152]

The implementation of the Convention is monitored by the Conference of the Parties to the Convention (COP).[153] The United Nations Office on Drugs and Crime (UNODC), originally established in 1997 through a merger between the United Nations Drug Control Programme and the Centre for International Crime Prevention, serves as its secretariat.[154]

In terms of the effectiveness of the Palermo Convention, it must be noted that with 190 State Parties, the convention has been almost universally accepted, and thus represents a major step forward in the criminalization and harmonization of legal norms.[155] The adoption of its definitions in other international legal documents, such as the European Council's 2008 Framework Decision on the Fight against Organized Crime, supports this view. The convention and its protocols provide a common framework for organized crime-related legal issues at the global level by stipulating the first consensus definitions of trafficking in persons and smuggling of migrants, as well as by introducing the first global legally binding instrument on small arms. In addition, the Convention overcomes previous blockades of transnational cooperation in criminal matters, extradition, and mutual assistance. Through defining organized criminal activities in its Protocols, the Convention provides a legal basis for additional norms to be added to the regime, thereby facilitating the criminalization of new organized criminal activities.[156] Furthermore, because of its broad jurisdictional rules, in sum, the Palermo Convention lays the legal basis for facilitated domestic prosecutions and international cooperation. However, it lacks an independent enforcement mechanism, and the COP as a review body is deeply political.[157]

151 *ibid.*, Articles 16–22 and 26–30; cited in Orlova and Moore 2005, 285.

152 Palermo Convention 2000, Article 15.

153 *ibid.*, Article 32(1).

154 A/RES/55/25 2000, para 11.

155 United Nations Treaty Collection 2019, Chapter XVIII: Penal Matters.

156 Marauhn and Meljnik 2007, 485–486.

157 Obokata 2010, 209.

Therefore, there is no transparency of the implementation and use of its provisions in the domestic systems of its State Parties. As a consequence, the differences in financial means and political will among the State Parties, which have not been addressed in the Convention, can hamper its effectiveness.[158] The need remains for further domestic legislation, increased use of international enforcement techniques, harmonized sentencing, and improved protection for victims worldwide.[159]

2.2.2.2 International Drug Control Conventions

With the internationalization of the markets for various illegal drugs as a consequence of colonial trade and improved methods of transportation, the first conferences and international treaties on drug control date back to the beginning of the 20th century, leading to a total of nine international drug control treaties negotiated between 1912 and 1953.[160] In 1961, this system was consolidated and expanded by the Single Convention on Narcotic Drugs, which was amended in 1972 and supplemented by the Convention on Psychotropic Substances in 1971 as well as the UN Convention against Illicit Traffic in Narcotic Drugs and Psychotropic Substances in 1988.[161] Because the negotiations were mainly driven by Western nations, especially the USA, whose societies suffered from increasing drug abuse, the designed system focuses on the supply side of international drug trade. The efficiency of this approach has been subject to debate, because the Western countries "earned political capital back home and shifted the cost and burden of drug control to predominantly [...] developing countries with no cultural inclination or resources to take on such an intrusive task—and no economic or military power to refuse what was imposed on them."[162] Thus, the resulting legal system in place today is focused on prohibition and criminalization. Nevertheless, with 186, 184, and 190 States Parties to the treaties, respectively, the regime enjoys almost universal support in the international community.[163]

158 Marauhn and Meljnik 2007, 486.

159 Enck 2003, 371. More detailed discussions of the provisions of the Palermo Convention can be found, e.g., in Clark 2004 and Obokata 2010, 39 *et seq.*

160 Sinha 2001, 2 *et seq.* The Convention for the Suppression of the Illicit Traffic in Dangerous Drugs 1936 was the first to criminalize certain conduct related to drug trafficking in its Article 2.

161 Single Convention 1961; Protocol amending the Single Convention 1972; Psychotropics Convention 1971; Drug Trafficking Convention 1988.

162 Sinha 2001, i.

163 United Nations Treaty Collection 2019, Chapter VI: Narcotic Drugs and Psychotropic Substances.

In addition to consolidation, the Single Convention extended the pre-existing regime to raw materials for drug production.[164] The Convention has tightened control of the trade of narcotics and aims at ensuring the availability of relevant substances for medical and scientific purposes.[165] The Psychotropics Convention integrated numerous synthetic psychotropic substances, such as amphetamines and hallucinogens, into the control regime. The Trafficking Convention complements the other two conventions by targeting the illicit trade in relevant substances. The Trafficking Convention is "one of the most detailed and far-reaching instruments ever adopted in the field of international criminal law."[166] It shows breadth not only regarding the substances included but also regarding the numerous aspects of the drug trade and of international cooperation addressed. The Convention criminalizes a broad set of activities, including cultivation, production, preparation, possession, offering, distribution, purchase, and sale; sets out requirements for domestic regulations such as for exports and free trade zones; contains extensive provisions on mutual legal assistance and extradition; and fosters additional methods of cooperation, such as training, assistance to transit States, and information-sharing.[167] Moreover, it includes a broad provision on jurisdiction similar to the UN Convention on Transnational Organized Crime, and recognizes the connection to other organized criminal activities.[168]

Concerning the breadth and specificity of the established legal norms as well as the high accession rates, the three major drug control treaties represent a powerful legal regime. However, the effectiveness of their implementation remains controversial.

The three Conventions attribute various functions to the Commission of Narcotic Drugs (CND) and the International Narcotics Control Board (INCB), both supported by the UNODC. Although the CND, composed of 53 members, is responsible for policy-making with regard to drug-related matters, including the addition, changes, and deletions of substances in the scope of the Conventions, the INCB is responsible for monitoring their implementation.[169] It is an independent body of 13 members which monitors illicit activities, identifies weaknesses in control systems, and monitors and promotes measures

164 Sinha 2001, 2.

165 Single Convention 1961, Articles 36 and, e.g., 4(c).

166 Steward 1990, 388.

167 Drug Trafficking Convention 1988, Articles 3, 16 and 18, 6 and 7, 9, 10 and 20 respectively; see section 2.1.2.1.

168 *ibid.*, Article 4 and Preamble.

169 E.g., Drug Trafficking Convention 1988, Articles 21–23.

taken by the governments of State Parties.[170] It publishes an annual report containing an overview of the global situation regarding the drug trade; an assessment of the functioning of the drug control systems, including the review of policies taken by specific States Parties; and different focus topics.[171] Although the independence of the body must be welcomed (for example, compared with the review mechanisms established in the Palermo Convention), the INCB still lacks teeth.[172] In its reports, it has increasingly moved away from its watchdog function in the direction of a " 'guardian' of the purity of the conventions" showing little flexibility considering different approaches to respond to the widespread use of illegal drugs.[173] In many jurisdictions, a view has emerged that both the focus on the supply side and the absolute prohibition of drugs have not been able to curtail global drug abuse or hamper drug trafficking. The issue of extradition from drug-producing to -consuming countries, such as that of Joaquín "El Chapo" Guzman to the USA, is illustrative of the challenges faced in drug-producing countries regarding the prosecution of drug traffickers. Moreover, the growth of the so-called harm reduction movement has increasingly pushed drug policies to a more tolerant and regulated end.[174] However, the flexibility of the conventions to encompass such approaches is limited.[175] Therefore, the drug control regime has been losing popularity regarding its effect on the health and well-being of drug users, and its constraint of national policy experimentation and the validity of its approach, especially with regard to its effectiveness, are questioned.[176]

2.2.2.3 Conventions against Corruption

Although corruption does not constitute a profit-generating activity of organized criminal groups, it is often an integral part of organized crime.[177] While corruption also occurs in other contexts, its criminalization is seen "as [a] significant and promising sign [...] in the fight against transnational crime."[178]

The first international instrument regarding corruption was the 1997 Convention on Combating Bribery of Foreign Public Officials in International Business Transactions, developed under the auspices of the Organization for

---

170 *ibid.*, Articles 22 and 23.
171 For the latest report, see International Narcotics Control Board 2019.
172 Guymon 2000, 70.
173 Bewley-Taylor and Trace 2006, 1.
174 Levine 2003, 145.
175 Bewley-Taylor and Trace 2006, 171.
176 Room and Reuter 2012, 84.
177 See section 2.1.2.5.
178 Guymon 2000, 72.

Economic Cooperation and Development (OECD) but open to non-OECD member States.[179] It entered into force in 1999 and currently has 44 States Parties, including Colombia, Russia, South Africa, and five other non-OECD countries.[180] The Convention "is the first and only [...] instrument focusing on the 'supply side'"[181] of a bribe, thereby requiring the criminalization of offering, promising, or giving a bribe for both natural and legal persons.[182] The Convention also provides for mutual legal assistance and extradition and installs a peer-driven monitoring mechanism conducted by the OECD Working Group on Bribery in periodical country monitoring reports.[183] Moreover, the OECD has developed further recommendations and guidelines, namely on tax measures, officially supported export credits, bilateral aid procurements, and multinational enterprises.[184]

In 2003, the OECD Convention was complemented by the UN Convention against Corruption. With 186 States Parties, a broad scope in terms of the types of corruption that are addressed and many mandatory provisions, it clearly goes beyond the OECD predecessor.[185] The Convention not only covers the criminalization of acts including bribery, embezzlement, trading in influence, abuse of functions, and illicit enrichment but also includes provisions on preventive measures, law enforcement, international cooperation, asset recovery, technical assistance, and information exchange.[186] The Conference of States Parties to the Treaty is charged with supporting the national implementation of the Convention and providing policy recommendations.[187] The implementation is monitored by the Implementation Review Mechanism, a unique peer-review process where each State Party is reviewed by two other State Parties and the results are summarized in country profiles.[188]

179 OECD Anti-Bribery Convention 1997.

180 OECD 2019b.

181 *ibid.*

182 OECD Anti-Bribery Convention 1997, Articles 1 and 2.

183 *ibid.*, Articles 9 and 10, 12 respectively; the country reports are available from OECD 2019a.

184 E.g., OECD 2006: Recommendation of the Council on bribery and officially supported export credits; OECD 2009a: Recommendation of the Council for further combating bribery of foreign public officials in international business transactions; OECD 2009b: Recommendation of the Council on tax measures for further combating bribery of foreign public officials in international business transactions; OECD 2011: OECD Guidelines for multinational enterprises; OECD 2016: Recommendation of the Council for development cooperation actors on managing the risk of corruption.

185 United Nations Treaty Collection 2019, Chapter XVIII: Penal Matters.

186 UN Convention against Corruption 2003, Articles 15 to 22 and chapters II, III, IV, V and VI, respectively; see section 2.1.2.5.

187 *ibid.*, Article 63.

188 Country profiles can be accessed at UNODC 2019.

Notably, in terms of effectiveness, the UN Convention was the first instrument in this context to include a provision on asset recovery, "one of the most important means of enforcement."[189] In addition, the Convention ends the one-sided approach that was apparent in the OECD text and that has often been criticized as being Western-focused, and thus, it expands the scope of criminalized conduct.[190] However, the peer-review mechanism is vulnerable to political influence. Moreover, a core component of corruption in many places—social embeddedness—remains unaddressed and seriously hampers domestic prosecutions of various forms of corruption.[191]

2.2.2.4 Provisions on Money Laundering and Related Instruments

To date, no dominant and universal treaty exists in international law focused on money laundering. Rather, the regime for years consisted of a combination of the money laundering provisions in the UN Drug Convention that only apply to proceeds from the drug trade, and the Council of Europe's 1990 Convention on Laundering, Search, Seizure and Confiscation of the Proceeds from Crime, which, although open for signature to countries outside Europe, was only ratified by five non-member States (the USA, Colombia, Canada, Australia, and Kazakhstan).[192] The regime was supported by guidelines developed by the Basel Committee on Banking Supervision, a global standard setter for banking regulation, and the Financial Action Task Force on Money Laundering (FATF), formed by the G-7 in 1989, which are sometimes considered soft law.[193] While the 1988 Basel Accord set forth a first set of rules for central banks, including "know your customer" and full cooperation with law enforcement, the Basel Committee continued its work and formulated several guidelines and standards for banks, such as those regarding customer due diligence, account opening, transparency in cross-border wire transfers, and risk management with regard to money laundering.[194] In 1990, the FATF first published 40 recommendations regarding national legal systems, the financial sector, and international cooperation in the fight against money laundering, updating them in 1996, 2003, and 2012 to account for new techniques and trends. The 2012

189 Snider and Kidane 2007, 710.

190 Posadas 2000, 409.

191 *ibid.*, 410.

192 CoE Laundering Convention 1990. The Convention was replaced by CoE Laundering Convention 2005.

193 Guymon 2000, 71.

194 Basel Accord 1988. For a collection of documents, see Bank for International Settlements 2021.

document includes recommendations regarding national policies and regulations, the criminalization of money laundering, secrecy laws for financial institution, customer due diligence, record-keeping, internal control mechanisms, reporting and transparency, supervision, law enforcement, and international cooperation.[195]

With the UN Convention on Organized Crime and UN Anti-Corruption Convention entering into force in 2003 and 2005, respectively, the scope of international anti-money laundering law was broadened. Crucially, the conventions request the criminalization of money laundering of the proceeds of all serious crimes, not only drug trafficking. Furthermore, both conventions request comprehensive domestic supervisory and regulatory regimes for financial and other vulnerable institutions that apply to natural and legal persons.[196]

In terms of effectiveness, the lack of universal implementation of the rules has a detrimental effect, which is greater than for other criminal activities discussed in this section. While opium poppy seeds cannot be grown anywhere in the world (e.g., because of the required climate), money laundering is completely independent from any jurisdiction or geography. Criminals move their proceeds to jurisdictions with less stringent laws or control or benefit from the focus on financial institutions in international regulations using money laundering techniques that utilize the banking system "in a secondary manner or only in passing it," such as by infiltrating business sectors that are cash-based.[197] Moreover, an additional complication in the fight against money laundering is the crucial role of a multitude of private sector financial institutions that are required to cooperate and implement internal policies and processes. The Director of Financial Crime of the UK Financial Services Authority Philip Robinson reportedly complained that, "I want them to defend against their firm being used by criminals, not against the regulator fining them."[198] In sum, monitoring and prosecuting money laundering as well as recovering assets in case of a conviction remain major challenges.

2.2.2.5 Other Transnational Criminal Law

In addition to the broad and more prominent transnational criminal law conventions discussed in previous subsections, several other treaties address specific illegal markets. Among them are the 1970 Convention on the Means of

195 Financial Action Task Force 2012.

196 UN Convention against Corruption 2003, Article 14; Palermo Convention 2000, Article 6.

197 Lilley 2006, 62–63.

198 *ibid.*, xi.

Prohibiting and Preventing the Illicit Import, Export and Transfer of Ownership of Cultural Property, which requires its State Parties to take various preventive measures against the illicit trade in cultural goods.[199] It currently has 140 State Parties and its implementation is reviewed in the course of UNESCO's periodic reporting cycles, where all member States submit national reports that are analyzed and presented at a session of the Subsidiary Committee of the Meeting of States Parties to the 1970 Convention.[200] Thus, no effective objective mechanism of review exists for the treaty. Its effectiveness is further hampered by its definition of cultural property, which lacks specificity, by its focus on exports, by its omission of a general prohibition on imports of illegally traded cultural goods, and by leaving the decision on sanctions and penalties for criminally responsible individuals to each State Party.[201]

Second, the 1973 Convention on International Trade in Endangered Species of Wild Fauna and Flora (CITES) sets rules to be implemented that are similar to the UNESCO Convention to control the trade in wildlife and prohibit trade that would put species in danger of extinction.[202] A total of 183 States are party to the Convention.[203] As with the UNESCO 1970 Convention, the focus of the CITES is regulating the trade in endangered species, not its criminalization. It merely stipulates that trade and possession of specimens covered by the treaty shall be penalized.[204]

Third, the 1979 Convention on the Physical Protection of Nuclear Material requests the criminalization of unlawful receipt, possession, use, transfer, and theft of nuclear material, among others.[205] Its 162 State Parties are required to inform the International Atomic Energy Agency, as the Depository, of the laws adopted to implement the Convention and provide a point of contact.[206] However, only 12 and 111, respectively, had complied with these obligations as of 2015, indicating serious shortcomings in the implementation of the treaty.[207]

---

199 Cultural Property Convention 1970; see section 2.1.2.4.

200 UNESCO 2021.

201 Cultural Property Convention 1970, Articles 1, 7(b)(i), 8; von Schorlemer 2016, 297 *et seq.*

202 CITES 1973; see section 2.1.2.4.

203 CITES 2021.

204 CITES 1973, Article VIII(1)(a).

205 Nuclear Material Convention 1979, Article 7. In 2005, the Convention was amended to include the protection of nuclear facilities and material used, stored or transported domestically and for nonmilitary purposes (entered into force 8 May 2016).

206 International Atomic Energy Agency 2020.

207 Rauf 2016.

2.2.3 *Other Relevant International Conventions*

In addition to transnational criminal law, other international treaties can become relevant in prosecutions of organized crime under specific circumstances. This is either because they may apply directly or because they are pertinent for the interpretation of the applicable criminal law. For the purpose of completeness of the overview, the most important treaties are noted herein. However, their effectiveness is not evaluated because their original aim is not the criminalization of organized crime.

First, the UN Convention on the Law of the Sea applies to cases of piracy, slave trade, and drug trafficking on the high sea, and sets out rules for the jurisdiction of crimes committed on the high sea.[208] Second, if organized crime occurs in a situation of armed conflict, especially if ties exist between the organized criminal group and groups recognized as armed groups under humanitarian law, the Geneva Conventions are relevant; for example, in cases of pillage.[209] Moreover, the UNSC has on several occasions shown itself to be "deeply concerned"[210] about the connection between organized crime and terrorism. Depending on specific circumstances, one of the numerous conventions relating to different acts of terrorism can become relevant to organized crime.[211] The same is true for human rights law, such as when violence and insecurity caused by organized crime interfere with the basic rights to security or freedom of movement, or in cases such as human trafficking where victims are subjected to slavery or inhuman treatment.[212]

2.2.4 *Regional Criminal Law*

Apart from international conventions, regional agreements to fight organized crime have been developed under the auspices of different multilateral organizations. "The second half of the 20th century witnessed the advent of regional agreements and schemes, often among States of the same region or those sharing common legal traditions."[213]

European organizations have developed the most extensive of all regional legal bodies in the areas of procedural and material transnational criminal

208 Convention on the Law of the Sea 1982, Articles 99, 101, 108.

209 First Geneva Convention 1949; Second Geneva Convention 1949; Third Geneva Convention 1949; Fourth Geneva Convention 1949; Protocol I to Geneva Conventions 1977; Protocol II to Geneva Convention 1977.

210 E.g., S/RES/2195 2014.

211 For a collection of relevant treaties, see UN Office of Counter-Terrorism 2019.

212 ICCPR 1966, Articles 9, 12, 8, 7 respectively; see also Universal Declaration of Human Rights 1948, Articles 3, 13, 4, 5 respectively (not binding).

213 United Nations 2015.

law. The Council of Europe has contributed to the "hodgepodge"[214] of treaties, with conventions on matters including Extradition (1957), Mutual Assistance in Criminal Matters (1959), the International Validity of Criminal Judgments (1970), the Transfer of Criminal Proceedings (1972), and Money Laundering (1990 and 2005).[215] Within the EU, all operational activities (i.e., persecution and prosecution) remain domestic responsibilities. However, the EU is active in both crime prevention and law enforcement through harmonizing legal texts, gathering and analyzing information, and financing specific projects. The latest EU document is the Council Framework Decision on the Fight against Organized Crime, which was adopted in 2008.[216] It builds on the Palermo Convention and replaced the 1998 Joint Action Plan. However, the alignment of national laws was slower than expected.[217] Overall, despite the high degree of legal integration within the European Union, incomplete adherence to non-EU treaties and numerous reservations as well as a lack of political readiness for closer collaboration have led to a high level of fragmentation of European criminal law.[218]

In the Americas, a number of agreements relevant to organized crime have been developed within the Organization of American States (OAS), including the Inter-American Convention on Extradition (1981), the Inter-American Convention on Mutual Legal Assistance in Criminal Matters (1992), the Inter-American Convention against Corruption (1996), and the Inter-American Convention against the Illicit Manufacturing of and Trafficking in Firearms, Ammunition, Explosives, and Other Related Materials (CIFTA, 1997).[219] The Inter-American Drug Abuse Commission, an autonomous policy forum within the OAS, has developed model legislation for anti-money laundering laws, and the Caribbean Financial Action Task Force develops recommendations for common countermeasures against money laundering and terrorism financing.[220]

214 Guymon 2000, 74.

215 European Convention on Extradition 1957; European Convention on Mutual Assistance in Criminal Matters 1959; European Convention on the International Validity of Criminal Judgments 1970; European Convention on the Transfer of Proceedings in Criminal Matters 1972; CoE Laundering Convention 1990; CoE Laundering Convention 2005.

216 EU Council Framework Decision 2008; see section 2.1.1.

217 Bakowski 2013.

218 Guymon 2000, 74–5. For a detailed discussion of organized crime legislation in the EU, see Calderoni 2010.

219 OAS Extradition Convention 1981 (Its first predecessor is the Inter-American Extradition Convention 1933) ; Convention on Mutual Assistance 1992 ; OAS Corruption Convention 1996 ; CIFTA 1997.

220 Guymon 2000, 77.

In the Hemispheric Plan of Action against Transnational Organized Crime of 2006, the OAS promotes the application of the Palermo Convention and accession of its member States to all relevant OAS treaties.[221] However, ineffective justice systems and socially embedded corruption, especially in some Latin American countries, hamper current efforts.[222]

The League of Arab States has sponsored several conventions on cooperation in criminal matters, including the Riyadh Arab Agreement on Judicial Cooperation.[223] The Regional Programme for the Arab States to Prevent and Combat Crime, Terrorism and Health Threats and Strengthen Criminal Justice Systems in Line with International Human Rights Standards (2016–2021) was set up to build a framework for cooperation between the League of Arab States, individual governments, and the UNODC.[224] It currently focuses on the reduction of human trafficking and migrant smuggling.[225]

The African Union (AU) developed the AU Convention on Preventing and Combating Corruption encompassing prevention, criminalization, and international cooperation, which entered into force in 2006 and has been signed by 49 countries thus far.[226] Moreover, the Economic Community of West African States has attempted to build regional mechanisms against organized crime, albeit without significant success.[227]

Within Asia, the ASEAN has limited itself to various declarations so far.[228]

2.2.5 *The International Enforcement Regime*

International police cooperation forms the basis of the international efforts against organized crime. In light of different justice and policing systems, uneven economic capacities, and political rivalries, engendering successful cooperation is no easy task.

The International Criminal Police Organization (INTERPOL) was founded as the International Criminal Police Commission in 1923 and re-established after World War II under its new name. It is the largest police organization worldwide with 194 members.[229] Based in Lyon, France, INTERPOL has an

221 Hemispheric Action Plan 2006.

222 Nagle 2002, 1711.

223 Riyadh Agreement 1983.

224 UNODC and League of Arab States 2016.

225 UNODC and League of Arab States 2018, 2.

226 AU Corruption Convention 2003; African Union 2021.

227 Council on Foreign Relations 2013.

228 ASEAN 2012; Emmers 2002, ii; Bukit 2016.

229 INTERPOL 2021.

international presence with seven regional offices and representation at the UN, EU, and National Central Bureaus in every member State.

INTERPOL's main legal document is its Constitution, which sets out the organization's aims, establishes the principle of neutrality and INTERPOL's commitment to human rights, and defines the organizational structure.[230]

INTERPOL has advanced the concept of international law enforcement in three ways: by providing a fast and reliable network that links police agencies on a global level, by establishing a professional association sharing best practices and new techniques, and by facilitating the harmonization of standards and tactics in national law enforcement.[231] While INTERPOL is first and foremost an information hub or clearinghouse, storing and organizing information in huge databases and sharing information (e.g., through their well-known notices), it also acts as a liaison for local police agencies, supports members in capability-building, and is moving increasingly into crime intelligence.[232] However, INTERPOL cannot conduct investigations independently or arrest suspects, and thus relies on domestic law enforcement institutions.[233]

Organized crime is one of INTERPOL's main focus areas. While a majority of INTERPOL's activity focuses on drugs, it also runs other specific projects.

At the regional level, the EU established its own Police Organization, the European Police Office (Europol) in 1998, the main tasks of which are to facilitate information exchange between member States, aid national law enforcement operations, and maintain a digital database.[234]

Although both INTERPOL and Europol provide valuable platforms for international cooperation in the field of organized crime, the reliance on domestic prosecution and law enforcement has not been overcome. While INTERPOL is criticized for the complexity of its procedures and remoteness of its officers,[235] limited competencies are at the core of its lack of effectiveness. Expanding its powers and increasing its independence from member States, one may argue, can "serve as a valuable resource in battling transnational crime."[236]

230 INTERPOL Constitution 1956.
231 Guymon 2000, 73.
232 Higdon 2001, 32 *et seq.*
233 Gilsinan 2014.
234 Europol Convention 1995, Article 3.
235 Balzer 1996.
236 Guymon 2000, 73. See also, e.g., Balzer 1996.

2.3 Organized Crime in International Criminal Law *Stricto Sensu*

Contrary to transnational criminal law, international criminal law *stricto sensu* creates criminal responsibility under international law and subjects crimes to international jurisdiction.[237] To lay the basis for the analysis of the applicability of international criminal law to organized crime in Chapter 3, the following sections provide an overview of the evolution of international criminal law *stricto sensu,* demonstrate its relevance to organized crime, and examine the role of organized crime in the history of international criminal law.

2.3.1 *The Evolution of International Criminal Law* Stricto Sensu

International criminal law finds its early origins in the *ius ad bellum* or theory of just war, establishing rules as to when it is permitted in international relations to use military force, in the international crimes of piracy and slavery that were developed as early as the mid-19th century, as well as in international humanitarian law.[238] However, until the Second World War, these norms lacked international enforcement mechanisms. As a consequence, the International Military Tribunals (IMT s) set up by the Allied Forces in Nuremberg and Tokyo in 1945 and 1946, respectively, are considered the birthplace of modern international criminal law.

The Nuremberg Charter, the legal basis for the IMT s, established jurisdiction for crimes against peace (aggression), war crimes, and crimes against humanity committed by "the major war criminals of the European axis."[239] The IMT for the Far East in Tokyo had jurisdiction over the same crimes, although over a longer period starting in 1931 with the Japanese invasion of Manchuria. Based on Control Council Law No. 10 of 1945 enabling the Allied powers to prosecute Nazi criminals beyond the IMT trials, subsequent trials were held by military tribunals in Nuremberg and elsewhere.[240] As the very first instance of international justice performed by tribunals *sui generis* and based on international agreements, the trials were a "revolutionary step"[241] and established many of the rules that have become integral components of international criminal law as it stands today. The Nuremberg Charter was the first to codify crimes against humanity, even if it represented no considerable innovation compared with criminal law encountered in national criminal codes of " 'civilized' nations."[242]

237 See section 2.2.

238 van Schaack and Slye 2007, 8–18.

239 Nuremberg Charter 1945, Articles 6, 1.

240 Control Council Law No. 10 1945, Articles 3–4.

241 Tomuschat 2006, 832.

242 *ibid.*, 834.

The Nuremberg Charter also established the insignificance of an official position of the defendants, including Heads of State, and removed the defense of superior order for the existence of individual criminal responsibility, contrary to most military codes existing at the time.[243]

During the Cold War, the development of international criminal law stalled and was only revived in the early 1990s when the UNSC acting under Chapter VII of the UN Charter established an *ad hoc* international criminal tribunal to prosecute crimes committed in the then ongoing conflict in the former Yugoslavia. The International Criminal Tribunal for the former Yugoslavia (ICTY) had limited territorial and temporal jurisdiction. Its jurisdiction *ratione materiae* included grave breaches of the Geneva Conventions of 1949, violations of the laws and customs of war, genocide, and crimes against humanity.[244] The *ad hoc* International Criminal Tribunal for Rwanda (ICTR) that was established by the same mechanism the following year was aimed at prosecuting the same crimes, with territorial and temporal jurisdiction limited to address the ethnic conflict between the Hutu and Tutsi.[245] Both tribunals made crucial contributions to the interpretation of these core crimes, such as the organizational requirements for crimes against humanity and gender-based crimes.

Furthermore, decade-long efforts within the UN system to create a permanent international criminal court regained momentum in the 1990s and led to the adoption of the Rome Statute of the International Criminal Court in 1998, which entered into force in 2002. Other than the IMTs, ICTY, and ICTR, the ICC's jurisdiction is not limited to specific conflicts. Rather, its jurisdiction can be triggered by a State Party or the ICC Prosecutor if a territorial or personal nexus exists between the alleged crime and a State Party, or by the UNSC without restrictions.[246] Cases are admissible before the ICC only if the State Party with jurisdiction is unable or unwilling to investigate or prosecute.[247] The Rome Statute contains detailed provisions on genocide, crimes against humanity, war crimes, and aggression, and for the first time codifies general principles of international criminal law.[248] ICC jurisdiction over the crime of aggression was activated by the Assembly of States Parties (ASP) as of 17 July

243 Nuremberg Charter 1945, Article 7, 8; Bassiouni 2013, 555.

244 ICTY Statute 1993 (S/RES/827), Articles 2–5.

245 ICTR Statute 1994 (S/RES/955), Articles 2–5.

246 Rome Statute 1998, Articles 12–15; see sections 3.1.1. and 3.1.2. Restrictions *ratione materiae, temporis* and *personae* apply to UNSC referrals as well.

247 *ibid.*, Article 17; see section 3.1.3.

248 *ibid.*, Articles 5–8, 22–33.

2018.[249] The Rome Statute currently has 122 State Parties, and 27 cases have been brought before the court thus far.[250] Because of its permanent and universal nature, it represents the most critical codification of international criminal law today.

In parallel to the establishment of the ICC, another type of international tribunal known as "hybrid" emerged, which combines international and domestic elements. Respective tribunals were aimed at addressing crimes that fell outside of ICC temporal jurisdiction; that is, those that occurred before the Rome Statute entered into force. For example, the Special Court for Sierra Leone (SCSL) was aimed at prosecuting crimes that occurred during the 10-year armed conflict characterized by brutal violence and atrocities and an illicit struggle over the country's natural wealth, in which Liberia's President Charles Taylor was deeply involved.[251] The SCSL was established based on an agreement between the UN and the government of Sierra Leone, and began operation in 2002. Domestic and international judges served together and the applicable law and mandate of the court was determined by a special statute.[252] The Court had jurisdiction over crimes against humanity and war crimes as well as certain domestic crimes relating to arson and the abuse of girls.[253] Similarly, the Extraordinary Chambers in the Courts of Cambodia, also known as the Khmer Rouge Tribunal, were established in 2003 by an agreement between the Royal Government of Cambodia and the UN, are staffed with both local and international judges and have jurisdiction over certain serious violations of Cambodian penal law, international humanitarian law, and international conventions recognized by Cambodia for crimes committed by the Khmer Rouge between 1975 and 1979. Other than the SCSL, the Chambers are integrated into the Cambodian court system and trials are held in Cambodia.[254] Other hybrid chambers can be found in East Timor and Bosnia and Herzegovina.[255]

---

249 ICC-ASP/16/Res.5 2017, para 1. Please note that jurisdiction over the crime of aggression is limited in Articles 8*bis*(1) and 25(3*bis*)of the Rome Statute to persons "in a position effectively to exercise control over or direct the political or military action of a State". Since actors in organized crime do not satisfy this criterion, the crime of aggression will not be analysed in this book.

250 United Nations Treaty Collection 2019, Chapter XVIII: Penal Matters.

251 Winter 2010.

252 *ibid.*, 102.

253 Statute for the SCSL 2002, Articles 2–5.

254 Bassiouni 2013, 548 *et seq.*

255 Other hybrid tribunals are, e.g. the Extraordinary African Chambers in Senegal prosecuting international crimes committed in Chad under Hissène Habré and the Special Tribunal for Lebanon set up for the prosecution of those responsible for the assassination of former Lebanese Prime Minister Rafic Hariri.

The latest hybrid court to be created, and the first in which core crimes and organized crime (in particular human trafficking) are dealt with by the same chambers, are the Kosovo Specialist Chambers and Specialist Prosecutor's Office (KSC). It is based on a Constitutional Amendment and its founding laws of 2015, and was established as a reaction to an EU report containing serious allegations against the Kosovo Liberation Army (KLA). It has jurisdiction over "grave transboundary and international crimes committed during and in the aftermath of the conflict in Kosovo," namely international customary law, war crimes, crimes against humanity, as well as selected crimes under Kosovo law.[256] It is staffed with international judges, prosecutors, and other personnel, financed by the EU and other State grants, and based in The Hague, Netherlands.

2.3.2 *The Relevance of International Criminal Law* Stricto Sensu *to Organized Crime*

Today, organized crime and international criminal law *stricto sensu* are rarely discussed together, but rather seen as separate concepts representing distinct legal frameworks with distinct purposes.[257] Testing this common understanding, two main questions determine the potential relevance of international criminal law to organized crime: (1) Is the fight against organized crime covered by the fundamental purpose or *telos* of international criminal law? (2) Does an approach separating organized crime and the core crimes addressed by international criminal law adequately reflect reality, and thus allow for an effective legal system in this realm? These questions are not aimed at analyzing the applicability of the current legal regime to organized crime but rather at examining if the application is sensible from a criminal policy perspective.

The following subsections first analyze the relevance of the *telos* of international criminal law "that the most serious crimes of concern to the international community as a whole must not go unpunished"[258]—to organized crime. They then proceed to examine the growing interdependencies between organized crime and conflict, such as those caused by the required funding of armed groups or exploitation of weak state institutions by organized criminal groups, as well as the implications for criminal prosecutions.

256 Law on KSC 2015, Articles 1(2), 12–14.

257 Discussions of organized crime in the context of international criminal law can be found, e.g., in Hauck 2016; van der Wilt 2016.

258 Rome Statute 1998, Preamble, para 4.

2.3.2.1 The *Telos* of International Criminal Law

The *telos* of international criminal law, as laid out in the Preamble of the Rome Statute, includes several components that must be satisfied for this law to come into play: the crimes prosecuted must be serious in nature, they must go unpunished in domestic systems, and they must be of concern to the international community as a whole.[259] Whether organized crime satisfies these criteria is analyzed in the following.

2.3.2.1.1 *The Most Serious Crimes Going Unpunished*

International criminal law *stricto sensu* is not designed to replace domestic institutions. Rather, it is confined to the most serious crimes, and more specifically to those serious crimes going unpunished without international prosecutions. To determine whether organized crime satisfies this criterion, its gravity and the effectiveness of current law enforcement must be discussed.

First, no clear definition or threshold exists for a serious crime in the context of international criminal law. While for any given court or tribunal its jurisdiction *ratione materiae* is clearly defined, these definitions as well as their interpretations have changed over time and depending on the situation addressed. To extract a more abstract meaning of the term "most serious crime," the history of international criminal law suggests a similar level of gravity as the genocidal experiences in World War II and crimes committed in the conflicts in former Yugoslavia and Rwanda. In connection to paragraph 3 of the Preamble of the Rome Statute, a serious crime must be grave enough to threaten the basic values of the international community.[260] Focusing on the social and legal goals of prosecutions, gravity can be determined by the scope of a crime as well as its negative effects on its victims, the affected community, and society as a whole.[261] However, given the contextual elements of some of the core crimes, especially the requirement of a "widespread or systematic attack" for crimes against humanity, a large scope cannot be a general prerequisite for international criminal law to apply. Therefore, it seems that the seriousness of a crime can be determined on the one hand by its scope, systematic nature, or effect on a large population, and on the other hand by a more abstract common understanding that the crime constitutes an outrageous affront to human dignity, such as genocide. Organized crime is broad in scope, of a systematic nature,

259 *ibid.*

260 Triffterer, Bergsmo, Ambos (Commentary edited by Triffterer and Ambos) 2016, 9; discussed in detail in section 2.3.2.1.2.

261 Keenan 2015, 426.: "Widespread harms and [...] conduct [that] affected as many people as possible, [...] those crimes that caused the greatest stigma to victims".

and has detrimental effects beyond the individual victim.[262] For example, drug trafficking has sparked intense violence in many countries in Middle and South America and weakened state institutions. Systematic illegal exploitation and trade in minerals in the Great Lake region undermine the legitimate economy. Illegal trade in cultural goods destroys large swathes of Syria's cultural heritage. Thus, organized crime can satisfy the criterion of seriousness laid out in the Preamble of the Rome Statute.

Second, international criminal law is a regime of last resort giving priority to domestic institutions.[263] Thus, it is complementary to the complex legal structures comprised of international and regional suppression regimes and domestic legislation relating to organized crime that have been previously discussed, and remains moot when domestic systems are working properly and consistently.[264] International criminal law only comes into play if shortcomings in domestic systems cause the most serious crimes to remain unpunished. With regards to organized crime, empirical data on the effectiveness of crime control strategies are scant, such as on failed prosecutions.[265] Furthermore, existing data are often limited in their reliability; for example, market size estimates are often based on the value of annual seizures.[266] Nevertheless, anecdotal evidence suggests that existing law enforcement efforts do not hamper illegal markets from flourishing. For example, global opium production increased by close to two-thirds in 2017 and cocaine manufacturing reached record levels in 2016.[267] Global convictions for trafficking in persons increased by 67% between 2007 and 2016; however, this increase broadly follows the rising numbers in detected trafficking victims.[268]

The main reasons for the lack of effective law enforcement are little international cooperation between law enforcement agencies and intelligence services, procedural challenges within domestic systems, as well as legal difficulties caused by the multitude of relevant legal texts.[269] Domestic prosecutors are often unable to secure sufficient evidence and arrest the accused, especially regarding cross-border crime. Provisions in transnational law, such as those regarding the illicit trade in cultural goods, are not implemented in

262 See section 2.1.5.
263 Rome Statute 1998, Article 17; see section 3.1.3.
264 See section 2.2.
265 Gabor 2003, 55 *et seq.*
266 E.g., UNODC 2018c, World Drug Report, Global overview of drug supply and demand.
267 *ibid.*, Analysis of drug markets, 12 and 30.
268 UNODC 2018a, Global Report on Trafficking in Persons, 7–8.
269 E.g., Marcus 1998; see section 2.2.1.

domestic systems or not applied.[270] Furthermore, organized crime intentionally moves to the jurisdictions with the weakest legal and policing systems where immunity from law enforcement is easier to obtain. In its 2016–2018 Strategy, the OTP of the ICC acknowledged a persisting impunity gap, stating that "a lack of coordination of efforts from all actors makes it difficult to close the impunity gap for ICC crimes and *related crimes, including transnational and organized crime.*"[271] The UNSC, in a similar voice to 2014, "stresses the importance of strengthening transregional and international cooperation on a basis of a common and shared responsibility to counter the world drug problem and related criminal activities."[272]

In sum, organized crime often constitutes a most serious crime that goes unpunished, thereby satisfying the *telos* of the Rome Statute in this regard.

2.3.2.1.2 *Concern to the International Community as a Whole*

International criminal law is based on the premise of respect of State sovereignty and the universality principle.[273] Therefore, a legitimate concern of the international community regarding a crime is paramount for international criminal law to come into play; that is, for the international community to interfere.

However, what constitutes a legitimate concern of the international community is subject to debate or treaty negotiations. In general, such a legitimate concern is triggered by a threat to one of the legally recognized values of the community of nations.[274] As for the definition of those values, the Preamble of the Rome Statute names the peace, security, and well-being of the world, as well as the territorial integrity and political independence of a State. It also references the purposes and principles of the Charter of the UN. These are laid out in Articles 1 and 2 of the UN Charter and include, among others, peace and security, friendly relations between all nations based on equal rights and self-determination of people, and the principle of sovereign equality.[275] Based on these values, the concept of *ius cogens* has developed over the last decades, meaning norms in international law from which no derogation is permitted, and thus are of particular concern to the international community.[276]

---

270 von Schorlemer 2016, 293 *et seq.*

271 Office of the Prosecutor of the International Criminal Court 2015, 6. Emphasis added.

272 S/RES/2195 2014.

273 Rome Statute 1998, Preamble, para 6–8.

274 Triffterer, Bergsmo, Ambos (Commentary edited by Triffterer and Ambos) 2016, 12.

275 The terms peace and security have their origin in the Preamble of the Covenant of the League of Nations; see also Wolfrum (Commentary edited by Simma *et al.*) 2012, 7 *et seq.*

276 Vienna Convention 1969, Article 53.

Recognized *ius cogens* norms include the crimes of aggression, genocide, torture, and slavery.[277] A related concept in international law is obligations *erga omnes* that arise from the violation of rights that all States have an interest in protecting. In *Barcelona Traction*, the International Court of Justice (ICJ) defined obligations *erga omnes* as "[b]y their very nature [...] the concern of all States." According to the Court, such obligations arise from acts of aggression, genocide, and basic human rights, including protection from slavery and racial discrimination.[278]

Thus, organized crime can be considered of concern to the international community as a whole if it poses a threat to any of the aforementioned values or violates any of the norms. Organized crime is a threat to peace and security because, for example, it sparks violence, has a deteriorating effect on State institutions, and has a perpetuating effect on armed conflict.[279] In many cases, such as human trafficking and the illegal exploitation and trade in natural resources, organized crime violates basic human rights. Furthermore, organized criminal groups directly violate some of the *ius cogens* norms, such as the prohibition of slavery in trafficking in persons. The UNGA confirmed a concern of the international community in resolution 55/25, expressing that it was "deeply concerned by the negative economic and social implications related to organized criminal activities."[280] Furthermore, the high numbers of ratifications of international suppression treaties are indicative of broad international concern for organized crime and the willingness to fight it on an international level.

Thus, the fight against organized crime is covered by the *telos* of international criminal law.

2.3.2.2 Empirical Interconnection: The Crime–Conflict Nexus

In addition to the relevance of international criminal law to organized crime based on the former's purpose, an increasing connection exists between organized crime and the core crimes because of an ever-closer interdependency between organized crime and conflict. Criminal groups not only exploit conflict situations to profit financially but also take up arms against the State or rival groups. Sometimes, they are contracted by parties to an armed conflict or create paramilitary units themselves.[281] "Such armed violence has become

277 Cassese 2005, 202–203.

278 ICJ Barcelona Traction 1970, 33–34; Funke 2014, 83.

279 See section 2.1.5.

280 A/RES/55/25 2000.

281 Peterke and Wolf 2016, 382.

astoundingly professional, causing death and destruction that, in extreme cases, is statistically on an equal footing with international armed conflicts."[282] A close interconnection between organized crime and the core crimes would support an integrated approach to their prosecution, and thus, underline the relevance of international criminal law to organized crime.

The nexus between organized crime and conflict consists of reciprocal effects concerning the beginning, duration, intensity, and end of a conflict as well as long-term economic, social, and democratic development. These are analyzed in the following paragraphs.

Regarding the role of organized crime at the outset of a conflict, the so-called "greed hypothesis" suggests that rent-seeking can lead to the mobilization of insurgents and become a primary cause of the outbreak of a conflict, which is not supported by empirical evidence.[283] Rather, the presence of organized crime is assumed to facilitate the outbreak of conflict.[284] On the one hand, informal trading networks and other established structures of illicit markets can be transformed and exploited by armed groups, as could be observed in Kosovo and Mali.[285] On the other hand, the opportunity to become involved in organized crime increases the financial capabilities of armed groups, and therefore "the challenge they pose to States."[286] Finally, the corruption and unfair wealth redistribution that often accompany organized crime are argued to be able to "trigger local grievances and provoke larger-scale violence."[287]

The evidence of the impact of organized crime on the duration of a conflict is clear. Quantitative research shows that civil wars in which parties to the conflict have access to financial resources from trade in contraband last significantly longer because of their dependable access to finance and weapons.[288] Furthermore, human trafficking is increasingly used to support the operations of armed groups through generating profits from sexual slavery, the extortion of victims' families, or forced labor, among others.[289] In Sierra Leone, trafficked individuals were exploited by being forced to mine diamonds.[290] From a qualitative perspective, regarding their involvement in organized crime, armed

282 *ibid.*

283 See E.g., Ballentine and Nietzschke 2003.

284 Boer and Bosetti 2015a, 7.

285 Ross 2003; Global Initiative against Transnational Organized Crime 2014.

286 Cornell 2005, 751.

287 Boer and Bosetti 2015a, 7.

288 Fearon 2004.

289 UNODC 2018b, Global report on trafficking in persons—in the context of armed conflict, 19–20.

290 *ibid.*

groups "affect the motivational structures [...] creating an economic function of war and vested interests in the continuation of armed conflict."[291] In a licit economy constrained by an ongoing conflict, illicit markets often provide the only source of income for the local population.[292] For example, this is the case for opium production in Afghanistan, for which the Taliban provide a certain degree of security.[293] The similar, quasi-governmental role of drug cartels in nonconventional conflicts in South America (e.g., Mexico and Brazil), where drug production and trafficking have become major parts of the local economy, also points to a consolidation of the situation over time.[294]

Whether the availability of finance from organized crime leads to more indiscriminate violence against civilians because of decreased dependency on popular support and more individualist attitudes of rent-seeking combatants is subject to discussion. However, the nexus between organized crime and a conflict's increased intensity is not automatic.[295]

In recent history, the risks of negotiating a peace agreement in a setting where organized crime is present have repeatedly been observed, such as in the failed Lomé Peace Agreement in Sierra Leone of 1999. However, robust research findings on how to best involve organized criminal groups' political agendas remain lacking.[296] By contrast, the interdependencies between post-conflict recovery and organized crime have been thoroughly studied. Post-conflict settings tend to ease the expansion and consolidation of organized crime: key factors for vulnerability to organized crime include the nature of "post-conflict aid economies," the lack of a long-term perspective on reforms and State legitimacy in strategic decisions made in the aftermath of a conflict, as well as the legacies of the war.[297]

Moreover, the existence of a conflict can boost some forms of organized crime, such as narcotics production, illegal trade in pillaged cultural goods, and illegal exploitation and trade in natural resources, including possible feedback loops between conflict and organized crime.[298] For example, Daesh systematically allowed organized criminal groups plunder and trade cultural goods from captured areas, reportedly gaining a 20% share of all revenues.[299]

291 Cornell 2005, 751.
292 Boer and Bosetti 2015a, 8.
293 Felbab-Brown 2009.
294 Desmond Arias 2006; Wennmann 2014.
295 Boer and Bosetti 2015a, 8–9.
296 *ibid.*, 11–12.
297 *ibid.*
298 Cornell 2005, 751; Boer and Bosetti 2015b.
299 von Schorlemer 2016, 72–73.

Organized criminal groups take advantage of weak state institutions and the vulnerability of their victims. Human trafficking, for example, increases in conflict situations that involve large numbers of refugees.[300]

Similar to the nexus between organized crime and conflict, "organized crime serves as a proximate cause of State failure by feeding off of and reinforcing other causes in a manner that propels weak States towards failure and provides obstacles to the re-establishment of a functional State."[301] Simultaneously, underdevelopment, the lack of liquidity, demographic trends, and the fast growth of cities have been identified as increasing vulnerability to organized crime.[302]

In particular, the nexus between organized crime and terrorism has become a topic of serious concern on the international stage.[303] A variety of collaborations between organized criminal groups and terrorists have been documented: direct engagement in illicit activities such as drug cultivation and trafficking, taxing of the illicit flows of illegal goods, money laundering, fraud, and cybercrime.[304] However, scientific "knowledge on the extent and nature of this relationship and the mechanisms that support this collaboration remain weak."[305] A major difficulty lies in the interaction or convergence of organized criminal groups on the one side and armed or terrorist groups on the other. While evidence exists that some armed groups such as the Colombian FARC, Al Qaeda, and the Sri Lankan Liberation Tigers of Tamil Eelam have developed " 'in house' criminal capabilities," it remains contested in terms of how far political or ideological differences preclude "fully symbiotic cooperation."[306] The rise of networked organizations without a clear chain of command and weakened group identity gives more independence to individual criminals, leading them to engage in activities previously seen as hurting the original endeavor of their group (either ideological or economic in nature) and creating a "leaderless nexus."[307] The emergence of hybrid groups can be described as

> either begin[ning] as organized criminal groups that appropriate terror tactics and simultaneously seek to secure political aims, or [...]

300 UNODC 2018b, Global report on trafficking in persons—in the context of armed conflict, 20–21.

301 West 2006, 1.

302 International Peace Institute 2013, 3.

303 S/RES/2195 2014.

304 Boer and Bosetti 2015a, 9.

305 *ibid.*

306 Hutchinson and O'Malley 2007, 1095. For an opposing view see Picarelli 2007.

307 Dishman 2005, 237.

> begin[ning] as terrorist groups that appropriate criminal capabilities to the point that they begin to use their political (ideological) rhetoric as a façade for perpetrating organized crime.[308]

Examples of such hybrid organizations include the "'narcoterrorist' drug cartels" of Peru and Colombia in the 1980s, the Kurdish *Partiya Karkerên Kurdistanê* (PKK), and Abu Sayyaf in the Philippines.[309]

In sum, the convergence of organized criminal groups and armed or terrorist groups leads to increasing overlaps of situations, victims and perpetrators of core crimes, and organized crime. The international prosecution of the latter along with the core crimes could facilitate the prosecution of crimes in their entirety, benefit from existing legal, political, and cultural expertise, and avoid a fragmented legal system.

2.3.3 *Organized Crime in the History of International Criminal Law* Stricto Sensu

In the short history of international criminal law, organized crime has only been touched peripherally. Still, examining its relevance is worthwhile in situations subjected to international justice, its in- or exclusion in arguments, and relevant case law developed in some international tribunals. During the drafting process leading to the adoption of the Rome Statute, organized crime played a more prominent role. The following subsections examine both the treatment of organized crime in selected international criminal tribunals and in the development of the ICC's jurisdiction. In Chapter 3, a detailed discussion of the *lex lata* in the Rome Statute follows.

2.3.3.1 Organized Crime Offenses in International Criminal Tribunals

2.3.3.1.1 *Post-World War II International Criminal Prosecutions*

In the aftermath of the Second World War, the UN War Crimes Commission (UNWCC), in charge of securing evidence and prosecutions between 1943 and 1948, as well as the International Criminal Tribunals in Nuremberg and Tokyo, were mainly concerned with the prosecution of crimes committed during the war by the Axis powers. Indeed, the chambers of the International Military Tribunal presupposed the requirement of a State policy to be a contextual element of crimes against humanity, making it impossible to try private individuals acting on their own behalf (e.g., organized criminals) for this category.[310]

---

308 West Sands Advisory LLP 2012, 36.

309 Boer and Bosetti 2015a, 10.

310 E.g., Justice Case 1947; Einsatzgruppen Case 1948.

This understanding remained dominant in national prosecutions until the early 1990s, when it was abandoned by the next generation of international criminal tribunals.[311] Nevertheless, some of the judgments of the IMT are of relevance considering international jurisdiction over organized crime.

For example, the Nuremberg Charter provided for judges to qualify an organization as criminal and subsequently bring individuals to trial for membership of that organization.[312] To counter the danger of guilt by association, the IMT additionally required either the defendant to have committed a crime or that the member knew that the organization was used for the commission of crimes.[313] Although many States, especially in civil law traditions, have been reluctant to adopt criminal liability based on membership, an increasing number of laws providing for organizational criminal responsibility have been enacted in recent years because of the spread of organized crime and terrorism.[314] Both the Palermo Convention and EU Framework Decision criminalize participation in an organized criminal group.[315] However, the IMTs only allusively touched on organized crime when distinguishing between groups and organizations as well as characterizing Nazi crimes as an "organized use of terror."[316]

While the IMTs did not charge individuals for the war crime of slave labor, the US Military Tribunal and a British War Crimes Court in Hong Kong did so in landmark cases against private industrialists.[317] In the arguments, no distinctions were drawn between slave labor and forced labor or other relevant notions.

Furthermore, several Nazi leaders were convicted for the war crime of pillage. Among them were Alfred Rosenberg, who was responsible of systematic and extensive plundering of art in the territories occupied by Nazi Germany as well as nine Nazi officials who excessively plundered Polish forests.[318]

Julius Streicher, the editor of the newspaper *Der Stürmer,* and Baldur von Schirach, Head of the *Hitlerjugend,* the Nazi youth organization, were convicted of the crime against humanity of persecution by the IMT for, among

311 For a more detailed discussion, see Smith 2009, 1124 *et seq.*

312 Nuremberg Charter 1945, Articles 9–10.

313 International Military Tribunal 1947, Vol. 1, 255 *et seq.* and 273.

314 Bassiouni 2013, 98.

315 Palermo Convention 2000, Article 5; EU Council Framework Decision 2008, Article 2.

316 Bormann Case 1946, Final arguments; Bormann Case 1946, Judgment, 64; Hauck 2016, 452.

317 Nuremberg Charter 1945, Article 6(2); Flick Case 1947; IG Farben Case 1948; Krupp Case 1948; Kinkaşeki Mine Case 1947.

318 IMT Rosenberg 1946; UNWCC Case 7150 1948.

others, the destruction of the Nuremberg synagogue in 1938 and extensive destruction of cultural goods in Great Britain, respectively.[319]

2.3.3.1.2 *ICTY and ICTR*

After the collapse of the Soviet Union, organized crime developed in the Balkans and flourished during the war because of economic blockades, weak State institutions, and a legal vacuum.[320] "Most of the organized crime groups were interlinked with State security forces and they nourished the (para)State apparatuses."[321] Organized crime is thus crucial to fully understanding crimes perpetrated during the Yugoslav conflict, and it continued to play a major role during ICTY investigations; for example, organized crime groups allegedly hid the Croatian Army General Ante Gotovina, who stood accused of war crimes by the tribunal.[322]

The situation in Rwanda with regard to organized crime was and remains different. Rwanda has, until today, not seen the emergence of major domestic organized criminal groups.[323] Although Rwanda's poorly controlled borders in some areas have allowed smuggling activities to strive in the Great Lake region, including the smuggling of cannabis, gold, and cassiterite, the genocidal conflict was largely conducted without support or involvement of organized crime.[324] Nevertheless, the main Hutu and Tutsi militias in the region, namely the Hutu *Forces démocratiques de libération du Rwanda* and the Tutsi *Congrès national pour la défense du peuple*, were involved in trafficking different goods.[325]

Organized crime, however, was not included in the (identical) jurisdiction *ratione materiae* of either the ICTY or ICTR. In fact, organized crime was only referenced with regard to two subjects: the first was the concept of indirect participation in German law (*mittelbare Täterschaft*), normally used in the context of organized crime and referenced in arguments on indirect (co-) perpetration, and the second concerned statistics on members of organized criminal groups portraying themselves as members of police or military, and

---

319 IMT Streicher 1946; IMT von Schirach 1946.

320 Stojarová 2007, 91.

321 Stojarová 2007, 113; see also Bovenkerk 2003.

322 Nielsen 2012; del Ponte 2005.

323 Overseas Security Advisory Council of the US Department of State 2012.

324 UNODC 2011a. Most of the violence was conducted with machetes and other readily available weapons and the arms that did play a role were purchased on the legal market. See also Gallimore, 2014.

325 UNODC 2011a, 62.

thus—according to the argument it was used in—hindering proper investigations by the accused.[326]

Nevertheless, both the ICTY and ICTR have developed case law that can be relevant to the context of organized crime regarding the definitions and elements of international crimes as well as individual criminal responsibility.

Especially regarding crimes against humanity, the ICTY and ICTR provided important interpretations. For example, the ICTY established that crimes against humanity can occur in times of peace, a view also taken by the negotiators of the Rome Statute.[327] Moreover, both tribunals altered the previously applied State policy requirement to a more general organizational policy requirement and rejected the policy element as part of customary international law.[328] Furthermore, both tribunals held that an attack, one of the contextual requirements for crimes against humanity, does not need to be violent and that even "exerting pressure on the population to act in a certain manner"[329] can qualify as an attack.

In addition, the *Kunarac* case before the ICTY is one of the milestone cases regarding modern forms of slavery, "blurr[ing] the conceptual borders between enslavement and trafficking in human beings."[330] The Trial Chamber held that enslavement as a crime against humanity may be "broader than the traditional [...] definitions of slavery, the slave trade and servitude or forced or compulsory labor found in other areas of international law."[331] The Trial Chamber identified the following factors relevant to limiting the crime of enslavement: physical and psychological control, the use or threat of force or other forms of coercion, cruel treatment and abuse, assertion of exclusivity, control of sexuality, and forced labor.[332] Thus, the Trial Chamber rendered the determination of a lack of consent or free will irrelevant. With regard to forced labor, the appeals Chamber in *Krnojelac* recognized that although a detainee's subjective opinion of having been forced to work is not sufficient to establish lack of consent, objective evidence for an atmosphere of fear making the expression of free consent impossible is indeed sufficient.[333]

---

326 ICTY Šainović *et al.* 2006, para 30; ICTR Gacumbitsi 2004, para 19; ICTY Prlić *et al.* 2011, para 289.

327 ICTY Tadić 1999, para 251 ; Smith 2009, 1137.

328 E.g., ICTY Kunarac 2002, para 98 and footnote 114; see section 3.2.2.1.1.

329 ICTR Akayesu 1998, 281; see also ICTY Kunarac 2002, para 86.

330 van der Wilt 2014.

331 ICTY Kunarac *et al.* 2001, para 541.

332 *ibid.*, para 542–3; see section 3.2.2.2.1.

333 ICTY Krnojelac 2003, para 231.

Moreover, the ICTY and ICTR developed jurisprudence judged "nothing short of revolutionary"[334] regarding gender-related crimes; that is, the characterization of rape as a possible instrument of genocide and the recognition of sexual violence as torture.[335] Moreover, the ICTY recognized the confiscation and destruction of cultural property as a possible manifestation of the crime of persecution, which may be relevant with regard to illicit trade in cultural goods.[336]

Regarding the interpretation of provisions concerning individual criminal responsibility, the ICTY and ICTR also played a major role. For example, the ICTY Trial Chamber in *Musema* held that the "definition of individual criminal responsibility [...] applies not only to the military but also to persons exercising civilian authority as superiors,"[337] thereby opening the possibility for business owners and heads of other nonmilitary hierarchies (e.g., organized criminal groups) to be held responsible for acts committed by their subordinates. Notably with regard to arms trafficking, the ICTR Trial Chamber held specifically that "by procuring means, such as weapons, [...] used to commit genocide, with the accomplice knowing that such means would be used for such a purpose,"[338] one may be liable as an accomplice in genocide.

2.3.3.1.3 *The Hybrid Chambers of the Court of Bosnia and Herzegovina*

While the same general developments could be observed in Bosnia and Herzegovina (BiH) as in the Balkans as a whole, BiH was affected more than other countries in the region. Organized crime and corruption remain major challenges of the country still today.[339] During the war, ethnically defined criminal networks expanded and, after the war, BiH attracted numerous groups from other parts of the region hoping to re-establish the Balkan trafficking route.[340] In a report prepared concerning BiH's ambitions for EU membership, a vast array of organized criminal activities were identified in the country, with trafficking in drugs and human beings, money laundering, and vehicle theft being the most dominant.[341] Organized crime is closely linked both to local

334 Askin 2003, 317.

335 ICTR Akayesu 1998; ICTY Delalić *et al.* 1998.

336 E.g., ICTY Blaškić 2000, para 22; ICTY Kupreškić *et al.* 2000, para 621; see also von Schorlemer 2016, 670 *et seq.*

337 ICTR Musema 2000, para 148.

338 ICTR Bagilishema 2001, para 69–70, citing Code Pénal du Rwanda 1977, Article 91(2).

339 Stojarová 2007, 5.

340 *ibid.*, 6.

341 Kržalić 2014, 7.

elites as well as terrorist groups, allegedly having supplied groups such as the Irish Republican Army with weapons.[342]

To supplement the work of the ICTY and continue judicially coping with crimes committed during the civil war after that work was completed, two special chambers were established within the BiH Criminal Court: one with jurisdiction over war crimes and one with jurisdiction over organized crime, economic crime, and corruption.[343] The chambers originally consisted of both domestic and international judges with the latter being phased out over time.[344]

Although the Chambers apply the 2003 BiH Penal Code and other domestic law, chapter 17 of the Code reiterates international offenses including genocide, crimes against humanity, war crimes, trafficking in persons, procuring prostitution, smuggling of persons, illicit trafficking in arms, nuclear materials and drugs, and terrorism.[345] Economic crime is addressed in chapter 18, different forms of corruption in chapter 19, obstruction of justice (in particular at the ICTY) in chapter 20, and organized crime in chapter 22.[346] It is exceptional that, first, the Court covers organized crime alongside the core crimes, and second, "national competencies [...] are both initiated and justified by international criminal law."[347]

Prosecuting core crimes, the War Crime Chamber has relied extensively on the ICTY's substantive and procedural jurisprudence as well as evidence.[348] Notably however, regarding the crimes of sexual slavery and enslavement as crimes against humanity, the BiH Penal Code mirrors the Rome Statute instead of the ICTY Statute and has thus been able to make "progressive determinations"[349] in these areas; for example, deciding that corroboration of the testimony of a victim of sexual violence is not necessarily required, and that the age of victims of sexual violence can be an aggravating circumstance.[350]

Between 2003 and 2018, the Chamber for organized and economic crime and corruption delivered more than 1100 final judgments on various offenses.[351]

---

342 Stojarová 2007, 8; Curtis and Karacan 2002.

343 Law of the Court of BiH 2009, Article 14.

344 *ibid.*, Article 24(2).

345 BiH Criminal Code 2003, chapter 17.

346 *ibid.*, chapters 18–20 and 22.

347 Hauck 2016, 457.

348 Reiger 2012, 305.

349 *ibid.*, 306.

350 BiH Criminal Code 2003, Article 172(c) and (g) ; Court of BiH Janković 2007, 58 ; Court of BiH Samardžic 2006, 39. For a more detailed account see Edman 2008.

351 The Court of Bosnia and Herzegovina 2021.

According to a 2012 study, trafficking in persons, drug trafficking, and tax evasion were the most prominent offenses prosecuted, followed by abuse of office and money laundering.[352] In most cases of organized criminal activity, the Court charged the defendants with a violation of the offense of organized crime in conjunction with the offense relevant in the concrete case, such as drug trafficking or smuggling of persons.[353] In its judgments, the Chamber also refers to the UN Convention against Transnational Organized Crime and its Protocols.[354]

Despite the largely domestic nature of the two hybrid sections of the BiH Criminal Court, their relevance to international prosecutions of organized crime is based on the fact that "organized group conduct incurs individual criminal responsibility by virtue of national jurisdiction but triggered essentially by international criminal law."[355]

2.3.3.1.4 *The Special Court for Sierra Leone*

In Sierra Leone, the illicit exploitation of natural resources, especially diamonds, was a main focus not only of the SCSL but also of the international community as it watched the tribunal commence operations. Two reports by Partnership Africa Canada and a UN Panel of Experts had blamed Liberia's President Charles Taylor for pulling the strings of the operations of the Revolutionary United Front (RUF), "with pillage a bigger objective than politics."[356] In his opening Statement, the Prosecutor announced:

> [The Prosecution will] prove that the accused is responsible for the development and execution of a plan that caused death and destruction in Sierra Leone. That plan [...] was to take political and physical control of Sierra Leone in order to exploit its abundant natural resources and to establish a friendly or subordinate government there to facilitate that exploitation.[357]

Although the provision on pillage is identical to the provision in the Rome Statute, it was interpreted much more broadly.[358] The SCSL Trial Chamber

352 Brady 2012, 29.
353 BiH Criminal Code 2003, Article 250; e.g., Court of BiH Mustafagić *et al.* 2011.
354 E.g., Court of BiH Bašić *et al.* 2008.
355 Hauck 2016, 435.
356 Smillie, Gberie and Hazleton 2000; UN Security Council Panel of Experts 2000; Gberie 2002, 2.
357 Cited in van den Herik and Dam-de Jong 2011, footnote 123.
358 Schabas (Commentary) 2016, 297; see sections 3.2.3.2.2.1 and 4.1.1.2.

explained that "the definition is framed to apply to a broad range of situations" and that, in its view, the requirement of "private or personal use" of pillaged property, as stated in the Elements of Crimes, was "unduly restrictive and ought not to be an element of the crime of pillage."[359] Pillage has been included in most indictments of the Court and has formed part of the convictions in all cases.[360]

However, the Prosecution encountered a series of difficulties holding defendants accountable for their actions related to the illicit diamond trade. Because the SCSL was the first international tribunal with jurisdiction over a conflict in which natural resources played a crucial role, the tribunal had to break new grounds. The Taylor Trial Chamber, for example, deliberated for a year on the question of whether the concept of joint criminal enterprise was applicable to what the Prosecution had presented as the common plan to exploit Sierra Leone's resources, a concept that the Defense had called "ill-defined at best."[361] The evidence presented by the Prosecution showed that Taylor had seen the exploitation of the diamonds as a benefit of the conflict from the beginning, but that they became more crucial as hostilities continued over years. The evidence also showed that Liberia was an important transit country for smuggled diamonds, which were critical for the RUF's funding for supplies and arms, but that, in fact, the majority of all funds went to Taylor for "safekeeping."[362] It was estimated that at the height of the conflict, Taylor owned assets of at least $400 million.[363]

The prosecution strategy of the joint criminal enterprise was similarly applied in the SCSL's cases regarding the RUF and the Armed Forces Revolutionary Council (AFRC). The Appeals Chamber, however, held that the objective of gaining control over the territory of Sierra Leone to exploit its resources did not constitute a crime under its statute itself, notwithstanding that crimes could have been committed on the way to achieving this objective.[364] It also refused to consider the charges concerning the systematic and unlawful appropriation of diamonds because they were not described in the part of the indictment that specifically referred to pillage.[365] Following these

359 Special Court for Sierra Leone AFRC Case 2007, 753–4.
360 An overview of cases until 2008 can be found in Rapp 2008, annex.
361 Cited in Marchuk 2009, 95.
362 Rapp 2008, 17.
363 Louth and Twort 2012, 14.
364 Special Court for Sierra Leone AFRC Case 2008, 82.
365 Special Court for Sierra Leone RUF Case 2009, 1339.

problems in earlier cases, the Taylor indictment was amended to exclude all references to diamonds.[366]

Although the SCSL Rules of Procedure provide for the recovery of assets, especially if they were obtained by proven criminal conduct, the Trial Chamber did not include forfeiture in its judgments, to the surprise of observers.[367] Only $7 million have been recovered from Taylor's personal assets. Moreover, David Crane, SCSL Prosecutor until 2005, stated that he has little hope that further asset recovery might still be possible at this late stage.[368]

2.3.3.1.5 *The Hybrid Kosovo Specialist Chambers and Specialist Prosecutor's Office*

After years of State organized oppression, Kosovar Albanians organized themselves into the KLA, which launched an insurgency in 1996 that led to the Kosovo War (1998–99). During that time, the KLA turned to various organized criminal activities to procure funding, including drugs, arms, and human trafficking.[369] Focused on political stability, the KLA was "upheld as a self-respecting nationalist movement" and *de facto* allies of the North Atlantic Treaty Organization (NATO) and other international forces despite their sound knowledge of the KLA's involvement in organized crime.[370] After the war and independence, "strong continuity between the former KLA and [...] the political and executive establishment"[371] persisted, as showcased by the 2017 indictment of former KLA commander and member of Parliament Azem Syla for leading an organized criminal group.[372]

However, following a 2011 Council of Europe Parliamentary Assembly report containing serious allegations with regard to war crimes, crimes against humanity, as well as human trafficking for the removal of organs committed by the KLA, the EU decided to establish a Special Investigative Task Force that in 2014 announced that sufficient evidence existed for an indictment relating to the crimes described in the report.[373] Since the alleged crimes continued after the official end of the war in 1999, the ICTY's restricted temporal jurisdiction made

366 van den Herik and Dam-de Jong 2011, 268.
367 SCSL Rules of Procedure and Evidence 2002; Gallant 2012, 5–6.
368 Cited in Louth and Twort 2012, 14 and 16. For a detailed discussion of organized crime in the post-conflict recovery of Liberia and Sierra Leone, see Vorrath 2014.
369 Athanassopoulou 2005, 43.
370 Chossudovsky 1999, 29.
371 Athanassopoulou 2005, 43.
372 State Prosecutor of the Republic of Kosovo 2016.
373 Marty 2011.

it necessary to prosecute these crimes in another forum.[374] After an exchange of letters between the President of Kosovo and the EU High Representative for Foreign Affairs and Security Policy, the establishment of a specialized institution was decided based on a Constitutional Amendment and the Law on Specialist Chambers and Specialist Prosecutor's Office.[375]

After the appointment of the judges in February 2017 and confirmation of the Rules of Procedure and Evidence in August 2017, the KSC became fully operational. At the time of writing, no charges have yet been filed.

2.3.3.2 Organized Crime Offenses and the Making of the Rome Statute

While several geographically and temporally restricted international criminal tribunals were established, the idea of a permanent and international criminal court gained momentum. Organized crime played a major role in related discussions. The following subsection summarizes the most critical steps leading to the adoption of the Rome Statute, focusing on the discussions on jurisdiction *ratione materiae*.

2.3.3.2.1 *The Draft Code of Crimes against Peace and Security of Mankind*

In 1947, after the Nuremberg and Tokyo tribunals had broken completely new ground, the UNGA asked the International Law Commission (ILC) to codify the legal principles that had evolved from the Nuremberg Charter and the tribunals' judgments, as well as to prepare a draft "code of offenses against the peace and security of mankind."[376] In 1954, the ILC submitted a draft containing 13 separate offenses, including aggression, annexation, intervention, State support of terrorist activities, genocide, war crimes, and inhuman acts committed against the civilian population.[377] While commentators leveled the criticism that "little progress has been made with the proposed code,"[378] the General Assembly tabled the discussion until 1981 because of the lack of a legal definition of aggression, when it requested the ILC to continue its work.[379]

New offenses entered the discussion based on nine reports prepared by a Special Rapporteur between 1983 and 1991, and in 1991 the ILC provisionally adopted the draft articles for the then-called Draft Code of Crimes against the

374 For a detailed discussion of the possibility of the ICTY to take over these cases see Holvoet 2017.

375 Kosovo Constitution Amendment 2015; Law on KSC 2015.

376 A/RES/177 (II) 1947.

377 International Law Commission 1954, Vol. II.

378 Johnson 1955, 447.

379 A/RES/36/106 1981; Bassiouni 1993, 259.

Peace and Security of Mankind.[380] From then on, offenses also included colonial domination, apartheid, mercenarism, international terrorism, illicit traffic in narcotic drugs, and crimes against the environment, which all remained part of the draft up to 1995.[381] Illicit traffic in narcotic drugs was defined as "undertaking, organizing, facilitating, financing or encouraging of illicit traffic in narcotic drugs on a large scale, whether within the confines of a State or in a transboundary context"[382] and included acquisition, holding, conversion, or transfer as well as production, manufacture, extraction, preparation, offering (for sale), distribution, sale, delivery, brokerage, dispatch, transport, and im- and exportation.[383] However, the draft articles were widely criticized as "an imperfect instrument"[384] "with significant shortcomings."[385] Bassiouni commented

> the specificity that would have been expected in that code has regressed in relationship to that which existed after World War II. Thus, the "Draft Code," which started with the expectation by the world community that it would initiate the codification of international criminal law, became nothing more than a frustrated attempt.[386]

In addition, ILC members were divided among themselves. On illicit drug trafficking, for example, some members felt that drug trafficking seriously affected sovereignty, especially of smaller States, whereas others held that it was unlikely to endanger international peace and security unless combined with other crimes, and pointed to the existing suppression regime.[387] Due to this internal opposition, the 1996 Draft Code was reduced to a few core crimes, namely aggression, genocide, crimes against humanity, crimes committed against UN personnel, and war crimes.[388] This decision was fiercely criticized.[389] The

---

380 Allain and Jones 1997, 100.

381 International Law Commission 1991, Articles 18, 20, 23, 24, 25, 26; International Law Commission 1995.

382 International Law Commission 1991, Article 25(1).

383 *ibid.*, Article 25(2) and (3).

384 Ferencz 1992, 380.

385 McCormack and Simpson 1994, 46.

386 Bassiouni 1993, 262.

387 International Law Commission 1995, para 112–3; see section 2.2.2.2.

388 International Law Commission 1996; Boister 1998, 27.

389 Rayfuse 1997, 85: "The decision to put the Code on a draconian diet in 1995 nearly drained all the life from it."; Allain and Jones 1997, 117: The ILC "lost its way in attempting to forge new ground".

parallel drafting of a statute for an international court, which in 1996/1997 went further in its substantive provisions than the 1996 Code, posed "something of a dilemma"[390] for the ILC's work on the Code. Thus, the ILC itself, after considering an international convention, the incorporation of the code in the statute of an international criminal court, or a General Assembly declaration, suggested to the General Assembly that it should decide which form the Code should take.[391] In response, the UNGA asked the Preparatory Committee on the Establishment of an International Criminal Court to consider the content of the draft Code for their work.[392] Whether considered or not for the drafting of the Rome Statute, the Code "die[d] a quiet death."[393]

2.3.3.2.2 *The 1993 and 1994 ILC Draft Statutes for an International Criminal Court*

Parallel to the ILC's work on the Code, a coalition of Caribbean States led by Trinidad and Tobago called upon the UN in 1989 to establish a permanent international criminal court with jurisdiction over illicit transnational trafficking in narcotic drugs, hoping that the corrupt influence of drug cartels would be weaker in a remote international system.[394] The UNGA requested that the ILC work on the issue, and in 1993 a first draft statute for an international criminal court was completed.[395]

The 1993 Draft Statute followed a number of basic ideas: that an international criminal court should be established by a treaty agreed by State Parties and be consensual in nature; that it should have jurisdiction over natural persons, not States; and that it should extend to treaties in force that define international crimes instead of being limited to the Code of Crimes against the Peace and Security of Mankind.[396] The Draft Statute included three categories of crimes: (1) crimes under a list of defined self-executing treaties, such as the Genocide and Geneva Conventions, as well as the Apartheid Convention and several treaties relating to specific acts of terrorism; (2) crimes under general international law; and (3) crimes under suppression regimes that are not self-executing but prescribe national jurisdiction, such as the UN Drug Convention.[397] The crimes in the third category had to meet an additional

390 Rayfuse 1997, 83.
391 International Law Commission 1996.
392 International Law Commission 1997.
393 Rayfuse 1997, 86.
394 UN General Assembly Sixth Committee 1989, A/C.6/44/SR.38; Boister 1998, 34.
395 A/RES/44/39 1989; International Law Commission 1993, annex.
396 Crawford 1994, 142.
397 International Law Commission 1993, annex, Articles 22, 26(2)(a) and (b).

threshold of exceptional seriousness. As for the first category, a State with jurisdiction over a crime under the relevant treaty, or in the case of genocide every State Party to the Genocide Convention, may confer its jurisdiction to the ICC.[398] For the acceptance of jurisdiction, the ILC provided three alternatives giving more or less importance to *ad hoc* acceptance of jurisdiction and restrictions to specific crimes.[399] As for the other two categories of crimes, the Draft Statute required "special consent," meaning that the acceptance of jurisdiction had to relate to specified persons or categories of persons, as well as that the requirements regarding the States accepting jurisdiction were higher than for the first category of crimes.[400] In particular, the inclusion of treaty crimes that were not self-executing was seen as a "considerable innovation."[401] On the one hand, the inclusion of these treaties was criticized because they "explicitly do not create or define crimes in international law" and lack sufficient specificity "covering a wide range of conduct," including local crimes that should be dealt with on a national level.[402] On the other hand, some members of the ILC argued that the Drug Convention in particular fulfilled the preconditions to be included in the first category of crimes.[403]

In 1994, the ILC adopted a new version of the Draft Statute, which reduced the number of categories of crimes to two: the first was crimes under general international law, namely genocide, aggression, war crimes, and crimes against humanity, and the second was treaty crimes as listed in the annex, which now all had to meet the additional threshold of "exceptionally serious crimes of international concern."[404] The annex included the same treaties as the 1993 Statute as well as the Torture Convention.[405] The criteria for inclusion in the annex were that the crimes were defined in the multilateral treaty, thereby upholding the *nullum crimen sine lege* guarantee, as well as that the treaty provided for universal jurisdiction based on the *aut dedere aut iudicare* principle or on a reference to the possibility of an ICC to take jurisdiction.[406] The 1994 Draft Statute also simplified the jurisdictional provisions. Whereas some authors saw the 1994 Draft as a "significant improvement on the models and proposals of the past" and as the "promise of an end to the world community's

398 *ibid.*, Article 24(1).
399 *ibid.*, Article 23.
400 *ibid.*, Article 26(1).
401 Crawford 1994, 145.
402 *ibid.*, 146.
403 International Law Commission 1993, 110.
404 International Law Commission 1994a, Article 20.
405 *ibid.*, annex II.
406 *ibid.*, 41.

current affair with *ad hoc* approaches to the establishment of international judicial bodies,"[407] the Draft Statute also faced criticism. First, the treaty approach was seen as contradictory because some crimes were codified but only partly recognized, whereas others formed part of international customary law but were not codified and thus would not fall under ICC jurisdiction.[408] Second, whether the enactment of new substantive crimes was not rather a matter of other instruments was debated, which among other reasons was because of the unwillingness of States to commit themselves to a more effective criminalization.[409] Third, inadequacies in existing definitions of crimes in treaties, of jurisdictional provisions, and provisions for extradition and mutual assistance were discussed both as an argument for and against the inclusion of treaty crimes.[410]

The Draft Statute was submitted to the General Assembly, which handed it over to an *Ad Hoc* Committee on the Establishment of an International Criminal Court.

2.3.3.2.3 *Work of the Ad Hoc and the Preparatory Committee and the 1998 Rome Conference*

The *ad hoc* Committee convened twice in 1995 to debate the most crucial substantive and administrative issues in the ILC's draft Statute, but did not negotiate or amend the draft itself.[411] In its report prepared for the UNGA, the Committee stressed the importance of limiting the crimes falling under ICC jurisdiction to promote broad acceptance and therefore increased effectiveness of the Statute, enhance its credibility and authority, avoid overburdening it, and limit its costs.[412] However, the delegations differed widely on concrete crimes to be included and the respective jurisdictional rules.[413] Treaty crimes were seen to be "of a lesser magnitude" than core crimes, thereby trivializing and overburdening the court.[414] Still, merit was found in keeping all crimes stated in the annex because of the consensual nature of jurisdiction and inability of smaller States to gather the intelligence necessary for the prosecution of terrorism and drug-related offenses in particular.[415] Nevertheless,

407 Berg 1996, 264.
408 Ambos 1996, 524.
409 Crawford 1994, 146; Boister 1998, 34.
410 Boister 1998, 34.
411 Bassiouni 1999, 443–444.
412 Ad Hoc Committee on the Establishment of an ICC 1995, para 54.
413 *ibid.*, para 55.
414 *ibid.*, para 81.
415 *ibid.*, para. 82.

a "clear trend emerged in favor of limiting the jurisdiction [...] to the core crimes,"[416] although some disagreement remained as to what crimes qualified as core crimes.[417] The UNGA decided to replace the *Ad Hoc* Committee with a Preparatory Committee (PrepCom) tasked to "prepare a widely acceptable consolidated text of a convention for an international criminal court [...] as a next step towards consideration by a conference of plenipotentiaries."[418] For its first year, however, the PrepCom did not engage in drafting and made no significant progress on the question of treaty crimes. In its 1996 report, the Committee discussed international terrorism, apartheid, torture, hostage-taking, illicit drug trafficking, attacks against the UN and associated personnel, as well as serious threats to the environment, but refrained from making recommendations or expressing majority views.[419] However, support for the inclusion of treaty crimes decreased with even Trinidad and Tobago representing the Caribbean Community and Common Markets supporting the emerging view that jurisdiction should be restricted to the most serious offenses.[420] Despite this apparent lack of progress, the UNGA "decided that a diplomatic conference [...] should be held in 1998, with a view to finalizing and adopting a convention on the establishment of an international criminal court."[421] Up until 1997, the PrepCom only produced "an unstructured and substantially unusable compilation of all governmental proposals."[422] During an intersessional meeting in January 1998, the compilation was streamlined. The resulting draft statute included genocide, war crimes, and crimes against humanity, as well as aggression, terrorism, crimes against the UN and associated personnel, and illicit drug trafficking in brackets; however, it noted that the three latter crimes were considered "without prejudice to a final decision on their inclusion"[423] and less thoroughly than the core crimes.[424] Overall, the draft consisted of numerous corrections, notes, and options, and was "essentially a cumbersome accumulation of alternative governmental proposals requiring additional technical work and more extensive negotiations, particularly with regard to fundamental issues such as the definition of crimes."[425] A last

416 von Hebel and Robinson 1999, 80.
417 E.g., United Nations Meetings Coverage and Press Releases 1996.
418 A/RES/50/46 1995.
419 Preparatory Committee on the Establishment of an ICC 1996, para 103–14.
420 Boister 1998, 27–29.
421 A/RES/51/207 1996.
422 Bassiouni 1999, 444.
423 Preparatory Committee on the Establishment of an ICC 1998a, 34.
424 *ibid.*, 16–36.
425 Bassiouni 1999, 444.

preparatory session was held in March and April 1998, and "after 19 weeks of formal meetings [...] the PrepCom sent to Rome a draft convention of 116 articles with 1,700 brackets containing disagreed language."[426] The preliminarily included crimes remained unchanged from the January draft.[427] After translation, 6 weeks remained to study the draft until the Rome Conference in July 1998, leaving many of the delegations of 160 participating States, 31 official organizations, and 134 NGO observers insufficiently prepared.[428] Throughout the negotiations, the delegations were aware that Part II of the Statute covering jurisdictional provisions comprised the "hardest and most intractable political and substantive problems."[429] Thus, "in an impressive display of his deft and thoughtful aggressiveness,"[430] Chairman Kirsch charged himself with the negotiations of part II, organized a debate in which he posed a couple of specific closed questions to the delegations, and published their votes, which clearly indicated that the option for part II enjoyed the broadest support.[431] The negotiated draft based on the poll was not reviewed by the Drafting Committee and was presented to the delegations on a take-it-or-leave-it basis.[432] It included the crimes contained in the Rome Statute today (genocide, aggression, war crimes, and crimes against humanity) and had left out all treaty crimes previously considered.

The Statute was adopted by 120 positive and seven negative votes with 21 abstentions, a moment representing the "culmination of the hopes and dreams of many generations [...] who aimed at seeing international law placed on a sounder basis than the voluntarist conceptions so characteristic of it."[433] Although resolution E of the Final Act of the Rome Conference recommended "that a Review Conference [...] consider the crimes of terrorism and drug crimes with a view to arriving at an acceptable definition and their inclusion in the list of crimes within the jurisdiction of the Court,"[434] the proposal has not been acted upon at the time of writing.

426 Washburn 1999, 362–3.
427 Preparatory Committee on the Establishment of an ICC, 1998b, 11–29.
428 Rosenne 2000, 387 ; Bassiouni 1999, 444–445.
429 Washburn 1999, 369.
430 *ibid.*, 370.
431 *ibid.*
432 Bassiouni 1999, 453 and 458.
433 Rosenne 2000, 387; Bassiouni 1999, 459–460.
434 UN Diplomatic Conference of Plenipotentiaries on the Establishment of an ICC 1998, section E.

2.4 Assessment

Although organized crime has never been prosecuted as an international crime before an international tribunal, this chapter demonstrated that it has a longstanding history not only in transnational criminal law but also in the development of international criminal law *stricto sensu.* Many offenses constituting organized crime are clearly defined in international conventions and enjoy high levels of support in the international community. However, existing efforts to contain organized crime have not been effective at curtailing the far-reaching detrimental effects of organized crime on societies worldwide. Thus, international criminal law, the purpose of which is to address "the most serious crimes of concern to the international community as a whole"[435] that currently remain unpunished, becomes relevant.

In this book, organized crime is defined as the commission of one or more crimes by a "structured group of three or more persons, existing for a period of time and acting in concert [...] to obtain, directly or indirectly, a financial or other material benefit."[436]

Among other crimes, this definition encompasses drug trafficking, trafficking in persons and subsequent exploitation, migrant smuggling, and illicit trade in arms and ammunition, natural resources, and cultural goods as defined in this book. Moreover, corruption, money laundering, and organized crime-related violence are covered by the definition. These offenses do not constitute profit-generating activities of organized criminal groups but frequently accompany them. They are perpetrated to enable the groups to operate in illegal markets, and thus represent key characteristics to differentiate illegal from legal market activities.

A large body of international and regional conventions, regimes, and soft law addresses these various activities of organized crime. The body of law mainly consists of transnational criminal law, or so-called suppression regimes, providing specific crime definitions and detailed rules for mutual legal assistance and other aspects of cooperation in the fields of law enforcement to be incorporated into the national laws of State Parties. Although transnational criminal law often contains the *aut dedere aut iudicare* rule, it does not establish international jurisdiction as a matter of international law. Because of the facilitating effects of globalization on organized crime and challenges in international cooperation, the existing legal regime does not currently hamper

435 Rome Statute 1998, Preamble, para 4.

436 Palermo Convention 2000, Article 2(a).

organized crime operations successfully. The results are negative effects on the legal economy, on the legitimacy of State institutions, and on society.

Therefore, organized crime meets the requirements of gravity, persisting impunity, and relevance to the international community that are inherent to the *telos* of international criminal law. Moreover, a growing interconnection exists between the crimes currently prosecuted at an international level and organized crime because of an increasing number of hybrid groups involved in both armed conflict or violence and organized criminal activities. The history of organized crime and international jurisprudence since the Second World War, and especially the role of organized crime throughout the drafting history of the Rome Statute of the International Criminal Court, underline the relevance of international criminal law in the fight against organized crime.

Hence, the applicability of the *lex lata* of international criminal law to organized crime is examined with regard to procedural and material aspects of jurisdiction in the following chapter. Subsequently, Chapter 4 discusses possible future developments facilitating the application of international criminal law to organized crime.

CHAPTER 3

Organized Crime under the Rome Statute of the International Criminal Court

Chapter 2 demonstrated the pertinence of international criminal law to organized crime as well as the historic interconnection between the two. The present chapter proceeds to analyze international jurisdiction over organized crime *de lege lata*, considering procedural as well as substantive law.

As the latest, most comprehensive, and most broadly applicable document of international criminal law, the Rome Statute of the International Criminal Court represents the most relevant legal framework in this regard. In terms of procedure, the Rome Statute establishes rules regarding the mechanisms for triggering ICC jurisdiction, the required jurisdictional nexus to a State Party, and the principle of complementarity to national jurisdiction. The substantive provisions on jurisdiction of the Rome Statute limit ICC jurisdiction *ratione materiae* to the crimes of genocide, crimes against humanity, war crimes, and aggression. Moreover, ICC jurisdiction is limited to the modes of participation incurring individual criminal responsibility under the Rome Statute.[1]

This chapter first analyzes whether organized crime fulfills the procedural requirements of the Rome Statute. It then examines in which particular cases the jurisdiction *ratione materiae* of the ICC applies to organized crime, namely regarding genocide, crimes against humanity, and war crimes. Lastly, the cases of organized crime that incur criminal responsibility under the Rome Statute are studied.

Recurring examples of organized criminal groups and activities used in this chapter include, among others, human trafficking by the Japanese Yakuza, reported organ trade by the KLA, migrant smuggling and migrant-related crimes reported from Libya, drug trafficking by large cartels from South and Central America, illicit excavations, plunder and illicit trade in cultural and historic sites in Syria and Iraq, illegal exploitation of and trade in diamonds in Sierra Leone, and organized crime-related violence in Mexico and Colombia before the Peace Agreement.

1 Furthermore, jurisdiction *ratione temporis* is limited by the entry into force of the Rome Statute on 1 July 2002, the date of accession of a new State Party or the date of acceptance of *ad hoc* jurisdiction by a State depending on the case. Jurisdiction *ratione personae* is limited to persons of a minimum age of 18 years. Rome Statute 1998, Articles 11 and 26.

 | DOI:10.1163/9789004462588_004

The analyses in this chapter focus on legal questions that are especially relevant to organized crime, that is, those that arise only in or to a greater extent in cases of organized crime than in conventional cases, meaning situations of armed conflict or violence not motivated by material gain.

3.1 Procedural Requirements for Jurisdiction

3.1.1 *Trigger Mechanisms*

Article 13 of the Rome Statute sets out the so-called trigger mechanisms for the ICC's exercise of jurisdiction, namely a referral of a situation by a State Party, a referral by the Security Council (UNSC), and a referral by the Prosecutor applying his or her *proprio motu* power to initiate an investigation. The referral by a State Party and a *proprio motu* investigation are addressed in detail in Articles 14 and 15 of the Rome Statute, respectively, whereas a referral by the UNSC is only addressed in Article 13(b) of the Rome Statute.[2]

First, Article 13 of the Rome Statute requires that one or more of the crimes under ICC jurisdiction *ratione materiae* appear to have been committed or, under Article 15, that a reasonable basis exists to believe that crimes were committed. Second, Article 13 requires that a "situation," not a case, be referred to the ICC. Because the UNSC is not limited by the Article 12 requirements of a territorial or personal nexus to a State Party to the ICC (discussed in detail in the next section), it enjoys wider discretion than a State Party in determining or delimiting the situation based on geography, the period in time, and the identification of certain crimes or of their authors.[3]

2 While the Rome Statute does not contain any provision outlining the cooperation between the UNSC and the ICC, the Relationship Agreement between the United Nations and the ICC sets out some procedural rules regarding information exchange and possible UNSC assistance, but without any binding obligation on the part of the UNSC. Negotiated Relationship Agreement Between the International Criminal Court and the United Nations 2004. Following the two UNSC referrals regarding the situation in Darfur in 2005 and in Libya in 2011, the Prosecutor informs the UNSC of the progress of the prosecutions in bi-annual reports. The ICC does not receive additional funding or assistance pertaining to non-cooperation of any of the States involved. Although neither South Sudan nor Libya are State Parties, the ICC has repeatedly held that an obligation to cooperate with the ICC exists based on Articles 103 and 25 of the UN Charter.

3 See section 3.1.2. The exclusion of certain categories of persons as included in the UNSC resolutions S/RES/1593 2005 and S/RES/1970 2011, para 6 respectively, are considered not to be compatible with the Rome Statute. Schabas (Commentary) 2016, 378; Condorelli and Villalpando (Commentary edited by Cassese, Gaeta and Jones) 2002, 632–633.

In addition, Article 13(b) of the Rome Statute requires the UNSC to act under Chapter VII of the Charter of the UN when referring a situation to the ICC. Therefore, the requirements of the UN Charter for the UNSC to act under Chapter VII must also be met when referring a situation involving organized crime. Thus, whether a situation of organized crime can trigger the UNSC's competences under Chapter VII must be determined.[4] This question is analyzed in the following paragraphs.

According to Article 39 of the UN Charter, the UNSC must first determine the existence of any threat to the peace, breach of the peace, or act of aggression. While a breach of the peace and act of aggression are usually understood to include armed conflict, the notion of a threat to peace is the broadest, and thus could cover various types of organized crime. Therefore, to determine if organized crime can trigger UNSC competences under Chapter VII, it is necessary to first interpret the term "threat to the peace" in Article 39.

Interpretations of "peace" vary from a narrow understanding as the absence of armed conflict between States to broad interpretations including friendly relations between States as well as economic, social, political, and environmental factors that can be relevant for sustainable peace.[5] The UNSC stressed, for example, that

> [t]he absence of war and military conflicts amongst States does not in itself ensure international peace and security. The non-military sources of instability in the economic, social, humanitarian and ecological fields have become threats to peace and security. [...] peace and prosperity are indivisible and [...] lasting peace and stability require effective international cooperation for the eradication of poverty and the promotion of a better life for all in larger freedom.[6]

While Article 39 of the UN Charter affords the UNSC a certain degree of flexibility required to "maintain [...] peace and security" in a preemptive manner, the UNSC's role in the UN system, especially its delimitation from other bodies such as the GA and UN Economic and Social Council (ECOSOC), as well as the need for justiciable meanings of the terms used in the UN Charter limits the interpretation.[7] Thus, although the UNSC is concerned with matters beyond

4 The ICTY Appeals Chamber laid the basis for the ICC reviewing the legality of a referral by the UNSC with regard to the UNSC acting under Chapter VII, including a verification that the UNSC acted in conformity with the conditions set up in the UN Charter. See ICTY Tadić 1995.

5 de Wet 2004, 138; Krisch (Commentary edited by Simma *et al.*) 2012, 1277.

6 UN Security Council 1992, S/23500, 3 and 5.

7 Krisch (Commentary edited by Simma *et al.*) 2012, 1277.

armed conflict, it can only act under Chapter VII if a situation, also internal and nonmilitary at that point in time, bears the serious risk of leading to the outbreak of conflict and therefore represents a threat to peace.[8] Reviewing UNSC practice, a "double strategy" can be observed where it utilizes the impact of a situation within a country on international relations to address the internal situation itself.[9] Weapons of mass destruction,[10] terrorism,[11] as well as internal armed conflict[12] can constitute a threat to the peace according to UNSC practice. The Appeals Chamber of the ICTY confirmed this view with regard to internal conflicts.[13] Moreover, the UNSC held that the deliberate targeting of civilians in armed conflicts may constitute a threat to peace.[14] With regard to organized crime, the UNSC has repeatedly addressed the close link between human trafficking and conflict as well as that between the illegal exploitation of natural resources and conflict; for example, the illegal diamond trade in Sierra Leone.[15] Regarding drug trafficking and organized crime in general, former UN Secretary-General Ban Ki-moon addressed the UNSC in 2010 with, "let us prevent drug trafficking and organized crime from threatening international peace and security and all our hard-won work, across our agenda."[16] Moreover, members of the UNSC have expressed their concern regarding organized crime as a threat to peace and security in several debates.[17] A 2013 report by the International Peace Institute as well as a commentary by the Stockholm International Peace Research Institute (SIPRI) also considered organized

8 de Wet 2004, 138–144.

9 E.g., S/RES/217 1965 that determined that the continuation of the minority regime in Southern Rhodesia constituted a threat to peace; S/RES/418 1977 regarding the acquisition of arms by South Africa; S/RES/713 1991 regarding fighting in Yugoslavia and explicitly referring to the effects on neighboring countries. See also de Wet 2004, 150–174.

10 E.g., S/RES/1540 2004; S/RES/1718 2006; S/RES/1977 2011. See also Krisch (Commentary edited by Simma *et al.*) 2012, 1280.

11 E.g., S/RES/731 1992; S/RES/1189 1998; S/RES/1989 2011. See also Krisch (Commentary edited by Simma *et al.*) 2012, 1281.

12 E.g., on the Yugoslav conflict S/RES/713 1991; on Rwanda S/RES/918 1994; on Sierra Leone S/RES/1132 1997. See also Krisch (Commentary edited by Simma *et al.*) 2012, 2182–1283.

13 ICTY Tadić 1995, para 30.

14 S/RES/1296 2000.

15 On human trafficking, e.g., S/RES/2388 2017. On illegal exploitation of resources, e.g., on Sierra Leone S/RES/1446 2002; on Liberia S/RES/1903 2009; on the Democratic Republic of Congo S/RES/1925 2010. See also Krisch (Commentary edited by Simma *et al.*) 2012, 1289. See sections 3.2.3.2.2.1. and 3.2.3.2.2.3.

16 Ki-moon 2010.

17 E.g., UN Security Council 2011, S/PV.6668; UN Security Council 2012, S/PV.6760.

crime a threat to peace and security.[18] However, a concrete risk of conflict must exist in any particular case.[19]

Hence, organized crime can trigger UNSC action under Chapter VII if it poses a concrete risk of conflict. This applies, for example, to situations where the international nature of organized crime has acute repercussions on the relationships between States; where organized crime is responsible for severe violence or causes internal conflict, including migration flows into other countries as a result; and where organized crime and armed groups or terrorists converge.

The second step in Article 39 of the UN Charter is for the UNSC to make recommendations or decide on measures to be taken. The question of whether the UNSC is acting *ultra vires by* applying judicial measures was reviewed by the ICTY Appeals Chamber following the SC's decision to establish the first *ad hoc* tribunal based on Chapter VII powers. The Defense of the first accused Duško Tadić had argued that the establishment of a tribunal was not included in the measures to be taken under the UN Charter, that the UNSC as an executive organ was inherently incapable of creating a judicial organ, and that the measure was not appropriate because it did not and could not promote peace in the former Yugoslavia.[20] The Appeals Chamber rejected all arguments and held that the tribunal "was lawfully established."[21] Given the subsequent State practice vis-à vis the *ad hoc* tribunals, an *opinio iuris* in support of the UNSC's competence to establish international criminal tribunals or lay the basis for international jurisdiction seems to have developed in the aftermath.[22] This applies to all threats to peace, and therefore, is also valid for relevant cases of organized crime.

Although not explicitly stated in Article 39 of the UN Charter, the UNSC has full discretion to choose the cases in which it deems Chapter VII actions most relevant and promising. In particular, the UNSC may have a special interest in referring a situation to the ICC if the national judicial authority is not able to "deal with crimes in their entirety"[23] due to difficulties in geographically locating a crime or conflicts between States on the *forum conveniens*. This underlines the relevance of international criminal law for the prosecution of organized crime.

---

18 Kemp, Shaw and Boutellis 2013; Kemp 2009.
19 Krisch (Commentary edited by Simma *et al.*) 2012, 1291.
20 ICTY Tadić 1995, para 32.
21 *ibid.*, para 33–40.
22 See also Tine (Commentary edited by Fernandez, Pacreau and Maze) 2012, footnote 29.
23 Condorelli and Villalpando (Commentary edited by Cassese, Gaeta and Jones) 2002, 639.

In sum, organized crime can constitute a threat to peace under Chapter VII of the UN Charter, and thus can be referred to the ICC by the UNSC.

3.1.2 *Preconditions to the Exercise of Jurisdiction*

The preconditions to the exercise of jurisdiction of the ICC were among the most contentious issues at the negotiations of the Rome Statute, and were finally decided by vote.[24] The resulting provision in Article 12 of the Rome Statute defines the required jurisdictional link by setting out the rule (in paragraph 2) of either a territorial or nationality nexus regarding the perpetrator of the crime. Such a nexus is required except for *ad hoc* acceptance of jurisdiction that can be limited with regard to territory, time, and types of crimes, as well as UNSC referrals under Chapter VII of the UN Charter.[25] Hence, contrary to the other trigger mechanisms, UNSC referrals are independent of a territorial or nationality nexus between the situation and the ICC; that is, the UNSC can refer any crime committed after the Rome Statute entered into force on July 1, 2002.[26] Thus, the Rome Statute's jurisdictional provisions "situate[…] the ICC on a continuum with the *ad hoc* international criminal tribunals […] which the Security Council established" and puts at the UNSC's "disposal a judicial instrument for the prosecution of international crimes, accessible in any and all future situations without the need to create new tribunals."[27]

Except for UNSC referrals and acceptance of *ad hoc* jurisdiction, either a territorial or nationality nexus to a State Party must therefore exist to establish ICC jurisdiction over organized crime. However, most organized crime today cannot be confined to a certain territory and organized criminal groups are rarely restricted in terms of nationality.[28] As a result, which national jurisdiction certain activities can be attributed to and how potential conflicts are to be resolved must be determined. Because of increasingly transnational criminal networks and technological advances, questions of the *forum conveniens* are becoming ever more relevant, as well as beyond organized crime, such as in relation to multi-stage cyberattacks.[29]

---

24 Schabas and Pecorella (Commentary edited by Triffterer and Ambos) 2016, 690–695.

25 See section 3.1.1.

26 Triffterer and Ambos 2016, 696. Some argue that the jurisdiction of the Court following an UNSC referral can be backdated further under certain circumstances. See Condorelli and Villalpando (Commentary edited by Cassese, Gaeta and Jones) 2002, 634–637.

27 *ibid.*, 628.

28 See also sections 2.1.3 and 2.1.4.

29 Some forms of multi-stage cyberattacks can also constitute organized crime. For a detailed discussion see Clark and Landau 2011.

The preconditions to the exercise of jurisdiction in the Rome Statute are much more restrictive than jurisdictional rules of international conventions directly addressing organized crime, such as the anti-drug conventions that apply both a subjective and objective approach (i.e., the effects doctrine, establishing jurisdiction in States that currently have no direct nexus to a crime except "a view to the commission within its territory.")[30] As Schabas indicated, "many national jurisdictions extend the concept of territorial jurisdiction to include crimes that create effects upon the territory of a State."[31] Crucially, neither the custodial State nor the State whose nationals have become the victim of a crime under ICC jurisdiction can provide a jurisdictional link under Article 12 of the Rome Statute.[32]

In cases where a crime has been committed on the territory or by nationals of two or more States, several scenarios are possible. First, all affected States can be State Parties to the Rome Statute, and thus serve as a jurisdictional link. In this case, jurisdiction over the different elements of a crime that have either been committed in different territories or by different nationals can be established separately through multiple referrals or by *proprio motu* investigations, and be grouped into one situation based on more than one jurisdictional link. In the case of two or more concurrent jurisdictional links to a crime, all provide an equal basis for jurisdiction unless the State Parties have acceded to the Rome Statute at different points in time, thereby establishing differing rules for ICC jurisdiction *ratione temporis* according to Article 11(2) of the Rome Statute.

A second possible scenario is where an individual accused of having committed a crime on two or more territories is a national of a State Party but not all States on whose territory the crime has been committed are State Parties. This "poses little difficulty and the exercise of jurisdiction by the Court is not in doubt"[33] because a single and continuous jurisdictional link exists based on nationality.

The issue becomes more complex in the third possible scenario, where neither the State of nationality of the perpetrator nor one of the States on whose territory the crime occurred are State Parties to the Rome Statute. If a third party exists that is a State Party to the Rome Statute and wishes to bring the crime before the Court, the possible scope of a referral must be determined. Two different approaches will now be examined. First, the crime in question

30 Drug Trafficking Convention 1988, Article 4(1). See section 2.2.2.2.

31 Schabas (Commentary) 2016, 353.

32 For a discussion of the implications of these omissions see Kaul (Commentary edited by Cassese, Gaeta and Jones) 2002, 613–614.

33 Bourgon (Commentary edited by Cassese, Gaeta and Jones) 2002, 567.

can be split into several elements and the Court can only exercise jurisdiction over those that were committed on the territory of the State Party. For example, in the case of human trafficking, the victims could be recruited on the territory of a State Party but be trafficked into and exploited in another jurisdiction. In such a case, the ICC would only consider the conduct before the victims crossed the border into a neighboring State. Indeed, several cases have occurred in which a crime was split into components because of jurisdictional constraints. For example, the case of the so-called Gaza Freedom flotilla, referring to the Israeli interception of a humanitarian aid flotilla bound for Gaza, was referred to the ICC by the Union of the Comoros; the OTP only considered the three vessels that were registered under the flag of a State Party.[34] Similarly, the OTP's preliminary investigations into Iraq only concerned crimes committed by British forces, because neither Iraq nor any of the allies of Great Britain are State Parties.[35] However, in both the *Gaza flotilla* situation as well as former Prosecutor Moreno Ocampo's first attempt at preliminary investigations in Iraq, the OTP decided not to proceed to open investigations because it considered the requirement of gravity to not be met.[36] A crime being partially considered because of jurisdictional constraints possibly renders it more difficult for the situation in question to meet the gravity threshold because atrocities are not considered in their entirety. Such an approach could incentivize criminals to move their criminal activities to the largest extent possible into the territory of a non-State Party. In cases of torture, for example, a State Party in whose territory people are abducted and brought outside the country to be tortured would not have the possibility to call upon the ICC.

Hence, from a teleological perspective, another approach to territorial jurisdiction is more pertinent. As early as 1935, the Draft Convention on Jurisdiction with Respect to Crime established that if a crime is committed "in whole or in part" within a territory, territorial jurisdiction exists.[37] A crime is committed "in whole within the territory when every essential constituent element is consummated within the territory" and "in part within the territory when any essential constituent element is consummated there."[38] This approach, subject to the *ne bis in idem* rule, has been adopted in national jurisdictions, such as in Article 693 of the French *Code de procedure pénale*, and is supported by recent scholarship, also with regard to the ICC.[39] With regard to international crimes,

34 Union of the Comoros 2013.

35 Office of the Prosecutor of the International Criminal Court 2014a.

36 Office of the Prosecutor of the International Criminal Court 2014c; Moreno Ocampo 2006.

37 Harvard Research in International Law 1935, Article 3.

38 *ibid.*, 466 *et seq.*

39 E.g., Bourgon (Commentary edited by Cassese, Gaeta and Jones) 2002; Blakesley 2008.

Schabas stated that a plan to commit genocide that has been developed outside of the territory of a State where the crime was to take place would still fall under the jurisdiction of that State.[40] Indeed, this view has been confirmed by Pre-Trial Chamber I in its Decision on its jurisdiction in the Bangladesh/Myanmar situation, in which Bangladesh, where many Rohingya refugees arrived in 2017, is a State Party to the Rome Statute, whereas Myanmar, the refugees' State of origin, is not. The Chamber noted that "the Court may assert jurisdiction pursuant to Article 12(2)(a) of the Statute if at least one element of a crime within the jurisdiction of the Court or part of such a crime is committed on the territory of a State Party."[41] Moreover, it confirmed its *Kompetenz-Kompetenz* to decide itself the scope of its jurisdiction.[42] Previously, in its decision on the request of the Union of Comoros to review the Prosecutor's decision not to initiate investigations into the *Gaza Freedom flotilla* situation, the Trial Chamber already criticized the OTP's decision not to consider evidence of cruel and abusive treatment of detained passengers occurring once they were taken off the vessels, over which the ICC has jurisdiction, and thus "erred in the determination of facts."[43] It can be inferred that the territorial jurisdiction of the ICC includes crimes of which one part is committed on the territory of a State Party, and in case of conspiracy for crimes that ought to take place on that territory. As for the scope of jurisdiction, the ICC must consider on a case-by-case basis the scope of a crime based on criteria such as temporal and geographic proximity, likeness of conduct, and consistency in terms of perpetrators and purpose.

With regard to organized crime, a territorial nexus can be established for conduct (e.g., sexual violence) that occurred on the territory of a non-State Party if another part of that crime was committed on that of a State Party; for example, if the victim was held in conditions of enslavement with sexual violence being a decisive factor for the subjective perception of a coercive environment.

However, if jurisdiction over crimes committed on the territory of a non-State Party can be established, this does not entail any legal obligations for that State; that is, it remains unbound by the obligation to cooperate with the ICC in Article 86 of the Rome Statute. Moreover, such a situation can have critical repercussions on the immunity of State officials and the surrender of accused individuals based on Articles 98(1) and (2) and 90 of the Rome Statute.[44]

40 Schabas (Commentary) 2016, 353.

41 ICC Bangladesh/Myanmar 2018, para 72.

42 *ibid.*, para 33.

43 International Criminal Court 2015, para 37–38.

44 For a more detailed discussion of the effects of these provisions see Akande 2003.

In sum, the preconditions to the exercise of jurisdiction by the ICC with regard to a territorial or nationality nexus are satisfied for any situation involving organized crime, if first the perpetrator is a national of a State Party, if all States on whose territory the crime was committed are State Parties, or if one part of the crime was committed on the territory of a State Party.

3.1.3 *The Principle of Complementarity*

The principle of the ICC's complementarity to national courts is one of the cornerstones of the system established in the Rome Statute. The relevant provisions are contained in Article 17 of the Rome Statute on the admissibility of a case. Paragraph 1 states that a case is inadmissible before the ICC if (a) the State is currently conducting investigations into or prosecutions of that case unless the State is unwilling or unable to genuinely carry them out; (b) the State has investigated the case and decided not to prosecute unless the decision resulted from the State's unwillingness or inability; (c) the *ne bis in idem* rule applies as stated in Article 20 of the Rome Statute; or (d) the case is not of sufficient gravity.[45]

Organized crime is often accompanied by high levels of corruption, including of the judicial variety.[46] Judicial corruption entails the intimidation of victims and judges as well as unnecessary delays in proceedings, and leads to impunity or lenient judgments.[47] Hence, whether the concept of complementarity as established in the Rome Statute allows for prosecutions of organized crime before the ICC in cases of judicial corruption must be determined.

In its jurisprudence, the Court established a two-step approach to determine the admissibility of a case in relation to national judicial proceedings. First, the ICC determines whether there are or have been investigations, prosecutions, or trials regarding the case in the State concerned. Although interpreted *a contrario* of article 17 of the Rome Statute, the ICC has taken the view that "in the absence of any acting State, the Chamber need not make any analysis of unwillingness and inability."[48] In *Lubanga*, the Chamber held that a case is admissible if the "States with jurisdiction over it have remained inactive in relation to that case *or* are unwilling or unable, within the meaning of Article 17(1)(a) to (c), (2) and (3) of the Statute."[49] Thus, in case of a State's inactivity, the ICC deems a case admissible.

45 In order to determine if the cases are congruent, the Court has established the so-called same-person-same-conduct test.

46 See section 2.1.2.5.

47 E.g., Buscaglia and van Dijk 2003.

48 ICC Lubanga 2006, footnote 19 and para 40.

49 *ibid.*, para 29. Emphasis added.

Second, the ICC must determine if the State with jurisdiction over a case is or was unable or unwilling to genuinely perform present or past proceedings. The interpretation of these terms is especially relevant with regard to organized crime because of its corruptive power. Judicial corruption cannot only affect judicial policemen, prosecutors, and judges but also clerks in various offices, court experts, interpreters, penitentiary workers, witnesses, and lawyers, all of which has various consequences for court proceedings and the legitimacy of State institutions.[50] "The judiciary is the ultimate protector of justice [...] [and] is also essential in the fight against transnational organized crime. Corruption in the judiciary robs citizens from that protection."[51]

However, judicial corruption is particularly difficult to assess for various reasons: First, the triadic nature of the judicial process with two of the parties in adversarial positions puts additional pressure on the parties not to reveal their corruptive activities; second, the extraordinarily high standards of impartiality for judges lead to a strong interest not to reveal any external influence; and third, the nature of judicial conflict resolution where the law is unclear and needs to be interpreted makes it extremely difficult to determine from a judgment whether the judge or any other actor in the system has been corrupted, especially in legal systems that are not yet fully developed.[52] It is thus necessary to assess whether the concepts of unwillingness or inability in the Rome Statute are fit to expose judicial corruption and allow the exercise of ICC jurisdiction in cases concerned.

Paragraphs (2) and (3) of Article 17 of the Rome Statute define the concepts of unwillingness and inability, respectively. According to Article 17(3) of the Rome Statute, a State is unable to genuinely perform judicial proceedings if "a total or substantial collapse or unavailability of its national judicial system" occurs that makes it "unable to obtain the accused or the necessary evidence and testimony" or to otherwise carry out its proceedings. Regarding the situation in the DRC, the Prosecution argued that the State was unable to prosecute based on a Statement of President Kabila in this direction.[53] Regarding the situation in the Central African Republic, the OTP based its decision to initiate an investigation on the confirmation of the State's inability by the Central African Republic's *Cour de Cassation*.[54] However, the inability of a State can

50 Danileţ 2010, 23–37.

51 Arvidsson and Folkesson 2010, 32.

52 Bedner 2002, 14.

53 ICC Lubanga 2006, para 36. The Pre-Trial Chamber found that this analysis did no longer wholly correspond to the situation in the DRC but deemed the case admissible due to the inactivity of the State.

54 Office of the Prosecutor of the International Criminal Court 2007.

also be assessed without this explicit determination by an authority of the State itself, as shown in the OTP's assessments of the situation in Darfur in its biannual reports to the UNSC.[55] More recently, Pre-Trial Chamber I found that the Libyan justice system was unavailable because the State was not able to secure the accused Saif Al-Islam Gaddafi, gather necessary evidence, or otherwise conduct proceedings because of "substantial difficulties in exercising its judicial powers fully across the entire territory."[56] By contrast, in the case against Abdullah Al-Senussi only 5 months later, the ICC determined that these security challenges had not affected the investigations against him in the same manner as in the *Gaddafi* case, and thus the Libyan State was not unable to genuinely conduct the proceedings.[57] Thus, case-by-case assessments regarding the impact of difficulties in the judicial system are necessary to determine inability. Regarding cases of judicial corruption in the absence of conflict or violent tensions, Article 17(3) of the Rome Statute renders cases admissible before the ICC only in extreme cases, such as where a legitimacy crisis of the judicial system has led to a complete or partial breakdown of the courts. The inability of a State becomes more relevant when organized crime has sparked civil unrest, severe violence, or armed conflict that render the judicial system of that State at least partly unavailable.

According to Article 17(2) of the Rome Statute, the ICC can determine the unwillingness of a State considering, as applicable and with regard to the principles of due process, (a) if proceedings were undertaken to shield the person accused from criminal responsibility for crimes within ICC jurisdiction; (b) if there has been an unjustified delay that is "inconsistent with an intent to bring the person concerned to justice;" and (c) if the proceedings are or were not conducted in an impartial and independent manner. These three indicators of unwillingness are not mutually exclusive.

As for paragraph (a), Schabas and El Zeidy indicated that "drawing an exhaustive list of all scenarios which reflect a State's intention to 'shield a person from criminal responsibility' is not possible."[58] They suggested that Article 17(2)(a) of the Rome Statute represents a test for discerning a State's bad faith through checking the effectiveness of national proceedings, where intentional deficiencies or serious negligence through acts or omissions that lead to negative results can reflect a State's intention within subparagraph (a).[59]

55 E.g. UN Security Council 2006, S/PV.5589, 2.

56 ICC Gaddafi and Al-Senussi 2013, para 205.

57 ICC Gaddafi and Al-Senussi 2013, para 297–303.

58 Schabas and El Zeidy (Commentary edited by Triffterer and Ambos) 2016, 819.

59 *ibid.*

The European Court of Human Rights (ECtHR) developed in its *Nachova* judgment, according to which national proceedings were effective if the following elements were present:

> The authorities must have taken the reasonable steps available to them to secure the evidence concerning the incident, including, inter alia, eye-witness testimony and forensic evidence. The investigation's conclusions must be based on thorough, objective and impartial analysis of all relevant elements and must apply a standard comparable to the "no more than absolutely necessary" standard required by Article 2 § 2 of the [European Convention on Human Rights].[60]

Similarly, in the *Mack* Case before the Inter-American Court on Human Rights, the Court determined after identifying various deficiencies relating to the manipulation of evidence, that "there was an attempt to cover-up those responsible."[61] Consequently, subparagraph (a) allows the ICC Chambers to deem a case admissible if there are intentional deficiencies or serious negligence in judicial proceedings that a State's bad faith can be discerned from. All of these are frequent manifestations of judicial corruption by organized criminal groups.

To assess the presence of the second indicator of unwillingness, unjustified delay, the ICC must determine if there was a delay, if the delay was unjustified, and if in the circumstances of the case the delay was inconsistent with an intent to bring the person to justice.[62] In the *Al-Senussi* Decision, although the ICC found that a period of 18 months between the commencement of investigations and the referral of the case to the Accusation Chamber does represent a delay under Article 17 (2)(b) of the Rome Statute, the Pre-Trial Chamber did not define general criteria for determining whether a delay renders a case admissible.[63] In fact, the ECtHR as well as the ICTR have stated that the question must be considered on a case-by-case basis and that the right to a trial without undue delay cannot be "translated into a fixed number of days, months or years."[64] However, the ECtHR referred to the complexity of the case, the conduct of the accused, and the conduct of the judicial authorities as criteria to

60 ECtHR Nachova 2005, para 113. Similar reasoning can also be found in ECtHR Timurtaş 2000, ECtHR Kuznetsov 2008.

61 IACtHR Mack 2003, para. 172.

62 Schabas and El Zeidy (Commentary edited by Triffterer and Ambos) 2016, 822.

63 ICC Gaddafi and Al-Senussi 2013, para 229.

64 ICTR Rwamakuba 2005, para 26. See also, e.g., ECtHR König 1978, para 99.

consider.[65] Hence, in cases of judicial corruption, Article 17(2)(b) of the Rome Statute prevents judicial authorities from continuing proceedings indefinitely without ever passing a judgment.

A third indicator of unwillingness, as stated in Article 17(2)(c) of the Rome Statute, is a lack of impartiality and independence in the proceedings. Similar to the question of unjustified delay, the question was raised in the *Al-Senussi* Case without which the Chamber provided an in-depth and more general analysis of the provision.[66] However, based on relevant human rights documents and jurisprudence, the ICTY held that "whether a court is independent and impartial depends [...] upon its constitution, its judges and the way in which they function."[67] In *Furundžija*, the ICTY Appeals Chamber developed a set of conditions to test impartiality based on the subjective and objective test developed by the ECtHR:[68]

A. A Judge is not impartial if it is shown that actual bias exists.
B. There is an unacceptable appearance of bias if:
   i) a Judge is a party to the case, or has a financial or proprietary interest in the outcome of a case, or if the Judge's decision will lead to the promotion of a cause in which he or she is involved, together with one of the parties [...]; or
   ii) the circumstances would lead a reasonable observer, properly informed, to reasonably apprehend bias.[69]

The subjective test in A relies on the personal convictions of a judge, whereas the objective test in B refers to the appearance of bias. The latter is especially critical regarding judicial corruption because it includes any financial or other interest in a case or the promotion of a certain cause. In the context of organized crime, the impartiality test also prohibits any bias based on kinship, other group identity, or shared interests with one of the parties. Although Article 17 establishes high standards, they are not impossible to satisfy; for example, the Court could rely on previous sham proceedings of other perpetrators, departures from the normal legal procedure, and the absence of sufficient qualified staff.[70]

65 *ibid.*
66 ICC Gaddafi and Al-Senussi 2013, para 241.
67 ICTY Tadić 1995, para 32.
68 E.g., ECtHR Piersack 1982.
69 ICTY Furundžija 2000, para 189. See also Schabas and El Zeidy (Commentary edited by Triffterer and Ambos) 2016, 825–827.
70 Holmes (Commentary edited by Cassese, Gaeta and Jones) 2002, 677–678.

Nevertheless, Article 17 has its limits. First, the ICC Chamber is not called upon to determine if a domestic case is strong enough on the merits to establish a person's criminal responsibility.[71] Second, Article 17 does not allow the ICC to base its admissibility decision on "an assessment of whether the due process rights of a suspect have been breached per se."[72] Instead, it is "limited to those considerations that have the potential to bear upon any of the scenarios envisaged under Article 17(2)."[73] Last, the Statute does not clearly preclude a scenario in which genuine domestic proceedings are conducted in relation to a conduct falling under the ICC's jurisdiction, but the convicted person is pardoned or paroled after a short or no incarceration.[74]

Overall, Article 17 of the Rome Statute provides the ICC with a mechanism to expose and act upon judicial corruption in a situation country based on inactivity, serious malfunctioning of the justice system, ineffectiveness of proceedings, unjustified delay, and personal bias of public officials.

3.2 Substantive Law: Jurisdiction *Ratione Materiae*

In this section, the applicability of the core crimes currently under ICC jurisdiction, namely genocide, crimes against humanity, and war crimes, to organized crime is analyzed. To avoid overlaps in terms of contents, the contextual and mental elements as well as overall material elements of the crimes are discussed in relation to organized crime in general as previously defined.[75] In the following subsections, the elements of the individual acts constituting a crime are analyzed in relation to concrete activities by organized criminal groups, notwithstanding that all elements—contextual, mental, and material—must be present at once for the Rome Statute to apply to organized criminal activities.[76] For example, the applicability of specific acts constituting crimes against

71 ICC Gaddafi and Al-Senussi 2013, para 122.

72 ICC Gaddafi and Al-Senussi 2014, para 230.

73 ICC Gaddafi and Al-Senussi 2013, para 243.

74 Holmes (Commentary edited by Cassese, Gaeta and Jones) 2002, 678–679.

75 See section 2.1.1.

76 The concrete organized criminal activities analyzed were chosen based on their relevance with regard to the crime definition in question after a preliminary assessment of applicability and a review of the scholarly debate. Child pornography, for example, is not discussed although sexual violence against children can constitute individual acts of crimes against humanity and war crimes. However, the production of child pornography, i.e. the sexual violence, is conducted in a decentralized manner as isolated acts against randomly selected individuals and thus does not satisfy the contextual elements of the crimes under the Rome Statute.

humanity, such as enslavement, rape, and forced prostitution, is examined with regard to human trafficking and subsequent exploitation of the victims. Furthermore, specific acts constituting war crimes (e.g., pillage) are examined in relation to the illicit trade in natural resources and cultural goods.

3.2.1 *The Crime of Genocide*

In Article 6 of the Rome Statute, genocide receives a short definition as well as an enumeration of individual acts constituting the crime. The definition establishes the *mens rea* requirement for the crime as well as the groups protected by this provision. Moreover, the Elements of Crimes specify its contextual elements that will be discussed in conjunction with the *dolus specialis*.

In this subsection, the offenses of organized crime that can constitute genocide are examined, as are the elements that must be present to prosecute them as such. The special intent requirement as well as protected groups are examined in light of the goals and activities of organized criminal groups. Regarding individual acts of genocide, the potential of human trafficking and organized crime-related violence to amount to genocide are studied because they provide the greatest overlap with the definition of genocide in the Rome Statute.

3.2.1.1 Mental Element: The *Dolus Specialis* of Genocide

For organized criminal groups and their members to commit genocide, the specific *mens rea* for the crime must be met. Thus, whether the special intent requirement can line up with the profit-driven motivation of organized crime must be determined.

The *mens rea* requirement for genocide amounts to what is commonly called special or specific intent, or *dolus specialis* "to destroy, in whole or in part, a [targeted] group,"[77] and thus, this is one of the most critical distinctions of genocide vis-à-vis other international crimes. International tribunals have repeatedly underlined the significance of this component of genocide. The ICTY Appeals Chamber stated that "its gravity [of genocide] is reflected in the stringent requirement of specific intent. Convictions for genocide can be entered only where that intent has been unequivocally established."[78] An ICTR Trial Chamber noted that the special intent is "a constitutive element of the crime, which demands that the perpetrator clearly seeks to produce the act charged."[79] The ICC has confirmed the significance of the "subjective

77 Rome Statute 1998, Article 6.
78 ICTY Krstić 2004, para 134.
79 ICTR Akayesu 1998, para 498.

element."[80] It follows that all forms of *dolus eventualis*, including negligence or recklessness, are excluded.[81]

The special intent toward the destruction of a targeted group is specified in Article 6 of the Rome Statute by the term "in whole or in part," which has been interpreted both quantitatively and qualitatively. Although Article 6 of the Rome Statute consistently speaks of "member*s* of the group,"[82] meaning at least more than one, there does not seem to be any additional requirement in terms of quantity. However, the expression "in whole or in part," directly adopted from the Genocide Convention, was drafted to exclude isolated acts of racially motivated violence while including cases where not an entire group but only a substantial portion of it is targeted.[83] According to ICTY jurisprudence,

> [t]he determination of when the targeted part is substantial enough to meet this requirement may involve a number of considerations. The numeric size of the targeted part of the group is the necessary and important starting point, though not in all cases the ending point of the inquiry. The number of individuals targeted should be evaluated not only in absolute terms, but also in relation to the overall size of the entire group. In addition to the numeric size of the targeted portion, its prominence within the group can be a useful consideration. If a specific part of the group is emblematic of the overall group, or is essential to its survival, that may support a finding that the part qualifies as substantial […].[84]

The Bosnian Muslim population in Srebrenica, approximately 40,000-strong, was deemed to meet the requirement despite the relatively small number relative to the total Bosnian Muslim population. This was because of the strategic importance of the location they occupied.[85]

Moreover, there is some support for the view that the significance of the targeted portion of the group could also satisfy the expression "in whole or in part." In its *Jelisić* judgment, the ICTY Trial Chamber held that genocidal intent could be inferred from the "desired destruction of a more limited number of persons selected for the impact that their disappearance would have upon the survival of the group as such."[86] Later, the Appeals Chamber stated that

80 ICC Bashir 2009, para 139.

81 Cassese (Commentary edited by Cassese, Gaeta and Jones) 2002b, 338.

82 Emphasis added.

83 Schabas (Commentary) 2016, 134.

84 ICTY Krstić 2004, para 12.

85 *ibid.*, para 15–16. See also Schabas (Commentary edited by Triffterer and Ambos) 2016, 134.

86 ICTY Jelisić 1999, para 82.

"selective targeting of leading figures of a community may amount to genocide and may be indicative of genocidal intent."[87]

Although not expressly required in Article 6 of the Rome Statute, the Elements of Crimes set out a contextual element for genocide, stating: "The conduct took place in the context of a manifest pattern of similar conduct directed against that group or was conduct that could itself effect such destruction."[88] Rejected by the *ad hoc* tribunals, the element was debated in the ICC Trial Chamber, but ultimately viewed as a teleological interpretation of the special intent requirement, namely that "the protection offered by the penal norm [...]—as an *ultima ratio* mechanism to preserve the highest values of the international community—is only triggered when the threat [...] becomes concrete and real, as opposed to just being latent or hypothetical."[89]

In the context of organized crime, defined as organized criminal groups "acting in concert [...] to obtain, directly or indirectly, a financial or other material benefit,"[90] it is debatable whether the interests of organized criminal groups are compatible with the requirement of special intent to destroy a group in whole or in part. It seems the destruction of the group, or parts thereof, would need to substantially further the organized criminal groups' economic interests.

To determine whether the notion of organized criminal groups committing or intending to commit genocide is plausible, studying the historical influence of economic interest in genocidal conflicts is instructive. In fact, economic interests in- and outside a conflict zone cannot only lead to the escalation of genocide but also influence decisions on possible interventions.[91] Economic interests can be of various natures; for example, State interests and individual interests, the need to finance a conflict, greed, or fear for survival. For example, both in the Armenian genocide and the Holocaust, a massive transfer of property occurred from the victims to the remaining population of the perpetrating States, namely Turkey and Germany, respectively, as well as to the State apparatuses. This not only greatly benefitted the receiving populations but also ensured popular support for the political regimes.[92] In addition, economic factors played a crucial role in the Rwandan genocide, namely for the

87 ICTY Tolimir 2015, para 263.

88 Elements of Crimes 2010, e.g., Article 6(a), para 4.

89 ICTY Krstić 2004, para 224; ICC Bashir 2009, 124. See also Schabas (Commentary edited by Triffterer and Ambos) 2016, 133.

90 Palermo Convention 2000, Article 2(a); see section 2.1.1.

91 Cormier *et al.* 2011, 283.

92 Üngör and Polatel 2011, 4–6.

different motivations of perpetrators. Micro-level evidence suggests that the main profiles of perpetrators were, first, the poor and landless, hoping to "gain from participation" and being subjected to "social and economic vulnerability," and second, landlords and employers, who had "something to defend."[93] Thus, economic interests play a role in cases of genocide.

Furthermore, organized criminal groups have a history of killing the leading figures and members of competitive groups, intending to weaken or eliminate the groups. Thus, notwithstanding the limitations regarding groups protected by the provision, it is possible for an organized criminal group to meet the special intent requirement of Article 6 of the Rome Statute in such a context.[94]

In addition, it is possible to be convicted of participation in genocide without meeting the special intent requirement.[95] According to ICTY case law, special intent is no longer required in cases of complicity in genocide.[96] Furthermore,

> [a]s long as those senior political and/or military leaders who planned and set into motion a genocidal campaign act with the requisite *dolus specialis*/ulterior intent, those others below them, who pass on instructions and/or physically implement such a genocidal campaign, will commit genocide as long as they are aware that the ultimate purpose of such a campaign is to destroy in whole or in part the targeted group.[97]

According to the ICC Pre-Trial Chamber, convictions for genocide without special intent can be passed under Article 25(3)(b) of the Rome Statute, ordering, soliciting, or inducing the commission of a crime; under Article 25(3)(d) of the Rome Statute, in any other way contributing to the commission of a crime; and under Article 28 of the Rome Statute on superior responsibility.[98] For example, the head of an organized criminal group whose members develop ideological or other goals and commit genocide with special intent may be criminally responsible for their inferiors' actions, or individuals abducted for the purpose of genocide might be trafficked by organized criminal groups, thereby contributing to the crime. Thus, in clearly defined cases, members of organized

93 Verwimp 2005, 390.
94 Protected groups will be discussed in section 3.2.1.2.1.
95 See section 3.3.2.
96 ICTY Krstić 2004, para 135–144; ICTY Brđanin 2004, para 5–10.
97 ICC Bashir 2009, footnote 154.
98 *ibid.* A detailed discussion of modes of liability follows in section 3.3. See also Schabas (Commentary edited by Triffterer and Ambos) 2016, 131–132.

criminal groups can be held responsible for genocide if they were aware of the genocidal plan but did not have special intent themselves.

In sum, organized criminal groups can satisfy the special intent requirement or incur criminal responsibility for participating in genocide without it in particular cases.

3.2.1.2 Material Elements

3.2.1.2.1 *Protected Groups*

In addition to the special intent requirement, the *chapeau* of Article 6 of the Rome Statute contains an exhaustive list of groups protected by the Statute, namely national, ethnic, racial, and religious groups. It is thus necessary for the purpose of this book to determine whether the groups within the meaning of the Rome Statute are relevant in the context of organized crime, as well as whether, as a consequence, it is plausible that organized criminal groups target them with committed crimes.

The list of groups included in the Rome Statute mirrors Article 2 of the UN Genocide Convention. As recognized by the ICTR Trial Chamber,

> [o]n reading through the *travaux préparatoires* of the Genocide Convention, it appears that the crime of genocide was allegedly perceived as targeting only 'stable' groups, constituted in a permanent fashion and membership of which is determined by birth.[99]

Mobile groups, especially those defined in social, political, or economic terms, were intentionally excluded.[100] Efforts to enlarge the definition during the drafting of the Rome Statute were unsuccessful, and an interpretation by an ICTR Trial Chamber stating that the aim of the provision was "to ensure the protection of *any* stable and permanent group"[101] was not adopted in later decisions by the ICTR itself or by other courts and tribunals.[102]

However, the definition and delineation of the four groups remain problematic, because "the concepts [...] have been researched extensively and [...], at present, there are no generally and internationally accepted precise definitions thereof. Each of these concepts must be assessed in the light of a particular political, social and cultural context."[103]

---

99 ICTR Akayesu 1998, para 511.

100 ICTR Rutaganda 1999, para 57; Schabas (Commentary) 2016, 136.

101 ICTR Akayesu 1998, para 516. Emphasis added.

102 Schabas (Commentary) 2016, 136.

103 ICTR Rutaganda 1999, para 56.

Several methods have been applied to identify a targeted group. First, the existence of a certain group has been assessed based on both objective and subjective factors. For example, in *Akayesu,* the existence of an ethnic Tutsi group was based on objective indicators such as identity cards, Rwanda's Constitution and Civil Code, as well as on the fact that "witnesses [...] identified themselves by ethnic group and generally knew the ethnic group to which their friends and neighbours belonged."[104] Self-identification by a group named in Article 6 of the Rome Statute has subsequently been accepted as an indicator for the existence of such a group by other Chambers.[105] However, the Chamber also stipulated that "[m]oreover, the Tutsis were considered an ethnic group by those who targeted them for killing."[106] Although this approach was criticized for allowing the characterization of a crime solely on the discriminative motive of the offender, ICTR and ICTY Trial Chambers adopted the method, arguing that "to define a [targeted] group today using objective and scientifically irreproachable criteria would be a perilous exercise whose result would not necessarily correspond to the perception of the persons concerned by such categorization."[107] Indeed, as the infamous alleged remark by Hermann Göring "*Wer bei mir Jude ist, bestimme ich*"[108] demonstrates, subjective and objective criteria for defining a group do not necessarily correspond; thus, basing the definition solely on objective criteria would represent an unwarranted reduction of the scope of protection.[109] Notably, however, this approach does not allow for any group perceived as such by the perpetrators of a crime to fall under the definition of Article 6 of the Rome Statute. Rather, the perpetrators must perceive the targeted group as a national, ethnic, racial, or religious group; these are attributes that by definition cannot be construed spontaneously to fulfill an immediate political or ideological purpose. Rather, the existence of such a group remains a social construct that must be established over time in the minds of perpetrators and victims alike.

Hence, in the context of organized crime, the subjective approach does not allow for a mass killing of members of a hostile criminal group to be qualified as genocide unless the criminal group had national, ethnic, racial, or religious

104 ICTR Akayesu 1998, para 171.

105 E.g., ICTR Kayishema and Ruzindana 1999, para 523–525.

106 ICTR Akayesu 1998, para 171.

107 See, e.g., Kreß 2006, 474; ICTY Jelisić 1999, para 70.

108 „Within my command, who is a Jew is my business", allegedly said with regard to Martin Wronsky remaining in office at Lufthansa despite his Jewish origin. Translated by the author. See also Berster (Commentary edited by Tams, Berster and Schiffbauer) 2014.

109 Berster (Commentary edited by Tams, Berster and Schiffbauer) 2014, 105.

ties, and furthermore, the mass killing not only contributed or was meant to contribute to the elimination of said criminal group but to the broader group as well.

Second, positive as well as negative approaches to defining the existence of a group have been applied, such as defining a group based on characteristics it possesses or on nonmembership of another distinct group. Although a negative definition was proposed by an ICTY Trial Chamber, it was later rejected by other ICTY Chambers as well as by the ICC Pre-Trial Chamber, which stated, "it is [...] a matter of who the targeted people are, not who they are not."[110]

Each of the four groups included in Article 6 of the Rome Statute must be considered individually. A national group has been defined by the ICJ as well as international criminal tribunals "as a collection of people who are perceived to share a legal bond based on common citizenship, coupled with reciprocity of rights and duties."[111] Moreover, the term has not only been construed based on nationality as such "but also [on] the fact of belonging to the opposing party in an armed conflict."[112] To date, no consensus has been reached on the question of whether genocide can also be committed against members belonging to the same group as the perpetrators, known as auto-genocide or geno-suicide.[113] This concept can be relevant in the case of massive violence or armed conflict between criminal groups or a government and an organized criminal group; for example, in the context of indiscriminate State violence against the population of a city or region siding with leading criminal figures.

An ethnic group has generally been understood as a group "whose members share a common language and culture,"[114] or, as stated by the ICC Pre-Trial Chamber, a group that "has its own language, its own tribal customs and its own traditional links to its lands."[115] Fundamentally, the Chambers are looking for "a group with a distinct identity."[116] Thus, the subjective elements of self-identification and identification of others discussed above become particularly crucial in this regard, as exemplified in the *Akayesu* case. There, it was

---

110 Negative approach: ICTY Jelisić 1999, para 71; Rejection: ICTY Brđanin 2004, para 685–686; ICTY Stakić 2006, para 22–24; ICC Bashir 2009, para 135. See also Schabas (Commentary) 2016, 137.

111 ICJ Nottebohm Case 1955; ICTR Akayesu 1998, para 512.

112 ICC Lubanga 2007, para 280.

113 See in favor Berster (Commentary edited by Tams, Berster and Schiffbauer) 2014, 101. For the opposing view see Beauvallet (Commentary edited by Fernandez, Pacreau and Maze) 2012, 412–413.

114 ICTR Kayishema and Ruzindana 1999, para 98.

115 ICC Bashir 2009, para 137.

116 ICTR Akayesu 1998, para 170.

argued that the ICTR Trial Chamber, by examining objective evidence such as identity cards and legislation, "merely endorsed artificial distinctions introduced by the colonial administration."[117] An argument could be made that certain criminal groups that have existed for decades or centuries and developed a strong subculture, including their own rites and accent or jargon, as well as a strong group identity, represent new ethnic groups. However, it would have to be demonstrated that such a group fulfills the requirement of permanence envisaged by the drafters of the provision, including the notion of membership by birth. In most cases, however, a majority of members are recruited as teenagers or adults and do not necessarily remain members all their lives.

Contrary to the cultural or traditional focus for defining an ethnic group, racial groups are defined "based on hereditary physical traits often identified with geography."[118]

Because organized criminal groups often have a geographically defined stronghold, such as the Medellín and Sinaloa cartels in Mexico that are named according to their original region of activity, they often also have a strong ethnic or racial bond. In intimidation or retaliation campaigns, large organized criminal groups often target the whole population of a competitor group's stronghold, which can thus qualify as a genocidal campaign if the destruction of that group in whole or in part is indeed the perpetrators' intent.

The fourth category, a religious group, defined as including "denomination or mode of worship or a group sharing common beliefs,"[119] is the most fluent type of group included because of the internationally protected right to change one's religion. Thus, determinations of the existence of a religious group must be made on a case-by-case basis considering both objective and subjective elements.

Notably, the exclusion of social and economic groups from the protection of the provision on genocide greatly limits the circumstances under which organized criminal groups' activities satisfy the requirements for genocide. However, as the ICTR Appeals Chamber stated, the provision does not "prohibit a conviction for genocide in a case in which the perpetrator was also driven by other motivations that are legally irrelevant in this context."[120] Thus, it is possible for an organized crime group to be held legally responsible for genocide when committing the crime based on economic considerations if the

117 Martin (Commentary edited by Gaeta) 2009, 123.

118 ICTR Kayishema and Ruzindana 1999, para 98.

119 *ibid.*

120 ICTR Niyitegaka 2004, para 53.

targeted group fulfills the requirements of Article 6 of the Rome Statute, as well as if the prerequisite *mens rea* can be established.

In sum, organized criminal groups frequently target protected groups as defined in Article 6 of the Rome Statute, especially ethnic and racial groups, although their ethnicity and race might not be the primary motivation, but rather factors such as loyalty to competitors or control of strategically critical geographies. Thus, organized criminal groups are not excluded from committing genocide against one of the protected groups.

3.2.1.2.2 *Individual Acts*

In addition to the *mens rea* and contextual requirements, Article 6 of the Rome Statute enumerates certain acts further defining genocide, namely killing, causing serious bodily or mental harm, inflicting conditions of life calculated to bring about the destruction of a group (in whole or in part), imposing measures to prevent births, and forcibly transferring children to another group. The following subsections analyze whether human trafficking and organized crime-related violence satisfy the elements of these crimes.

3.2.1.2.2.1 Individual Acts of Genocide in Trafficking in Persons, Including Forced Prostitution and Labor and Organ Trafficking

In relation to organized crime, different forms and aspects of human trafficking can constitute acts enumerated in Article 6 of the Rome Statute. Both the initial act of trafficking (i.e., recruiting and removing the victims from their homes) and subsequent abuse and exploitation of the victims are discussed.[121]

First, the act of removing victims from their homes could meet the requirements of inflicting conditions of life calculated to bring about the destruction of the group under Article 6(c) as well as of causing serious physical or mental harm under Article 6(b). The former is usually understood to include a subsistence diet, lack of medical care, or lack of sufficient living accommodation; furthermore, it has also been interpreted to include "systematic expulsion from homes"[122] and deportation.[123] Both imply the use or threat of force. Moreover, the expression "systematic" implies that such conduct requires a certain number of victims and does not refer to individual cases. On the other hand, ethnic cleansing, that is, "the forcible expulsion of civilians belonging to a particular group from an area, village, or town," was intentionally omitted by

121 See also section 2.1.2.2.

122 ICTY Mladić 2017, para 3434.

123 ICTR Akayesu 1998, para 506. See also Schabas (Commentary edited by Triffterer and Ambos) 2016, 139.

the drafters of the Genocide Convention and is generally not considered genocide.[124] However, ICJ Judge *ad hoc* Lauterpacht took a contrary view regarding the conflict between Serbs and Bosnian Muslims.[125] Thus, a case-by-case assessment seems necessary. Crucially, deportation and forcible transfer are also enumerated in Article 7 of the Rome Statute as crimes against humanity. For them to qualify as genocide, the required *mens rea* and other material elements must be prevalent. In particular, the goal of the deportation must be the destruction of the deported group. This is usually not the case for human trafficking, and furthermore, human trafficking for the purpose of exploitation normally concentrates on young men, women, or children and not on entire groups. Although this subset also plays an essential role in the reproduction of a group, human trafficking can only be a byproduct of deportations amounting to genocide; it does not satisfy in and of itself the elements of inflicting conditions of life calculated to bring about the destruction of a group.

Nevertheless, in the case of forced transfer of the population in Srebrenica, the Trial Chamber concluded that "the forced displacement of women, children and elderly people was itself a traumatic experience, which [...] reaches the requisite level of causing serious mental harm."[126] Thus, the removal of trafficking victims from their home can constitute an act of causing serious mental harm under Article 6(b) of the Rome Statute depending on the circumstances and psychological effects.

Moreover, trafficking victims are often subjected to cruel treatment regardless of the specific form of exploitation they must endure, such as violence, threats of violence, and psychological abuse, as well as a lack of food, decent housing, and medical care. If these acts reach the prerequisite gravity, they constitute the crime of causing serious mental or bodily harm within the meaning of Article 6(b) of the Rome Statute.

Furthermore, trafficking in children in particular could satisfy the requirements of forcibly transferring children to another group. According to the Elements of Crimes, the act is not restricted to physical force but can include

---

124 During the drafting phase of the Genocide Convention, Syria proposed a sixth class of acts of genocide, namely "measures intended to oblige members of a group to abandon their homes in order to escape the threat of subsequent ill-treatment". The proposal was rejected. UN General Assembly 1948, A/C6/234; Cassese (Commentary edited by Cassese, Gaeta and Jones) 2002b, 338.

125 ICJ Application of the Genocide Convention 1993, Separate Opinion by Judge *ad hoc* Lauterpacht, 68–70. See also Cassese (Commentary edited by Cassese, Gaeta and Jones) 2002b, 338.

126 ICTY Blagojević and Jokić 2005, para 650. In ICTY Mladić 2017, para 2988, the forcible transfer in Srebrenica is considered as a crime against humanity.

the "threat of force or coercion, such as that caused by fear of violence, duress, detention, psychological oppression or abuse of power, against such person or persons or another person, or by taking advantage of a coercive environment."[127] This definition excludes any cases of trafficking in children where the children are voluntarily handed to the traffickers, unless consent has been reached by abuse of power or by taking advantage of a coercive environment, such as in armed conflict. Although children are defined as any person under 18 years of age, the provision refers to the transfer of children who, as a consequence, lose their group identity, which becomes less likely with increasing age.[128] In the Statute it remains unclear whether the group the children are transferred to must meet any specific criteria. Presumably, the group of destination can be any other group.[129] In the case of human trafficking, the individuals or families purchasing the trafficked children are determined by market dynamics and do not necessarily share any common features. However, the expression "to another group" in Article 6(e) of the Rome Statute primarily seems to underline a transfer into another cultural, traditional, or social context. Thus, it seems detrimental to its protection to unduly restrict the definition of the group of destination, as long as it is not the same as the targeted group. Trafficking in children, if based on a forced transfer as described in the Elements of Crimes, can thus constitute genocide or contribute thereto.

Second, the exploitation of trafficking victims once they are removed from their homes can also fall under individual acts constituting genocide given genocidal intent. Human trafficking for the purpose of organ removal and trade could meet the requirements of (a) killing and (b) causing serious bodily and mental harm. For example, the report on "Inhuman treatment of people and illicit trafficking in human organs in Kosovo" indicated that

> [t]he testimonies [...] spoke credibly and consistently of a methodology by which all of the captives were killed, usually by a gunshot to the head, before being operated on to remove one or more of their organs. We learned that this was principally a trade in "cadaver kidneys," i.e. the kidneys were extracted posthumously.[130]

127 Elements of Crimes 2010, footnote 5.

128 Schabas (Commentary edited by Triffterer and Ambos) 2016, 140.

129 Beauvallet (Commentary edited by Fernandez, Pacreau and Maze) 2012, 404.

130 Marty 2011, para 162. See also section 2.3.3.1.5.

As specified in the Elements of Crimes of the ICC, killing is synonymous with "causing death."[131] Although there has been a controversy as to the difference in meaning between the English word "killing" and French word *"meurtre,"* they are both construed "as referring to intentional but not necessarily premeditated murder."[132] Killing a person to remove one or more organs clearly meets this criterion of intent. However, it is possible for kidneys in particular to be removed without causing the death of the donor. In this case, it can fall under the act of causing serious physical or mental harm. The Elements of Crimes specify that this "include[s], but is not necessarily restricted to, acts of torture, rape, sexual violence, or inhuman or degrading treatment,"[133] the former being defined as "severe physical or mental pain or suffering [inflicted upon a person] in the custody or under the control of the perpetrator."[134] While the removal of an organ causes severe physical suffering, it does not necessarily have long-term consequences for the survival or well-being of the victim. However, the ICTR stated that serious physical or mental harm does not necessarily entail permanent or irremediable harm.[135] Moreover, the trauma caused by the forced removal of an organ amounts to serious mental harm within the meaning of Article 6(b) of the Rome Statute. Thus, organ removal for the aim of organ trafficking can amount to an act of genocide.

Furthermore, physical and sexual exploitation, including forced prostitution, meet the criteria of inflicting serious physical or mental harm. While rape and sexual violence are expressly included in the Elements of the Crime, forced labor and the particular situation of victims of such exploitation can cause severe physical and mental suffering within the meaning of Article 6(b) of the Rome Statute.

Overall, specific elements of human trafficking fall under the enumerated acts of genocide. These are forced transfer, cruel treatment, physical and sexual exploitation, and organ removal under Article 6(b) of the Rome Statute (causing serious bodily or mental harm). Organ removal can also fall under Article 6(a) of the Rome Statute (killing). Moreover, trafficking in children can fall under Article 6(e) of the Rome Statute (forcibly transferring children to

---

131 Elements of Crimes 2010, footnote 2.

132 ICTR Kayishema and Ruzindana 1999, para 151. See also Schabas (Commentary edited by Triffterer and Ambos) 2016, 138.

133 Elements of Crimes 2010, footnote 3.

134 *ibid.*, Article 7(1)(f), para 1–2.

135 ICTR Rukundo 2009, para 489. For more details see Schabas (Commentary edited by Triffterer and Ambos) 2016, 138.

another group). Notwithstanding the required *mens rea* and restrictions on protected groups, human trafficking can constitute and contribute to genocide.

3.2.1.2.2.2 Individual Acts of Genocide in Organized Crime-Related Violence

As outlined above, a high prevalence of organized crime is often accompanied by increased violence because of conflicts between various criminal groups, between the State and criminal groups, or as a strategy to secure smooth business flows.[136] In some cases, long-term, widespread, severe and indiscriminate violence has reached such a level that it draws frequent comparisons to a war situation, at least in colloquial language, such as the so-called "drug wars" in Colombia, Mexico, and the Philippines. Killings, rape, and trauma are manifest elements of such violent campaigns. In Mexico, approximately 200,000 people are estimated to have been killed and 28,000 disappeared between 2007 and 2016.[137] Both government groups and cartels allegedly make frequent use of torture and rape.[138] Moreover, violence is inflicted publicly and visually, causing trauma not only to the victims but also to the population living in the area or those exposed to continuous and visual news coverage. Such conduct satisfies the requirements of individual acts of genocide, namely killings and causing serious physical or mental harm as interpreted above, and can have a critical impact on group identity, national or other.[139] However, ethnic cleansing *per* se is not considered genocide. Moreover, all of these crimes can fall under Article 7 of the Rome Statute, which describes crimes against humanity.[140] The special intent of the perpetrator as well as the actual potential of the acts to generate the destruction of a group is thus decisive to qualify these acts as genocide.

In sum, organized crime-related violence can constitute genocide if the victims belong to a protected group and if special intent is present.

3.2.1.3 Summary

While certain organized criminal activities satisfy the elements of individual acts of genocide, namely elements of human trafficking and severe violence perpetrated by organized criminal groups to facilitate or defend their business, both the restriction of the protected groups as well as the special intent requirement greatly limit the cases in which organized criminal activities can qualify as genocide.

---

136 See section 2.1.2.7.

137 Lakhani 2016.

138 E.g., Human Rights Watch 2019, 393; Associated Press 2007.

139 See, e.g., Dennis 2006.

140 See discussion above in section 3.2.2.2.5.

In relation to protected groups, organized criminal groups usually commit crimes against competing criminal groups or agents of the State; that is, economically or politically defined groups. Furthermore, they commit crimes against individuals chosen based on market dynamics and vulnerability, such as for human trafficking, or against a random population, such as in the case of indiscriminate violence. Thus, the victims are usually not targeted based on their membership of a national, ethnic, racial, or religious group, although it is feasible that an economically or politically defined group targeted by organized crime also possesses links of that nature, which would be sufficient to satisfy this element of Article 6 of the Rome Statute.

Relating to the special intent requirement, organized criminal groups are driven by economic motives. For an organized crime group to intend to destroy a group, in whole or in part, there must be business-related reasons that justify the effort and risk of genocide. Thus, situations in which genocide is committed by an organized criminal group as the only or decisive actor are limited, although it is possible that an execution campaign against a competitor, for example, constitutes the crime.

Nevertheless, given the growing interdependencies between armed groups, terrorists, and organized crime as outlined above, an increasing likelihood exists of organized crime exploiting the economic opportunities of conflict as well as of diverging economic and ideological interests.[141] As part of such a crime–conflict conglomerate, organized criminal groups can thus contribute to a genocidal campaign in a manner that entails individual criminal responsibility, in some cases without satisfying the *mens rea* requirements.[142]

3.2.2 *Crimes against Humanity*

Crimes against humanity are defined in Article 7 of the Rome Statute that contains a *chapeau* with contextual elements and a *mens rea* requirement, an enumeration of individual acts that can constitute crimes against humanity and additional legal definitions clarifying the former.

In this section, the contextual elements and the *mens rea* requirement are discussed in light of organized crime. Moreover, it examines whether particular acts of organized crime, namely human trafficking, migrant smuggling and migrant-related crimes, drug trafficking, illicit trade in cultural goods, and organized crime-related violence, are covered by the enumerated acts of crimes against humanity.

---

141 See section 2.3.2.2.

142 Discussed in detail in section 3.3.

3.2.2.1 Contextual Elements

For the individual crimes enumerated in Article 7(a)-(k) of the Rome Statute to qualify as crimes against humanity, they must fulfill the contextual requirements set out in the *chapeau*. Specifically, the crime must be "part of a widespread or systematic attack directed against any civilian population," and the perpetrator of the individual crime must know of the attack. Through stipulating a nexus between a crime and a "widespread or systematic attack directed against any civilian population," the provision excludes isolated acts from the definition.[143] The nexus to the attack is "the internationalizing factor that transforms acts, [...] which otherwise would be simply ordinary crimes under national law, into crimes against humanity."[144] Thus, a single criminal act can constitute a crime against humanity if a sufficient nexus exists to a broader attack.

3.2.2.1.1 *Widespread or Systematic Attack*

The contextual element of a widespread or systematic attack can be subdivided into the attack itself and the qualifying adjectives. First, the crime must be committed as part of an attack. To determine if such an attack can be committed by organized criminal groups or if such groups can commit crimes in the context of such an attack, the exact meaning of the legal term as well as the required nexus between different acts constituting the attack must be examined.

An attack is defined in Article 7(2)(a) of the Rome Statute as a multiplicity of criminal acts. Although the Statute does not specify the required nature of the nexus, a case-by-case evaluation based on criteria similar to those set forth by the ICTY to examine the link of a crime to an armed conflict can be applied.[145] Specifically, possible indicators of a nexus can be the similarity between the acts committed by the accused and those committed during the attack, the nature of events and circumstances surrounding the acts by the accused, temporal and geographical proximity, and the nature and extent of the accused's knowledge of the attack, in particular the connection to the underlying policy.[146] However, these criteria are indicative; the acts do not necessarily have to occur simultaneously to the commission of any part of the attack or represent the same conduct as acts committed in the attack.[147] Thus,

143 Elements of Crimes 2010, Article 7, Introduction, para 3: "multiple commission of acts"; This imposes a weaker requirement than the term widespread, see section 3.2.2.1.1.

144 Hall and Ambos (Commentary edited by Triffterer and Ambos) 2016, 165.

145 ICTY Tadić 1997, para 629–633.

146 *ibid.;* Hall and Ambos (Commentary edited by Triffterer and Ambos) 2016, 167.

147 ICTY Tadić 1997, para 632.

organized criminal groups can be involved in an attack without fully executing it themselves. This can be especially important in a case of cooperation between armed or terrorist groups and organized crime as well as organized crime operating in, benefiting from, and possibly actively prolonging situations of conflict or instability. Although the Rome Statute stipulates that the acts must occur "as part of an attack," they can also constitute the attack as a whole.[148] Thus, mass killings by organized criminal groups, for example, could qualify as an attack themselves.

The Elements of Crimes specify that an attack under the Statute must not necessarily be a military attack.[149] Furthermore, the *ad hoc* tribunals established that an attack does not need to involve armed conflict, and can in fact occur during peacetime.[150] In the context of organized crime, this widens the scope of applicability of the concept of an attack to different activities of organized criminal groups, which often do not amount to or depend on armed conflict; for example, violence that does not meet the intensity threshold of armed conflict. Notably, only few organized criminal groups have paramilitary wings that would be able to carry out a military attack.

However, the Elements of Crimes introduce an important restriction on the interpretation of the term "attack." They stipulate that an attack "is understood to mean a course of conduct [...] pursuant to or in furtherance of *a State or organizational policy* to commit such attack."[151] Although crimes against humanity were interpreted by the Nuremberg Tribunals to require a State policy, the so-called policy requirement subsequently evolved in international customary law and was questioned by national courts as well as the *ad hoc* tribunals in light of the increasing role of internal conflicts and asymmetric warfare.[152] In the *Nikolić* case before the ICTY, the Trial Chamber recognized that a policy need not be "established at State level, in the conventional sense of the term."[153] Later, ICTY Trial Chambers questioned whether customary international law had evolved not to include any policy requirement, a view that was confirmed by the Appeals Chamber in *Kunarac* and adopted in all subsequent

148 ICTR Akayesu 1998, para 581.

149 Elements of Crimes 2010, Article 7, Introduction, para 3.

150 ICTY Kunarac 2002, para 86; ICTY Tadić 1999, para 251. The negotiators of the Rome Statute also rejected a link to armed conflict. See von Hebel and Robinson 1999, 92–93; Hall and Ambos (Commentary edited by Triffterer and Ambos) 2016, 166.

151 Elements of Crimes 2010, Article 7, Introduction, para 3. Emphasis added.

152 International Military Tribunal 1947, Judgment; Jurovics (Commentary edited by Fernandez, Pacreau and Maze) 2012, 461–462.

153 ICTY Nikolić 1995, para 26.

Decisions.[154] Thus, the ICC Elements of Crimes' restriction of crimes against humanity to acts pursuant to or in furtherance of State or organizational policies is narrower than customary international law.[155]

The term "organizational" is not defined by the Statute or Elements of Crimes. However, the ordinary meaning of organization being "a group of people who work together in an organized way for a shared purpose"[156] suggests that the term requires a certain degree of structure, but does not limit the kind of group included, such as to only political, public, or State-like groups. This view is supported by the fact that the word organization is repeated in the Elements of Crimes relating to forced disappearance, where they specify a required involvement of a "State or political organization."[157] Because the drafters in this case chose to add the adjective "political" to specify the term "organization," it can be deduced that for the organizational policy element of crimes against humanity, all types of organizations are included. Pursuant to this interpretation, organized criminal groups, which fulfill the criterion of having a certain structure *per definitionem*, would qualify as an organization, and thus not be excluded from committing crimes against humanity.

Still, the drafting history of the provision reveals that the organizational policy element was included to encompass those non-State organizations that the case law at the time had suggested, namely the *Tadić* Decision, including in the policy element "forces which, although not those of the legitimate government, have *de facto* control over, or are able to move freely within, defined territory."[158] This would apply, for example, to Mexican drug cartels that have significant territorial influence, especially near their production centers and main trafficking routes.[159] Professor M. Cherif Bassiouni, Chair of the Drafting Committee, argued: "Article 7 does not bring a new development […], namely its applicability to non-State actors. If that were the case, the mafia […] could be charged […] and that is clearly neither the letter nor the spirit of Article 7."[160] However, the ICC Pre-Trial Chamber rejected the restriction to State-like actors, commenting

154 ICTY Kunarac *et al.* 2001; ICTY Kordić and Čerkez 2001; ICTY Kunarac 2002, para 98. For a detailed discussion of the customary international law see Smith 2009.

155 Cassese (Commentary edited by Cassese, Gaeta and Jones) 2002a, 375–376.

156 Cambridge Dictionary 2019c.

157 Elements of Crimes 2010, Article 7(1)(i), para 4–5.

158 ICTY Tadić 1997, para 654; von Hebel and Robinson 1999, 97.

159 Beittel 2018, 1.

160 Bassiouni 2005, Vol. I, 151–152.

> [w]hereas some have argued that only State-like organizations may qualify, the Chamber opines that the formal nature of a group and the level of its organization should not be the defining criterion. Instead, as others have convincingly put forward, a distinction should be drawn on whether a group has the capability to perform acts which infringe on basic human values.[161]

The Chamber expressly cited purely private criminal organizations, private individuals with *de facto* power, and criminal gangs or groups as possibly meeting the organization requirement of Article 7 of the Rome Statute, and set out several considerations to consider for case-by-case assessments:

> (i) whether the group is under a responsible command, or has an established hierarchy;
> (ii) whether the group possesses, in fact, the means to carry out a widespread or systematic attack against a civilian population;
> (iii) whether the group exercises control over part of the territory of a State;
> (iv) whether the group has criminal activities against the civilian population as a primary purpose;
> (v) whether the group articulates, explicitly or implicitly, an intention to attack a civilian population;
> (vi) whether the group is part of a larger group, which fulfils some or all of the abovementioned criteria.[162]

Although Judge Hans-Peter Kaul formulated a dissenting opinion stating that "non-State actors […] are not able to carry out a policy of this nature, such as groups of organized crime, a mob, groups of (armed) civilians or criminal gangs,"[163] it is unlikely that the term organization will be restricted in future Decisions beyond the criterion of "moving freely within a territory"[164] as pronounced in the *Tadić* Decision at time of the drafting of the Rome Statute.

Organized criminal groups are often highly structured with a clear chain of command or a well-functioning network structure. They possess significant financial resources and are often well-armed, satisfying the criteria set out by the Pre-Trial Chamber to the extent that they are "capable of performing acts

161 ICC Republic of Kenya 2010, para 90.

162 *ibid.*, para 90–91 (citing M. Di Fillippo and the International Law Commission) and 93.

163 ICC Republic of Kenya 2010, para 38; See also Hauck 2016, 455, arguing that the provision only applies to state-like organizations.

164 ICTY Tadić 1997, para 654.

that infringe on basic human values."[165] In some cases, such as the hybrid FARC, organized criminal groups control territory. In other cases, they do not have *de facto* control but move freely due to police corruption and strong bonds to the local population (e.g., drug cartels in Mexico), meaning that these groups also possess characteristics as mentioned in the *Tadić* Decision.

Second, the contextual element of an "attack" is specified in Article 7 of the Rome Statute using the adjectives "widespread or systematic." Although an attack requires a multiplicity of acts, the two adjectives clarify the meaning of "attack" and simultaneously raise the threshold for a course of conduct to qualify as such. "Only the attack, not the individual acts of the accused, must be widespread or systematic."[166] Nevertheless, the crimes committed by organized criminal groups must either satisfy one of the criteria themselves or have a sufficient nexus to a widespread or systematic attack for the ICC to have jurisdiction.

Critically, the terms "widespread" and "systematic" are disjunctive elements. Although they only first appeared as part of the definition of crimes against humanity in Article 3 of the ICTR Statute, they had already been mentioned in Nuremberg and have been incorporated as alternative elements in ICTY jurisprudence.[167] However, a contradiction seems to exist between the alternative formulation in Article 7(1) of the Rome Statute and the requirements of "multiple acts" *and* of a policy in Article 7(2)(a).[168] Whereas a systematic attack usually satisfies the policy requirement, a widespread attack does not necessarily. However, the policy requirement is an element that must be proven separately regardless of whether an attack is widespread or systematic. As Schabas indicated, "in practice, [...] 'widespread' and 'systematic' tend to overlap, and manifest themselves in many of the same factors."[169] Although a Chamber must consider both quantitative and qualitative aspects, an attack must only satisfy the threshold of either being systematic or widespread, in both cases in addition to fulfilling the definition of an attack understood as multiple criminal acts as well as the policy element.[170]

165 ICC Republic of Kenya 2010, para 90.

166 ICTY Kunarac 2002 para 96.

167 International Military Tribunal 1947, Judgment; ICTY Tadić 1997; although the French version of the ICTR Statute indicated that the attack needs to be „genéralisée *et* systématique", the Chambers followed the disjunctive approach, see ICTR Akayesu 1998; Hall and Ambos (Commentary edited by Triffterer and Ambos) 2016, 168.

168 Ambos 2001, 406–407.

169 Schabas (Commentary) 2016, 166.

170 ICC Bemba 2009, para 82.

The term "widespread" is mainly understood in quantitative terms to refer to the scale of an attack or the numbers of victims, thereby "cover[ing] various situations involving a multiplicity of victims, for example, as a result of the cumulative effect of a series of inhumane acts or the singular effect of an inhumane act of extraordinary magnitude."[171] The element has been interpreted broadly in ICTR and in late ICTY jurisprudence, as well as by the ICC Pre-Trial Chamber, adding that "[t]he assessment is neither exclusively quantitative nor geographical, but must be carried out on the basis of the individual facts."[172][173] In the case of Darfur, the attack was held to be widespread because it "affected hundreds of thousands of individuals and took place across large swathes of the territory of the Darfur region."[174]

In the context of organized crime, such as involvement in a conflict between other forces, large-scale violence against public officers or the population, or massive suffering directly caused by organized criminal groups' market operations (e.g., migrants detained in severe conditions or forced labor), can satisfy the "widespread" element.[175]

While the term "systematic" has initially been interpreted by the *ad hoc* tribunals as setting a very high threshold of "a pattern or methodical plan"[176] or as "thoroughly organized and following a regular pattern on the basis of a common policy involving substantial public and private resources,"[177] such interpretations have given way to more expansive definitions.[178] According to recent case law, the term "systematic" means "the organized nature of the acts of violence and the improbability of their random occurrence,"[179] with a "non-accidental repetition of similar criminal conduct on a regular basis."[180] According to the ICC Trial Chamber, the requirement of being systematic refers to the nature of the attack and "therefore goes beyond the existence of any policy seeking to eliminate, persecute or undermine a community."[181] Because organized criminal groups are designed to earn profit on a continuous basis,

171 International Law Commission 1996, 47.

172 ICC Republic of Kenya 2010, para 95.

173 E.g., ICTY Blaškić 2000; ICTY Krnojelac *et al.* 2002; ICTR Muvunyi 2006. See also Hall and Ambos (Commentary edited by Triffterer and Ambos) 2016, 170.

174 ICC Bashir 2009, para 84.

175 For an analysis of these crimes in detail, see sections 3.2.2.2.1.-2. respectively.

176 ICTY Tadić 1997, para 648.

177 ICTR Akayesu 1998, para 580.

178 Hall and Ambos (Commentary edited by Triffterer and Ambos) 2016, 170–171.

179 ICTY Kordić 2004, para 94; ICTR Muvunyi 2006; ICC Republic of Kenya 2010.

180 ICTY Kordić 2004, para 94; ICC Katanga and Ngudjolo 2008.

181 ICC Katanga 2014, para 1113.

their operations are always systematically directed toward this goal. Although organized criminal groups might occasionally benefit from a specific market opportunity that does not repeat itself, for example plundering a historic site that has recently been abandoned and trading the plundered artefacts, or perpetrate acts of violence only once, such as for the purpose of intimidation, their activities are usually not only nonaccidental but also repetitive and similar in nature. Thus, the requirement of a systematic attack is pertinent to the analysis of ICC jurisdiction over organized criminal activities under Article 7 of the Rome Statute.

In sum, organized criminal groups frequently commit widespread or systematic attacks as defined in Article 7 of the Rome Statute.

3.2.2.1.2 *A Civilian Population as the Object of an Attack*

In addition to the abovementioned requirements, Article 7 of the Rome Statute states that for a crime to qualify as a crime against humanity, it must be part of an attack "against any civilian population." Thus, an organized criminal activity must also satisfy this element to fall under ICC jurisdiction under Article 7.

The term consists of three distinct elements: the terms "population," "civilian," and "directed against," which will be studied separately in the following paragraphs.

The term population has been interpreted broadly, as underlined by the word "any." Pre-Trial Chamber I of the ICC stated that based on ICTY jurisprudence the potential victims can belong to any population, "regardless of their nationality, ethnicity or other distinguishing feature."[182] Crimes against humanity can thus be committed against a population "of the same nationality as the perpetrator or those who are Stateless, as well as those of a different nationality."[183] While a population is understood to refer to a group of individuals sharing common features, the type of attributes to be shared is not specified and can also include "(perceived) political affiliation."[184][185] The term population has been interpreted not to mean "the entire population of the geographical entity in which the attack is taking place."[186] Rather, "it is sufficient to show that enough individuals were targeted [...], or that they were targeted in such a way as to satisfy the Chamber that the attack was [...] [not directed]

182 ICC Katanga and Ngudjolo 2008, para 399.
183 ICTY Tadić 1997, para 635.
184 ICC Ruto *et al.* 2012, para 164.
185 Hall and Ambos (Commentary edited by Triffterer and Ambos) 2016, 172; ICC Katanga and Ngudjolo 2008, para 399.
186 ICTY Kunarac 2002, para 90.

against a limited and randomly selected number of individuals."[187] The term population thus implies the collective nature of crimes against humanity.[188] Article 7 does not require any discriminatory intent or motive against the collective.[189] A formulation including the words "on political, racial, ethnic or religious grounds or any other arbitrarily defined grounds"[190] in the Preparatory Committee's draft for the Rome Statute did not receive support.[191] Therefore, the term population only excludes a small number of randomly selected individuals as the object of an attack. Broad categories such as women, children, or young men in good health, often the groups targeted for human trafficking, can thus also qualify as a population in the sense of Article 7.

The term "civilian" has been interpreted in accordance with international humanitarian law (IHL) to comprise "all persons who are civilians as opposed to members of armed forces and other legitimate combatants."[192] This group includes

> members of a resistance movement and former combatants—regardless of whether they wore wear [sic] uniform or not—but who were no longer taking part in hostilities when the crimes were perpetrated because they had either left the army or were no longer bearing arms or, ultimately, had been placed *hors de combat*, in particular, due to their wounds or their being detained.[193]

Because the underlying purposes of prosecuting crimes against humanity are to safeguard human values and protect human dignity, "a broad interpretation should [...] be placed on the word 'civilians.' "[194] Thus, "the specific situation of the victim at the moment the crimes were committed, rather than his status, must be taken into account in determining his standing as a civilian."[195] The population must be "predominantly civilian in nature," although combatants

187 *ibid.*

188 ICTR Bagilishema 2001, para 80. Hall and Ambos comment: "[...] the population requirement does not add anything to the attack requirement, since the multiplicity of victims is already covered by the 'widespread' or 'systematic' elements." Hall and Ambos (Commentary edited by Triffterer and Ambos) 2016, 173.

189 Cassese (Commentary edited by Cassese, Gaeta and Jones) 2002a, 369.

190 Preparatory Committee on the Establishment of an ICC 1998a, 90.

191 Schabas (Commentary) 2016, 171–172. See also ICTY Tadić 1999, para 297.

192 ICC Bemba 2009, para 78.

193 ICTY Blaškić 2000, para 214.

194 ICTY Kupreškić *et al.* 2000, para 547.

195 ICTY Blaškić 2000, para 214.

might be present.[196] Thus, crimes committed by organized criminal groups against combatants cannot be prosecuted as crimes against humanity without prejudice to the question of whether organized criminal groups meet the requirements of Article 8 of the Rome Statute to commit a war crime.[197]

In the absence of an armed conflict, the principles of humanitarian law do not apply, and thus the term civilian should be interpreted more broadly, including every person, even members of the armed forces and policemen.[198] Therefore, attacks against the police force by organized criminal groups, such as those that frequently occur in Mexico, can qualify as crimes against humanity in the absence of armed conflict.

Lastly, the term "directed against" has been interpreted as requiring that "the civilian population [...] be *the primary object* of the attack and not just an incidental victim."[199] To determine whether this element is satisfied, the ICTY Appeals Chamber developed several criteria:

> *inter alia*, the means and method used in the course of the attack, the status of the victims, their number, the discriminatory nature of the attack, the nature of the crimes committed in its course, the resistance to the assailants at the time and the extent to which the attacking force may be said to have complied or attempted to comply with the precautionary requirements of the laws of war.[200]

The term "directed" thus specifies the intention of the attack, not its result or the context of individual crimes committed as a part thereof.[201]

The directional requirement draws a distinction between attacks qualifying as crimes against humanity and war crimes as well as civilian casualties in armed conflicts. In the absence of an armed conflict, however, all nonaccidental attacks against a civilian population have an intentional

196 ICC Katanga 2014, para 1104–1105.

197 See section 3.2.3.1.1.

198 Hall and Ambos (Commentary edited by Triffterer and Ambos) 2016, 174; Ambos 2014, 64–67; SCSL Norman *et al.* 2008, para 261. Regarding the history of the armed conflict nexus for crimes against humanity and its elimination in recent general practice see Ford 2006. *Contra*: Hauck 2016, 455. Hauck argues that crimes against humanity can only be committed in a military context of an armed conflict where a clear distinction can be made between combatants and non- or "no longer"-combatants. The author of this book sees no support for this view in recent case law and literature.

199 ICC Bemba 2009, para 76. Emphasis added.

200 ICTY Kunarac 2002, para 91.

201 *ibid.*, para 103; ICTY Blaškić 2000, footnote 401.

direction, as well as in the context of organized crime where economic interests prevail.

Generally, crimes against humanity can be committed against a much broader range of victims than can genocide and war crimes, which facilitates prosecutions of crimes against humanity committed by organized criminal groups.[202] For example, victims of human trafficking are often chosen from a specific area and based on their economic situation. The systematic creation of insecurity and fear by organized criminal groups is addressed to a geographically or politically defined population. Thus, such conduct would satisfy the requirement of an attack to be directed against any civilian population.

3.2.2.1.3 *Mental Element: Knowledge of the Attack*

Article 7 of the Rome Statute in its *chapeau* explicitly requires that a crime against humanity be committed "with knowledge of the attack." For organized criminal activities to fall under this provision, the actors must be aware that their "conduct [is] part of or intend […] the conduct to be part of a widespread or systematic attack against a civilian population."[203]

This *mens rea* requirement is customary international law and consistent with the jurisprudence of the *ad hoc* tribunals.[204] It constitutes a mental element that is required in addition to the specific intent and knowledge required for the underlying offense according to Article 30 of the Rome Statute and, in the case of persecution, the required *dolus specialis* or discriminatory animus as laid out in the Elements of Crimes for Article 7(1)(h) of the Rome Statute. In addition to the required factual nexus between an individual act and the attack, the mental element of Article 7 thus ensures the perpetrator's awareness of the nexus. Therefore, acts that happen to be carried out contemporaneously with the attack are excluded from the provision.

However, the Rome Statute does not require that the "perpetrator had knowledge of all characteristics of the attack or the precise details of the plan or policy of the State or organization."[205] *Dolus eventualis*, meaning that the perpetrator was aware of the likelihood of becoming instrumental in the execution of an attack, is sufficient.[206] This argument was essential in the conviction

---

202 Hall and Ambos (Commentary edited by Triffterer and Ambos) 2016, 174.

203 Elements of Crimes 2010, e.g., Article 7(1)(a), para 3.

204 ICTY Kordić 2004; ICTY Kunarac 2002; ICTR Musema 2000; ICC Katanga and Ngudjolo 2008; Cassese (Commentary edited by Cassese, Gaeta and Jones) 2002a, 373; Schabas (Commentary) 2016, 167.

205 Elements of Crimes 2010, Article 7, Introduction, para 2.

206 Hall and Ambos (Commentary edited by Triffterer and Ambos) 2016, 176.

of Bruno Tesch and others who, through a legal enterprise, sold the legal pesticide Zyklon B to the Nazi regime "know[ing] of this wholesale extermination of human beings in the eastern concentration camps by the S.S. using Zyklon B gas."[207] Organized crime, providing the means to commit crimes against humanity knowing of an attack, can thus be held responsible for contributing to crimes against humanity.

The *mens rea* does not require a "concrete idea of the consequences [...] or an 'abominable attitude' ".[208] Moreover,

> the motives of the accused [...] are irrelevant and a crime against humanity can be committed for purely personal reasons. Furthermore, the accused need not share the purpose or goal behind the attack. It is also irrelevant whether the accused intended his acts to be directed against the targeted population or merely against his victim.[209]

Furthermore, "neither does the person charged need to be the leader, or even a member, of the organization"[210] bearing the policy to commit the attack. As a consequence, "it is only necessary to establish that the person had knowledge of the attack in general terms,"[211] or "knowledge of the wider context in which his acts occur."[212] In cases where the attack itself is not planned or perpetrated mainly by an organized criminal group, members of the group can consequently still be held responsible for criminal conduct in furtherance of the underlying policy, regardless of their motivation, attitude, or involvement with the goal of the attack or the perpetrating group, as long as they were aware of the overall setting of their actions. This might be the case, for example, when organized criminal groups abduct persons from an area that is or has recently been attacked by an armed group that informed the organized criminal group of the attack.

A purely risk-based approach adopted by the *Blaškić* Trial Chamber of the ICTY, whereby it "suffices that [the perpetrator] knowingly took the risk of participating in the implementation of the ideology, policy or plan," was rejected by the Appeals Chamber.[213] However, the situation of a perpetrator in

207 British Military Court "Zyklon B Case" 1946, para 3.

208 Oberster Gerichtshof für die Britische Zone in Strafsachen 1949, Case 16, para 60–62.

209 ICTY Kunarac 2002, para 103. (Footnote omitted).

210 ICC Muthaura *et al.* 2012, para 223.

211 ICC Gbagbo 2014, para 214.

212 ICTY Kordić and Čerkez 2001, para 185.

213 ICTY Blaškić 2004, para 126.

the context of crimes against humanity committing crimes "*dans la complète ignorance du plan criminel*" is "*improbable,*" the claim of not having known the plan or its consequences "*peu crédible*"[214] Thus, the jurisprudence has established that "circumstantial evidence, such as: the accused's position in the military"[215] can be used to prove the requisite *mens rea*, imposing a presumption of knowledge, or "*quasi obligation de savoir*"[216] based on the circumstances. Factors that the requisite knowledge can be inferred from include:

- the historical and political circumstances in which the acts of violence occurred;
- the functions of the accused when the crimes were committed;
- his responsibilities within the political or military hierarchy;
- the direct and indirect relationship between the political and military hierarchy;
- the scope and gravity of the acts perpetrated;
- the nature of the crimes committed and the degree to which they are common knowledge.[217]

In sum, if a general nexus exists between organized crime and the group planning or perpetration of an attack, such as continual arms trade with a militia, it might be sufficient to infer the requisite *mens rea* requirement of Article 7 of the Rome Statute. Especially in cases where the victimization of a multitude of individuals to gain a profit constitutes the attack itself, anyone involved in the business must be aware of the attack.

3.2.2.2 Material Elements: Individual Acts

Article 7(1) of the Rome Statute contains in subparagraphs (a) to (k) an exhaustive list of 11 separate offenses that can constitute crimes against humanity. Each is further defined in the Elements of Crime. Notwithstanding the contextual and *mens rea* requirements analyzed above, the following subsection examines which offenses committed by organized criminal groups fall under these 11 offenses and can thus be brought before the ICC.[218] The section focuses on human trafficking, migrant smuggling and migrant-related crimes, drug

214 Jurovics (Commentary edited by Fernandez, Pacreau and Maze) 2012, 476. "In complete ignorance of the criminal plan", "unlikely", "little credible". Translated by the author.

215 ICC Katanga and Ngudjolo 2008, para 402.

216 Jurovics (Commentary edited by Fernandez, Pacreau and Maze) 2012, 476. "Quasi obligation to know". Translated by the author.

217 ICTY Blaškić 2000, para 259. See also ICC Katanga and Ngudjolo 2008, para 402.

218 See section 3.2.2.1.

trafficking, illicit trade in cultural goods, and organized crime-related violence because their elements provide the broadest basis for potential jurisdiction.[219]

3.2.2.2.1 *Individual Acts of Crimes against Humanity in Trafficking in Persons, Including Forced Prostitution and Labor and Organ Trafficking*

Human trafficking is one of the most lucrative illegal markets worldwide.[220] Specific components of it can constitute several of the individual acts of crimes against humanity defined in Article 7 of the Rome Statute. For the purpose of analysis, this study subdivides human trafficking into the initial act of trafficking (i.e., recruiting and removing individuals from their home and transferring them to another location); the general living conditions of trafficking victims (i.e., enslavement and any form of cruel treatment); and the most common purposes of trafficking (i.e., forced labor, sexual exploitation, and organ trade).

First, the initial act of removing trafficking victims from their home environment can fall under Article 7(1)(d) of the Rome Statute—deportation or forcible transfer of a population. The Elements of Crimes specify that "[t]he perpetrator deported or forcibly transferred [...] one or more persons to another State or location, by expulsion or other coercive acts."[221] Deportation commonly refers to a forced transfer of a person from one country to another, whereas forcible transfer refers to movements within the same country.[222] Both imply the use of force.

Trafficking victims are often recruited based on deception; for example, a method commonly used by the Japanese Yakuza is where local recruiters, often friends or relatives of the victims, approach women in financial difficulties with job opportunities in Japan.[223] Thus, whether deception satisfies the coercive nature required by Article 7(1)(d) of the Rome Statute must be analyzed. The Elements of Crimes specify in a footnote that

> [t]he term "forcibly" is not restricted to physical force, but may include threat of force or coercion, such as that caused by fear of violence, duress, detention, psychological oppression or abuse of power against such person or persons or another person, or by taking advantage of a coercive environment.[224]

219 For a detailed discussion of cultural genocide by way of the illegal exploitation and trade in cultural goods, see von Schorlemer 2016, 687 *et seq.*

220 See section 2.1.2.2.

221 Elements of Crimes 2010, Article 7(1)(d), para 1 (Footnotes omitted).

222 Hall and Stahn (Commentary edited by Triffterer and Ambos) 2016, 192.

223 Dinan 2002, 5.

224 Elements of Crimes 2010, footnote 5.

The ICTY Trial Chamber interpreted the term "forced" as meaning "not voluntary" or based on "an individual's own genuine wish" and required that "the persons had *no real choice*."[225] The Chamber went on stating that "in assessing whether the displacement of a person was voluntary or not, it should look beyond formalities to all the circumstances surrounding the person's displacement, to ascertain that person's genuine intention."[226] The term forcible should thus be given a broad reading.[227] The provision of false information, vulnerable (financial) situation of the victim, and systematic exploitation of the personal relationship between the recruiter and victim, often paired with indirect psychological pressure on the victim and her family members as well as the psychological pressure based on promises of a better life (in the case of Yakuza recruitment strategies) impair the victim's genuine intention. Deception, if paired with such a coercive environment, can thus satisfy the requirement of a forcible transfer.

Moreover, the ICC Pre-Trial Chamber required a link between the perpetrator's acts and the "effect of forcing the victim to leave."[228] Victims of trafficking are provided with necessary travel documents and their transport is arranged for them, clearly establishing a close nexus—in addition to the deception by the local recruiter—between the perpetrators' acts and the victims leaving their homes.

While the term "population" in the provision suggests that the crime must be committed against a multitude of victims, the Elements of Crimes clearly state that one victim is sufficient for the crime to be established, as long as it is part of a widespread or systematic attack as outlined above.[229]

The initial act of transferring victims of human trafficking away from their homes can consequently fall under the crime of deportation or forcible transfer if deception, psychological and social pressure as well as exploitation of the victims' economic or other vulnerability do not leave the victim with a real choice.

Second, regardless of the type of exploitation the victims are subjected to, their general living conditions once they have been removed from their familiar environment can also constitute a crime against humanity. Specifically, their living conditions can amount to the crimes of enslavement or other inhumane acts under Article 7(1)(c) and (k) of the Rome Statute, respectively. These are analyzed as follows.

The Elements of Crimes define enslavement as a situation in which

225 ICTY Simić 2003, para 125.

226 *ibid.*, para 126.

227 Hall and Stahn (Commentary edited by Triffterer and Ambos) 2016, 196.

228 ICC Ruto *et al.* 2012, para 245.

229 See section 3.2.2.1.1.

> [t]he perpetrator exercised any or all of the powers attaching to the right of ownership over one or more persons, such as by purchasing, selling, lending or bartering such a person or persons, or by imposing on them a similar deprivation of liberty.

A footnote specifies that "[i]t is also understood that the conduct described in this element includes trafficking in persons."[230] Thus, the provision is not limited to traditional forms of slavery but meant to cover slavery-like practices often defined as servitude, such as serfdom and debt bondage.[231] In the *Kunarac* Appeals Judgment, the Chamber formulated a nonexhaustive list of indicia of enslavement:

> control of someone's movement, control of physical environment, psychological control, measures taken to prevent or deter escape, force, threat of force or coercion, duration, assertion of exclusivity, subjection to cruel treatment and abuse, control of sexuality and forced labour.[232]

The ICC Pre-Trial Chamber later added "the personal circumstance of the victim, including his/her vulnerability"[233] to the list. In the case of trafficking by the Yakuza, the victims are sold into specific placements and demanded to work off exorbitant debts for their travel, food, and lodging. They are also threatened with violence and increased debt if they attempt to escape and are made to believe that the Japanese police will treat them as illegal aliens, especially since their passports are confiscated by the perpetrators.[234] Such treatment, especially in light of the vulnerability the victims were recruited for as well as language and cultural barriers, clearly satisfies the requirements of enslavement.

Moreover, trafficking victims are often subjected to other cruel treatment regardless of the specific form of exploitation they must endure. Such treatment involves, for example, violence, threats of violence, psychological abuse, and a lack of food, decent housing, and medical care. Such acts can fall under the residual clause in subparagraph (k), covering other inhumane acts intentionally causing great suffering, or serious injury to the body or to mental or

230 Elements of Crimes 2010, footnote 18.

231 For a more detailed discussion of legal and historical reasons to include slavery-like practices see Hall and Stahn (Commentary edited by Triffterer and Ambos) 2016, 190–191.

232 ICTY Kunarac 2002, para 119.

233 ICC Ntaganda 2014, footnote 209.

234 Dinan 2002, 7–8.

physical health, described as "*serious* violations of international customary law and the basic rights pertaining to human beings, drawn from the norms of international human rights law."[235] The acts must be committed with intent and be serious enough in nature to be judged of similar character as the explicitly enumerated acts in subparagraphs (a) to (j). However, case law provides little guidance on how the similarity is determined and suggests a case-by-case approach.[236] For example, serious physical or mental injury, acts of sexual violence that caused mental suffering to eye-witnesses, and mutilations have been qualified as inhumane acts.[237] Notably, the enumerated acts under Article 7 of the Rome Statute are not mutually exclusive and have been interpreted differently by different Chambers. Thus, drawing a distinction between other inhumane acts as defined in subparagraph (k) and explicitly enumerated acts is particularly difficult and depends on the individual case.[238] Nevertheless, cruel treatment of victims of human trafficking can amount to inhumane acts under Article 7(1)(k) of the Rome Statute but must be considered on a case-by-case basis.

Third, once trafficking victims have arrived in their work placement, they are exploited for different sources of income for the organized criminal group. The most frequent are forced labor and sexual exploitation, including forced prostitution. Trafficking for organ trade is less frequent.[239]

Sexual exploitation is covered by subparagraph (g), which defines "rape, sexual slavery, enforced prostitution, forced pregnancy, enforced sterilization, or any other form of sexual violence of comparable gravity" as crimes against humanity. All provisions in the Rome Statute referring to sexual violence are deliberately phrased in gender-neutral terms, refer to biological and social aspects, and apply to both men and women, as explicitly stated in Article 7(3).[240] Sexual slavery is defined as a subset of enslavement, where "[t]he perpetrator caused [the victim] to engage in one or more acts of a sexual nature."[241] The provision thus applies to all situations of enslavement in which

235 ICC Katanga and Ngudjolo 2008, para 448. Emphasis added.

236 ICTR Bagilishema 2001, para 92.

237 ICTY Blaškić 2000, para 239; ICTR Kajelijeli 2003, para 916; ICC Muthaura *et al.* 2012, para 270–273; see also Hall and Stahn (Commentary edited by Triffterer and Ambos) 2016, 238.

238 For example, see Hall and Stahn (Commentary edited by Triffterer and Ambos) 2016, 239, for a discussion of the qualification of forced marriage as an inhumane act, a form of enslavement or sexual violence.

239 See section 2.1.2.2.

240 For a detailed discussion of the definition of gender see Hall, Powderly and Hayes (Commentary edited by Triffterer and Ambos) 2016b, 292–294.

241 Elements of Crimes 2010, Article 7(1)(g)-2, para 2.

the victim's ability to decide matters relating to her sexual activity is impaired, including rape by her captors, forced (temporary) marriage (e.g., of young girls to soldiers), and detention in so-called rape camps.[242] In *Katanga*, the Chamber underlined that neither a commercial transaction nor force, threat of force, or coercion are necessary to constitute the crime of sexual slavery. Rather, the victim's "perception of his or her situation as well as his or her reasonable fear" are decisive, including situations where the inability to exercise personal autonomy or escape from the situation is based on socioeconomic inequality between victim and perpetrator.[243] The provision thus covers several different situations of sexual exploitation of trafficking victims, namely those where sexual exploitation is the source of profit itself, either in an exclusive setting (i.e., in a forced marriage) or in the form of prostitution, or where sexual violence accompanies other forms of servitude. However, for a situation to constitute sexual slavery, the conditions of enslavement as outlined above must be satisfied. As shown above, this clearly applies to trafficked women sold into establishments operated by Yakuza gangs.

Situations of sexual exploitation in the context of organized crime that do not amount to enslavement are covered by the crimes of rape, enforced prostitution, and other forms of sexual violence of comparable gravity. Rape is defined as an invasion of "the body of a person by conduct resulting in penetration, however slight, of any part of the body of the victim or of the perpetrator with a sexual organ, or of the anal or genital opening of the victim with any object or any other part of the body" that

> was committed by force, or by threat of force or coercion, such as that caused by fear of violence, duress, detention, psychological oppression or abuse of power, against such person or another person, or by taking advantage of a coercive environment, or the invasion was committed against a person incapable of giving genuine consent.[244]

Absence of consent is only relevant where a perpetrator profits from a victim's inability to give genuine consent because of natural, induced, or age-related incapacity.[245] In all other cases the existence of coercive conditions as defined in *Katanga* and cited above is sufficient.[246] Rule 70 of the Rules of Procedure

242 McDougall 1998, para 8.
243 ICC Katanga 2014, para 976–978.
244 Elements of Crimes 2010, Article 7(1)(g)-1, para 1–2.
245 *ibid.*, footnote 16.
246 ICC Katanga 2014, para 966.

and Evidence states that consent cannot be inferred in any way from the victim's words or conduct.

While rape must involve some form of penetration, other forms of sexual violence of comparable gravity are included in a residual provision that "is not limited to physical invasion of the human body and may include acts that do not involve penetration or even physical conduct," such as forced nudity.[247] However, the assessment of comparable gravity must be done on a case-by-case basis. In *Bemba*, for example, the Chamber found that allegations of women being forced to undress in public did not constitute sexual violence of comparable gravity.[248] Moreover, "not every act of violence which targets parts of the body commonly associated with sexuality should be considered an act of sexual violence."[249] In a much-disputed Decision, the ICC Pre-Trial Chamber re-characterized forcible circumcision and penile amputation of Luo men as other inhumane acts.[250]

Enforced prostitution is defined as a situation where "[t]he perpetrator caused one or more persons to engage in one or more acts of a sexual nature" and "obtained or expected to obtain pecuniary or other advantage in exchange for or in connection with the[se] acts."[251] Most cases of enforced prostitution would also fall under sexual slavery. Although it was suggested that the provision is meant to capture situations that lack slavery-like conditions, such conduct would also fall under rape or other acts of sexual violence of comparable gravity.[252] Nevertheless, the provision leaves no doubt that sexual acts performed under any coercive circumstances and for the actual or expected benefit of a third person constitute crimes against humanity. This is frequently the case for the illegal market of sexual services supplied by organized crime.[253]

Overall, subparagraph (g) covers a wide range of conduct associated with sexual exploitation in the context of human trafficking with various degrees of control and coercion by the perpetrator, including sexual slavery, forced prostitution, rape, and other forms of sexual violence of comparable gravity.

---

247 ICTR Akayesu 1998, para 688; Office of the Prosecutor of the International Criminal Court 2014b.

248 ICC Bemba 2008, para 40.

249 ICC Muthaura *et al.* 2012, para 265–266.

250 *ibid.* Also see remarks relating to the distinction between other inhumane acts and enumerated acts above. For a critique see Hall, Powderly and Hayes (Commentary edited by Triffterer and Ambos) 2016a, 217.

251 Elements of Crimes 2010, Article 7(1)(g)-3, para 1–2.

252 Hall, Powderly and Hayes (Commentary edited by Triffterer and Ambos) 2016a, 214–215.

253 Legal prostitution and voluntary illegal prostitution are not included.

Forced labor is not explicitly mentioned in Article 7 of the Rome Statute. However, compulsory and forced labor have been considered in connection with enslavement as early as 1926, when Article 5 of the Slavery Convention demanded all State Parties to put an end to all forced labor that is not exacted for public purposes. The Nuremberg Charter included enslavement under crimes against humanity as well as deportation for forced labor under war crimes.[254] Thus, according to customary international law, the crime of enslavement has encompassed forced labor "at least since the end of the Second World War."[255] The Elements of Crimes specify that the deprivation of liberty associated with enslavement

> may, in some circumstances, include exacting forced labour or otherwise reducing a person to a servile status as defined in the Supplementary Convention on the Abolition of Slavery, the Slave Trade, and Institutions and Practices Similar to Slavery of 1956.[256]

Forced labor by trafficking victims therefore constitutes a crime against humanity if the conditions for enslavement outlined above are satisfied. However, contrary to sexual exploitation, Article 7 of the Rome Statute does not explicitly provide recourse for victims of forced labor in coercive contexts that do not amount to enslavement. It is questionable, however, whether forced labor in and of itself is not an act sufficiently related to the exercise of the right of ownership. Nevertheless, it could otherwise be argued that forced labor is covered by subparagraph (k) because of the long-term effects on the physical health of a victim, especially in cases of physical labor, severe working conditions, and a lack of adequate food, housing, and medical care, as well as the psychological harm done to the victim through continuous coercion, lack of autonomy, and humiliation. For example, in the case of so-called truck wages, which usually refers to workers in small communities being paid in goods or direct credit to be used in a store held by their employer, the assessment must be made on a case-by-case basis based on the circumstances as well as reasonable subjective perceptions of the victim.

Overall, forced labor can be prosecuted under Article 7(1)(c) or (k) of the Rome Statute.

Human trafficking for the purpose of organ trade is covered by the crimes of murder as well as other inhumane acts under subparagraphs (a) and (k).

254 Nuremberg Charter 1945, Article 6.

255 Hall and Stahn (Commentary edited by Triffterer and Ambos) 2016, 190.

256 Elements of Crimes 2010, footnote 18.

As in the case of the KLA, most organized criminal groups trafficking individuals for the purpose of removing their organs do not possess adequate medical equipment to remove them without causing the victim's death.[257] In such cases, the crime would amount to murder under subparagraph (a). According to ICC case law, for murder to occur, "the victim has to be dead and the death must result from the act of murder [...] committed by action or omission."[258] As indicated by the French wording "*meurtre*" instead of "*assassinat,*" the provision does not require premeditation.[259] Death can be inferred from factual circumstances regardless of whether the corpse has been found based on, for example, "the location of the alleged murder, its approximate date, the means by which the act was committed with enough precision, the circumstances of the incident, and the perpetrator's link to the crime."[260] Killing a victim for the purpose of organ removal clearly satisfies these elements. The example of the KLA's practice of running a clinic for organ removal as part of other detention centers clearly shows how such organized criminal activity can become part of a widespread or systematic attack and exemplifies the relevance of the crime–conflict nexus in this regard. Lastly, in the rare circumstances of a victim surviving the organ removal, such conduct falls under other inhumane acts because it causes severe physical suffering in addition to a high probability of psychological trauma. Moreover, mutilations, commonly defined as "damage[ing] something severely, especially by violently removing a part,"[261] have previously been held to constitute other inhumane acts under Article 7(1)(k) of the Rome Statute.[262]

Thus, human trafficking for organ removal can be prosecuted as a crime against humanity under Article 7 of the Rome Statute.

Overall, the initial act of trafficking (forcibly removing individuals from their home and transferring them to another location), conditions of slavery and cruel treatment, and the most common purposes of trafficking (forced labor, sexual exploitation, and organ trade), can all constitute crimes against humanity under Article 7 if the contextual elements are met, and thus can be brought before the ICC.

257 See section 3.2.1.2.2.1.
258 ICC Bemba 2009, para 132.
259 Hall and Stahn (Commentary edited by Triffterer and Ambos) 2016, 181.
260 ICC Bemba 2009, para 133; ICC Katanga 2014, para 768.
261 Cambridge Dictionary 2019a.
262 ICC Muthaura *et al.* 2012, para 270–273.

3.2.2.2.2 *Individual Acts of Crimes Against Humanity in Migrant Smuggling, Including Migrant-Related Crimes*

The market for the smuggling of migrants, defined in Article 3(a) of the Additional Protocol to the UN Convention against Transnational Organized Crime as "the procurement, in order to obtain, directly or indirectly, a financial or other material benefit, of the illegal entry of a person into a State Party of which the person is not a national or a permanent resident," has significantly grown in recent years, and there are frequent reports of deaths and inhumane conditions before and during the illegal transfers.[263] Especially in the light of a 2017 Statement by ICC Prosecutor Fatou Bensouda announcing that her Office is "carefully examining the feasibility of opening an investigation into migrant-related crimes in Libya,"[264] which was confirmed in the OTP's latest report to the UNSC, whether migrant smuggling satisfies the requirements of the enumerated crimes of Article 7 of the Rome Statute must be analyzed.[265] For the purpose of analysis, migrant smuggling can be subdivided into the isolated act of smuggling, the conditions under which the transfers are occurring, as well as the broader circumstances before and during the transfer. These are analyzed in the following paragraphs.

First, the act of smuggling migrants into another State's territory could qualify as deportation or forcible transfer under Article 7(1)(d) of the Rome Statute.[266] Notably, the requirement of the crime of deportation or forcible transfer that the transferred persons be "lawfully present in the area from which they are so deported or transferred"[267] refers solely to international law, and thus excludes the possibility of a State merely declaring a population to be deported unlawfully present on its territory.[268] The provision does not require that the persons transferred are removed from their homes or long-term places of residency. Rather, the provision is "intended to exclude only those situations where the individuals are occupying houses or premises unlawfully or illegally and not to impose a requirement for 'residency' to be demonstrated as a legal standard."[269] Non-refoulement obligations warranting the legal presence of asylum seekers and refugees, such as Article 33 of the 1951 Refugee Convention, can thus be of particular importance in cases of migrant

263 See also section 2.1.2.3.

264 Bensouda 2017, para 29.

265 Office of the Prosecutor 2019b, para 31.

266 See also the analysis of the crimes with regard to human trafficking in section 3.2.2.2.1.

267 Elements of Crimes 2010, Article 7(1)(d), para 2.

268 Hall and Stahn (Commentary edited by Triffterer and Ambos) 2016, 263–264.

269 ICTY *Popović et al.* 2010, para 900.

smuggling. For example, the absence of a functioning asylum system and the miscategorization of certain internationally recognized refugee groups in Libya do not exclude the applicability of Article 7(1)(d) of the Rome Statute to asylum seekers and refugees present on Libyan territory.[270]

However, the crime of deportation or forcible transfer requires that the transfer be of a coercive nature, interpreted by international tribunals to mean "involuntary," or not "motivated by an individual's own genuine wish to leave an area."[271] The Elements of Crimes specify that

> [t]he term 'forcibly' [...] may include threat of force or coercion, such as that caused by fear of violence, duress, detention, psychological oppression or abuse of power against such person or persons or another person, or by taking advantage of a coercive environment.[272]

An assessment of a person's genuine intention must be made based on "all the circumstances surrounding the person's displacement."[273] Migrant smuggling is a service provided to the person transferred in exchange for a financial or material benefit. Willingness to provide such a payment is a clear indication of the person's intention to leave. Nevertheless, it could be argued that the smuggler has benefitted from the vulnerability of the smuggled individual, abusing his power, or generally benefitted from the coercive environment of armed conflict. However, considering the high costs of being smuggled, the importance of the coercion relative to the individual's wish to leave does not seem to satisfy the requirement of coercion in Article 7(1)(d) of the Rome Statute. Moreover, the ICC Pre-Trial Chamber required a direct link between the perpetrator's acts and the "effect of forcing the victim to leave."[274] In this regard, it must be noted that many, if not all refugees and migrants, leave their homes with a destination in mind or decide on a destination based on the circumstances in the place in which they are present at a certain moment. In North Africa, for example, for many migrants this destination is the EU, although only few can afford the transfer. The person being smuggled is thus leaving because of causes having affected his or her decision before the smuggling is initiated, and smuggling is reduced to a means to the end of leaving the current place of residency. Consequently, migrant smuggling does not satisfy the requirement

270 Tucci 2012, 50–51.
271 ICTY Simić 2003, para 125.
272 Elements of Crimes 2010, footnote 12.
273 ICTY Simić 2003, para 126.
274 ICC Ruto *et al.* 2012, para 245.

of coercion under Article 7(1)(d) of the Rome Statute, and thus, does not constitute a crime against humanity if considered as an isolated act.

Second, however, migrant smuggling often involves conditions that could amount to other crimes under Article 7. It was estimated that 5,000 persons died in 2016 trying to illegally cross the Mediterranean Sea from North Africa to Europe.[275] These deaths are substantially caused by the inadequacy of the boats used and a lack of safeguard methods, especially life vests. Therefore, whether the smugglers responsible for these conditions can be held responsible for murder under Article 7(1)(a) of the Rome Statute must be analyzed. It can be noted at the outset that for smugglers to be held responsible for murder under the Rome Statute, a risk-based approach to *dolus eventualis* would have to be deemed sufficient because they do not intentionally kill the passengers but knowingly accept the risk of their death, and in some cases, such as during bad weather conditions, they might even be aware of the likelihood of their deaths and might be reckless as to whether death occurs. According to ICTY and ICTR jurisprudence, murder can be charged if the victim died because of an act or omission by the perpetrator with the intention "to kill, or to inflict grievous bodily harm or to inflict serious injury, in the reasonable knowledge that such act or omission was likely to cause death."[276] However, smugglers do not inflict either grievous bodily harm or serious injury, and in most cases, the death of a passenger is possible but not likely. Nevertheless, it could be argued that the concept of likelihood should be considered in the collective context instead of regarding a single individual. If, for example, a smuggler knows that 1% of persons smuggled over the Mediterranean drowned in recent years and runs a business with 10,000 passengers per year, the smuggler reconciles himself with 100 annual deaths, even if any given individual cannot be said to have a high likelihood of dying during passage. However, the collective aspect of crimes against humanity is covered by the contextual requirements and application of collective reasoning to individual criminal responsibility conflicts with the very nature of international criminal law. Moreover, ICC Trial Chambers have underlined that murder "encompasses, first and foremost, cases of *dolus directus* of the first and second degree,"[277] that is, intent and knowledge. Knowledge, defined in Article 30(3) of the Rome Statute as "awareness that a circumstance exists or a consequence will occur in the ordinary course of events," could thus

275 Nebehay 2016.

276 ICTY Krnojelac *et al.* 2002, para 324 (citing ICTY Kordić and Čerkez 2001 and ICTY Delalić *et al.* 1998).

277 ICC Katanga and Ngudjolo 2008, para 423.

encompass circumstances of likelihood. However, this approach has been rejected by the ICC Appeals Chamber, which stated that

> these provisions [article 30(2)(b) and (3)] do not refer to the notion of "risk" [...]. The Appeals Chamber considers that the words "[a consequence] will occur" refer to future events. The verb 'occur' is used with the modal verb 'will', and not with 'may' or 'could'. Therefore, this phrase conveys [...] certainty about the future occurrence. However, absolute certainty about a future occurrence can never exist; therefore the Appeals Chamber considers that the standard for the foreseeability of events is *virtual certainty*.[278]

ICC practice is thus stricter than the jurisprudence of the *ad hoc* tribunals and excludes *dolus eventualis* from Article 30 of the Rome Statute.[279] Consequently, migrant smugglers do not commit the crime of humanity of murder by accepting the risk of passengers drowning or otherwise dying during passage.

For the same reasons, deaths or serious harm caused by insufficient safety measures during transfer or passage do not satisfy the requirements of the crime against humanity of other inhumane acts, since Article 7(2)(k) of the Rome Statute requires that these acts *intentionally* cause great suffering or serious injury to body or to mental or physical health. As outlined above, the mental element of intent requires at least virtual certainty of the occurrence of the consequence, in this case serious harm, and excludes risk.

Finally, ICC Chief Prosecutor Fatou Bensouda expressed concern about

> reports that thousands of vulnerable migrants, including women and children, are being held in detention centers across Libya in often inhumane conditions. Crimes, including killings, rape, torture, deprivation of liberty, abduction for ransom, extortion, and forced labor are alleged to be commonplace.[280]

These, what Bensouda calls migrant-related crimes, could constitute crimes against humanity regardless of the act of smuggling. That is, they could constitute imprisonment, torture, rape, or other sexual violence, as well as other inhumane acts under Article 7 of the Rome Statute.

---

278 ICC Lubanga 2014, para 447. See also ICC Bemba 2009, para 362.

279 It should be noted that previous Decisions have taken different views, e.g., ICC Lubanga 2007; ICC Lubanga 2012; see section 4.1.1.1.

280 Bensouda 2017, para 26; Office of the Prosecutor 2019b, para 31.

Thousands of migrants are being held in detention centers in Libya, some run by smugglers and some by the government.[281] Such detention could constitute the crime of imprisonment or other severe deprivation of physical liberty within the meaning of Article 7(2)(e) of the Rome Statute, defined as "arbitrary or otherwise unlawful detention or deprivation of liberty"[282] "without due process of law"[283] or "if no legal basis can be called upon [for justification]."[284] The term deprivation of liberty has been interpreted broadly in accordance with international customary law to include a variety of restrictions of physical liberty, including house arrest or restrictions of movement to a certain city or area, such as a ghetto.[285] In *Krnojelac*, the Trial Chamber stated that "any form of arbitrary physical deprivation of liberty of an individual may constitute imprisonment."[286] Although the reference to due process suggests that perpetrators have some kind of connection to the State, the crime of deprivation of liberty was not added "to distinguish deprivations of liberty carried out by persons who were not State officials or acting at their instigation or with their consent or acquiescence, since the *chapeau* [...] makes clear that persons unconnected with a State can be guilty of any of the acts prohibited under article 7."[287] In situations of armed conflict, the detention must not be permitted under IHL, such as by Article 42 of the Fourth Geneva Convention allowing for internment of civilians, if the security situation makes it absolutely necessary. In the case of Libya, a Chamber would thus need to assess the security situation in any particular case. Moreover, Article 7 of the Rome Statute requires that the deprivation of liberty be severe. Since the term is not defined, severity must be considered on a case-by-case basis taking factors into account, such as whether the detainee was subjected to torture, inhuman treatment, punishment or intimidation, the detainee's ability to connect to the outside world, duration, and whether the detention was part of a series of repeated short-term detentions.[288] As stated by Bensouda, inhuman treatment, torture, and rape are reportedly commonplace in Libyan detention centers. Thus, the deprivation of liberty can be defined as severe and the detention of migrants can constitute the crime of humanity of imprisonment, unless the security situation

281 Office of the Prosecutor 2019b, para 34.

282 ICTR Ntagerura 2004, para 702.

283 ICTY Kordić 2004, para 114.

284 ICTY Krnojelac *et al.* 2002, para 114.

285 Working Group on Arbitrary Detention 1993; Hall and Stahn (Commentary edited by Triffterer and Ambos) 2016, 198–199.

286 ICTY Krnojelac *et al.* 2002, para 112.

287 Hall and Stahn (Commentary edited by Triffterer and Ambos) 2016, 201, footnote 340.

288 *ibid.*, 202.

makes the detention absolutely necessary. However, an analysis of commensurability will also consider the dangers to individuals from inhumane detention conditions versus the security concerns of the Libyan authorities.

Moreover, any of the acts described by Bensouda relating to the detention conditions, namely rape, sexual violence, torture, and inhuman treatment, can also be tried as separate offenses under Article 7 of the Rome Statute. It should be noted in this regard that the crime of torture as defined in Article 7(2)(f) contains neither a requirement of official capacity of the perpetrator nor a purpose element; it merely stipulates that the victim must be "in the custody or under the control" of the perpetrator, which is the case in refugee detention facilities.[289] Moreover, the ICC Pre-Trial Chamber has specified that severe physical or mental pain or suffering satisfying the requirements for torture can simultaneously constitute another crime under Article 7, namely rape, and decided that torture was subsumed by the more specific material elements of rape.[290] In addition to rape, sexual violence, and torture, acts such as mutilations and other types of severe bodily harm, beatings and inflicting severe harm on somebody in front of the victim's family members have been deemed to fall under the crime of inhuman treatment, and thus could also be tried as migrant-related crimes by the ICC.[291] Accordingly, such migrant-related crimes may constitute crimes against humanity.

Overall, the isolated act of smuggling and the harm caused through risks taken during transfers do not meet the requirements of crimes against humanity, whereas migrant-related crimes, namely deprivation of liberty and different forms of cruel treatment, as for example reported from Libya, can constitute crimes against humanity under Article 7 of the Rome Statute if the contextual elements are satisfied.

3.2.2.2.3 *Individual Acts of Crimes against Humanity in Drug Trafficking*

Over the last decades, drug trafficking's inclusion on the list of internationally prosecuted crimes as well as under the category of crimes against humanity in particular has been continually requested and discussed. Repeatedly, especially during the 1980s, when the negative effects of drug trafficking and drug abuse multiplied and international treaty negotiations took place, public officials of several countries publicly stated that they considered drug trafficking

289 Cassese (Commentary edited by Cassese, Gaeta and Jones) 2002a, 374.

290 ICC Bemba 2009, para 204–205.

291 E.g., ICTY Blaškić 2000, para 239; ICTR Kajelijeli 2003, para 916; ICC Muthaura *et al.* 2012, para 270–273; see also Hall and Stahn (Commentary edited by Triffterer and Ambos) 2016, 238; see section 3.2.2.2.1.

a crime against humanity and demanded the UN declare it as such.[292] Their argument about the gravity of drug trafficking "seriously affect[ing] people's lives, health and welfare, ha[ving] a negative effect on the economic and social system and pos[ing] a danger to the stability of democratic processes"[293] was repeated at the Rome Conference but did not lead to an explicit inclusion of the crime of drug trafficking.[294] Thus, for drug trafficking offenses, specifically all acts along the value chain of the drug trade, to fall within ICC jurisdiction, they would need to be covered by other crimes enumerated in Article 7 of the Rome Statute.[295] This is analyzed as follows.

Drug trafficking could constitute several offenses enumerated as crimes against humanity in Article 7, namely the crimes of murder, if drug users die as a consequence of their drug consumption, or of other inhumane acts. However, two main issues are shared by both these acts listed in Article 7(2)(a) and (k) of the Rome Statute.

First, drug trafficking does not meet the *mens rea* requirements of the crimes. While Article 7(2)(k) of the Rome Statute requires intent to cause great suffering, or serious injury to the body or to mental or physical health, Article 7(2)(a) requires intent or knowledge that death will occur in the ordinary course of events. Article 30(2)(b) of the Rome Statute defines intent in relation to a consequence as the perpetrator meaning to cause the consequence or being aware that it will occur in the ordinary course of events. As for actors such as drug traffickers and producers, their main objective is profit; they do not mean to cause drug consumers to die. However, given the high numbers of deaths caused by overdoses or continuous drug abuse, they are aware of the risk. Still, as outlined above, the term "in the course of ordinary events" in Article 30 has been interpreted in ICC jurisprudence to require "virtual certainty"[296] that a consequence will occur.[297] Such certainty is not manifest regarding drug consumption or abuse given the small proportion of deaths caused, even if confined to particularly harmful drugs.

Second, drug trafficking has an insufficient causal link to the harm it causes, affecting both *actus reus* and *mens rea*. For the crime of murder, it is established case law that "the death resulted from an unlawful act or omission of

292 Permanent Representatives of Argentina, Bolivia, Brazil, Colombia, Ecuador, Peru and Venezuela 1984.

293 *ibid.*

294 See section 2.3.3.2.3.

295 See section 2.1.2.1.

296 ICC Lubanga 2014, para 447.

297 See section 3.2.2.2.2.

the accused or a subordinate."[298] Subparagraph (k) requires that both the act performed by the perpetrator was inhumane and that it caused great suffering or serious injury. Drug trafficking, including all components of the value chain, supplies drugs and could be said to also work to create additional demand. However, the purchase of drugs, usually the last contact of persons involved in drug trafficking with the drug before its consumption, neither kills nor inflicts great suffering on the buyer. Rather, drug-related death or suffering results from drug abuse or consumption, which is voluntary. Even in cases of addiction, where one could argue that drug traffickers abuse the vulnerability of the addicted individual, the act of consumption causing death or suffering is performed by the individual possibly under the influence of mental and physical pressure caused by addiction, but in the absence of external pressure or coercion by a person involved in drug trafficking. In relation to *mens rea*, the trafficker's intent is to sell the drug against a profit and he or she lacks interest in subsequent actions of the buyer. Moreover, the sale of drugs, however grave its societal and individual consequences, cannot be said to constitute an inhumane act. Subparagraph (k) requires that an inhumane act be of a similar character to the other enumerated acts. The Elements of Crimes specify that "character" refers to the "nature and gravity of the act."[299] There is little guidance in the case law on how the similarity of an act should be determined.[300] According to Article 22(2) of the Rome Statute, "a crime shall be strictly construed and shall not be extended by analogy. In case of ambiguity, the definition shall be interpreted in favour of the person being investigated, prosecuted or convicted" to safeguard the *nullum crimen sine lege* principle. Although the other subparagraphs in Article 7(2) protect different interests and values, the enumerated acts share the characteristic of being forced upon the victim. As a consequence, there is a clear distinction in the nature of these acts and drug trafficking because of the aforementioned voluntary element.

In support of the argument and as a supplementary means of interpretation in accordance with Article 32 of the Vienna Convention on the Law of Treaties, the discussions surrounding the crime of drug trafficking during the *travaux préparatoires* should be noted.[301] In particular, previous drafts of the Rome Statute included drug trafficking as an additional offense and several delegations remained in favor of its inclusion throughout the negotiations.[302] This

298 ICTR Akayesu 1998, para 589.

299 Elements of Crimes 2010, footnote 30.

300 E.g., ICTR Bagilishema 2001, para 92, „this should be determined on a case-by-case basis".

301 Vienna Convention 1969, Article 32.

302 See sections 2.3.3.2.2 and 2.3.3.2.3; Kirsch and Robinson (Commentary edited by Cassese, Gaeta and Jones) 2002, 78–79.

indicates a deliberate decision and clear intention of the drafters that drug trafficking not be covered by the Rome Statute.[303] Moreover, the fact that the recommendation of the Rome Conference to work toward the inclusion of the crime of drug trafficking in the Rome Statute has not been acted upon suggests that this view persists.[304]

The only precedent determining that drug trafficking constitutes a crime against humanity is a Decision by the Supreme Court of Venezuela arguing based on the gravity of negative effects for individuals and societies. With regard to the Rome Statute, the Chamber stated that "[a]rticle 7 lists crimes against humanity, and letter K of such law defines conducts that in the opinion of this Chamber encompasses the illicit traffic of drugs" without providing further analysis.[305] The Supreme Court reiterated this opinion in later Decisions stating that

> crimes [...] related to the traffic and transportation of illicit narcotic and psychotropic substances [...] seriously threaten physical, mental and economic integrity of an unknown number of people. It similarly generates social violence in the areas where such criminal action takes place. In this regard, the Chamber considers such crimes as crimes against humanity.[306]

However, in addition to a lack of legal argument, the Decisions have been widely criticized and not been adopted by other courts or international legal scholars.[307]

Hence, drug trafficking does not constitute a crime against humanity.

3.2.2.2.4 *Individual Acts of Crimes against Humanity in the Illicit Trade in Cultural Goods*

The illicit trade in cultural goods has received much attention lately because of the extensive destruction of cultural sites in Iraq and Syria and the associated

303 E.g., Zimmermann (Commentary edited by Triffterer and Ambos) 2016, 115–116.

304 UN Diplomatic Conference of Plenipotentiaries on the Establishment of an ICC 1998, section E; *ibid.*, 116.

305 Supreme Court of Venezuela 2001 „en su artículo 7 se enumeran los crímenes de lesa humanidad; y en el literal K de dicha norma, se tipificaron las conductas que a juicio de esta Sala engloban el tráfico ilícito de estupefacientes". Translated by the author.

306 Supreme Court of Venezuela 2006. Translated by the author.

307 E.g., Sainz-Borgo 2012; Yacoubian 2007.

trade in cultural goods.[308] While especially in Syria, the plunder of cultural sites is often perpetrated in connection with the ongoing armed conflict and constitutes a war crime, cases also exist in which either cultural sites are destroyed or plundered in the absence of an armed conflict, such as because of weak institutional oversight, or that lack a sufficient nexus to an armed conflict, such as if the crime is not committed against cultural property belonging to the adversary in an armed conflict.[309] In such a case, the appropriation or (part) destruction of cultural sites or property for the purpose of illicit trade in cultural goods can constitute a crime against humanity. Specifically, it may satisfy the elements of the crime of persecution under Article 7(1)(h) of the Rome Statute.

The crime of persecution consists of an *actus reus* and a *mens rea* requirement. The *actus reus* is defined in Articles 7(1)(h) and 7(2)(g) of the Rome Statute as an act or omission that is discriminatory and severely infringes or denies a fundamental right laid down in international law.[310] Examples of where such fundamental rights are laid down include in the International Covenant on Civil and Political Rights (ICCPR), the International Covenant on Economic, Social and Cultural Rights, and in the Universal Declaration of Human Rights.[311] They include the right to freedom of religion, minority rights, and the right to take part in cultural life.[312] The right to property has also been recognized with regard to the crime of persecution.[313] According to Article 7(2)(g) of the Rome Statute, the infringement must be severe; that is, there must be a clear disadvantage to an identifiable group.[314] Since cultural sites are usually associated with a certain religious, ethnic, or other group, and the appropriation or (part) destruction of a cultural site for the purpose of illicit trade can deprive or severely infringe on one or more persons' rights (named above), such acts can constitute the *actus reus* of persecution. The ICTY recognized, in particular, that the destruction of religious buildings can constitute

308 See section 2.1.2.4. At the time of writing, the OTP of the ICC was finalising a new policy on the protection of cultural heritage within the Rome Statute legal framework. Office of the Prosecutor 2019a, para 37.

309 See section 3.2.3.2.2.2.

310 ICTY Krnojelac *et al.* 2002, para 431.

311 Schabas (Commentary) 2016, 195. From a strictly positivist perspective, only the treaties can be considered as a source of international law, while the Universal Declaration is not legally binding. See also Hall and Powderly (Commentary edited by Triffterer and Ambos) 2016, 281–282.

312 ICCPR 1966, Articles 18, 27; ICESCR 1966, Article 15(1)(a).

313 ICC Ntaganda 2014, para 58; ICTY Kupreškić *et al.* 2000, para 631.

314 Hall and Powderly (Commentary edited by Triffterer and Ambos) 2016, 276.

the crime of persecution.[315] Moreover, in *Blaškić,* the Trial Chamber held that the destruction of symbolic buildings belonging to an identifiable group, in this case places of worship and education belonging to the Bosnian Muslim population, also constituted the crime of persecution.[316] With regard to the destruction of religious buildings and cultural sites, the ICTY Trial Chamber noted that "all of humanity is indeed injured by the destruction of a unique religious culture and its concomitant cultural objects."[317]

In addition, Article 7(1)(h) of the Rome Statute stipulates that persecution can only be perpetrated in connection with another crime under the Statute. This requirement can be understood as a gravity threshold for the perpetrated acts.[318] For example, in the situation in Darfur, the alleged acts of persecution consisted of, among others, murder, rape, pillage, and destruction of property.[319]

Furthermore, the crime of persecution as defined in Article 7(1)(h) requires that the act must be committed "against any identifiable group or collectivity on political, racial, national, ethnic, cultural, religious, gender [...] or on other grounds that are universally recognized" in international law. The Elements of Crimes specify that the crime of persecution can either target an individual based on these grounds or target any identifiable group or collectivity as such based on these grounds.[320] Thus, a clear distinction exists between the *dolus specialis* of genocide, whose target is always the group, and the *mens rea* requirement for persecution.[321] Other grounds universally recognized can be interpreted based on international human rights documents, such as the Universal Declaration on Human Rights and the ICCPR, as well as on case law concerning discrimination.[322] Article 2(1) of the ICCPR, for example, includes language, religion, social origin, property, birth, or other status.[323] Notably, with regard to the plunder and destruction of cultural sites for illicit trade, Article 7(1)(h) of the Rome Statute not only requires that the targeted site be

315 ICTY Kordić and Čerkez 2001, para 203; ICTY Kupreškić *et al.* 2000, para 621; see also von Schorlemer 2016, 671 *et seq.*

316 ICTY Blaškić 2000, para 22.

317 ICTY Kordić and Čerkez 2001, para 207.

318 Schabas (Commentary) 2016, 199–200.

319 ICC Harun and Abd-Al-Rahman 2007, para 74.

320 Elements of Crimes 2010, Article 7(1)(h), para 2; Schabas (Commentary) 2016, 197.

321 ICTY Kupreškić *et al.* 2000, para 636.

322 Schabas (Commentary) 2016, 198. Discrimination, however, is less severe than persecution.

323 There must not be a consensus between all States regarding a certain ground for persecution but rather wide recognition. Hall and van den Herik (Commentary edited by Triffterer and Ambos) 2016, 226.

associated with a certain group but that the perpetrator has the specific intent to "cause injury to a human being because he belongs to a particular community or group."[324] Hence, plunder for the pure goal of profit and being ignorant of or indifferent toward the group whose cultural property is hurt does not fall under the crime of persecution.

In sum, the appropriation or (part) destruction of cultural sites or goods for the purpose of illicit trade can constitute the crime of persecution if the concrete acts amount to crimes under the Rome Statute, as well as if it is perpetrated with the intent to cause injury to an individual or the group that the site or cultural good is associated with based on discriminatory grounds. In the case of Syria, for example, the plunder and destruction of cultural sites may amount to war crimes and were committed partly with the intention of manifesting the domination of the people living in the area and their former culture by Daesh and their ideology.[325] Thus, such conduct can constitute persecution under the Rome Statute.

3.2.2.2.5 *Individual Acts of Crimes against Humanity in Organized Crime-Related Violence*

In addition to crimes committed as part of the core business of organized criminal groups, they also use violence to deter competitors, manifest their power in a certain territory, divert attention from their core business, and defend themselves against State policing, among others.[326] Moreover, the lines between armed groups and organized criminal groups has become increasingly blurred in today's conflict situations, leading organized criminal groups to be increasingly involved in violence and armed conflicts.[327] Such violence can be characterized as organized crime-related violence or crimes, as opposed to migrant-related crimes, for example, which have a direct link to the organized criminal group's profit-generating activity of migrant smuggling. The most notorious examples of organized crime-related violence are the so-called "drug war" in Mexico and the situation in Colombia before the 2016 peace agreement, which in the following analysis are used as illustrative examples. Reported conduct by organized criminal groups (and other actors) in both cases can amount to various crimes against humanity, namely murder, extermination, forced disappearance, torture, rape and other sexual violence, severe deprivation of liberty, persecution, and other inhumane acts. Each of them is examined separately.

---

324 ICTY Blaškić 2000, para 235.

325 See section 3.2.3.2.2.2; von Schorlemer 2016, 713 *et seq.*

326 See section 2.1.2.7.

327 See section 2.3.2.2.

The violence in Mexico reportedly claimed a high of 29,000 lives in 2017, or 150,000 between 2006 and 2017, only counting organized crime-related homicides.[328] During the presidential campaign in 2017/2018, 114 candidates and politicians were allegedly killed by organized criminal groups with the goal of intimidation.[329] Many of these deaths meet the *actus reus* as well as the *mens rea* requirements of murder under Article 7(2)(a) of the Rome Statute, namely that death occurred and resulted from an unlawful act or omission by the perpetrator, who had intent or knowledge under Article 30 of the Rome Statute.[330] In some cases, mass killings, such as those evidenced by recoveries of numerous mass graves throughout Mexico,[331] amount to the crime of extermination under Article 7(2)(b) of the Rome Statute. Mass graves are concentrated in States that have a high presence of organized criminal activity.[332] Extermination and murder consist of "closely related criminal conduct," but extermination "by its very nature is directed against a group of individuals [...] [and] involves an element of mass destruction."[333] Mass killings, in contrast to murder, require "a substantial degree of preparation and organization."[334] The individuals who constitute the targeted group do not need to share any additional common characteristics and the perpetrator does not need to know who the victims are.[335] Thus, killings and mass killings perpetrated by organized criminal groups may amount to the crimes against humanity of murder or extermination under Article 7(1)(a) and (b) of the Rome Statute.

Moreover, mass graves in Mexico are symptomatic of the large numbers of enforced disappearances, defined as a crime against humanity in Article 7(2)(i) of the Rome Statute. According to official records, almost 38,000 persons were reported missing in Mexico between December 2006 and October 2017. While some of them were found in clandestine graves, the whereabouts of most remain unknown.[336] According to the Elements of Crimes, enforced disappearance consists of the act of and refusal to acknowledge or give

328 Beittel 2018, 1–2.

329 *ibid*, 1.

330 ICTR Akayesu 1998, para 589. See sections 3.2.2.2.1 and 3.2.2.2.2. for previous analyses of the crime of muder under Article 7(1)(a) of the Rome Statute.

331 For a study of the almost 2,000 mass graves discovered between 2006 and 2016 see Guillén, Torres and Turati 2018.

332 *ibid.*

333 International Law Commission 1996, 97.

334 ICTY Krstić 2001, para 501.

335 International Law Commission 1996, 97; Hall and Stahn (Commentary edited by Triffterer and Ambos) 2016, 187.

336 Human Rights Watch 2019, 394.

information on arrest, detention, or abduction of one or more persons.[337] Both the act as well as the refusal to acknowledge or provide information constitute the crime if the other element was present simultaneously. Article 7 of the Rome Statute also requires that the perpetrator intended to "remove such person or persons from the protection of the law for a prolonged period of time" and that the crime be "carried out by, or with the authorization, support or acquiescence of, a State or a political organization."[338] Compared with customary international law, the Rome Statute adds the requirement of a specific purpose, namely removing the person from the protection of the law, as well as of the temporal element of a prolonged period of time.[339] The inclusion of political organizations also differs from customary international law.[340] While the elements of arrest, detention, abduction, special purpose, and prolonged period of time are less controversial in the context of organized crime and frequently conducted, whether a sufficient nexus to a State or political organization can be established must be determined. Organized criminal groups do not constitute a State organization. A political organization is not equivalent to the type of organization required for an organizational policy in the *chapeau* of Article 7 as indicated by the additional adjective, and thus must be interpreted more narrowly.[341] Because of the purpose of the safeguard of effective access to the administration of justice, it is held that the term "political organization" in this context can only include organizations that can grant that access and thus perform certain state functions.[342] Organized criminal groups do not fall under this definition. Therefore, the authorization, support, or acquiescence by the State must be present. Acquiescence is defined as "the inaction of a State which is faced with a situation constituting a threat to or infringement of its rights" or "silence or absence of protest in circumstances which generally call for a positive reaction signifying an objection."[343] In Mexico, investigations into disappearances are reported to be routinely neglected. A specialized office opened in 2013 has opened more than 1,000 investigations but reported no conviction.[344] In many cases, State acquiescence for arrests, detentions, and abductions in the sense of Article 7(1)(i) of the Rome Statute can thus

337 Elements of Crimes 2010, Article 7(1)(i), para 1.

338 *ibid.*, Article 7(1)(i), para 4–5.

339 Hall and van den Herik (Commentary edited by Triffterer and Ambos) 2016, 286.

340 *ibid.*

341 *ibid.*, 288.

342 Ambos 2014, 111.

343 MacGibbon 1954, 145.

344 Human Rights Watch 2019, 394.

be established and organized criminal groups be prosecuted for enforced disappearances.

In addition, organized criminal groups commit rape and other sexual violence,[345] torture[346] and other inhumane acts, such as attempted murder or serious physical and mental injury.[347] For example, in Colombia, the OTP found a reasonable basis to believe that hybrid organizations such as the FARC committed torture, rape, and other forms of sexual violence among others.[348] Thus, organized criminal groups may be prosecuted for committing these crimes.

In some cases, the crimes committed by organized criminal groups could also amount to persecution under Article 7(1)(h) of the Rome Statute. According to the Elements of Crimes, persecution is committed in connection with any act defined as a crime under the Rome Statute if it is part of a conduct that targets a particular group.[349] Notably, in connection with organized criminal groups, economic grounds are not expressly cited. Political grounds—concerning the State, its government, public affairs in general, membership of a political party, or adherence to a certain ideology—could apply to struggles over territorial control, or certain policy issues such as extradition.[350] The distinction of social origin could apply to attacks against certain geographically defined groups that are seen as supporting a competing organized criminal group because of social bonds. Pure struggles over market share or influence in an illegal market do not seem to fall under the cited grounds, and thus cannot constitute the crime of persecution.

Hence, organized criminal groups may commit the crime of persecution under Article 7(1)(h) of the Rome Statute if discriminatory grounds recognized in international law are present.

Finally, organized criminal groups can also commit the crime of imprisonment or severe deprivation of liberty, such as in the case of abductions, to exert pressure on the government for the purpose of prisoner exchanges or to gain an additional source of funding through extortion.[351] In Colombia, for example, the OTP of the ICC has found evidence that

345 For a detailed discussion see section 3.2.2.2.1.

346 For a detailed discussion see section 3.2.2.2.2.

347 ICTY Blaškić 2000, para 239 *et seq*. For a more detailed discussion see section 3.2.2.2.1.

348 Office of the Prosecutor of the International Criminal Court 2018, para 131.

349 For a detailed discussion see section 3.2.2.2.4.

350 ICTR Akayesu 1998, para 583. See also Hall Hall, Powderly and Hayes (Commentary edited by Triffterer and Ambos) 2016a, 223.

351 For a more detailed discussion see section 3.2.2.2.2.

> FARC, ELN [*Ejército de Liberación Nacional*] and paramilitary groups have resorted to imprisonment in order to obtain resources to finance their activities in relation to the internal armed conflict […], to assert their presence and authority in a particular area or to exert pressure over the Colombian State […] Severe deprivation of liberty is reportedly committed through different methods, including abductions in multiple locations such as victims' residences, checkpoints or public places. While in captivity, victims are subjected to severe conditions, including long periods of detention, ill-treatment, deprivation of communication from the outside world, and placing of chains around their bodies.[352]

In *Krnojelac*, the Trial Chamber stated that "any form of arbitrary physical deprivation of liberty of an individual may constitute imprisonment."[353][354] Therefore, the conduct described above satisfies the requirements of Article 7(1)(e) of the Rome Statute and organized criminal groups may be prosecuted for that crime.

Overall, many forms of organized crime-related violence, including murder, extermination, forced disappearance, torture, rape and other sexual violence, severe deprivation of liberty, persecution and other inhumane acts (for example, those reported in Mexico and Colombia) constitute crimes against humanity under various subparagraphs of Article 7(1) of the Rome Statute if they satisfy the contextual elements.

3.2.2.3 Summary

Crimes against humanity as defined in Article 7 of the Rome Statute encompass various types of conduct by organized criminal groups that consequently fall under the jurisdiction of the ICC.

First, organized criminal groups are capable of committing or forming part of a widespread or systematic attack against a civilian population as required by the *chapeau* of Article 7. The term attack has been interpreted broadly and must not be military or even violent in nature. The civilian population must be targeted based on common features, but without further limitations on what type of feature is required. The disjunctive elements of the attack being either widespread or systematic aim at excluding any random or small-scale occurrence of acts. Moreover, the Rome Statute requires a State or organizational policy to underlie the attack. Although restrictive interpretations of the term

352 Office of the Prosecutor of the International Criminal Court 2012, para 69–70.

353 ICTY Krnojelac *et al.* 2002, para 112.

354 For a more detailed discussion see section 3.2.2.2.2.

"organizational" have been proposed, recent jurisprudence has established a broad understanding of the term, based on capability to cause harm rather than on organizational features. In line with the objective of the ICC to prosecute only the most serious crimes going unpunished, the contextual elements of crimes against humanity favor crimes committed by large organized criminal groups with sufficient financial resources, a higher degree of organization, and the potential for significant impacts rather than local and small gangs; however, these are not categorically excluded.

Moreover, Article 7 of the Rome Statute only requires that the perpetrator of a crime had knowledge of the attack the crime is part of. This mental element has been interpreted broadly and is frequently established based on circumstantial evidence, such as a formal position or continuous interaction between various actors.

In terms of the concrete organized criminal activities constituting crimes against humanity, the core business activities of organized crime covered are limited; human trafficking, including different forms of exploitation for labor, sex, and organ trade, meet the requirements for several of the enumerated acts in Article 7 of the Rome Statute. The appropriation or (part) destruction of cultural property in connection with the illicit trade in cultural goods falls under the crime of persecution if discriminatory intent is present. By contrast, drug trafficking and migrant smuggling are not covered. Nevertheless, Article 7 applies to many forms of ill-treatment, sometimes even of voluntary customers of organized crime (e.g., to the reported treatment of migrants in Libya).

Finally, Article 7 of the Rome Statute encompasses many forms of organized crime-related violence. Although the related conduct does not represent the core of organized criminal activities, examples such as Mexico and Colombia demonstrate the possible magnitude of such crimes that can indeed become the aspect of organized crime under which the civilian population, especially in drug-producing countries, suffers the most.

Overall, Article 7 of the Rome Statute is not designed to cover organized criminal activities, and thus does not apply to a broad range of conduct. Nevertheless, its importance can be subsumed, by trend, to the fact that the criminal activities it is applicable to are those directly causing the greatest human—as opposed to economic—suffering related to organized crime.

3.2.3 *War Crimes*

Over the past years,

> it [has become] a disturbing reality [...] that criminal groups not only try to profit financially from armed conflicts, but take up arms against the

> State or rival groups if such interfere in their illicit businesses [...]. On occasion, they are also contracted by parties to an armed conflict or create paramilitary units themselves. Such armed violence has become astoundingly professional, causing death and destruction that, in extreme cases, is statistically on an equal footing with international armed conflicts.[355]

Therefore, this chapter analyzes whether and in what circumstances members of organized criminal groups can be criminally responsible for committing war crimes under Article 8 of the Rome Statute.

Article 8 requires that a nexus exists to an armed conflict, that the crime is "committed as part of a plan or policy or as part of a large-scale commission"[356] of crimes, and that the perpetrator is aware of the armed conflict. The applicability of these requirements to crimes committed by organized criminal groups is examined in the following subsections.

Moreover, paragraph 2 of Article 8 contains an exhaustive list of acts that can constitute a war crime. Article 8 is in large part based on IHL and distinguishes between war crimes in international and noninternational armed conflict.[357] The crimes referred to in Article 8(2)(a) and (b) of the Rome Statute are applicable to international armed conflict, the latter referring to the grave breaches regime of the four Geneva Conventions. The crimes in Article 8(2)(c) and (e) of the Rome Statute are applicable to noninternational armed conflict, the latter referring to common Article 3 of the Geneva Conventions. Subparagraphs (b) and (e) must be interpreted "within the established framework of international law."[358] This chapter examines which particular offenses of organized crime fall under these provisions. Furthermore, it focuses on the illicit exploitation and trade in natural resources, illicit trade in cultural goods, human trafficking, migrant smuggling, and migrant-related crimes as well as organized crime-related violence.

3.2.3.1 Contextual Elements

3.2.3.1.1 *Armed Conflict and a Nexus Thereto*

For war crimes to be committed by members of organized criminal groups, it must be established, first, that there is an armed conflict and, second, that the

355 Peterke and Wolf 2016, 382.

356 Rome Statute 1998, Article 8(1).

357 The legal definitions and distinction will not be discussed in detail here since they are not unique to the issue of organized crime. For a detailed discussion, see, e.g., Schabas (Commentary) 2016, 228 *et seq.*

358 Rome Statute 1998, Article 8(2)(b) and (e).

crime has a sufficient nexus to that conflict. This subsection first examines the notion of international armed conflict and how far organized criminal groups can participate in it, then applies the same analysis to noninternational armed conflict, and finally examines the required nexus that a war crime committed by organized criminal groups must have to an armed conflict.

Armed conflict has been defined as

> whenever there is resort to armed force between States or protracted armed violence between governmental authorities and organized armed groups or between such groups within a State. International humanitarian law applies from the initiation of such conflicts and extends beyond the cessation of hostilities until [...] in the case of internal conflicts, a peaceful settlement is reached.[359]

As for international armed conflict, Article 2 common to the Geneva Conventions limits the applicability to armed conflict between States, including military occupation. The Additional Protocol I of 1977 as part of the established framework of international law referred to in subparagraph (b) of Article 8 of the Rome Statute extends this definition to include "armed conflicts in which peoples are fighting against colonial domination and alien occupation and against racist régimes in the exercise of their right of self-determination."[360] However, many of the crimes in subparagraph (b) are not derived from the Additional Protocol and no indication exists in the *travaux préparatoires* that distinct definitions of armed conflict for subparagraphs (a) and (b) have been considered.[361] International armed conflict has thus been interpreted to take place only between States.[362]

However, if an armed group, or a dual-purpose group, is under effective or overall control by a State other than the State of the forces it is fighting, this constitutes an international armed conflict.[363] Moreover, a State can recognize

359 ICTY Tadić 1995, para 70; see also Pictet (Commentary) 1958, 20 *et seq.*

360 Protocol I to Geneva Conventions 1977, Article 1(4).

361 Schabas (Commentary) 2016, 229–230.

362 ICC Lubanga 2007, para 209.

363 "Effective control": ICJ Nicaragua 1986; Draft Articles on the International Responsibility of States; "Overall control": ICTY Tadić 1999. The ICJ in the Genocide Case determined that the overall control test "may well be [...] applicable and suitable" to the questions whether or not an armed conflict is international, but not appropriate for the determination of State responsibility. ICJ Application of the Genocide Convention 2007, para 404.

the belligerent status of insurgents, such as where an organized criminal group has sustained control over a certain territory, and thus trigger the law of international armed conflict. However, such recognition would give privileged legal status to the insurgents and possibly confer political legitimacy, making recognition from a parent State unlikely. As a consequence, despite some theoretical exceptions, IHL and the Rome Statute essentially exclude organized criminal groups as a party to an international armed conflict.

Nevertheless, individual members of organized criminal groups can participate in international armed conflicts as combatants if they fulfill the criteria set out in Article 4(A)(2) of the Third Geneva Convention.[364] Moreover, a member of an organized criminal group can directly participate in hostilities as indicated in Article 51(3) of the Additional Protocol I, meaning conduct that likely affects the military operations or capacities of a Party to the conflict, that has a direct causal link to the harm that is expected and is designed to cause harm in support of one and be to the detriment of the other party to the conflict.[365] In this case, the person does not lose his or her civilian status but only the protection afforded for the time they participate in the armed conflict.[366] Although the US Pentagon interpreted the provision to include drug traffickers who had contact with the Taliban, legal scholars have criticized such an interpretation as "an absurdly broad reading of the threshold of harm."[367][368]

As a consequence, members of organized criminal groups can participate in an international armed conflict as combatants belonging to a Party to a conflict or as civilians taking direct part in hostilities. Organized criminal groups are essentially excluded from representing a Party to the conflict unless they are under effective or overall control of a State or recognized as insurgents.

Noninternational armed conflict is not defined in the Rome Statute but subjected to two limitations. First, Article 8(2)(d) and (f) of the Rome Statute

364 "Members of other militias and members of other volunteer corps, including those of organized resistance movements, belonging to a Party to the conflict and operating in or outside their own territory, even if this territory is occupied, provided that such militias or volunteer corps, including such organized resistance movements, fulfil the following conditions:(a) that of being commanded by a person responsible for his subordinates; (b) that of having a fixed distinctive sign recognizable at a distance; (c) that of carrying arms openly; (d) that of conducting their operations in accordance with the laws and customs of war." Third Geneva Convention 1949, Article 4(A)(2).

365 Melzer 2009, 46.

366 *ibid.*, 20.

367 Gallahue 2010, 15.

368 Committee on Foreign Relations, United States Senate 2009.

require a certain intensity of conflict, excluding "internal disturbances and tensions, such as riots, isolated and sporadic acts of violence or other acts of a similar nature." Subparagraph (f) adds that the provision applies to cases of "protracted armed conflict between governmental authorities and organized armed groups or between such groups," also called the organization requirement. Despite an unresolved debate as to whether Article 8 establishes two distinct definitions for noninternational armed conflict, case law supports the view that there is only one threshold in the Rome Statute.[369] The organization requirement has been interpreted as focusing on armed groups' "ability to plan and carry out military operations for a prolonged period of time."[370] Indicative factors are, *inter alia*,

> the force or group's internal hierarchy; the command structure and rules; the extent to which military equipment, including firearms, are available; the force or group's ability to plan military operations and put them into effect; and the extent, seriousness, and intensity of any military involvement.[371]

Similarly, indicators for the required intensity of a conflict have been developed that are applied on a case-by-case basis, namely

> the number, duration and intensity of individual confrontations; the type of weapons and other military equipment used; the number of [and] caliber of munitions fired; the number of casualties; extent of material destruction; and the number of civilians fleeing combat zones.[372]

Although making a definitive legal assessment goes beyond this section, the intense violence that has taken place in Mexico, such as in Juarez, as well as the substantial resources and capabilities and the strict internal organization, namely of the Sinaloa Cartel and Los Zetas (before its recent fragmentation), show that organized criminal groups have a growing potential to satisfy the organization requirement, and hence to become a party to a noninternational armed conflict. In the case of Colombia, the OTP has found *Los Urabeños*, a Colombian drug cartel and paramilitary group, to satisfy the organization requirement because "its members are well-disciplined; there is a hierarchical

369 ICTY Boškoski and Tarčulovski 2008, para 197; ICC Bemba 2009, para 232.

370 ICC Lubanga 2007, para 234.

371 ICC Lubanga 2012, para 537.

372 ICTY Haradinaj *et al.* 2008, para 49.

structure; effective control is exercised over its members; it exercises control over territory; it has the capacity to recruit and acquire weapons; and it has a significant number of personnel."[373]

Similar to international armed conflicts, members of organized groups can be involved in the fighting if the organized criminal group itself is not a party to the conflict. Specifically, an individual is considered to gain the status of a fighter (as opposed to combatants in international armed conflicts with attached privileges) if he or she assumes a continuous combat function in the armed group.[374]

Overall, organized criminal groups can thus be party to noninternational armed conflict if the organization and intensity requirements are satisfied. Individual members of organized criminal groups can participate as fighters under the command of a party to the conflict.

In addition to the existence of an armed conflict, a sufficient nexus between the crime and armed conflict is required for war crimes to be committed. The Elements of Crimes require that "the conduct took place in the context of and was associated with an armed conflict."[375] While the armed conflict

> must play a substantial role in the perpetrator's decision, in his ability to commit the crime or in the manner in which the conduct was ultimately committed [...] it is not necessary, however, for the armed conflict to have been regarded as the ultimate reason for the criminal conduct, nor must the conduct have taken place in the midst of the battle.[376]

It has been established that war crimes do not have to happen in the same place and/or at the same time as fighting occurs.[377] Factors for establishing a sufficient relationship between a crime and the conflict are, *inter alia,*

373 Office of the Prosecutor of the International Criminal Court 2013, para 129.

374 ICTY Strugar 2008, para 177 defines direct participation in hostilities as, among others, "bearing, using, or taking up arms, taking part in military or hostile acts, activities, conduct or operations, armed fighting or combat, participating in attacks against enemy personnel, property or equipment, transmitting military information for the immediate use of a belligerent, transporting weapons in proximity to combat operations" (footnotes omitted) and indirect participation as, among others, "selling goods to a party to a conflict" (footnotes omitted); Zimmermann and Geiß (Commentary edited by Triffterer and Ambos) 2016b, 548; Melzer 2009.

375 E.g., Elements of Crimes 2010, Article 8(2)(a)(i), para 4.

376 ICC Lubanga 2007, para 287.

377 ICTY Kunarac 2002, para 57.

> the fact that the perpetrator is a combatant; the fact that the victim is a non-combatant; the fact that the victim is a member of the opposing party; the fact that the act may be said to serve the ultimate goal of a military campaign; and the fact that the crime is committed as part of or in the context of the perpetrator's official duties.[378]

The ICTR Appeals Chamber criticized an approach that includes

> only [...] individuals [...] belonging to the armed forces under the military command of either of the belligerent parties, or to individuals who were legitimately mandated and expected, as public officials or agents or persons otherwise holding public authority or *de facto* representing the government, to support or fulfil the war efforts,[379]

thereby establishing that war crimes can also be committed by civilians.[380] In *Kunarac*, the Appeals Chamber established that a war crime must be shaped by or be dependent of an armed conflict, meaning that the armed conflict must at least have played a substantial role in the perpetrator's ability or decision to commit the crime or in the manner in which it was committed.[381] The exploitation of the circumstances and chances of war, especially of its coercive environment, can also be an indication of a nexus between an individual crime and armed conflict.[382] In the case of plundering and subsequent illicit trade, for example, organized criminal groups often operate in the aftermath of fighting and benefit from the insecurity and chaos left behind. Daesh probably plundered the museum of Mosul months after the conquest of the city. However, the nexus to the armed conflict can be established based on two arguments: first, Daesh used the destruction and plunder of cultural sites to manifest its power and further oppress the local population and, second, it was used to fund ongoing military operations.[383] Interestingly, the OTP argued that regarding the situation in Colombia for so-called "new illegal armed groups," often meaning armed organized criminal groups, to commit war crimes, they must either be a party to the existing conflict between the government, FARC,

378 *ibid.*, para 58–59.

379 ICTR Akayesu 2001, para 425.

380 Cottier (Commentary edited by Triffterer and Ambos) 2016, 316; Zimmermann and Geiß (Commentary edited by Triffterer and Ambos) 2016b, 548.

381 ICTY Kunarac 2002, para 58.

382 Cottier (Commentary edited by Triffterer and Ambos) 2016, 316.

383 von Schorlemer 2016, 712.

and ELN, or there must be a distinct armed conflict between these groups and the government or only between these groups.[384] The OTP did not consider if crimes were committed based on the coercive environment of the existing armed conflict. The OTP argued that the intensity of violence between these groups and the parties to the existing conflict did not meet the requisite threshold and that, although the fighting between different groups was sufficiently intense, most of them did not satisfy the organization requirement.[385]

In sum, with regard to a nexus to an armed conflict, members of organized criminal groups can commit war crimes if they form part of a party to the conflict, that is, as combatants or fighters or directly participating in hostilities, if the organized criminal groups are a party to a noninternational armed conflict themselves, requiring that both the intensity threshold and organization requirement are met, or if the crimes committed were shaped by or dependent on an armed conflict.

3.2.3.1.2 *Plan or Policy or Large-Scale Commission of Crimes*

Contrary to customary international law as well as to statutes applied in previous international tribunals, Article 8(1) of the Rome Statute contains a contextual element in addition to the requirement of the existence of an armed conflict.[386] The provision stipulates that the ICC shall have jurisdiction over war crimes "in particular when committed as part of a plan or policy or as part of a large-scale commission." The implications of this provision for organized crime are examined in the following paragraphs.

The term "in particular" has been interpreted as "mak[ing] it clear that the existence of a plan, policy or large-scale commission is not a prerequisite for the ICC to exercise jurisdiction over war crimes but rather serves as a practical guideline for the Court."[387] Single acts can thus also amount to war crimes under the Rome Statute if committed in the context of and associated with an armed conflict.[388] ICC Chambers have hardly included the provision in their arguments.[389] Indeed, a Decision of Pre-Trial Chamber I in the situation of the DRC was overturned by the Appeals Chamber, which leveled the criticism that the jurisdictional requirements of crimes against humanity and war crimes were blurred by interpreting the terms plan or policy to mean "systematic." The

384 Office of the Prosecutor 2013, para 128–129.
385 *ibid.*
386 Schabas (Commentary) 2016, 225–226.
387 ICC Bemba 2009, para 211.
388 ICC Mbarushimana 2011, para 94.
389 Schabas (Commentary) 2016, 227.

Chamber underlined that large-scale commission was an alternative to commission as part of a plan or policy and that the provision was "not absolute but qualified by the expression 'in particular.' "[390] The Prosecutor, however, based several of his decisions to proceed or not with investigations on the threshold in Article 8(1) of the Rome Statute. For example, concerning alleged war crimes in Iraq, he explained that the "specific gravity threshold [...] provide[s] Statute guidance that the Court is intended to focus on situations meeting these requirements. [...] it did not appear that any of the criteria of Article 8(1) were satisfied."[391]

The threshold underlines the spirit of Article 5 of the Rome Statute, limiting jurisdiction to "the most serious crimes of concern to the international community as a whole"[392] and the complementarity principle as expressed in Article 17. Furthermore, it indicates the limited resources of the ICC and discretion of the Prosecutor to consider other factors, such as the egregiousness of a particular crime, the seriousness and scale of a single crime, or the official function of an alleged perpetrator.[393] However, in terms of legal analysis, the threshold has "practical insignificance" and can be seen as "an expedient to be invoked opportunistically rather than a meaningful legal norm."[394]

Therefore, with regard to organized crime, the gravity threshold in Article 8(1) of the Rome Statute has no legal relevance as to the ICC's jurisdiction *ratione materiae,* and adds nothing to the limitations imposed by the principle of complementarity and the ICC's overall nature and purpose.

3.2.3.1.3 *Mental Element: Awareness of the Conflict*

In addition to the required factual nexus between a war crime and an armed conflict, Article 8 of the Rome Statute requires a certain *mens rea,* namely "awareness of the factual circumstances that establish the existence of an armed conflict."[395]

---

390 ICC Democratic Republic of Congo 2006, para 70.

391 Moreno Ocampo 2006, 8. Conversely, the Prosecutor argued regarding an attack on the African Union Mission in Sudan that "the issues of the nature, manner and impact of the attack are critical" and thus found that "intentional [sic!] directing attacks against peacekeeping operations constitute exceptional serious offenses": ICC Situation in Darfur, Sudan 2008, para 7.

392 Rome Statute 1998, Article 5 and Preamble, para 4.

393 E.g., Bothe (Commentary edited by Cassese, Gaeta and Jones) 2002, 380; Dörmann (Commentary edited by Triffterer and Ambos) 2016, 322; Eudes (Commentary edited by Fernandez, Pacreau and Maze) 2012, 493.

394 Schabas (Commentary) 2016, 228.

395 Elements of Crimes 2010, Article 8, Introduction, para c.

The introduction to Article 8 in the Elements of Crimes specifies that no requirement exists "for a legal evaluation by the perpetrator as to the existence of an armed conflict or its character as international or non-international," nor of the facts that establish such a character.[396] It merely requires "the awareness of the factual circumstances that established the existence of an armed conflict that is implicit in the terms 'took place in the context of and was associated with,'"[397] a formulation that is rather ambiguous and has been interpreted as setting a threshold of knowledge below the standard of Article 30 of the Rome Statute, namely "knew or should have known."[398] In many situations, the existence of and a crime's nexus to an armed conflict are obvious enough that objective proof is sufficient.[399]

With regard to organized crime, the *mens rea* is especially relevant when the perpetrator is not directly involved in the fighting. In this case it must be established that he was aware of the circumstances and the nexus of his conduct to those circumstances, which can form part of the argument that his actions were shaped by or dependent on the armed conflict.

3.2.3.2 Material Elements

3.2.3.2.1 *Protected Groups*

As indicated above, the war crime provisions in the Rome Statute are based on IHL and largely follow its logic as it has historically developed. As a consequence, in Article 8 of the Rome Statute, not only are crimes committed in international and noninternational conflicts separated into different subparagraphs, but some subparagraphs also apply to specific groups of protected persons. Thus, whether organized criminal groups can commit crimes against these protected groups must be determined.

Subparagraph (8)(2)(a), applicable to international armed conflict and based on the grave breaches regime in IHL, encompasses "acts against persons or property protected under the provisions of the relevant Geneva Convention." Contrary to the Hague Conventions, which are mainly concerned with the rights of combatants, the Geneva Conventions are meant to protect the victims of war, namely the wounded and sick in armed forces in the field; the wounded, sick and shipwrecked members of armed forces at sea; prisoners of war; and civilians. It must thus be shown that a crime under subparagraph (a) has been committed against an individual belonging to one of these

396 *ibid.*, Article 8, Introduction, para a and b.

397 Dörmann (Commentary edited by Triffterer and Ambos) 2016, 328.

398 Dörmann 2003, 362.

399 *ibid.*, 362–363.

categories of protected persons. While neither the concept of soldiers nor of soldiers *hors de combat* (i.e., wounded, sick, and shipwrecked) are specified in the Geneva Conventions, prisoners of war are defined in detail in Article 4 of the Third Geneva Convention. Prosecutions of crimes committed against civilians have been the most frequent in international tribunals and are most relevant in the context of organized crime. Civilians are defined in the Fourth Geneva Convention as "those who, at a given moment and in any manner whatsoever, find themselves, in case of a conflict or occupation, in the hands of a Party to the conflict or Occupying Power of which they are not nationals."[400] Additional Protocol I in Article 50 defines civilians as any person who is not a member of the armed forces. With respect to nationality. the Elements of Crimes of the Rome Statute require only that the perpetrator knows that the victim belongs to an adverse party.[401] Moreover, concerning Bosnian Muslims persecuted by individuals of the same nationality, the term nationality was interpreted as referring to genuine allegiance.[402] The term can thus be interpreted broadly. Nationals of neutral States and of co-belligerent States of the State in whose territory a person finds him/herself are also excluded from protection under IHL.

This represents a critical limitation with regard to crimes committed by members of organized criminal groups in international armed conflicts concerning crimes under Article 8(2)(a) of the Rome Statute: Only crimes against a person with genuine allegiance to an adverse party can qualify as war crimes.

Subparagraph 8(2)(c), applicable to noninternational armed conflict and drawn from common Article 3 of the Geneva Conventions, does not refer to protected persons but uses the analogous concept of "persons taking no active part in the hostilities, including members of armed forces who have laid down their arms and those placed *hors de combat* by sickness, wounds, detention or any other cause." The enumeration is nonexhaustive.[403] The Elements of Crimes specify that this includes persons "*hors de combat*, or [...] civilians, medical personnel or religious personnel taking no active part in the hostilities."[404] Critically, the ICC Trial Chamber decided in *Ntaganda* that the war crimes of rape and sexual violence under Article 8(2)(e)(vi) of the Rome Statute can also be committed against members of the perpetrator's own group, arguing that the characterization of protected persons in common Article 3 of the Geneva

400 Fourth Geneva Convention 1949, Article 4.

401 Elements of Crimes 2010, footnote 33.

402 ICTY Tadić 1999, para 166–169.

403 Zimmermann and Geiß (Commentary edited by Triffterer and Ambos) 2016b, 547.

404 For the interpretation of active participation in hostilities see section 3.2.3.1.1.

Conventions was not intended to limit their protection.[405] The same would apply, for example, to forced prostitution in military camps organized and traded by organized criminal groups. Although this interpretation was made with regard to "the established framework of international law" required by subparagraph (e), subsequent decisions may adopt this view as a general rule for common Article 3 of the Geneva Conventions, and hence also for subparagraph (c) of Article 8 of the Rome Statute. Such an interpretation, in turn, can have important repercussions on the rules on international armed conflict.

With regard to organized crime, widening the scope of war crimes in noninternational armed conflict to include victims of the organized criminal group's own group would facilitate prosecutions. Organized crime is motivated by profit and less by military or other allegiance, and thus does not follow the traditional logic of war crimes.

Overall, organized criminal groups commit crimes against protected persons in the sense of Article 8(2)(a) and (c) of the Rome Statute as well as against other persons, namely victims who belong to the same group as the organized criminal group. This is a crucial limitation. The inclusion of crimes against members of the same group widens the applicability of the Rome Statute to organized crime, but the evolution of this interpretation remains to be seen.

3.2.3.2.2 *Individual Acts*

3.2.3.2.2.1 Individual Acts of War Crimes in Illicit Exploitation of and Trade in Natural Resources

The illicit trade in natural resources is a major global market. In many cases, the exploitation of resources benefits from weak State institutions and a lack of export controls as well as of other regulations.[406] If the resources are exploited and subsequently traded by organized criminal groups in situations of armed conflict, such as so-called blood diamonds from Sierra Leone, such conduct can fall under war crime provisions aimed at the protection of property in conflict situations. Specifically, Article 8 of the Rome Statute contains five definitions of war crimes relating to property. These are examined and evaluated in the following paragraphs with regards to the illicit exploitation and trade in natural resources.

First, subparagraph (2)(a)(iv) prohibits "extensive destruction and appropriation of property, not justified by military necessity and carried out unlawfully and wantonly." The provision is part of the grave breaches regime under

---

405 ICC Ntaganda 2017, para 45 *et seq.*

406 See section 2.1.2.4.

the Geneva Conventions and thus only applies to international armed conflict. Moreover, the *chapeau* of subparagraph (a) specifies that the enumerated crimes refer to "acts against persons or property protected under the provisions of the relevant Geneva Conventions." These provisions are "*aussi nombreuses qu'éparses*"[407] and protect property related to medical care, such as hospitals and medical convoys; objects indispensable to the survival of the civilian population, such as water supply systems; cultural objects and places of worship; and installations containing dangerous forces, such as nuclear plants.[408] Although Article 53 of the Fourth Geneva Convention also refers to "real or personal property situated in an occupied territory" more generally, the provision only applies to destruction and not appropriation. While destruction of property is less applicable in the case of illegal trade, appropriation is understood as taking away property for a relevant period of time without the consent of the owner. It distinguishes itself from pillage, which is analyzed below, only in the specific intent.[409]

In sum, Article 8(2)(a)(iv) of the Rome Statute mainly covers property that does not lend itself to appropriation for profit-seeking. However, notwithstanding the following analyses, it may cover cases of organized crime, such as where hospitals of the adversary side are plundered extensively to sell the medical supplies to hospitals held by the perpetrator's own group.

Second, subparagraphs (2)(b)(xiii) and (2)(e)(xii) prohibit the destruction or seizure of the enemy's or adversary's property unless imperatively demanded by military necessity. This is a certain duplication of subparagraph (a)(iv), although the latter contains a higher threshold for criminal behavior, that is, *extensive* destruction or appropriation.[410] Moreover, the provision on destruction or seizure is applicable in both international and noninternational armed conflict. According to the *Katanga* Trial Chamber, the provisions protect all types of property that do not constitute military objectives, defined in Article 52(2) of Additional Protocol I as "those objects which by their nature, location, purpose or use make an effective contribution to military action and whose total or partial destruction, capture or neutralization,

407 Eudes (Commentary edited by Fernandez, Pacreau and Maze) 2012, 512. „As numerous as scattered". Translated by the author.

408 First Geneva Convention 1949, Articles 19, 33–35; Second Geneva Convention 1949, Articles 22, 24–25, 27; Fourth Geneva Convention 1949, Articles 18–19, 21–22, 33, 53, 57; Protocol I to Geneva Conventions 1977, Articles 53, 54, 56; Protocol II to Geneva Convention 1977, Article 16; *ibid.*

409 Ambos 2014, 171.

410 *ibid.*

in the circumstances ruling at the time, offers a definite military advantage."[411] Moreover, the destruction or seizure of property is punishable unless it was imperatively demanded by the necessities of war. The definition of military necessity was formulated in Article 14 of the Lieber Code, which stated that "military necessity [...] consists in the necessity of those measures which are indispensable for securing the ends of war, and which are lawful according to the modern law and usages of war."[412] The term "imperatively" has been interpreted as meaning that the perpetrator had no other option.[413] However, total or part destruction of property is less relevant in the context of appropriation for illicit trade. Moreover, the term "seizure" is understood as appropriation by legal right or process.[414] Organized criminal groups are consequently not capable of seizure unless they act on behalf or with the authorization of a State. Moreover, the term must be interpreted in light of the relevant provisions in the Hague Convention, namely Articles 53 and 55, which allow for seized property to be administered in accordance with the rules of usufruct for the duration of the conflict only and proscribe restoration or compensation when peace is made. Organized criminal groups benefiting from conflict situations to exploit and trade natural resources do not envisage such a relation to the property they appropriate.

In sum, subparagraphs (b)(xiii) and (e)(xii) do not represent the most appropriate provision to prosecute property crimes committed by organized criminal groups in armed conflict.

Third, Article 8 of the Rome Statute also prohibits the crime of pillage in subparagraphs (2)(b)(xvi) and (2)(e)(v) in international and noninternational armed conflicts, respectively. The crime of pillage is usually understood as the "unauthorized appropriation or obtaining of property in order to confer possession of it on oneself or on a third party against the will of the rightful owner."[415] The Elements of Crimes define pillage accordingly as an appropriation of property without the owner's consent. Furthermore, the Elements of Crimes introduce a *dolus specialis* requirement. Specifically, they require that "the perpetrator intended to deprive the owner of the property and to appropriate it *for private or personal use*."[416] This definition seems to most specifically

411 ICC Katanga 2014, para 893.

412 Lieber Code 1863; ICC Katanga 2014, para 894; ICTY Kordić 2004, para 686; ICTY Boškoski and Tarčulovski 2008, para 357.

413 ICC Katanga 2014, para 894.

414 Ambos 2014, 171.

415 Zimmermann and Geiß (Commentary edited by Triffterer and Ambos) 2016a, 452.

416 Elements of Crimes 2010, Article 8(2)(b)(xvi), para 2. Emphasis added.

describe the circumstances of illicit resource exploitation due to the overarching goal of profit-seeking.

The crime of pillage applies to all types of property, "moveable or immovable, private or public," as long as it belongs to "individuals or entities who are aligned with or whose allegiance is to a party to the conflict who is adverse or hostile to the perpetrator."[417] Thus, exploitation of natural resources in the territory of the group the perpetrator is associated with is not covered. Pillage can be perpetrated not only by combatants but by any individual without restriction.[418] In the *IG Farben*, *Flick* and *Krupp* trials before the IMT, for example, the private owners of major German companies were convicted for pillage for their confiscation of plants and mines in occupied territories.[419] In the *Armed Activities* Case, the ICJ referred to the crime of pillage as enshrined in IHL with regard to the exploitation of resources in the DRC by the State of Uganda.[420]

The ICC Pre-Trial Chamber held that for the war crime of pillage to occur, the property must necessarily have come under the control of the perpetrator, though the scope of the crime is not limited to occupation *stricto sensu*, but can also occur during ongoing hostilities or belligerent occupation.[421] Pillage encompasses "isolated acts committed by individual soldiers for their private gain as well and acts committed as part of a systematic campaign to economically exploit a targeted area."[422] In Case 7150, for example, the UNWCC, in charge of investigating and prosecuting war crimes by the Axis powers between 1943 and 1948, found nine German administrators guilty of systematic pillage of Polish forests by exploiting them "to an extent far in excess of what was necessary to preserve the resources of the country, with a loss to the Polish nation […], [and] without the least regard to the basic principles of forestry."[423][424]

ICC Chambers have interpreted the term "serious violation" in the *chapeau* of paragraph (b) as an indication that mere sporadic acts of property expropriation might be excluded, and that a case-by-case assessment of seriousness must be made.[425] Moreover, the crime of pillage is limited by a belligerent's

417 ICC Katanga and Ngudjolo 2008, para 329.

418 Zimmermann and Geiß (Commentary edited by Triffterer and Ambos) 2016a, 454.

419 McGregor 2009.

420 International Court of Justice Armed Activities Case 2005, 252.

421 ICC Katanga and Ngudjolo 2008, para 330.

422 ICTY Gotovina *et al.* 2011, para 1778; Zimmermann and Geiß (Commentary edited by Triffterer and Ambos) 2016a, 453.

423 Cited in: Lundberg 2008, 519.

424 UNWCC Case 7150 1948; see section 2.3.3.1.1.

425 ICC Bemba 2009, para 317; ICC Katanga 2014, para 908; Zimmermann and Geiß (Commentary edited by Triffterer and Ambos) 2016a, 453.

rights to seizure and requisition, as indicated by footnote 47 of the Elements of Crimes that states that appropriations justified by military necessity do not constitute pillage.[426] Military necessity is always excluded in the case of resource exploitation with the purpose of profit-seeking trade.

The special intent requirement that the property be pillaged for personal or private use is not part of customary international law and has not been included in the Statutes or jurisprudence of previously established international tribunals.[427] Trial Chambers of the SCSL, whose Statute contained an identical provision to the Rome Statute, interpreted the term based on the accompanying footnote, stating that "the inclusion of the words 'for private or personal use' excludes the possibility that appropriation justified by military necessity might fall within the definition. Nevertheless, the definition is framed to apply to a broad range of situations."[428] In addition, the SCSL Chamber stated that this requirement was "unduly restrictive and ought not to be an element of the crime of pillage."[429] Personal or private use as applied by the ICC Chambers, however, goes beyond the mere exclusion of acts justified by military necessity. The ICC Pre-Trial Chamber confirmed the *dolus specialis* requirement and found that evidence relating to combatants carrying away furniture and other goods to appropriate it for their private or personal use or sell it to a third party was sufficient to establish substantial grounds to believe the *dolus specialis* requirement was satisfied.[430] As for trade in natural resources by organized criminal groups, the intent to appropriate property for private or personal gain can be inferred by the overall goal of financial profit.

However, it is unclear whether the crime of pillage as defined in Article 8 of the Rome Statute also covers situations where the proceeds of the exploitation and trade in pillaged resources are reinvested in the military or militias' capabilities, creating a "self-sustained war economy in which hostilities create win-win situations for all belligerents."[431] In cases of hybrid organizations or criminal conduct that benefits both private individuals as well as military or State institutions, a case-by-case assessment is necessary. However, in practice, leaders of (hybrid) armed groups who systematically pillage natural resources and conduct illicit trade also benefit personally. For example, the Prosecution in the case against Charles Taylor showed that smuggled diamonds were critical

426 For the definition of military necessity, see above.
427 Zimmermann and Geiß (Commentary edited by Triffterer and Ambos) 2016a, 452–453.
428 Special Court for Sierra Leone AFRC Case 2007, para 753.
429 *ibid.*, para 754.
430 ICC Katanga and Ngudjolo 2008, para 332 and 336.
431 Steward 2010, 319.

for the RUF's funding of supplies and arms, but that, in fact, the majority of all funds went to Taylor for "safekeeping."[432] It can be assumed that the entirety of such conduct may be prosecuted as pillage under articles 8(2)(b)(xvi) and (2)(e)(v) of the Rome Statute.

Overall, the property-related provisions in Article 8 of the Rome Statute apply to the illegal exploitation of natural resources for the purpose of illicit trade by organized criminal groups if the contextual elements are satisfied; that is, if the act has a sufficient nexus to the armed conflict that the perpetrator is aware of as well as if the resources belong to an adverse or hostile party. Because of the special intent requirement, pillage under Articles 8(2)(b)(xvi) and (2)(e)(v) of the Rome Statute seems to be the most pertinent provision, although especially extensive appropriation of property protected by the Geneva Conventions in international armed conflict can also trigger Article 8(2)(a)(iv) of the Rome Statute.

3.2.3.2.2.2 Individual Acts of War Crimes in Illicit Trade in Cultural Goods

In recent years, archeological sites in Syria and Iraq were systematically targeted for clandestine excavations and plundered by well-organized and often armed groups. Reportedly, Daesh installed a system for plundering historic and cultural sites after their capture on an industrial scale by giving out licenses to organized criminal groups that paid 20% of their revenues in return for the license.[433] Thus, the issue of trafficking in cultural goods by organized criminal or hybrid groups is of pertinent interest.[434] Moreover, pillaging of art treasures was prosecuted as a war crime before international criminal tribunals as early as 1946, when Alfred Rosenberg received a death sentence for his excessive and systematic plunder of museums and cultural sites on territories occupied by Nazi Germany.[435] The applicability of the war crimes in Article 8 of the Rome Statute to the illicit exploitation and trade in cultural goods is analyzed in the following paragraphs.

Trafficking in cultural goods can generally fall under the same war crime provisions relating to property as the aforementioned exploitation and trade in natural resources.[436] However, international law, particularly IHL, recognizes the unique threat to the cultural heritage of a population posed by property crimes relating to cultural goods. There are therefore several partly

432 Rapp 2008, 17.
433 von Schorlemer 2016, 72–73.
434 See sections 2.1.2.4 and 3.2.2.2.4.
435 IMT Rosenberg 1946.
436 See section 3.2.3.2.2.1.

overlapping provisions whose applicability to and suitability for a concrete case must be determined on a case-by-case basis according to its factual circumstances as well as the perpetrators' *mens rea*.

First, traffic in cultural goods is covered by the war crime of pillage if the property belongs to an adverse or hostile party as well as if the conduct has a sufficient link to the armed conflict. Alfred Rosenberg was indicted by the IMT for being responsible "for a system of organised plunder of both public and private property [...] []and organis[ing] and direct[ing] the 'Einsatzstab Rosenberg', which plundered museums and libraries, confiscated art treasures and collections and pillaged private houses."[437] Thus, pillage under Articles 8(2)(b)(xvi) and (2)(e)(v) of the Rome Statute is applicable to the illegal plunder and trade in cultural goods in international and noninternational armed conflict.

Second, cultural goods are part of the property protected under the grave breaches regime, paragraph (2)(a) of Article 8 of the Rome Statute, applicable to international armed conflicts. Subparagraph (iv) criminalizes "extensive destruction and appropriation of property, not justified by military necessity and carried out unlawfully and wantonly." The Elements of Crimes require that "such property was protected under one or more of the Geneva Conventions of 1949" and that "the perpetrator was aware of the factual circumstances that established that protected status." Article 53 of Additional Protocol I to the Geneva Conventions prohibits "any acts of hostility directed against the historic monuments, works of art or places of worship which constitute the cultural or spiritual heritage of peoples, to use such objects in support of the military effort, and to make such objects the object of reprisals." An act of hostility is understood as "any act arising from the conflict which has or can have a substantial detrimental effect on the protected objects."[438] Since the provision does not prohibit the detrimental effect but rather an act directed against the object, no actual damage must occur.[439] The prohibition of the use of cultural objects in support of the military effort is designed to prevent such objects from becoming a military objective. Although Article 8(a)(iv) of the Rome Statute prohibits the appropriation and destruction of protected property, it only does so to the extent the particular type of property is also protected under the Geneva Conventions.[440] Thus, with regard to cultural goods, such property is protected from appropriation and destruction in any case where it

437 IMT Rosenberg 1946.

438 Wenger (Commentary edited by Sandoz, Swinarski and Zimmermann) 1987, 647.

439 *ibid.*

440 ICC Gaza Flotilla 2015, para 83–89.

is used for military purposes that put the cultural property in danger of becoming a military objective. This protection covers, *inter alia*, cases of pillage and trade in cultural goods that do not meet the *dolus specialis* requirement of personal or private use in the Rome Statute because the proceeds are reinvested in the military. Furthermore, the term "act of hostility" must be interpreted as encompassing conduct beyond military attacks. Attacking the territory of and around a cultural site to exploit it, for example, constitutes an act of hostility. Moreover, appropriations, if arising from the conflict, are also prohibited under Article 53 of Additional Protocol I.[441] The required *mens rea*, namely intent or knowledge, as well as awareness of the factual circumstances establishing the status of property as cultural goods can, in the context of organized crime, be inferred from the purpose of trafficking the property for profit.[442] Hence, Article 8(2)(a)(iv) also applies to illicit plunder and trade in cultural goods. Compared with the crime of pillage, the provision applies to all cases of extensive appropriation regardless of the purpose. Moreover, the provision might be more pertinent in cases of extensive destruction *and* appropriation of a certain cultural site, which was the case, e.g., for the main museum in Mosul.[443]

Third, the ICTY Statute in Article 3(d) criminalized "the seizure of, destruction or willful damage done to institutions dedicated to religion, charity and education, the arts and sciences, historic monuments and works of art and science." Based on this provision, the tribunal entered two convictions for the destruction caused by bombardments of the fortified city of Dubrovnik.[444] Although the Rome Statute lacks a provision specifically referring to the destruction or seizure of such protected property, they are covered by subparagraphs (2)(b)(xiii) and (2)(e)(xii) that relate to the destruction and seizure of the enemy's or adversary's property.[445] However, in the case against Al Mahdi for the destruction of mausoleums and mosques in Timbuktu, Mali, the accused was charged before the ICC for attacking protected objects under Article 8(2)(e)(iv) of the Rome Statute rather than for their destruction under paragraph (e)(xii), which was considered to be the more general crime.[446] An attack was understood to encompass "any acts of violence against protected objects."[447] The criminal

441 Although, in cases of illicit traffic, the war crime of pillage might be the *lex specialis*.

442 According to ICTY jurisprudence, recklessness is sufficient. See ICTY Kordić and Čerkez 2001, para 335–341; Dörmann (Commentary edited by Triffterer and Ambos) 2016, 342.

443 In 2015, Daesh published a video of its destruction.

444 ICTY Strugar 2005; ICTY Jokić 2004.

445 For more details see section 3.2.3.2.2.1.

446 ICC Al Mahdi 2016, para 12.

447 *ibid.*, para 15.

conduct as well as requisite *mens rea* thus differ between the crimes of directing an attack against and destroying cultural property.

The adequacy of these different provisions for a crime committed in the course of trafficking cultural goods in a situation of armed conflict depends on the particular circumstances of the case. While pillage is most appropriate to underline an accused's intention to draw personal benefit from the crime, extensive appropriation is most adequately described as a grave breach. Moreover, whether the removal of cultural objects from a site for the purpose of trafficking can also constitute the total or part destruction of the site must be determined on a case-by-case basis. This can, for example, be the case for critical spiritual artefacts at a religious site whose removal nullifies the holiness of the place. However, the provisions on destruction of property are most relevant where at least part of a site has been destroyed or damaged.

Overall, Article 8 of the Rome Statute prohibits the trafficking in cultural goods and related conduct, such as damaging or destroying cultural property, in international and noninternational armed conflicts, as long as the property belongs to another party to the conflict.

3.2.3.2.2.3 Individual Acts Of War Crimes in Trafficking in Persons, Including Forced Prostitution and Labor and Organ Trafficking

Depending on the contextual elements of the crime, human trafficking cannot only constitute a crime against humanity as analyzed above but also a war crime.[448] Indeed, the UNSC recognized that "persons forcibly displaced by armed conflict, including refugees, can be especially vulnerable to trafficking in persons in armed conflict and to [...] exploitation."[449]

Although some of the elements overlap, others must be discussed separately. For the purpose of analysis, human trafficking can again be subdivided into the initial act of trafficking (i.e., recruiting and removing individuals from their home and transferring them to another location); the general living conditions of trafficking victims (i.e., enslavement and any form of cruel treatment); and the most common purposes of trafficking (forced labor, sexual exploitation, and organ trade). The applicability of Article 8 of the Rome Statute to these components of human trafficking is analyzed in the following paragraph.

First, the removal of trafficking victims from their homes can constitute the crimes of unlawful deportation, transfer, or displacement under Article 8(2)(a)(vii), (b)(viii), and (e)(viii) of the Rome Statute in international and

448 See sections 2.1.2.2 and 3.2.2.2.1.

449 S/RES/2388 2017.

noninternational armed conflict, respectively. Since these provisions originated from IHL, especially Article 49 of the Fourth Geneva Convention and Article 17 of the Additional Protocol II, the elements of the crimes are not necessarily the same as for the similar crime against humanity of deportation or forcible transfer of a population under Article 7(1)(d) of the Rome Statute.[450] While Article 8(2)(b)(viii) of the Rome Statute refers to the deportation or transfer of individuals present in an occupied territory, the provision "does double duty"[451] with the more general prohibition under subparagraph (a)(vii). To establish an offense under the latter, the perpetrator must have intentionally carried out an act or omission to affect the deportation or transfer.[452] The requisite *mens rea* is implied by the systematic nature of human trafficking operations. Although the Elements of Crimes do not repeat the element of force or coercion named in Article 7 of the Rome Statute, it is required by Article 49(1) of the Fourth Geneva Convention as well as considered an integral element of the provision of the Rome Statute.[453] However, the term "forcibly" has been interpreted broadly as covering any situation where the transfer is not "motivated by an individual's own genuine wish to leave."[454] This interpretation is the same for the crime of humanity and the war crime of deportation or forcible transfer, thereby limiting the applicability of the provision to cases of human trafficking where a coercive element is present.[455] Subparagraph (a) applies in international armed conflicts and is limited to persons protected under the Geneva Conventions. By contrast, subparagraph (e)(viii) applies in noninternational armed conflicts but has the same origins in IHL. The provisions exclude deportations, transfers, and displacements justified by the security of the individuals involved or by military necessity. However, neither is relevant in the context of human trafficking unless traffickers take advantage of a legal transfer of individuals, in which case they cannot be charged for the initial act of removing the persons from their homes.

Furthermore, the living conditions trafficking victims must endure regardless of the type of exploitation they are trafficked for, especially if they amount to slavery, can also constitute war crimes. However, unlike Article 7 of the Rome Statute, Article 8 does not explicitly prohibit enslavement. Nevertheless, Article 8(2)(b)(xxii) and (e)(vi) of the Rome Statute prohibit sexual slavery,

450 See section 3.2.2.2.1.
451 Schabas (Commentary) 2016, 272.
452 ICTY Naletilić and Martinović 2003, para 519–521.
453 Cottier and Baumgartner (Commentary edited by Triffterer and Ambos) 2016, 414.
454 *ibid.*, para 519; ICTY Krnojelac *et al.* 2002, para 475.
455 For a detailed discussion see section 3.2.2.2.1.

which is considered a subcategory of enslavement. Because sexual slavery in the context of armed conflict has the same basis in international law as the corresponding crime against humanity, and the elements regarding *actus reus* and *mens rea* are identical in Articles 7 and 8 of the Rome Statute, the only difference lies in the contextual elements.[456] Moreover, the prohibition of slavery is included in the Lieber Code, presupposed by the provisions of the Geneva Conventions relating to labor of civilians and prisoners of war and forced allegiances of persons in occupied territory, and is thus considered a *ius cogens* norm in customary international law.[457] In *Krnojelac*, the accused was charged with slavery as a crime against humanity as well as a war crime.[458] Thus, enslavement violates IHL and constitutes a war crime in international law. However, Article 8 of the Rome Statute contains an exhaustive list, as indicated by the word "namely." For enslavement to constitute a war crime under the Rome Statute, it thus needs to be subsumed in another crime definition. There are several more general provisions that can apply to enslavement, namely the prohibition of inhuman treatment or willfully causing great suffering under subparagraphs (2)(a)(ii) and (iii), outrages upon personal dignity under subparagraphs (2)(b)(xxi) and (c)(ii), and cruel treatment under subparagraph (2)(c)(i).[459] Outrages upon personal dignity prohibited in international and non-international armed conflicts, however, seem to be the most appropriate provision; as the Elements of Crimes specify, "the perpetrator humiliated, degraded or otherwise violated the dignity of one or more persons. The severity [...] was of such a degree as to be generally recognized as an outrage upon personal dignity." The standard for identifying treatment falling under this provision is objective and must be assessed based on the form, severity, and duration of the treatment, as well as on the suffering caused and intensity of the act.[460] The Trial Chamber described the crime as "a species of inhuman treatment that is deplorable, occasioning more serious suffering than most prohibited acts falling within the *genus*."[461] Because of the absolute nature of enslavement and the treatment of the victim as an object rather than a human being, as well as the nature of the crime involving mental suffering, humiliation, and degradation

456 See section 3.2.2.2.1.

457 International Committee of the Red Cross 2019, Rule 94; Cottier and Mzee (Commentary edited by Triffterer and Ambos) 2016, 490.

458 ICTY Krnojelac *et al.* 2002, para 349.

459 As Schabas points out, "there is inevitably some overlap because the drafters of the Rome Statute made no serious effort to effect a new and internally coherent codification of war crimes". Schabas (Commentary) 2016, 242.

460 ICTY Aleksovski 1999, para 56–57.

461 *ibid.*, para 54–56.

rather than physical violence, enslavement meets this threshold for outrages upon personal dignity and is best described by its elements. Notably, to establish enslavement as a war crime under the Rome Statute, proving all elements of enslavement defined in Article 7 of the Rome Statute is not necessary, but it must be demonstrated that the factual circumstances amount to outrages of personal dignity and meet the specific requirements of this crime.

Moreover, victims of trafficking are often subjected to violence and other inhuman treatment, which fall under the other abovementioned more general provisions. As outlined, outrages upon personal dignity have been interpreted to require a higher gravity threshold than inhuman treatment. For example, forcing father and son to beat each other, brothers to perform oral sex on each other being watched by other prisoners, or victims to dance naked on a table, as well as creating an atmosphere of constant fear of violence have been judged outrages upon personal dignity.[462] Inhuman and cruel treatment applicable to international and noninternational armed conflict, respectively, are both defined as "inflict[ing] severe physical or mental pain or suffering upon one or more persons."[463] While inhuman treatment encompasses the grave breaches not explicitly listed in Article 8(2)(a) of the Rome Statute, cruel treatment is set out in common Article 3 (paragraph 1(a)) of the Geneva Conventions.[464] However, the PrepCom and ICTY jurisprudence both determined that the crimes have identical elements.[465] Unlike the crime of willfully causing great suffering under subparagraph (a)(iii), inhuman or cruel treatment does not require serious mental or physical injury. Temporary unhappiness, embarrassment, or humiliation can be sufficient.[466]

Thus, under Article 8 of the Rome Statute, the physical or mental abuse, violence, pressure, and fear (among others) that victims of human trafficking are subjected to can constitute the war crimes of outrages on personal dignity, inhuman or cruel treatment, or willfully causing suffering, depending on the particular acts as well as the context if they are sufficiently associated with an armed conflict.

In addition to removal from their home environment and general treatment of trafficked individuals, the type of exploitation they are trafficked for, namely

462 ICC Katanga and Ngudjolo 2008, para 371; ICTY Delalić *et al.* 1998, para 1067–1070 and 1062–1066; Arnold and Wehrenberg (Commentary edited by Triffterer and Ambos) 2016, 473.

463 Elements of Crimes 2010, Articles 8(2)(a)(ii)-2, para 1, and 8(2)(c)(i)-3, para 1, respectively.

464 ICTY Blaškić 2000, para 154–155.

465 ICTY Delalić *et al.* 1998, para 443.

466 ICTY Kordić and Čerkez 2001, para 245.

sexual exploitation, labor exploitation, and organ trade, can also constitute war crimes.

First, sexual exploitation is covered by subparagraphs (2)(b)(xxii) and (e)(vi) applicable in international and noninternational armed conflict, respectively. Sexual exploitation is prevalent in many armed conflicts and the vulnerability of the victims as well as a culture of virility among soldiers are a breeding ground for organized crime in this market. The enumerated acts of sexual violence are identical to the crime of humanity defined in Article 7(1)(g) of the Rome Statute. As for "any other form of sexual violence," Article 7 of the Rome Statute requires gravity comparable to the other acts listed in the provision, whereas Article 8(2)(a) requires that it also constitutes a grave breach of the Geneva Conventions, and Article 8(2)(e) of the Rome Statute refers to common Article 3 of the Geneva Conventions. However, Trial Chambers have treated the crimes as indistinguishable except for their contextual elements.[467] Hence, as indicated by the analysis of the applicable crime against humanity that will not be reproduced here, different forms of sexual exploitation of trafficked individuals constitute the war crimes of rape, sexual slavery, forced prostitution, and other forms of sexual violence if committed in the context of and in association with an armed conflict.[468]

Second, labor exploitation is not explicitly prohibited under Article 8 of the Rome Statute. However, forced labor is considered part of the customary crime of enslavement.[469] The ICTY Trial Chamber stated, "the exaction of forced or compulsory labor or service is an indication of enslavement, and a factor to be taken into consideration in determining whether enslavement was committed."[470] As outlined above, forced labor must be charged under another crime included in Article 8, namely outrages upon personal dignity or inhuman or cruel treatment. As for enslavement, the strong mental component of forced labor and its impact on self-worth and independence meet the gravity threshold of outrages against personal dignity under subparagraphs (b)(xi) and (c)(ii). However, forced labor does not need to be shown to meet the requirements for enslavement; rather, the conduct must satisfy the elements of the specific crime charged, such as of inhuman or cruel treatment. It should be noted, however, that civilians deprived of their liberty in noninternational

467 ICC Katanga 2014, para 961–972; ICC Ntaganda 2014, para 49–57; Schabas (Commentary) 2016, 252.

468 See section 3.2.2.2.1.

469 *ibid.*

470 ICTY Krnojelac *et al.* 2002, para 359.

armed conflicts may be compelled to work under specific circumstances, as indicated in Article 5(1)(e) of the Additional Protocol II.

Lastly, human trafficking for organ removal, as reported from Kosovo for example, constitutes a violation of the prohibition of physical mutilation that causes death to or seriously endangers the health of victims under the identical subparagraphs (2)(b)(x) and (e)(xi) of Article 8 of the Rome Statute. Although the crime of mutilation under subparagraph (c)(i) as well as willful killing under subparagraph (a)(i) and murder under subparagraph (c)(i), which are essentially the same, as well as the prohibitions on outrages against personal dignity, inhuman or cruel treatment, or willfully causing severe mental or physical suffering are also applicable, the abovementioned prohibition on physical mutilations represents the *lex specialis*, since the main objective is organ removal, not death.[471] The Elements of Crimes specify that mutilation takes place "in particular by permanently disfiguring the person or persons, or by permanently disabling or *removing an organ* or appendage."[472] They also require that the mutilation "caused death or seriously endangered the physical or mental health" of the victim, necessarily a member of the adverse party, and was "neither justified by the medical, dental or hospital treatment of the person or persons concerned nor carried out in such person's or persons' interest." Consent is not a valid defense for these crimes. Human trafficking for the purpose of organ removal satisfies the element of mutilation and, in most cases, causes death. In the rare cases of a victim surviving the procedure, the mental harm caused by the experience alone would satisfy the element of seriously endangering the victim's health, let alone the physical consequences of operations usually not conducted under the optimal medical conditions and with respect and care for the victim. The crime is thus covered by article 8(2)(b)(x) and (e)(xi) of the Rome Statute.

Overall, human trafficking, including the initial act of trafficking (i.e., recruiting and removing individuals from their home and transferring them to another location), their treatment and slavery-like living conditions, as well as their exploitation for sex, labor, or organ trade constitute war crimes in international and noninternational armed conflict under Article 8 of the Rome Statute if the crimes are committed in the context of and associated with an armed conflict.

---

471 As for the applicability of the crime against humanity of murder, which is identical to the war crimes except for the contextual elements, see section 3.2.2.2.1.

472 Elements of Crimes 2010, Article 8(2)(b)(x)-1, para 1. Emphasis added.

3.2.3.2.2.4 Individual Acts of War Crimes in Migrant Smuggling, Including Migrant-Related Crimes

Migrant smuggling, and migrant-related crimes as described by Prosecutor Bensouda with regard to the situation in Libya, can fall under both crimes against humanity and war crimes.[473] This subsection analyzes that under war crimes. For the purpose of analysis, migrant smuggling is again subdivided into the isolated act of smuggling, the conditions under which the transfers occur, as well as the broader circumstances before and during the transfer.

For migrant smuggling and migrant-related crime to constitute a war crime, they must take place in the context of and be associated with an armed conflict.[474] Notably, the fact that migrants have fled an armed conflict is not sufficient to establish a nexus as such, because the act constituting the crime, not the victim, needs to be associated with the armed conflict.

First, as discussed with regard to the crime of humanity of deportation or forcible transfer under Article 7(1)(d) of the Rome Statute, as well as to the war crimes of unlawful deportation and transfer under Article 8(2)(a)(vii) and (b)(viii) and displacement under (e)(viii) concerning human trafficking, for a transfer to constitute a war crime it is required to be against the victim's "genuine wish to leave."[475][476] Because migrants, especially in the context of armed conflict, decide to leave an area for reasons independent of and possibly some time before the act of smuggling and express their wish by paying the smuggler, these crimes do not apply to the smuggling of migrants.

Second, death or serious harm caused by insufficient security measures taken by the smugglers could also constitute a war crime. However, the war crimes of willful killing or murder under subparagraphs (2)(a)(i) and (c)(i), of inhuman or cruel treatment under subparagraphs (a)(ii) and (c)(i), or of willfully causing great suffering under subparagraph (a)(iii), are subjected to the same *mens rea* requirements as crimes against humanity.[477] Murder and willful killing possess the same elements as the crime against humanity of murder under article 7(1)(a) of the Rome Statute, including the required *mens rea* of *dolus directus* of first or second degree. Similarly, the Article 30 standard applies to the other abovementioned crimes.[478] Following the interpretation of the Trial Chambers, intent or "virtual certainty"[479] that harm will occur

---

473 See sections 2.1.2.3 and 3.2.2.2.2.
474 See sections 3.2.3.1.1. and 3.2.3.1.3.
475 ICTY Simić 2003, para 125.
476 See sections 3.2.2.2.1–2. and 3.2.3.2.2.3.
477 See section 3.2.2.2.2.
478 See, e.g., ICTY Kordić and Čerkez 2001, para 265.
479 ICC Lubanga 2014, para 447.

must thus be established. Consequently, the risk taken by smugglers applying insufficient security measures does not suffice to constitute a war crime.

However, the circumstances under which migrants are detained, such as those reported from Libya, could fall under the prohibition of unlawful confinement in Article 8(2)(a)(vii) of the Rome Statute. Notably, the provision only applies to international armed conflict and requires that the victims be protected under the Geneva Conventions. Under these circumstances, the provision prohibits the confinement or continuation of confinement of one or more persons to a certain location.[480] The Fourth Geneva Convention allows internment of civilians only under specific conditions. Specifically, Article 42 of the Fourth Geneva Convention requires that the internment is absolutely necessary for the security of the detaining power. Article 43 of the Fourth Geneva Convention contains procedural guarantees for the interned individual. As noted by the ICTY Appeals Chamber, "there must be an assessment that each civilian taken into detention poses a particular risk to the security of the State. [...] [T]he mere fact that a person is a national of, or aligned with, an enemy party cannot be [...] a valid reason for interning him."[481] An internment is unlawful if it is not absolutely necessary for security reasons, thereby violating Article 42 of the Fourth Geneva Convention, as well as if the safeguards of Article 43 of the Fourth Geneva Convention are not upheld, even if the internment was initially justified.[482] Although Libya argues that the internment of migrants is necessary for State security, no evidence exists that individual assessments have been made or that Article 43 safeguards are upheld neither in State-run nor privately-run detention facilities.[483] Thus, smugglers or other organized criminals responsible for detaining migrants belonging to the adverse party to a conflict can be held responsible for unlawful internment.

Moreover, human rights law suggests that unlawful confinement cannot only be established because of the illegality of the confinement itself but also because of inhumane conditions of detention that violate international standards.[484] As a consequence, the crime of unlawful confinement is also perpetrated in situations that do not constitute violations of Articles 42 and 43 of the Fourth Geneva Convention but involve, for example, "various forms of mistreatment, including severe beatings, electrocution, acts of sexual violence

480 Elements of Crimes 2010, Article 8(2)(a)(vii)-2, para 1.

481 ICTY Delalić *et al.* 2001, para 322, 327.

482 *ibid.*

483 UN Support Mission in Libya 2016. Note that the characterization of the armed conflict in Libya as international or noninternational has been disputed, Milanovic 2011.

484 In favor Schabas (Commentary) 2016, 254.

and rape, solitary confinement, deprivation of food and water, inhumane conditions of detention, mock executions, and threats of killing and rape"[485] as reported from Libya.

Furthermore, acts constituting the aforementioned inhumane detention conditions can—depending on the exact circumstances—also constitute other war crimes, namely torture under subparagraphs (a)(ii) and (c)(i); mutilation under subparagraphs (c)(i), (b)(x), and (e)(xi); rape and all other forms of sexual violence included in subparagraphs (b)(xxii) and (e)(vi); outrages against personal dignity under subparagraphs (b)(xxi) and (c)(ii); and inhuman or cruel treatment or willfully causing great suffering under subparagraphs (a)(ii), (c)(i), and (a)(iii) of Article 8(2) of the Rome Statute, respectively. It should be noted that while the elements of rape and all other sex-related war crimes are identical to the corresponding crimes against humanity, the war crime of torture in international and noninternational armed conflicts differs from the crime against humanity. First, the Elements of Crimes omit the reference to the victim being under the control of the perpetrator, although this circumstance seems to be implied in the conduct. Second, the war crime of torture includes a specific intent requirement, namely the conduct must have been committed "for such purposes as: obtaining information or a confession, punishment, intimidation or coercion or for any reason based on discrimination of any kind."[486]

The distinctions between outrages upon personal dignity, inhuman or cruel treatment, and willfully causing great suffering have been discussed above.[487] For example, case law has identified injuries and mistreatment of detainees as being inhuman treatment; beatings as cruel treatment; and forcing detainees to urinate in their clothing and imposing constant fear of violence as outrages upon personal dignity.[488] The Prosecutor has also deemed being denied access to toilet facilities or being watched while on the toilet, denial of medication, limited access to food and drink, physical and verbal harassment, threats and intimidation involving dogs, and being blindfolded and hooded as sufficiently serious to constitute outrages upon personal dignity.[489]

Thus, members of organized criminal groups can be held responsible for unlawful confinement as well as other crimes committed against migrants if

485 Bensouda 2017, para 26; Office of the Prosecutor 2019b, para 31.

486 Elements of Crimes 2010, Articles (8)(2)(a)(ii) and (c)(i), para 2.

487 See section 3.2.3.2.2.3.

488 ICTY Kordić and Čerkez 2001, para 256; ICC Kony 2005, 17; ICC Katanga and Ngudjolo 2008, para 370 respectively; Schabas (Commentary) 2016, 245, 250.

489 Office of the Prosecutor of the International Criminal Court 2014c, para 64.

the contextual elements are satisfied; however, they cannot be held responsible under Article 8 of the Rome Statute for the act of smuggling or death and injuries that occur as a consequence of insufficient safety measures taken during transfers.

3.2.3.2.2.5 Individual Acts of War Crimes in Organized Crime-Related Violence

As discussed in relation to genocide and crimes against humanity, organized criminal groups use violence to deter competitors, manifest their power in a certain territory, divert attention from their core business, and defend themselves against State policing, among other reasons.[490] Such criminal conduct without a direct link to the core business (e.g., illicit trade) can be characterized as organized crime-related violence.

Especially in the context of armed conflict, organized criminal groups arm themselves or merge with armed groups, and armed groups enter organized crime creating hybrid groups involved in both organized crime and armed conflict.[491] As previously mentioned, the most notorious examples of organized crime-related violence are the situation in Colombia prior to the 2016 peace agreement and the so-called drug war in Mexico. While the situation in Colombia was recognized as a noninternational armed conflict, the legal qualification of the violence in Mexico remains disputed.[492]

The FARC is a prime example of a hybrid group, as the difficulties in distinguishing between former guerilla fighters and drug traffickers in the course of demobilization illustrated.[493] Because these groups do not act solely on the basis of economic motivations, the war crimes they commit are not limited by an underlying functional logic as, for example, in Mexico where crimes are specifically designed to hurt competitors and the State and manifest a cartel's power. In the case of Colombia, the Prosecution found that a reasonable basis exists to believe that the FARC and ELN committed murder pursuant to subparagraph (e)(i), torture and cruel treatment pursuant to subparagraph (c)(i), outrages upon personal dignity pursuant to subparagraph (c)(ii), rape and other forms of sexual violence pursuant to subparagraph (e)(vi), as well as conscripting, enlisting, and using child soldiers pursuant to subparagraph (e)(vii).[494] Moreover, the Prosecutor found reasonable grounds to believe that the

---

490 See section 2.1.2.7, 3.2.1.2.2.2, and 3.2.2.2.5.

491 See section 2.3.2.2.

492 Office of the Prosecutor of the International Criminal Court 2012, para 128; in favor of the qualification as an armed conflict in Mexico see, e.g., Bergal 2011; against see Gallahue 2011.

493 Bargent 2017.

494 Office of the Prosecutor of the International Criminal Court 2012, para 132 *et seq.*

crime of hostage-taking under subparagraph (c)(iii) was committed. Unlike the crime against humanity of deprivation of liberty or the war crime of unlawful confinement, the crime of taking hostages requires the special intent "to compel a State, an international organization, a natural or legal person or a group of persons to act or refrain from acting as an explicit or implicit condition for the safety or the release of such person or persons."[495] Hostages are often used by guerillas and organized criminal groups alike, such as the Medellín Cartel, to exert political pressure.

If the situation in Mexico should indeed constitute a noninternational armed conflict, all crimes identified by the Prosecution in Colombia would also apply.[496] Other acts in organized crime-related violence constitute crimes, such as those of mutilation and attacks against the civilian population under subparagraphs (c)(i) and (e)(i).[497] The latter requires intent by the perpetrator and is an absolute prohibition, that is, the crime cannot be justified by military necessity.

Overall, organized crime-related violence is largely covered by Article 8 of the Rome Statute if it occurs in the context of and is associated with an armed conflict.

3.2.3.3 Summary

The individual acts defined in the war crime provision of Article 8 of the Rome Statute encompass various activities by organized criminal groups, notably illicit trade in natural resources and cultural goods, human trafficking, migrant-related crimes, and organized crime-related violence. However, the contextual elements required for these activities to qualify as war crimes, especially a sufficient nexus to an armed conflict and the requirement in some provisions that the victims belong to certain protected groups, limit the jurisdiction of the ICC over organized crime.

For war crimes to occur, an armed conflict must be present, and the crime must be associated with that conflict. Such an association can first be based on the participation of organized criminal groups or their members in the conflict. While international armed conflicts are limited to States as parties to a conflict, members of organized criminal groups can be combatants or directly participate in hostilities. Noninternational armed conflicts require that a certain intensity threshold be met and that the involved armed groups possess an internal organization sufficient to maintain protracted armed conflict. Strictly

495 Elements of Crimes 2010, Article 8(2)(a)(viii) and (c)(iii), para 3.

496 For more detail see sections 3.2.1.2.2.2. and 3.2.2.2.5.

497 Human Rights Watch, 2017.

organized and well-equipped organized criminal groups can thus be a party to a noninternational armed conflict. Moreover, members of organized criminal groups can be fighters if they assume a continuous combat function. In addition, war crimes can be committed by civilians.[498] Second, the required nexus can be established if the crime was shaped by the conflict or was dependent on the conflict. The context must have played a substantial role for the perpetrator's ability, his decision to commit the crime, or for the way in which it was committed.[499] Although such a nexus can be established for, for example, illegal trade that plays a substantial role in funding one of the armed groups or dependents in the insecurity created by armed conflict, it includes all cases of organized crime that operate independently of the armed conflict.

Moreover, the limitation of the protection of certain war crimes to a group of protected people, particularly victims belonging to the adversary, limit the applicability of some provisions of Article 8 of the Rome Statute. This excludes, for example, all crimes committed by organized criminal groups against members of their own group, such as the illicit exploitation of natural resources on the territory of the group they are associated with.

Nevertheless, the enumerated acts constituting war crimes cover a range of conduct relevant to organized crime. In contrast to crimes against humanity, war crimes cover property-related crimes and thus apply to illegal exploitation of natural resources and cultural goods for the purpose of illegal trade. The war crime of pillage in particular criminalizes all appropriation of property for the purpose of personal or private use. While this special purpose requirement is applicable to situations of organized crime acting for economic profit only, the provision excludes cases where proceeds of the illegal trade benefit a belligerent State or military. In such cases, however, extensive appropriation may still be covered by other provisions.

Similar to crimes against humanity under Article 7 of the Rome Statute, Article 8 prohibits human trafficking in armed conflicts, including sexual and labor exploitation as well as organ removal. However, migrant smuggling is not covered; migrant-related crimes such as torture, sexual violence, and forms of inhuman treatment are prohibited in different war crime provisions in Article 8. That is, the elements of unlawful confinement often apply more specifically to the situation of migrant detention than the crime against humanity of imprisonment or deprivation of liberty, though the crime is only defined for international armed conflicts.

498 Cottier (Commentary edited by Triffterer and Ambos) 2016, 316; Zimmermann and Geiß (Commentary edited by Triffterer and Ambos) 2016b, 548.

499 ICC Lubanga 2007, para 287.

Furthermore, war crimes under Article 8 of the Rome Statute are highly relevant in relation to organized crime-related violence, especially regarding criminal and armed hybrid groups. Violence in the course of conflicts between organized criminal groups, in particular well-financed drug cartels, and the government or between such groups can satisfy the elements of war crimes under the Rome Statute depending on the intensity of the violence and internal organization of the groups involved, or on their association with another party to a conflict.

Overall, the war crime provisions in Article 8 of the Rome Statute establish jurisdiction over some of the crimes committed by organized criminal groups in the context of armed conflicts. Contrary to crimes against humanity under Article 7, the conduct covered is not confined to acts causing direct human suffering, but Article 8 also applies to property-related crimes. Thus, the illicit trade in natural resources and cultural goods in particular can be addressed in war crime prosecutions before the ICC.

3.3 Substantive Law: Attribution of a Crime

According to Article 25(1) and (2) of the Rome Statute, the ICC has jurisdiction over natural persons who are individually responsible and liable for punishment if committing crimes under Article 5 of the Rome Statute. Therefore, regarding possible prosecutions of members of organized criminal groups before the ICC, whether their actions entail individual criminal responsibility under the relevant provisions of the Rome Statute must be analyzed.

In Articles 25 and 28, the Rome Statute distinguishes between several modes of liability. The provisions are based on "an eclectic combination of sources from several national legal traditions"[500] and their interpretation "is far from being uncontentious or settled."[501][502] As a consequence, and similar to the jurisprudence of the *ad hoc* tribunals, judges have departed from the text and developed concepts of perpetration not explicitly included in the Statute, such as that of indirect co-perpetration or the "control over the crime" theory.[503] Moreover, whether Article 25 of the Rome Statute constitutes a hierarchy with perpetration entailing more blameworthiness than participation in a crime

500 ICC Ngudjolo 2012, para 13.

501 ICC Katanga 2013, para 15.

502 Eser (Commentary edited by Cassese, Gaeta and Jones) 2002, 781 *et seq.*; Schabas (Commentary) 2016, 562–563.

503 See section 3.3.1.

remains unclear.[504] At the time of writing, the types of participation included in subparagraphs (e) and (f), namely incitement to genocide and attempt, have not been applied before the ICC.

Based on this jurisprudence, the application and relevance of the pertinent provisions with regard to organized crime are analyzed in the following section. Members of organized criminal groups can bear criminal responsibility under the Statute as (indirect) perpetrator or co-perpetrator under Article 25(3)(a) of the Rome Statute, as a secondary perpetrator or accessory under Article 25(3)(b) to (f), and as a commander or superior under Article 28. The analyses focus on perpetration, the different modes of participation in subparagraphs (b) to (d) of Article 25(3), and superior responsibility under Article 28.[505]

3.3.1 *Perpetration*

Article 25(3)(a) of the Rome Statute distinguishes three types of perpetration, namely direct perpetration as an individual, co-perpetration jointly with another person, and indirect perpetration through another person. This section examines these concepts with regard to organized crime.

Direct perpetration, meaning that the perpetrator physically carried out the objective elements of a crime with the requisite *mens rea,* is the exception before the ICC because of its usual practice of accusing the leaders of groups whose members physically carried out crimes. Nevertheless, this practice is based rather on prosecutorial discretion than on a provision in the Statute. Consequently, from a purely legal perspective, members of criminal groups can be held responsible for the direct perpetration of any of the crimes discussed in the previous sections.

Co-perpetration is characterized by "the division of essential tasks for the purpose of committing a crime between two or more persons acting in a concerted manner."[506] It requires, first, "an agreement or common plan" between the co-perpetrators and, second, an "essential contribution" by each co-perpetrator to the realization of the crime.[507] The existence of an agreement or plan may be "inferred from the subsequent concerted action of the co-perpetrators."[508] Moreover, the common plan must not be specifically directed

504 In favor ICC Lubanga 2014, para 462; against ICC Katanga 2014, para 1386–1387; Eser (Commentary edited by Cassese, Gaeta and Jones) 2002, 787.

505 Incitement of genocide as well as attempted commission of a crime under Article 25(3)(e) and (f) of the Rome Statute have no particularities with regard to organized crime.

506 ICC Lubanga 2007, para 342.

507 *ibid.*, para 343, 346; ICC Lubanga 2012, para 999; Ambos (Commentary edited by Triffterer and Ambos) 2016, 992.

508 ICC Lubanga 2007, para 345.

at the commission of the crime but it is sufficient to involve "a critical element of criminality," which makes it virtually certain that the implementation of the plan leads to the commission of the crime.[509] Each co-perpetrator can be held responsible for the crime as a whole because the common plan provides for the possibility of a mutual attribution of the various contributions.[510] The essential contribution can be made both at the planning or preparation stage, including when the common plan is conceived, and at the execution stage of the crime.[511] Furthermore, the co-perpetrators must "share control [over the offense] because each of them could frustrate the commission of the crime by not carrying out his or her task."[512] Control over the crime has been applied as the determinant factor in distinguishing criminal responsibility as a principal perpetrator under subparagraph (a) from forms of accessorial liability or participation under the other subparagraphs.[513] Two members of an organized criminal group can be held responsible for a crime as co-perpetrators, for example, for enslavement, if they have a common plan to operate in a certain illegal market, such as offering forced prostitution, and if both have control over the crime and could frustrate their commission, such as through recruiting the victims and coercing them to perform sexual intercourse with a client. The existence of a common plan can be presupposed if the co-perpetrators are both members of an organized criminal group and if the crime they commit represents the core business of that group.

Indirect perpetration requires that the indirect perpetrator exerts control over a crime engendered by one or more other persons (direct perpetrators) who are used as instruments by the principal perpetrator.[514] The direct perpetrators can be innocent agents, such as minors and persons acting erroneously, suffering from mental defects, or excused for acting under duress (*Nötigungsherrschaft*).[515] It is also possible, however, that the direct perpetrator commits the crime with the required *mens rea* and is aware of its illegality. Such is the case, for example, when the indirect perpetrator controls the direct perpetrators by virtue of a hierarchical organizational structure (*Organisationsherrschaft*). In this case, indirect perpetration requires control

509 ICC Lubanga 2014, para 446, 451.

510 Ambos (Commentary edited by Triffterer and Ambos) 2016, 991 *et seq.*

511 ICC Lubanga 2014, para 7, 469, 473; Ambos (Commentary edited by Triffterer and Ambos) 2016, 991 *et seq.*

512 ICC Lubanga 2007, para 342.

513 ICC Katanga 2014, para 1396; ICC Lubanga 2014, para 469; Ambos (Commentary edited by Triffterer and Ambos) 2016, 991–992.

514 ICC Katanga 2014, para 1399.

515 Ambos (Commentary edited by Triffterer and Ambos) 2016, 994.

over the organization, an "organized and hierarchical apparatus of power," and automatic compliance by interchangeable executors.[516] According to the Trial Chamber, "persons wielding control over the apparatus of power, therefore, are unquestionably those in the organization who conceived the crime, oversaw its preparation at different hierarchical levels, and controlled its performance and execution."[517] Indirect perpetration is especially relevant in well-organized, hierarchical organized criminal groups, such as in drug cartels that frequently exhibit structures similar to a conventional company. If the crime under the Rome Statute consists of the profit-generating activities of an organized criminal group, such as plundering and trade in conflict diamonds, the whole organization is perceived to commit that crime and the leaders will normally be criminally responsible as indirect perpetrators based on their *Organisationsherrschaft*.

Judges have applied the notion of indirect co-perpetration to cases where the elements of co-perpetration (i.e., a common plan and an essential contribution) and indirect perpetration (i.e., control over a crime carried out by another person) were both present.[518] Furthermore, joint indirect perpetratorship has been applied to situations where several indirect perpetrators jointly exercised control over a hierarchical organization.[519] Both are situations that can frequently occur in organized criminal organizations, such as a cartel being run jointly by several leaders.

Overall, co-perpetration, indirect perpetration, and indirect co-perpetration are especially relevant with regard to organized criminal groups due to the large scope of operation and the organizational features of organized criminal groups.

3.3.2 *Participation*

In addition to (in-)direct (co-)perpetration, Article 25 of the Rome Statute contains several modes of liability characterized as secondary or accessorial, or distinguished from perpetration as participation in the commission of a crime. Trial Chambers have used the "control over the crime" test to delineate participation from perpetration.[520] Thus, accessorial responsibility requires a lower threshold than an essential contribution to a crime. In the context of organized

516 ICC Katanga and Ngudjolo 2008, para 498–518; *ibid.*, 994–995.

517 ICC Muthaura *et al.* 2012, para 1412.

518 ICC Katanga and Ngudjolo 2008, para 492, 521–522; Ambos (Commentary edited by Triffterer and Ambos) 2016, 997.

519 ICC Blé Goudé 2014, para 136.

520 ICC Lubanga 2007, para 342; see section 3.3.1.

crime, Article 25(3)(c) of the Rome Statute on aiding, abetting, or otherwise assisting the commission of a crime, and Article 25(3)(d) on contributing in any other way to a group committing a crime, are relevant accessorial modes of liability, especially with regard to the provision of the material or financial means to commit a crime, such as through trade. Giving the order to commit a crime, as included in Article 25(b) of the Rome Statute, is also relevant in relation to the criminal responsibility of leaders of organized criminal groups. These provisions are examined in the following paragraph.

With regard to participation in a crime through supplying the means to commit it, a few cases exist that involve commercial transactions in illegal markets. One example is the case against the Dutch businessman Van Anraat before the District Court of The Hague. In this case, the accused was convicted of complicity in war crimes for selling the chemical thiodiglycol (TDG) to the Iraqi regime under Saddam Hussein, which subsequently used it to produce mustard gas to attack Kurdish villages.[521] In a 2017 Decision by the Den Bosch Court of Appeal, another Dutch businessman, Van Kouwenhoven, was convicted for complicity in war crimes for his involvement in smuggling arms to the Liberian government under Charles Taylor.[522]

Members of organized criminal groups can be held responsible for similar conduct, first, under Article 25(3)(c) of the Rome Statute for aiding, abetting, and otherwise assisting the commission of a crime. While accessorial liability, especially the concept of complicity, are defined differently in various domestic legal systems, the notion of aiding and abetting has already been used under the *ad hoc* tribunals and is based in customary international law.[523] Aiding can be understood as referring to physical assistance, whereas abetting refers to encouragement or moral suasion.[524] Although the formulation in the Rome Statute adding "otherwise assists" suggests that they are understood as distinct acts, aiding, abetting, and assisting are frequently discussed together.[525] The *ad hoc* tribunals required a substantial effect on the commission of the crime, that is, some causal relationship between the contribution

521 District Court of the Hague 2005.

522 Den Bosch Court of Appeals 2017.

523 ICTY Tadić 1997, para 666.

524 ICTY Furundžija 1998, para 231; ICTR Akayesu 1998, para 484.

525 ICTR Rutaganda 1999, para 43 ; ICC Blé Goudé 2014, para 167 ; Ambos (Commentary edited by Triffterer and Ambos) 2016, 1006–1007; Eser (Commentary edited by Cassese, Gaeta and Jones) 2002, 799: "Instead of exchanging synonyms, which are in any case rather unclear, it appears preferable to resort to the umbrella term of 'assistance' […]."

and resulting crime.[526] However, no explicit reference to a certain threshold for the contribution's significance is made in the Rome Statute. As the ICC Pre-Trial Chamber noted, to date "[t]here is [...] scholarly disagreement as to whether the *actus reus* required [by the Rome Statute] should likewise differ from the *ad hoc* tribunals' 'substantial contribution' requirement."[527] The contribution does not need to be tangible or indispensable in the sense of a condition *sine qua non*.[528] Moreover, the assistance can consist of an omission, such as where such an omission constitutes official tolerance of certain crimes and can thus be interpreted as encouragement.[529]

The contribution to the crime under Article 25(3)(c) of the Rome Statute does not require a geographical link, although presence at the crime scene may constitute the act of abetting if the person holds a position of "*autorité incontestée*."[530] Moreover, an act of assistance can be performed before and during the commission of the crime.[531] There is support in the *travaux préparatoires* that *ex post facto* assistance has deliberately been excluded from the provision.[532] Nevertheless, the ICC Pre-Trial Chamber noted that such exclusion would only apply to the interpretation of subparagraph (c) and be without prejudice to the application of subparagraph (d) to assistance after the act.[533]

Regardless of whether the substantiality threshold will be applied by the ICC, the *actus reus* of aiding and abetting constitutes one of the "weakest form[s] of complicity,"[534] and thus, covers a broad range of contributions to international crimes by organized criminal groups. This can include, for example, the supply of arms and other material contributions, financial support of armed groups favorable to illicit market activities, or, in some cases, the failure of an organized criminal group's leader to condemn extreme violence perpetrated by the group's members.

However, subparagraph (c) also establishes a *mens rea* requirement for aiding, abetting, and assisting, namely that the perpetrator acts "for the purpose of facilitating the commission of such a crime." This specific subjective

526 ICTY Tadić 1997, para 691–692. For an overview of ICTY and ICTR jurisprudence see Ambos (Commentary edited by Triffterer and Ambos) 2016, 1003–1006.

527 ICC Mbarushimana 2011, para 281.

528 ICTR Kayishema and Ruzindana 1999, para 200–201.

529 ICTR Akayesu 1998, para 548; Ambos (Commentary edited by Triffterer and Ambos) 2016, 1007.

530 ICTY Aleksovski 1999, para 63. "Uncontested authority". Translated by the author.

531 ICTY Vasiljević 2002, para 70.

532 Schabas (Commentary) 2016, 578.

533 ICC Mbarushimana 2011, para 286.

534 Ambos (Commentary edited by Triffterer and Ambos) 2016, 1003.

requirement differs from the approach of the *ad hoc* tribunals, which only required knowledge that the acts concerned assist the commission of the specific crime.[535] However, the specific purpose requirement only refers to the act of facilitation, whereas the mental element required for the main crime remains the one required for that crime.[536] Especially in the case of abetting, where some kind of expression by the perpetrator is usually involved, the specific purpose can be deduced from the conduct of the accused. For aiding and assisting, in turn, the requirement is more critical, especially in the case of ambiguous acts whose criminal nature depends on the accused's awareness of the principal perpetrator's intentions. This example highlights the contrasts: under ICTR jurisprudence, an arms trafficker who knew that the supplied weapons would be used to commit a crime was found liable for aiding the commission of that crime. The Rome Statute, in turn, requires the trafficker to act with the motive of facilitating the crime. As a consequence, Article 25(3)(c) of the Rome Statute excludes all forms of assistance to a crime based purely on alternative motives (e.g., profit), even if the assistant knew that his acts contributed to the commission of a crime. Hence, the supply of material or financial means to armed groups by organized criminal groups resulting in the commission of a crime does not constitute aiding, abetting, or assisting under the Rome Statute unless the organized criminal groups have the particular intent to facilitate the commission of such crime.

Nevertheless, cases not qualifying for subparagraph (c) may be covered by the "residual form of accessory liability"[537] of Article 25(3)(d) of the Rome Statute. Case law has developed three objective elements of subparagraph (d): first, a crime under the ICC's jurisdiction was committed; second, the persons who committed the crime form a group with a common purpose; and third, the accused has contributed significantly to the commission of the crime.[538]

With regard to the second element, the group does not need to be part of a military, political, or administrative structure and the common purpose may be established spontaneously and can be inferred from concerted conduct.[539] While the common purpose "need not be specifically directed at the

535 ICC Mbarushimana 2011, para 286.

536 Ambos (Commentary edited by Triffterer and Ambos) 2016, 1010.

537 ICC Lubanga 2007, para 337.

538 ICC Katanga 2013, para 16; Eser (Commentary edited by Cassese, Gaeta and Jones) 2002, 802–803.

539 ICC Katanga 2014, para 1620.

commission of a crime [...] nor must the group pursue a purely criminal purpose or must its ultimate purpose be criminal,"[540]

> [o]nly those crimes which the group harboured the intention to commit (the common purpose being to commit the crime or encompassing its execution), and falling within the ordinary course of events, can therefore [...] incur the accused's liability under article 25(3)(d).[541]

The accused does not need to be a member of the group.[542] As a consequence, subparagraph (d) also applies to supplying weapons to a militia, for instance, who subsequently use them to commit war crimes—even if the arms dealer has no connection to that group other than business.

With regard to the third element, the significant contribution must be connected directly to the crime, not only to the general activities of the group.[543] Concerning the threshold of significance, a Pre-Trial Chamber took the view that it is lower than the substantiality threshold potentially required for aiding, abetting, and assisting.[544] Another Chamber identified various relevant factors:

> the sustained nature of the participation after acquiring knowledge of the criminality of the group's common purpose, any efforts made to prevent criminal activity or to impede the efficient functioning of the group's crimes, whether the person creates or merely executes the criminal plan, the position of the suspect in the group or relative to the group [and] perhaps most importantly the role the suspect played vis-à-vis the seriousness and scope of the crimes.[545]

Notably, Judge Fernández disagreed with the requirement of significance due to the term "in any other way" in subparagraph (d).[546] Thus, the objective elements of subparagraph (d) cover at least the conduct by organized criminal groups that significantly contributes to the commission of a crime, such

540 *ibid.*, para 1627.
541 *ibid.*, para 1630.
542 ICC Mbarushimana 2011, para 278; Ambos (Commentary edited by Triffterer and Ambos) 2016, 1013.
543 ICC Katanga 2014, para 1632.
544 ICC Ruto *et al.* 2012, para 354. For the opposite opinion see Ambos (Commentary edited by Triffterer and Ambos) 2016, 1011–1012.
545 ICC Mbarushimana 2011, para 284. (Footnotes omitted).
546 ICC Mbarushimana 2012.

as supplying weapons or funds. It must be noted in this regard, however, that not all illicit trade with armed groups committing international crimes satisfy the objective elements of a contribution under Article 25(3)(d) of the Rome Statute. For example, supplying drugs to a militia can result in voluntary drug consumption by individual fighters, which does not constitute a war crime, or in the use of drugs as a means of torture or humiliation of persons associated with the adversary party, which may constitute a war crime under Article 8 of the Rome Statute.

Moreover, subparagraph (d) contains *mens rea* requirements that differ from those for aiding, abetting, and assisting. Specifically, the contribution must be made intentionally and must either be made in furtherance of the group's criminal activity or in the knowledge of an intent of the group to commit a crime.[547] The requirement of intent thus only applies to "the conduct which constitutes the contribution and not the activity, purpose or criminal intention" of the group.[548] With regard to the second element, knowledge of the intention to commit a specific crime is sufficient and "it is therefore not required for the contributor to have the intent to commit any specific crime and not necessary for him or her to satisfy the mental element of the crimes charged."[549] Therefore, members of organized criminal groups supplying arms or financial means to armed groups in the knowledge that such group frequently commits crimes under the Statute are liable under Article 25(3)(d) of the Rome Statute. The intent of the conduct can be inferred from the economic purpose of organized criminal groups; for example, they mean to sell arms because it is their primary purpose. In the case of arms trade, as well as in the case of providing financial means to armed groups, both directly or via some form of economic cooperation, organized criminal groups are also aware of their contribution to the activities of the armed group. Knowledge of the group's criminal intention can be inferred from circumstantial evidence, such as if the frequent commission of crimes by that group is common knowledge, as in the situation of an arms embargo. Nevertheless, this last requirement cannot automatically be inferred from the fact that material or financial means are accessed through an illegal channel (i.e., through organized crime).

In addition to the relevance of participatory modes of liability with regard to the contribution of organized crime to crimes committed by other groups, they are also crucial for establishing the individual criminal responsibility of

547 ICC Katanga 2013, para 16.

548 ICC Katanga 2014, para 1638; Eser (Commentary edited by Cassese, Gaeta and Jones) 2002, 803.

549 ICC Mbarushimana 2011, para 289.

leaders of organized criminal groups for the actions of their subordinates, particularly for ordering the commission of crimes.[550] The elements of ordering a crime have been described as

> (a) the person is in a position of authority, (b) the person instructs another person in any form to either: (i) commit a crime which in fact occurs or is attempted or (ii) perform an act or omission in the execution of which a crime is carried out, (c) the order had a direct effect on the commission or attempted commission of the crime, and (d) the person is at least aware that the crime will be committed in the ordinary course of events as a consequence of the execution or implementation of the order.[551]

An order can be explicit or implicit, must not be given directly to the perpetrator and can be proven through circumstantial evidence.[552] Depending on the structure of an organized criminal group, the participatory mode of ordering a crime can be relevant to holding managers on every organizational level criminally responsible for operations conducted by other members of the group.

Overall, aiding, abetting, and assisting a crime under Article 25(3)(c) of the Rome Statute are especially relevant to contributions to international crimes by organized criminal groups, where the acting member has the intent to contribute to the commission of such a crime. The residual clause of participation under Article 25(3)(d) of the Rome Statute covers significant contributions to crimes committed by a group of people who lack this special intent. Knowledge of the intention of the group to commit a crime is sufficient. Lastly, members of organized criminal groups can be held criminally responsible for ordering the commission of a crime.

3.3.3 *Superior Responsibility*

In addition to individual criminal responsibility incurred as a result of control over the commission of a crime or participation therein, the Rome Statute holds superiors responsible for the actions of their subordinates without any active contribution by the superior. In particular, Article 28 establishes the criminal responsibility of superiors failing to act under certain circumstances. Leaders of organized criminal groups who do not commit or assist in

550 See also section 3.3.3.
551 ICC Ntaganda 2014, para 145.
552 ICTY Blaškić 2000, para 281–282.

committing a crime under Article 5 can thus be held responsible for failing to prevent, repress, or submit a crime to the relevant authorities.

Article 28 of the Rome Statute has been described as "an archetypal form of omission liability for superiors,"[553] and thus no act by the accused is required. Although superior responsibility is framed in the Rome Statute as a "*sui generis* form of liability,"[554] it is also sometimes treated as a distinct crime.[555] The principles of superior responsibility form part of customary international law, although whether its application to civilian superiors in Article 28(b) and the standards of liability required correspond to the customary standard is debated.[556]

Where an omission by a superior also constitutes a form of direct participation, such as when a superior's presence at a crime scene qualifies as abetting the commission of the crime, active participation under Article 25 of the Rome Statute prevails as *lex specialis*.[557]

Article 28 of the Rome Statute applies to military commanders or persons effectively acting as such in addition to other superior and subordinate relationships. The latter category, described in subparagraph (b), is commonly referred to as civilian superiors and encompasses all other superior–subordinate relationships. Leaders of organized criminal groups are thus usually covered by subparagraph (b). Nevertheless, it has been established that the superior–subordinate relationships can be both *de iure* and *de facto*, and that superior responsibility applies regardless of the official rank or other nonmilitary functions of the accused.[558] An ICC Pre-Trial Chamber held that persons effectively acting as a military commander (i.e., *de facto* military commanders or military-like commanders) include

> superiors who have authority and control over regular government forces such as armed police units or irregular forces (non-government forces) such as rebel groups, paramilitary units including, inter alia, armed resistance movements and militias that follow a structure of military hierarchy or a chain of command.[559]

---

553 ICTY Milutinović *et al.* 2009, para 79.

554 ICTY Halilović 2007, para 78.

555 Schabas (Commentary) 2016, 610; Laucci (Commentary edited by Fernandez, Pacreau and Maze) 2012, 864.

556 For more detail see Schabas (Commentary) 2016, 611.

557 ICC Bemba 2009, para 34 and 402; ICTY Stakić 2003, para 466; Triffterer and Arnold (Commentary edited by Triffterer and Ambos) 2016, 1096.

558 ICTY Delalić *et al.* 2001, para 191–192; Special Court for Sierra Leone AFRC Case 2007, para 784 ; ICC Bemba 2009, para 408; Schabas (Commentary) 2016, 612.

559 *ibid.*, para 410.

As a consequence, leaders of organized criminal groups could also be held responsible as military-like commanders under subparagraph (a) if the organized criminal group possesses an armed wing that satisfies the structural requirements outlined by the Chamber.

For both military and civilian superiors to be criminally responsible, Article 28 of the Rome Statute requires that the subordinates committing the crime are under effective control and command or authority of the accused; belonging to a chain of command is not sufficient *per se*.[560] No meaningful distinction exists between effective command and effective authority, required for *de iure* military commanders and all other superiors, respectively, although the term command means "authority, especially over armed forces."[561] Both are understood to refer to "the power to give orders and enforce obedience," whereas the term control is perceived as the "material ability or power to prevent and punish" the commission of a crime or submit it to the competent authorities.[562] A superior position of effective authority and control can be indicated by the person's official position, for example in the military or other hierarchical structure, the power to give orders, including to engage in hostilities, the capacity to enforce compliance with these orders, the person's actual tasks, and the power to promote, replace, remove, or discipline subordinates.[563] While an ICC Trial Chamber stated that the accused must have effective control "at least when the crimes were about to be committed,"[564] it remains controversial if effective control at the point in time when the superior failed to prevent or punish can suffice.[565] Effective authority and control is decisive, not the hierarchical or formal superior–subordinate relationship. Thus, superior responsibility is also applicable to superior–subordinate relationships across borders or different armed groups, such as when a State relies on guerilla groups to prevent incurring State responsibility.[566] For leaders of organized criminal groups to be responsible under Article 28 of the Rome Statute, they must have effective authority and control over subordinates committing a crime. While this requirement for superior–subordinate relationships is not problematic in well-structured hierarchical organizations, such as the Yakuza, it can be

560 ICTY Aleksovski 1999, para 73 *et seq.;* Triffterer and Arnold (Commentary edited by Triffterer and Ambos) 2016, 1086.
561 ICC Bemba 2009, para 412–413.
562 *ibid.*, para 413, 415; Schabas (Commentary) 2016, 614.
563 *ibid.*, para 417.
564 *ibid.*, para 419.
565 *ibid.*, para 418.
566 Triffterer and Arnold (Commentary edited by Triffterer and Ambos) 2016, 1086.

difficult to establish authority as well as control of leaders over criminal networks that function primarily due to its members' profit-based motivation or abstract threats of violence, such as in drug sales networks or Chinese triads.

Furthermore, to incur criminal liability under Article 28 of the Rome Statute, a superior must have failed to either prevent crimes or repress or submit them to the competent authority. The failure to fulfill any one of these duties can constitute a distinct violation.[567] The assessment of what constitutes necessary and reasonable measures must be made based on the superior's material ability, bearing in mind the degree of his effective control on a case-by-case basis.[568] Preventive measures can include the training of armed forces in IHL, issuing orders that bring certain practices in accord with the rules of war, or taking disciplinary measures.[569] Repression can take the form of stopping the commission of crimes or punishing those already committed.[570] Based on the formulation "as a result of" in the *chapeau* of both subparagraphs (a) and (b), and contrary to the jurisprudence by the *ad hoc* tribunals, the ICC Pre-Trial Chamber found a component of causality in Article 28 of the Rome Statute.[571] Given that repressing or submitting a matter to the competent authorities occur during or after the crime, the requirement of causality is confined to the duty of prevention. Thus, it must be shown that the "failure to exercise [the] duty to prevent crimes increased the risk"[572] of crimes being committed.

Article 28 of the Rome Statute establishes a *mens rea* requirement that differs from Article 30. For both military and civilian superiors, two alternatives exist. The first is knowledge that the forces or subordinates were committing or about to commit crimes. Knowledge cannot be presumed but must be established through evidence, such as through

> the number of illegal acts, their scope, whether their occurrence is widespread, the time during which the prohibited acts took place, the type and number of forces [or subordinates] involved, the means of available communication, the modus operandi of similar acts, the scope and nature of the superior's position and responsibility in the hierarchical

567 ICC Bemba 2009, para 436.

568 ICTY Blaškić 2004, para 395.

569 ICC Bemba 2009, para 437.

570 *ibid.*, para 439.

571 *ibid.*, para 421–423; Ambos (Commentary edited by Cassese, Gaeta and Jones) 2002, 860–861.

572 ICC Bemba 2009, para 426.

> structure, the location of the commander [or superior] at the time and the geographical location of the acts.[573]

The second *mens rea* alternative laid out in subparagraph (a) for military or military-like commanders is that the accused should have known that crimes were committed or about to be committed. This has been interpreted as involving negligence in failing to acquire information of the subordinates' crimes.[574] In the Chamber's view,

> the "should have known" standard requires more of an active duty on the part of the superior to take necessary measures to secure knowledge of the conduct of his troops and to inquire, regardless of the availability of information at the time, on the commission of the crime.[575]

By contrast, the alternative *mens rea* for nonmilitary superiors in subparagraph (b) requires that the superior "consciously disregarded information which clearly indicated" subordinates were committing or about to commit crimes. This is more demanding than the standard for military commanders, negligence, and rather amounts to a form of recklessness.[576] It is required that the civilian superior received information "putting a superior on notice of the risk that crimes might subsequently be carried out by his subordinates."[577] Thus, leaders of organized criminal groups who knew that crimes were committed or about to be will be liable under Article 28 of the Rome Statute regardless of their characterization of civilian or military-like superiors. In case actual knowledge cannot be proved, however, only leaders of military-like armed wings of organized criminal groups can be held responsible under the "should have known" standard. In all other cases, which will be the usual case for leaders of organized criminal groups, the leaders must have received and disregarded information as to the possible commission of crimes. This represents a significant additional burden on the Prosecution compared with the standard for military commanders.[578] However, in many cases of crimes committed by organized criminal groups, as discussed above, these crimes are either a constitutive part of the illicit business of the group or systematic in nature.[579] Both

---

573 *ibid.*, para 429.

574 *ibid.*, para 433.

575 *ibid.*

576 Ambos (Commentary edited by Cassese, Gaeta and Jones) 2002, 870.

577 ICTY Strugar 2008, para 304.

578 Ambos (Commentary edited by Cassese, Gaeta and Jones) 2002, 870.

579 See sections 3.2.1.2.2., 3.2.2.2 and 3.2.3.2.2.

circumstances would suggest that the leader of the relevant organized criminal group had knowledge of the crimes, and thus is liable under Article 28 of the Rome Statute.

Overall, superior responsibility under Article 28 facilitates prosecutions of leaders of organized criminal groups for crimes committed by subordinates under their effective control, including profit-generating activities such as human trafficking, plundering of and trade in cultural artefacts, as well as organized crime-related violence, especially if the internal hierarchy of an organized criminal group's armed wing is comparable to a military structure. Los Zetas in Mexico, for example, were created out of an elite group of the Mexican army and functioned in a similar manner to a military group.

3.4 Assessment

Current legal mechanisms for combating organized crime, including domestic prosecution, lack effectiveness.[580] The Rome Statute, designed to "put an end to the impunity for the perpetrators of [...] the most serious crimes of concern to the international community,"[581] has thus far not been used as a mechanism to combat organized crime and is often estimated not to provide an adequate forum to this end.[582] However, the detailed analysis of the ICC's jurisdiction over organized crime in the present chapter generates a more differentiated picture.

In fact, the Rome Statute's jurisdiction extends to various activities of organized criminal groups that currently remain unpunished, and is underexploited as a mechanism to address some of the most pressing issues of international cooperation. First, the ICC's international and complementary character is advantageous to organized crime prosecutions, especially in light of the impunity gap persisting in the current system dominated by domestic prosecutions. Second, the crimes named in Article 5 of the Rome Statute cover different and significant portions of the harm caused by organized crime. Third, the different modes of liability represent effective mechanisms to do justice to

580 See section 2.2.1.

581 Rome Statute 1998, Preamble, para 4.

582 Hauck 2016, 452. Hauck comments, "the *lex lata* brings us down to the fact that only in special cases transnational offenses show such heinous misconduct that they may even fit the definition of a core crime. [...] Trying only the grave cases [...] covers nothing but a small percentage of the whole range, similar to the tip of an iceberg".

various forms of involvement of organized crime in the commission of crimes, especially in hybrid crime–conflict settings.

Regarding the admissibility of cases, the ICC follows the principle of complementarity; that is, the ICC is an institution of last resort. Its role becomes crucial in situations where domestic judicial institutions do not function properly ("unable") or if their correct functioning is impeded by political or other considerations ("unwilling"). One important mechanism for organized crime to escape law enforcement is corruption, which includes judicial corruption. Where a legal system declines to investigate and prosecute specific powerful leaders of organized crime, Article 17 of the Rome Statute offers a vital method of delivering justice. In fact, in such a case, the ICC is often the only competent forum.

Moreover, with regard to preconditions to the exercise of jurisdiction, Article 12 of the Rome Statute provides for both a personality and territorial nexus to a State Party. In cases where organized criminal activities are spread over several jurisdictions, a crime can be prosecuted in its entirety regardless of whether several State Parties are involved or whether only part of the crime was perpetrated on the territory of a State Party. In addition, referring such a case to an international forum might increase the perception of legitimacy in all States involved and can solve disagreements as to the *forum conveniens*. The nexus requirement is nullified if a situation is referred to the ICC by the UNSC based on its determination of the existence of a breach or threat to international peace and security under Chapter VII of the UN Charter. As indicated by UNSC discussions as well as the establishment of the *ad hoc* tribunals, organized crime and its consequences, especially in connection with terrorism or armed conflicts, can amount to a threat to international security. In that case, a referral does not constitute an act *ultra vires*.

Regarding the jurisdiction of the ICC *ratione materiae*, several activities of organized criminal groups amount to crimes under Article 5 of the Rome Statute. With regard to genocide, it must be noted that although organized criminal groups can perpetrate enumerated acts in the course of their business activities, especially in the course of human trafficking and organized crime-related violence, the *dolus specialis* requirement as well as the protected groups are not in line with the usual economic interests of organized crime. Contributions to genocide as accessories that require a lower *mens rea* threshold are consequently more relevant in the context of organized crime than principal perpetratorship.

However, if the thresholds of a widespread or systematic attack based on an organizational policy are met, crimes against humanity cover a broader range of organized crime-related conduct because of the looser standards regarding the type of population to be attacked and the required *mens rea*. Human trafficking as well as victims' subsequent exploitation for labor, sex, or organ trade, illicit trade in cultural goods, and organized crime-related violence can be prosecuted as crimes against humanity. Moreover, when it comes to ill-treatment of customers or other stakeholders in the criminal value chain, such conduct can also constitute a crime against humanity, as is the case with migrant-related crimes reported from Libya.

The commission of war crimes by organized criminal groups requires a nexus to an armed conflict. Although war crimes can be committed by both combatants and civilians, the crime must be associated with the armed conflict. Members of organized criminal groups can form part of a party to the conflict (i.e., as combatants or fighters or directly participating in hostilities), and furthermore, organized criminal groups can be a party to a noninternational armed conflict themselves if both the intensity threshold and organization requirements are met. Moreover, a nexus can be established if the crimes committed were shaped by or dependent on an armed conflict. Under such limitations, organized criminal groups can commit war crimes related to human trafficking and organized crime-related violence, as well as other ill-treatment, often based on the same or similar enumerated acts as for crimes against humanity. Furthermore, organized criminal groups can be held responsible for property-related crimes in armed conflicts, namely with regard to the illicit trade in natural resources and cultural goods.

Additionally, the Rome Statute provides for several modes of responsibility that members of organized criminal groups can incur depending on their contribution to the commission of a crime. Article 25 defines as a principal perpetrator not only the direct perpetrator but also a person acting jointly with another or through another person. Chambers have interpreted these modes as also encompassing possible combinations of indirect and co-perpetration. Indirect co-perpetration can occur, *inter alia*, when a person controls an organization whose members commit a crime. Superior responsibility in Article 28 of the Rome Statute provides for criminal responsibility of a leader in a position of effective control and authority as a consequence of a failure to prevent, repress, or submit a crime by his subordinates to the relevant authorities. Moreover, different accessory modes of liability provide for criminal liability, such as for ordering, aiding, abetting, assisting, and contributing to the commission of a crime by a group acting with a common purpose. Consequently, a member of an organized criminal group can incur criminal responsibility for crimes committed by his subordinates as well as by other direct perpetrators given he provided a significant or essential contribution to the commission of the crime and has the required *mens rea*. In some cases, the person accused based on accessory modes of liability is not required to meet the *mens rea* requirements of the crime itself, such as the *dolus specialis* requirement for genocide, but it is sufficient that the perpetrator intentionally made the contribution and knew of the criminal intent of the group committing the crime. Thus, members of organized criminal groups can be held responsible for a large range of contributions to crimes committed by others, especially material or financial in nature.

Nevertheless, four general observations can be made as to the limitations of the Rome Statute vis-à-vis organized crime prosecutions. First, the Rome Statute imposes gravity thresholds relevant for prosecutorial discretion as well as the ICC's jurisdiction, namely in the contextual elements of the crimes. Although they not only limit the Rome Statute's application to organized crime but also to criminal conduct in general, the thresholds have often been interpreted in relation to organizational qualities, such as the policy element in crimes against humanity or the nexus and intensity requirement for war crimes. Such an interpretation poses a particular challenge to organized criminal organizations because of their network structure, which partly protects their leaders from law enforcement. However, Chambers recently began to place greater emphasis on organizational capability rather than structure. Concerning post-election violence in Kenya and the organizational quality of the perpetrators, the ICC Pre-Trial Chamber noted "that the formal nature of a group and the level of its organization should not be the defining criterion. Instead [...], a distinction should be drawn on whether a group has the capability to perform acts which infringe on basic human values."[583] The organizational requirement for noninternational armed conflict has been interpreted as focusing on the armed groups' "ability to plan and carry out military operations for a prolonged period of time,"[584] assessed based on factors such as "the extent to which military equipment, including firearms, are available; the force or group's ability to plan military operations and put them into effect; and the extent, seriousness, and intensity of any military involvement."[585] In relation to organized crime, the interpretation focusing on the ability to cause harm instead of the internal hierarchy encompasses a broader range of criminal conduct.

Second, the crimes listed in Article 5 of the Rome Statute generally focus on direct human suffering. Most of the enumerated acts describe violations of the physical or mental integrity of an individual. Only few crimes take a long-term

583 ICC Republic of Kenya 2010, para 90.

584 ICC Lubanga 2007, para 234.

585 ICC Lubanga 2012, para 537. See also ICC Lubanga 2007, para 234.

perspective on suffering caused as a consequence of another form of criminal conduct. Exceptions include the war crimes of extensive destruction of property, especially of cultural relevance, the denial of the right to a fair trial, or the transfer of a population into occupied territory. Very few crimes in the Rome Statute are more generally concerned with property or economic crimes. This approach excludes many of the core business activities of organized criminal groups, such as trade in contraband goods, systematic theft and handling of stolen goods, and evasion of tax and customs regulations. Nevertheless, activities covered by the Rome Statute, especially trafficking in persons and their exploitation for forced prostitution or labor and organ removal, illicit exploitation and trade in natural resources and cultural goods, as well as widespread organized crime-related violence as a byproduct, represent crucial illicit markets and are some of the most pressing issues in conflict zones and societies.

Third, the Rome Statute applies *mens rea* requirements that only rarely fall short of *dolus directus*; that is, intent and knowledge. Forms of *dolus eventualis*, such as recklessness or knowledge of the likelihood that certain conduct leads to the commission of a crime, are generally excluded. With relation to organized crime, this approach excludes all crimes committed by organized criminal groups as a consequence of a general lack of respect for human life but without virtual certainty. This includes the death of smuggled migrants or hostages that result from a substantial risk consciously taken by organized criminal groups from ICC jurisdiction.

Fourth, for a person to be liable, the Rome Statute requires a clear link between a person's conduct and the crime committed, namely causality or a significant contribution at minimum. In most cases, except for when the victim is a minor or in another way unable to make decisions independently, an element of voluntariness breaks the required link; this is because the nature of the crime changes (i.e., no crime exists) if an act is willfully caused by the victim alone, or the crime is re-characterized, such as in the case of the crime of drug consumption versus that of causing physical or mental suffering. This is especially relevant for traffic in drugs, because the organized criminal group knows that at least the most harmful and addictive drugs will lead to physical and mental decay in the course of ordinary events. However, such decay is caused by the victim herself, and thus does not incur criminal responsibility under the Rome Statute.

In the following chapter, possible developments in the field of international criminal law are examined that counteract some of the aforementioned challenges, or otherwise facilitate the reduction of the current impunity gap with regard to organized crime through applying international criminal law.

CHAPTER 4

Organized Crime and International Criminal Law *De Lege Ferenda*

In Chapter 2, a legal definition of organized crime was provided, its characteristics as a real-world phenomenon as well as relevant international regimes were discussed, and an overview of the role of organized crime in previous international tribunals and the negotiations leading to the Rome Statute was given. In Chapter 3, an in-depth analysis of all relevant questions regarding organized crime relating to admissibility, exercise of jurisdiction, jurisdiction *ratione materiae*, and modes of liability under the Rome Statute *de lege lata* was conducted. The current chapter builds on this content and discusses what developments *de lege ferenda* could facilitate a wider application of international criminal law to fill the impunity gap that remains in relation to organized crime. First, it analyzes the possibility of departing from current interpretations of the Rome Statute, possibly including an amendment of the Elements of Crimes, based on customary international law as well as precedence within the current framework of the core crimes. Second, the possibility to introduce selected crimes committed by organized criminal groups as an addition to Article 5 of the Rome Statute will be examined (i.e., expanding jurisdiction *ratione materiae*). Finally, the establishment of a new separate tribunal dedicated to prosecutions of organized crime will be envisaged and its key features outlined.

4.1 Potential Developments within the Current Jurisdictional Framework

As the in-depth analysis of the *lex lata* in Chapter 3 indicated, certain aspects of ICC practice currently complicate prosecutions of members of organized criminal groups, although the practice conflicts with customary international law and/or relevant precedence and leaves legal uncertainty. This is the case, in particular, for the general exclusion of *dolus eventualis* by the current interpretation of Article 30 of the Rome Statute, for the special purpose requirement for pillage laid out in the Elements of Crimes and for the inclusion of human trafficking in the crime of enslavement. The (re-)interpretation of the Rome Statute by the ICC Judges and possibly amendments to the Elements of Crimes

 | DOI:10.1163/9789004462588_005

that would align the Rome Statute with customary international law and previous case law could alleviate these difficulties, and will be examined in the following sections.

Interpretation and re-interpretation are integral parts of the functioning of the Rome Statute. Despite the work of the *ad hoc* and other international or hybrid criminal tribunals, the Rome Statute at the time of its drafting (and to a lesser extent still today) constituted a major development in international criminal law, and thus included numerous progressive provisions. Over the years, the exact interpretation of these provisions needed to be established in the Elements of Crimes or be developed by the jurisprudence of the Court. For this purpose, ICC Judges may apply the law as outlined in Article 21 of the Rome Statute, namely (in order of priority) the Statute, Elements of Crimes and Rules of Procedure and Evidence, applicable treaties and the principles and rules of international law, as well as general principles of law derived by the Court from national legal systems. They may base their interpretations on the precedence of the ICC as well as on the means of interpretation outlined in Articles 31 and 32 of the Vienna Convention on the Law of Treaties. The former includes "any subsequent practice in the application of the treaty which establishes the agreement of the parties regarding its interpretation."[1] Thus, the Rome Statute not only provides for adding specificity to its provisions through interpretation but also for adapting established interpretations in case of new legal or technological developments.

Furthermore, the Elements of Crimes provide guidance as to the constitutive elements, subjective and objective, of the crimes named in Article 5 of the Rome Statute. Except for the primacy of the Statute, the same rules of interpretation apply. Moreover, the Rome Statute provides for their amendment. Amendments to the Elements of Crimes are governed by Article 9; "[t]hey are a somewhat flexible instrument capable of adjusting the subject-matter provisions of the Rome Statute [...] without the need for full-blown amendment."[2] There exists an ongoing controversy regarding the relationship of the Elements of Crimes to the Statute in general and the binding force of the Elements in particular: both the ICTY and SCSL have rejected the binding character of the Elements of Crimes, the SCSL arguing that they contradict customary international law.[3] The ICC Trial Chamber held in *Bashir* that the Elements of Crimes are binding unless there is an irreconcilable contradiction to the

1 Vienna Convention 1969, Article 31(3)(b).

2 Schabas (Commentary) 2016, 322.

3 ICTY Krstić 2004, para 224, footnote 366; Special Court for Sierra Leone AFRC Case 2007, para 753.

Rome Statute.[4] Judge Usacka dissented.[5] Nevertheless, as the Trial Chamber indicated, the application of the Elements of Crimes as they stand, or amending them if necessary, provides the best safeguard for the *nullum crimen sine lege* principle.[6] Amendments can be proposed by any State Party, an absolute majority of the Judges or the Prosecutor and submitted by the latter two to the Advisory Committee on Legal Texts.[7] Amendments are adopted by a two-thirds majority in the Assembly of States Parties.[8]

Although treaty law differing from customary international law prevails as *lex specialis,* an interpretation of the Rome Statute and Elements of Crimes in line with customary international law decreases the complexity of the international legal system and increases legal certainty.[9] Customary international law, one of the sources of international law according to Article 38(1)(b) of the Statute of the ICJ, requires "evidence of a general practice accepted as law",[10] or, put differently,

> for a new customary rule to be formed, not only must the acts concerned 'amount to a settled practice', but they must be accompanied by the *opinio juris sive necessitatis.* Either the States taking such action or other States in a position to react to it, must have behaved so that their conduct is 'evidence of a belief that this practice is rendered obligatory by the existence of a rule of law requiring it.'[11]

It is generally subdivided into the material element of State practice and the psychological factor of *opinio iuris.*[12] Amendments or re-interpretations based on customary international law can address provisions in the Rome Statute and Elements of Crimes that already differed from international customary law at the time of their drafting, as well as provisions that differ from customary international law because of a recent evolution of the latter.

The following analyses study current interpretations of the Rome Statute, compare them with customary international law and precedence, and discuss

4 ICC Bashir 2009, para 117–120.
5 ICC Bashir 2009 (Dissent).
6 ICC Bashir 2009, para 131.
7 Rome Statute 1998, Article 9(2); Regulations of the Court 2004, Regulation 5.
8 *ibid.*
9 ICJ Nicaragua 1986, para 180–181.
10 ICJ Statute 1945, Article 38(1)(b).
11 ICJ Nicaragua 1986, para 207 citing ICJ North Sea Continental Shelf 1069, para 77.
12 For more detail see Shaw 2008, 72 *et seq.*

possible re-interpretations and amendments and their implications for prosecutions of organized crime.

4.1.1 *Mental Elements*

4.1.1.1 *Dolus Eventualis*

Organized criminal groups are motivated *per definitionem* by economic profit.[13] Therefore in most cases, inflicting human suffering is not their primary goal. For example, the primary goal of organ trade is economic gain, that of organized crime-related violence is intimidation, and that of low-quality boats for migrant smuggling is cost reduction. Some of the activities of organized criminal groups discussed in Chapter 3 clearly lead to crimes under Article 5 of the Rome Statute; for example, the trade in cadaver kidneys always entails the crime of murder or willful killing, and the perpetrator knows that death will occur in the ordinary course of events.[14] In other cases, however, such as organized crime-related violence and migrant smuggling under extreme weather conditions, the acting members of organized criminal groups may merely reconcile themselves with a high probability that death or other forms of human suffering will occur.[15] Thus, the exclusion of *dolus eventualis* under the current interpretation of Article 30 of the Rome Statute excludes many crimes perpetrated by organized criminal groups and is especially relevant in this context. A potential re-interpretation as well as its implications for organized crime prosecutions are examined in the following paragraph.

For the first time in the history of international criminal law, the Rome Statute codifies in Article 30 a mental element generally required to trigger individual criminal responsibility. Although Article 30 requires intent and knowledge "unless otherwise provided," the exact meaning of intent and knowledge remains unsettled, in particular regarding the question of whether it includes *dolus eventualis* and what alternative sources the term "unless otherwise provided" permits. However, a strict interpretation of Article 30 of the Rome Statute, as has been applied in recent judgments of the ICC requiring at least "virtual certainty"[16] that an act will lead to the commission of a crime, differs from the jurisprudence of the *ad hoc* tribunals and many national penal laws.[17] A strict interpretation of Article 30 excludes criminal responsibility for organized and other crimes committed as a consequence of a perpetrator

13 See section 2.1.1.

14 See, e.g., section 3.2.2.2.1.

15 See, e.g., sections 3.2.2.2.2. and 3.2.2.2.5.

16 ICC Lubanga 2014, para 447.

17 Werle and Jessberger 2005, 38.

reconciling himself with a high probability of a crime being committed, if the likelihood of the occurrence of the crime does not amount to virtual certainty.

Although Article 30 of the Rome Statute establishes the default rule for the *mens rea* requirement for crimes under ICC jurisdiction, it leaves space for differing requirements for particular crimes and modes of liability. In the Statute as well as in the Elements of Crimes, a number of exceptions exist both below and above the threshold of intent and knowledge, the so-called article 30 standard.[18] Moreover, the term "unless otherwise provided" in Article 30, in contrast to terms such as "other grounds [...] provided for *in this Statute*"[19] in Article 31(1), allows for modifications based on sources other than the Statute, in particular the Elements of Crimes and, secondarily according to Article 21(1), customary international law. Given the latter's critical role in the evolution and thus in the interpretation of *mens rea* requirements, such as for the war crime of willful killing, a broad interpretation of the term "unless otherwise provided" does not violate the *nullum crimen sine lege* principle.[20] It is therefore pertinent to interpret *mens rea* requirements and criticize current jurisprudence based on customary international law, as expressed in previous jurisprudence, national legal systems, and scholarly writings.

However, the understanding of subjective elements in criminal law varies significantly, especially between civil law and common law countries and in particular with regard to *dolus eventualis*. While recklessness is often equated with *dolus eventualis*, *dolus eventualis* in fact originates in Romano-Germanic law systems and entails an element of foreseeability and a volitional element, often described as the perpetrator reconciling himself with the prohibited result.[21] Recklessness is a common law concept denoting the conscious creation of unjustifiable risk and is distinct from intent because of the lack of a volitional element.[22] Still, the threshold for the volitional element in *dolus eventualis* is not identical in different civil law systems, ranging from an awareness of a substantial or high degree of *probability* to substantial or serious *risk*.[23] The attempts to define *dolus eventualis* and recklessness were abandoned early during the negotiations of the Rome Statute, although it is controversial

18 Rome Statute 1998, e.g., Articles 6, 7(1)(h), 28.

19 *ibid.*, Article 31(1). Emphasis added.

20 Werle and Jessberger 2005, 45–46. *Contra*: Fletcher and Ohlin 2005, 555 *et seq.* arguing that customary international law is insufficiently stable to be used in criminal law.

21 Cassese 2003, 168; Roxin 1997, 376; McAuley and McCutcheon 2000, 301–303; Badar 2008, 498–499.

22 Badar 2012, 425; Badar 2008, 497–498.

23 Piragoff and Robinson (Commentary edited by Triffterer and Ambos) 2016, footnote 67.

whether their exclusion was merely because of different national conceptions or whether it was indicative of an intent of the drafters to exclude the concepts from the *mens rea* requirements of the Statute altogether.[24] Nevertheless, a comparative analysis reveals that a strictly construed understanding of *dolus eventualis* requiring a high degree of probability is a common denominator of civil law countries and can be defined as follows:[25]

> It is a form of criminal intent which satisfies the threshold for the mental element of intentional crimes. It is an unfocused intent that occurs when the perpetrator foresees the possibility that the consequence of his act exceeds the goal he intended—whether legitimate or illegitimate—to another unlawful goal which he did not intend initially, and nevertheless performs the act, reconciling himself with the consequences.[26]

Thus, three distinct possible views exist. First, based on the abovementioned definition, *dolus eventualis* may indeed be a form of intent and hence be included in Article 30 of the Rome Statute because of its volitional element. Second, the application of *dolus eventualis* can only be based on the term "unless otherwise provided," or, third, the applicability of *dolus eventualis* is excluded in the Rome Statute altogether unless explicitly stated in the Statute or Elements of Crimes.[27] Based on the third possibility, Antonio Cassese leveled the following critique:

> It appears questionable to have excluded recklessness as a culpable mens rea under the Statute. One fails to see why, at least in the case of war crimes, this last mental element may not suffice for criminal responsibility to arise. Admittedly, in the case of genocide, crimes against humanity and aggression, the extreme gravity of the offence presupposes that it may only be perpetrated when intent and knowledge are present. However, for less serious crimes, such as war crimes, current international law must be taken to allow for recklessness: for example, it is admissible to convict a person who, when shelling a town, takes a high and unjustifiable

24 In favor of the former: *ibid.*; Goy 2012, 25; in favor of the latter: ICC Bemba 2009, para 365 *et seq.*

25 See Badar 2009 for a discussion of Egypt, France, Italy, South Africa, Germany and Islamic Jurisprudence.

26 Cited in *ibid.*, 15.

27 i. Piragoff and Robinson (Commentary edited by Triffterer and Ambos) 2016; Badar 2012; Goy 2012; Ambos 2009; ii. Werle and Jessberger 2005; iii. Fletcher and Ohlin 2005.

> risk that civilians will be killed—without, however, intending, that they be killed—with the result that the civilians are, in fact, thereby killed. [...] Hence, on this score the Rome Statute marks a step backwards with respect to *lex lata*, and possibly creates a loophole: persons responsible for war crimes, when they acted recklessly, may be brought to trial and convicted before national courts, while they would be acquitted by the ICC.[28]

The ICTY defined the subjective element required for committing a crime, other than by way of a joint criminal enterprise, as the "intent to commit the crime, or [...] awareness of the probability, in the sense of the substantial likelihood, that the crime would occur as a consequence of [the accused's] conduct."[29] The Appeals Chamber noted "that an awareness of a higher likelihood of risk and a volitional element must be incorporated into the legal standard"[30] of the *mens rea* requirement. It defined the standard as awareness of substantial likelihood and stated that the volitional element could be inferred from acting with this awareness.[31] The ICTY referred to *dolus eventualis*; for example, in relation to ordering, participation in a criminal enterprise, killing, and extermination.[32] Regarding extermination, this opinion concurred with ICTR jurisprudence stating that "the act(s) or omission(s) may be done with intention, recklessness, or gross negligence."[33]

Early Decisions at the ICC adopted the ICTY's approach. In the *Lubanga* Confirmation Decision, the Pre-Trial Chamber noted that in addition to *dolus directus* of the first and second degree, Article 30 of the Rome Statute included "situations in which the suspect (a) is aware of the risk that the objective element of the crime may result from his or her actions or omissions, and (b) accepts such an outcome by reconciling himself or herself with it or consenting to it."[34] The Pre-Trial Chamber distinguished between two scenarios:

> Firstly, if the risk of bringing about the objective elements of the crime is substantial (that is, there is a likelihood that it "will occur in the ordinary

28 Cassese 1999, 153–154.
29 ICTY Limaj *et al.* 2005, para 509.
30 ICTY Blaškić 2004, para 41.
31 *ibid.*, para 42.
32 *ibid.*; ICTY Tadić 1999; ICTY Kupreškić *et al.* 2000; ICTY Stakić 2003.
33 ICTR Kayishema and Ruzindana 1999, para 146.
34 ICC Lubanga 2007, para 352.

> course of events"), the fact that the suspect accepts the idea of bringing about the objective elements of the crime can be inferred from:
> (i) the awareness by the suspect of the substantial likelihood that his or her actions or omissions would result in the realization of the objective elements of the crime; and
> (ii) the decision by the suspect to carry out his or her actions or omissions despite such awareness.
>
> Secondly, if the risk of bringing about the objective elements of the crime is low, the suspect must have clearly or expressly accepted the idea that such objective elements may result from his or her actions or omissions.[35]

In *Katanga and Ngudjolo*, the majority of the Chamber agreed with the *Lubanga* Decision but found elaborating on it unnecessary because their Decision was based on *dolus directus*.[36] However, the *Bemba* Pre-Trial Chamber found that *dolus eventualis* was not included in Article 30 of the Rome Statute and that the term occurring "in the ordinary course of events" requires a minimum threshold of virtual certainty.[37] This interpretation was later followed by the *Lubanga* Appeals Chamber.[38] This approach was criticized based on the following argument:

> [i]n order not to undervalue people's lives and interests, particularly in contemporary armed conflicts where civilians and their properties become the main targets, [...] it becomes inevitable to adopt the concept of *dolus eventualis* as the basis of intentional crimes under the ICC Statute, particularly in cases where there is clear evidence from which the Court can infer the perpetrator's acceptance of the illegitimate consequences of his act or his underestimation of the gravity of such consequences.[39]

This debate is highly relevant in light of, for example, the severe violence against the civilian population carried out by armed wings of drug trafficking organizations (e.g., in Mexico), as well as concerning migrant-related crimes and criminal conduct by hybrid groups in conflict zones.

---

35 *ibid.*, para 353.
36 ICC Katanga and Ngudjolo 2008, footnote 329 and para 531.
37 ICC Bemba 2009, para 369.
38 ICC Lubanga 2014, para 447.
39 Badar 2009, 489.

As is evident in the jurisprudence of the *ad hoc* tribunals and the ICC as well as the debate outlined in this section, the acceptance of a restrictive understanding of *dolus eventualis,* at least with regard to selected crimes and participatory modes of liability, has significant support in national and international practice and would facilitate prosecutions of organized crime before the ICC. Thus, loosening the interpretation of the Article 30 standard forms part of the *lex ferenda* in the context of organized crime prosecutions before the ICC.

4.1.1.2 The *Dolus Specialis* Requirement for Pillage

Pillage is the most relevant property-related crime in the Rome Statute with regard to organized crime because its elements describe most closely the conduct of appropriation of a victim's property for subsequent profit-generating trade.[40] However, the Elements of Crimes of the war crime of pillage contain the *mens rea* requirement of appropriating property "for personal or private use." The element is at odds with previous case law as well as customary international law. In addition, it creates uncertainty in cases of systematic pillage, if there is State involvement or if the proceeds of a subsequent trade do not only benefit individual perpetrators. Therefore, this section examines a possible reinterpretation or amendment of the Elements of Crimes.

The war crime of pillage is part of customary international law for international and noninternational armed conflict, and has been included in various international and national legal documents as well as military codes and the statutes of international criminal tribunals.[41] As early as the 19th century, it was recognized by the Lieber Code, the Brussels Declaration, and the Oxford Manual.[42] The Hague Convention of 1907 prohibits "[t]he pillage of a town or place, even when taken by assault"; the provision was copied *verbatim* in the Rome Statute. The Fourth Geneva Convention simply states in its Article 33 that "pillage is prohibited," and Additional Protocol II prohibits pillage against protected persons "at any time and in any place whatsoever."[43] The official commentary on the Fourth Geneva Convention underlines the deliberately chosen absolute character of the provision as well as its general scope,

40 See section 3.2.3.2.2.1 and 3.2.3.2.2.2.

41 For a detailed list of national legislation and military codes, see International Committee of the Red Cross 2019, Rule 52, footnotes 6 and 7; Nuremberg Charter 1945, Article 6; ICTY Statute 1993, Article 3(e); ICTR Statute 1994, Article4(f); UNTAET Regulation 2000, section 6.1.(b)(xvi); Statute of the Iraqi Special Tribunal 2003, Article 13(b) No. 17; Statute for the SCSL 2002, Article 3(f).

42 Lieber Code 1863, Article 44 ; Brussels Declaration 1874, Article 18 and 39 ; Oxford Manual 1880, Article 32.

43 Protocol II to Geneva Convention 1977, Article 4(2).

including systematic and petty, authorized and unauthorized acts of pillage of public and private, movable and immovable property.[44]

The Elements of Crimes of the Rome Statute, however, introduce a *dolus specialis* to the definition that was not part of any previously written documents or custom. The Elements of Crimes of Articles 8(2)(b)(xvi) and 8(2)(e)(v) of the Rome Statute stipulate that the perpetrator of pillage must have "intended to deprive the owner of the property and to appropriate it *for private or personal use.*"[45] Footnotes 47 and 62 clarify that appropriations justified by military necessity do not constitute the crime of pillage. However, there is no further guidance as to the interpretation of personal or private use.

Case law of international tribunals has established that pillage may affect both private and public property. The term is general in scope, comprising not only large-scale seizures of property within the framework of systematic economic exploitations of occupied territory but also acts of appropriation committed by individual soldiers for their private gain.[46]
The consequences for the victims, not the value of the pillaged property is decisive.[47] Therefore, the SCSL Trial Chamber, based on the SCSL Statute containing an identical provision to the Rome Statute, stated that the mental element of "personal or private use" is at variance with previous case law "since it may not include 'organized' and 'systematic' seizure of property."[48] According to the Trial Chamber, the element is "unduly restrictive and ought not to be an element of the crime of pillage."[49] Indeed, the element was contested during the drafting period of the Elements of Crimes but ultimately accepted to distinguish the crime of pillage more clearly from the crime of destroying or seizing property in Article 8(2)(b)(xiii) of the Rome Statute.[50]

With regard to organized criminal activities in conflict zones, the mental element raises important questions, such as: what criteria can be applied to distinguish public or military from personal or private use? For example, if the booty allocated to each soldier is considered part of his salary, as was the case in many wars up to the 20th century, is it the individual soldier or rather the

44 Pictet (Commentary) 1958, 226–227.
45 Elements of Crimes 2010, Articles 8(2)(b)(xvi) and 8(2)(e)(v), para 2. Emphasis added.
46 ICTY Naletilić and Martinović 2003, para 612.
47 *ibid.*, para 612–617. Also, e.g., ICTY Delalić *et al.* 1998, para 59;. ICTY Gotovina *et al.* 2011, para 1778; IG Farben Case 1948; Flick Case 1947; Krupp Case 1948; International Court of Justice Armed Activities Case 2005.
48 Special Court for Sierra Leone AFRC Case 2007, para 754.
49 *ibid.*
50 Hosang 1999, 176–177 and footnote 99.

military gaining from the plunder?[51] If the financial or material gain from pillage is distributed between individuals and an armed group, as was the case for proceeds from conflict diamonds in Sierra Leone, under which circumstances does the provision apply? Can a third party profit from the personal or private gain? Does the provision also prohibit plunder benefiting a public agency other than the military?

The understanding of pillage under customary international law as elaborated by case law provides guidance on these questions. Aligning the definition of the war crime of pillage in the Rome Statute with its definition under customary international law would therefore increase legal certainty and reduce grey areas in interpretation.

Concerning organized crime, deleting the term "for personal or private use" from the Elements of Crimes or establishing a broad interpretation would open up the application of the Rome Statute to all kinds of systematic or organized pillage, focusing on the consequences for the victims rather than the perpetrators' exact intentions.

4.1.2 *Material Elements: Trafficking in Persons and Enslavement*

Trafficking in persons is the only profit-generating activity by organized criminal groups expressly included in the Rome Statute, which defines it as covered by the crime of enslavement.[52] However, enslavement is a crime with a longstanding history in international law and its legal definition differs from that of human trafficking.[53] Therefore, it is not entirely clear how the inclusion of human trafficking in the crime of enslavement can be understood and what elements need to be proved, consequently reducing legal certainty for prosecutions of human trafficking by organized criminal groups. The following section analyzes how a clear and consistent interpretation of the meaning of human trafficking under the Rome Statute can be developed.

The Rome Statute includes enslavement as an *actus reus* of crimes against humanity in Article 7(1)(c). The Elements of Crimes define enslavement as a status or condition where "[t]he perpetrator exercised any or all of the powers attaching to the right of ownership over one or more persons, such as by purchasing, selling, lending or bartering such a person or persons, or by imposing on them a similar deprivation of liberty."[54] A footnote adds: "It is also understood that the conduct described in this element includes trafficking in

51 Pictet (Commentary) 1958, 226.

52 See section 3.2.2.2.1.

53 See section 2.1.2.2.

54 Elements of Crimes 2010, Article 7(1)(c), para 1.

persons, in particular women and children."[55] However, despite "strong overlaps between the crime of slavery and trafficking,"[56] crucial distinctions exist between the two concepts, in particular the absence of a constitutive element of ownership in the definition of human trafficking. The provision of the Rome Statute originated from the Slavery Convention of 1926 that defines slavery as "the status or condition of a person over whom any or all of the powers attaching to the right of ownership are exercised."[57] It defines the slave trade as

> all acts involved in the capture, acquisition or disposal of a person with intent to reduce him to slavery; all acts involved in the acquisition of a slave with a view to selling or exchanging him; all acts of disposal by sale or exchange of a slave acquired with a view to being sold or exchanged, and, in general, every act of trade or transport in slaves.[58]

Human trafficking, on the other hand, is defined in the Trafficking Protocol supplementing the Palermo Convention as

> recruitment, transportation, transfer, harbouring or receipt of persons, by means of the threat or use of force or other forms of coercion, of abduction, of fraud, of deception, of the abuse of power or of a position of vulnerability or of the giving or receiving of payments or benefits to achieve the consent of a person having control over another person, for the purpose of exploitation. Exploitation shall include, at a minimum, the exploitation of the prostitution of others or other forms of sexual exploitation, forced labour or services, slavery or practices similar to slavery, servitude or the removal of organs.[59]

There remains some degree of uncertainty regarding the definition of trafficking, for instance concerning the relationship between smuggling and trafficking, the requirement of passing international borders, and the meaning of coercion.[60] Nevertheless, trafficking, as opposed to slavery, does not explicitly

---

55 *ibid.*, footnote 53.
56 Heintze and Lülf 2016, 159.
57 Slavery Convention 1926, Article 1(1).
58 *ibid.*, Article 1(2).
59 Protocol on Human Trafficking 2000, Article 3(a).
60 Bassiouni *et al.* 2010. Hauck, on the contrary, argues that the crime is clearly defined in Article 3 of the Protocol on Human Trafficking and in many domestic jurisdictions, but that the crime lacks in state practice. Hauck 2016, 464.

or implicitly require an element of ownership. The juxtaposition of slavery and slavery-like practices and other forms of exploitation in the second sentence of the Palermo definition underlines the distinct definitions of the two crimes. Therefore, "if this provision [the trafficking provision in the Rome Statute] [...] is to have any meaning at all, then the concept of exercising the power of ownership must be given a broad reading."[61]

In this context, however, the status of human trafficking as part of the customary norm prohibiting slavery is subject to discussion. The prohibition of slavery constitutes a norm of customary international law as well as an *ius cogens* norm.[62] However, the customary norm in its original form was restricted to chattel slavery, and the *travaux préparatoires* regarding the relevant codifications of the prohibition of slavery clearly indicate that States did not mean the norm to encompass human trafficking.[63] Moreover, the relevant State practice is inconclusive; while most States have outlawed slavery in their national legislation, the resulting laws are rarely used to prosecute cases of human trafficking.[64] In fact, many States are implementing legislation on human trafficking in addition to and independently of laws on slavery.[65] Nevertheless, significant scholarly support exists for the argument that the customary norm has evolved to encompass all forms of human trafficking.[66] Indeed, the work of representative organs of the UN as well as developments in treaty law, which may adduce evidence for State practice along with the necessary *opinio iuris*, exhibit a tendency toward including human trafficking in the definition of slavery. For example, the Human Rights Committee welcomed the Italian judiciary treating "offences concerning trafficking in women and others for the purposes of prostitution as acts which can be assimilated to slavery"[67]; the Commission on Human Rights has identified trafficking in children, the sale of children, child prostitution, and child pornography as "modern forms of slavery"[68]; and the Working Group on Contemporary Forms of Slavery declared that transborder trafficking of women and girls for sexual exploitation constitutes a contemporary form of slavery.[69] The UNGA dedicated the 1996 International Day for the Abolition of Slavery to the problem of trafficking in humans and repeatedly

61 Hall (Commentary edited by Triffterer and Ambos) 2016, 247.

62 International Committee of the Red Cross 2019, Rule 94; Bassiouni *et al.* 2010.

63 United Nations Economic and Social Council 1953; Bossuyt 1987.

64 Gallagher 2008, 411–412.

65 *ibid.*, 412.

66 Farrior 1997; Bunch 1995; Inglis 2001; Malone 2001; Bassiouni 2002.

67 Report of the Human Rights Committee 1998, A/53/40, para 333.

68 Commission on Human Rights 1992.

69 Working Group on Contemporary Forms of Slavery 1998, B(4)(1).

called upon UN member States to ratify and implement international slavery conventions in their considerations of human trafficking.[70] The 1999 Convention of the International Labor Organization (ILO) concerning the prohibition and immediate action for the elimination of the worst forms of child labor prohibits in its Article 3(a) "all forms of slavery or practices similar to slavery, such as the sale and trafficking of children, debt bondage and serfdom and forced or compulsory labour, including forced or compulsory recruitment of children for use in armed conflict," suggesting that trafficking in children is a practice at least similar to slavery. The European Convention on Trafficking in Human Beings recognizes in its preamble that human "trafficking can lead to slavery," and the Charter of Fundamental Rights of the EU in its Article 5 entitled "Prohibition of slavery" contains a specific provision on human trafficking. However, the validity of the abovementioned treaties for establishing customary international law was criticized because of the existence of reservations, small number of ratifications, and lack of a legally binding character.[71] The references to slavery and slavery-like practices in the Trafficking Protocol supplementing the Palermo Convention (as cited above) as well as the reference to human trafficking in the provision on enslavement in the Elements of Crimes of the Rome Statute indicate an increasing tendency to relate slavery and trafficking to each other, although they do not provide guidance on the exact relationship between the two concepts. In sum, a customary norm including human trafficking in all its manifestations in the definition of slavery cannot be unequivocally established.

In *Kunarac*, however, the ICTY Appeals Chamber established indicative factors for determining whether a particular situation is a form of enslavement, namely the

> control of someone's movement, control of physical environment, psychological control, measures taken to prevent or deter escape, force, threat of force or coercion, duration, assertion of exclusivity, subjection to cruel treatment and abuse, control of sexuality and forced labour.[72]

The ICC Pre-Trial Chamber later added "the personal circumstance of the victim, including his/her vulnerability"[73] to the list. This broad understanding of

70 E.g., A/RES/50/167 1995, para 6 and 12.

71 E.g., Hauck 2016, 464.

72 ICTY Kunarac 2002, para 119.

73 ICC Ntaganda 2014, footnote 209.

the exercise of rights of ownership includes human trafficking as defined in the Additional Protocol to the Palermo Convention.

Hence, although a customary norm on human trafficking cannot be clearly detected at this point, significant evidence exists of an ongoing evolution of the interpretation of enslavement. Already in 2008, it seemed

> clear that international law is in a State of flux and that changes to the customary norms are currently underway. […] However, on balance, and taking into account recent developments in international criminal law, it appears that […] linking the two practices and their relevant legal frameworks, is on the ascendancy.[74]

Overall, establishing a clear and consistent interpretation of enslavement that gives the element of ownership a broad reading, so as to encompass the definition of human trafficking in all its manifestations, will open the door for prosecutions related to one of the most valuable illegal markets today; furthermore, it will provide a mechanism for overcoming current shortcomings in international law enforcement. The indicative factors for enslavement identified by the ICC Pre-Trial Chamber can be taken as a basis for further elaboration.

4.2 Expanded Jurisdiction *Ratione Materiae*

Amendments to the Rome Statute were envisaged from the outset of its drafting and the corresponding procedure set out in the Statute itself to ensure that it can incorporate and reflect legal, technological, and other developments. Expanding the ICC jurisdiction *ratione materiae* to use existing expertise and infrastructure for an increased scope of international crimes could subject a broader range of organized crime to international justice. After a short overview of the amendment process, the following section discusses criteria for the introduction of new crimes, and then examines and proposes first drafts for possible definitions for contextual elements of new crimes and, if relevant, for the material elements of the crimes of drug trafficking; illicit trade in arms and ammunition, natural resources, and cultural goods; migrant smuggling; corruption; and money laundering.

74 Gallagher 2008, 418.

The procedure to amend substantial provisions of the Rome Statute is set out in its Article 121.[75] Any State Party can propose an amendment by submitting it to the Secretary-General of the UN who circulates it to all State Parties. After a minimum of three months, the Assembly of States Parties can decide with a two-third majority of those present and voting to take up the proposal, either directly or by convening a Review Conference. Review Conferences are governed by Article 123 of the Rome Statute, which is closely related to Article 121 and which it references with regard to the adoption and entry into force of any amendments. As a consequence, a Review Conference "is really nothing more nor less than a special meeting of the Assembly of States Parties, albeit with an agenda focused on amendment of the Statute."[76] An amendment must be adopted with a two-thirds majority of States Parties and enters into force for all States Parties a year after the deposit of the instruments of ratification or acceptance by seven-eighths of them. A State Party disagreeing with the amendment may withdraw from the Rome Statute with immediate effect. An exception is provided for amendments to Articles 5 to 8 of the Rome Statute, that is, the ICC's jurisdiction *ratione materiae*. Such amendments enter into force only for those States accepting the amendments one year after the deposit of their instrument of ratification or acceptance and do not apply to any other State Party.

While this special procedure facilitates the use of the ICC infrastructure for the prosecution of additional crimes for those States willing to accept jurisdiction, it also bears the risk of reducing the effectiveness of newly introduced crimes because of fragmentation and reduced incentivization to negotiate a broad consensus.

Thus far, amendments have been introduced during the first Review Conference in Kampala in 2010 in relation to the definition of the crime of aggression in Article 8*bis* of the Rome Statute, as well as to the introduction of additional elements to the war crimes provision in Article 8 of the Rome Statute and its Elements of Crimes.[77]

4.2.1 *Criteria for the Introduction of New Offenses*

International criminal law, in particular its jurisdiction *ratione materiae*, represent an evolution of the concept of universal jurisdiction as it has existed for centuries. Universal jurisdiction, established by customary international law

75 Amendments to provisions of an institutional nature are dealt with in Article 122 of the Rome Statute that establishes a simplified procedure.

76 Schabas (Commentary) 2016, 1502.

77 Review Conference Resolution 5 2010; Review Conference Resolution 6 2010.

or by treaty, allows a State without a conventional jurisdictional nexus to a crime (i.e., a nationality or territorial nexus) to prosecute it before its domestic courts or for the crime to be prosecuted before an international tribunal.[78] The invasion of national sovereignty this represents has always necessitated strict limitations on crimes covered by the concept, as is also reflected in the rules regarding ICC jurisdiction and in the principle of complementarity. Moreover, considering the introduction of new crimes, one must be careful not to overburden the ICC and to safeguard its original purpose to prosecute only "the most serious crimes of concern to the international community as a whole," which otherwise go unpunished.[79] Crimes to be included in the Rome Statute *de lege ferenda* must thus be selected based on common restrictive criteria.

During the drafting process of the Rome Statute, the ILC identified two criteria for the inclusion of treaty crimes.[80] First, it required that an existing treaty already subjects the crime in question to universal jurisdiction, either based on the principle *aut dedere aut iudicare* or on the possibility of an ICC to take jurisdiction.[81] One step ahead, there are two prerequisites for a crime to be subjected to universal jurisdiction: first, a pragmatic rationale requires the actual existence of an impunity gap, and second, a humanitarian rationale establishes a gravity threshold, meaning that the crime in question must be sufficiently heinous or detrimental to the global community that it becomes of concern to the international community as a whole.[82] Second, the ILC required that a crime in question is sufficiently defined in an existing treaty so as not to violate the *nullum crimen sine lege* principle.[83]

Building on these criteria, the crimes examined in the following subsection are selected based on the gravity of and persisting impunity in relation to that crime as well as its current status in international law with regards to the specificity of its definition and universal jurisdiction. The analyses will focus on their material elements *de lege ferenda*.[84]

4.2.2 *Common Contextual Elements*

In addition to criteria applied for the selection of crimes to be subjected to international justice in general, contextual elements can ensure that the acts

78 See section 2.2.

79 Rome Statute 1998, Preamble, para 4.

80 See section 2.3.3.2.2.

81 International Law Commission 1994b.

82 Geraghty 2004, 380 *et seq.*

83 International Law Commission 1994b.

84 It is assumed that the modes of liability as established in Articles 25 and 28 of the Rome Statute will apply.

committed in a specific case meet the requisite thresholds concerning gravity and scope. For example, while rape is included in the enumerated acts in Articles 7 and 8 of the Rome Statute, the crime only falls under ICC jurisdiction *ratione materiae* if it is committed as part of a widespread or systematic attack directed against a civilian population or in the context of and associated with an armed conflict.

Both the ILC and the ICC Preparatory Committee have discussed contextual elements in the Draft Code of Crimes against the Peace and Security of Mankind as well as in drafts of the Rome Statute, suggesting that, for example, "an individual who commits [a crime] [...] on a large scale, whether within the confines of a State or in a transboundary context."[85] A Caribbean draft introduced as part of the discussion on the inclusion of drug trafficking in the Rome Statute suggested that the acts must be committed

> (a) On a large scale (and) (or) in a transboundary context;
> (b) Within the framework of an organized and hierarchical structure;
> (c) With the use of violence and intimidation against private persons, judicial persons or other institutions, or members of the legislature, executive, or judicial arm of government, (thereby) creating fear and insecurity within a State or disrupting its economic, social, political, or security structures, or with other consequences of a similar nature; or
> (d) In a context in which corrupt influence is exerted over the public, the media and public institutions.[86]

However, this highly restrictive suggestion must be viewed in the light of diminishing support for the inclusion of drug trafficking in the Rome Statute during the negotiations. Rather than focusing on the organizational qualities of the perpetrating group and additional crimes committed in conjunction with a crime charged, a more common approach ensures the exclusion of singular or random acts, such as for crimes against humanity.

Along this line and building on the proposals advanced by the ICC Preparatory Committee, as well as by the ILC with regard to the treaty crimes discussed above, the following phrase could be applied to limit new crimes added to ICC jurisdiction *ratione materiae* to the worst crimes of concern to the international community as a whole *de lege ferenda*:

---

85 International Law Commission 1995, footnote 63; see section 2.3.3.2.

86 Barbados, Dominica, Jamaica and Trinidad and Tobago 1998, A/CONF.183//C.1/L.48; see also Robinson (Commentary edited by Cassese, Gaeta and Jones) 2002, 504.

> «[Crime in question] means any of the following acts if their commission is widespread or systematic: [Enumeration of acts]»

While these contextual requirements exclude the small-scale or random occurrence of crimes from ICC jurisdiction, they are not the same as the "widespread or systematic" element for crimes against humanity: here, the elements apply directly to the act charged; for example, drug trafficking must be of a systematic nature, whereas a crime against humanity (e.g., rape) can occur only once as long as it is part of a widespread or systematic attack. Nevertheless, the interpretation of the terms widespread and systematic can build on existing Decisions regarding the quality of an attack in crimes against humanity.

4.2.3 *Potential Offenses and Their Material Elements*

Based on the analyses of the *lex lata* in Chapter 3, common offenses by organized criminal groups that are not or only partially covered by ICC jurisdiction are examined in the following subsections as to their inclusion in Article 5 of the Rome Statute. Furthermore, the crimes of drug trafficking, illicit trade in arms and ammunition, natural resources, and cultural goods, migrant smuggling, corruption, and money laundering are discussed. First, a short overview of the status of each crime in international criminal law is given. Second, each crime is studied with regard to the criteria set out above, namely gravity, impunity, the specificity of its definition in international law, and universal jurisdiction.[87] If a crime meets the criteria, a suggestion for its material elements is developed.

4.2.3.1 The Crime of Drug Trafficking

The process for the establishment of an international criminal court that ultimately resulted in the creation of the ICC began with a request by Trinidad and Tobago to include the discussion on such a court with the purpose of prosecuting illicit trafficking in narcotic drugs in the agenda of the 44th session of the UNGA in 1989.[88] Following the proposal, the crime of drug trafficking represented a constant subject of debate throughout the drafting process of the ILC Draft Code of Crimes against the Peace and Security of Mankind as well as the Rome Statute.[89] After almost two decades, the negotiating parties at the Rome Conference finally decided not to include drug trafficking in the Statute but referred the topic to a future Review Conference under Article 111

87 See section 4.2.1.

88 UN General Assembly Sixth Committee 1989, A/C.6/44/SR.38.

89 See section 2.3.3.2.

of the Rome Statute "with a view to arriving at an acceptable jurisdiction and their [the crimes of drug trafficking and terrorism] inclusion in a list of crimes within the jurisdiction of the Court."[90] To date, this referral has not been acted upon. Because conduct related to drug trafficking is not covered by any of the crimes included in the Statute, drug trafficking is currently excluded from ICC jurisdiction.[91]

However, the offense of drug trafficking may satisfy the criteria for the inclusion of crimes in the ICC Statute as set out above:

With regard to gravity, it can be argued that drug trafficking constitutes a crime less serious than the four core crimes due to the voluntary element that drug abuse entails. However, this view is difficult to uphold given the magnitude of the global market, and the levels of corruption, violence, and social costs associated with the drug trade:[92] "There can be no doubt that the global trafficking in narcotic drugs has for the past forty years been the most pressing of all criminal justice issues."[93]

In relation to the criterion of persisting impunity, the numerous international treaties and cooperative efforts as well as the failure to effectively constrain the global drug market are evidence of the existence of an impunity gap.[94] Moreover, drug trafficking as a transnational offense involving multiple jurisdictions is generally more international in character than many core crimes, thereby posing an additional challenge to domestic law enforcement.[95]

Concerning its status in international law, drug trafficking is defined in several suppression conventions that contain *aut dedere aut iudicare* rules.[96] The definitions are detailed and specific. Moreover, support exists for the view that the crime of drug trafficking has reached the status of customary international law. International practice can be traced back to the 1936 Convention for the Suppression of the Illicit Traffic in Dangerous Drugs that obliged States to criminalize various acts associated with drug trafficking in their national systems and contained the *aut dedere aut iudicare* principle. The regime was complemented with administrative as well as substantive norms regarding drug control, jurisdiction, and mutual legal assistance among others by the conventions

---

90 UN Diplomatic Conference of Plenipotentiaries on the Establishment of an ICC 1998, section E.
91 For a detailed analysis see section 3.2.2.2.3.
92 See also section 2.1.2.1.
93 Schloenhardt 2004, 9; Ambos and Timmermann 2014, 320.
94 See section 2.2.2.2.
95 Schloenhardt 2004, 9.
96 See section 2.2.2.2.

subsequently developed. The relevant conventions enjoy almost universal support with 186 States adhering to the Single Convention on Narcotic Drugs of 1961, 184 States adhering to the Convention on Psychotropic Substances of 1971, and 190 States Party to the UN Convention against Illicit Traffic in Narcotic Drugs and Psychotropic Substances of 1988, with no relevant reservations.[97] Correspondingly, the State practice of including universal jurisdiction for drug traffickers in domestic legal systems is widespread.[98] Moreover, a view has emerged that drug trafficking as an international phenomenon requires domestic as well as international responses. Evidence can be found in the conventions, such as in Article 4 of the 1988 Trafficking Convention establishing universal jurisdiction, as well as in the practice of representative UN bodies and scholarly writings.[99] It is argued that after the year 2008 was set as the target date for all States to eliminate illicit drug trafficking, "State treatment of drug trafficking as an international crime by virtue of customary international law has been a proven fact."[100] However, no universal support exists for this view. For example, the 2001 Princeton Principles on Universal Jurisdiction do not include drug trafficking.[101] It is argued that a customary norm is in the process of development, or that drug trafficking *stricto sensu* is customary international law but that other parts of the regime, such as the prohibition of money laundering, lack in *opinio iuris*.[102] Nevertheless, notwithstanding its status in customary international law, drug trafficking constitutes an international crime and universal jurisdiction over it can be established by treaty.[103]

Thus, the offense of drug trafficking could be included in the Rome Statute *de lege ferenda*.

Regarding its material elements, the crime of drug trafficking can be defined according to Article 3 of the 1988 Trafficking Convention, as well as proposals

97 United Nations Treaty Collection 2019, Chapter VI: Narcotic Drugs and Psychotropic Substances; see section 2.2.2.2.

98 For a detailed discussion see Geraghty 2004, 28 *et seq. Contra:* Ambos and Timmermann 2014, 321. It is argued that universal jurisdiction for drug trafficking is not recognized since Article 4(1)(a) of the Drug Trafficking Convention requires a territorial or nationality nexus and Article 4(1)(b), applicable to all perpetrators in custody of the State, is only facultative. However, other drug control conventions do not contain such limitations.

99 E.g., A/RES//S-20/2 1998. For a complete list of all resolutions and decisions by the UNGA, ECOSOC and the Commission on Narcotic Drugs see UNODC 2021; Wise 1999; Jiménez de Aréchaga 1978.

100 Hauck 2016, 463.

101 Princeton Project on Universal Jurisdiction 2001.

102 E.g., Geraghty 2004; Jordan 2000; McConville 2000; Robinson (Commentary edited by Cassese, Gaeta and Jones) 2002; Ambos and Timmermann 2014.

103 Geraghty 2004; Robinson (Commentary edited by Cassese, Gaeta and Jones) 2002.

advanced during the work of the Preparatory Committee and by the ILC for the Draft Code of Crimes against the Peace and Security of Mankind:

> For the purposes of the present Statute, crimes involving the illicit traffic in narcotic drugs and psychotropic substances include any of the following acts:
> (i) The production, manufacture, extraction, preparation, offering, offering for sale, distribution, sale, delivery on any terms whatsoever, brokerage, dispatch, dispatch in transit, transport, importation or exportation of any narcotic drug or any psychotropic substance contrary to the provisions of the 1961 Convention, the 1961 Convention as amended or the 1971 Convention;
> (ii) The cultivation of opium poppy, coca bush or cannabis plant for the purpose of the production of narcotic drugs contrary to the provisions of the 1961 Convention and the 1961 Convention as amended;
> (iii) The possession or purchase of any narcotic drug or psychotropic substance for the purpose of any of the activities enumerated in (i) above;
> (iv) The manufacture, transport or distribution of equipment, materials or of substances listed in Table I and Table II [of the annex to the 1988 United Nations Convention against Illicit Traffic in Narcotic Drugs and Psychotropic Substances] knowing that they are to be used in, or for the illicit cultivation, production or manufacture of narcotic drugs or psychotropic substances;
> (v) The organization, management or financing of any of the offences enumerated in (i), (ii), (iii) or (iv) above[104]

This definition excludes subparagraph (b) and (c) of Article 3(1) of the 1988 Trafficking Convention that cover laundering of proceeds from drug trafficking and oblige States Parties to criminalize the enumerated acts only "subject to [their] constitutional principles and the basic concepts of [their] legal system."

Furthermore, a new provision in the Rome Statute may incorporate the current drug policies that show an increasing tendency toward "soft defection" from the international drug regime through creative interpretation, ranging

104 Drug Trafficking Convention 1988, Article 3(a) and (b); see also Preparatory Committee on the Establishment of an ICC 1998b, 29; International Law Commission 1995.

from the decriminalization of certain conduct, in particular in relation to cannabis (e.g., in the Netherlands) to harm reduction policies favored by the World Health Organization and the ICRC.[105] An exception could be provided, for example,

> «…for acts that are legal in the State Party in which they take place and are aimed at medical use, the reduction of harm caused by preexisting drug addiction or are conducted with regard to cannabis in a legal market…»

4.2.3.2 Illicit Trade in Arms and Ammunition, Natural Resources, and Cultural Goods

While illicit trade in specific goods, especially in drugs and human beings, has been identified as an important subject of international coordinated efforts in the field of criminal law, other illegal markets have been attributed less priority or been addressed using other approaches, often with a preventive or regulative focus.[106] However, the gravity of the consequences as well as the magnitude of some illicit markets provide a basis for substantiating or complementing current efforts by means of international penal law.

The Rome Statute represents one of the available avenues for addressing these crimes from an international criminal law perspective. However, the *lex lata* only provides limited possibilities for the prosecution of property or trade-related crimes. Specifically, the war crime provision in Article 8 of the Rome Statute provides protection against the extensive destruction of civilian property, the natural environment and cultural buildings, extensive seizure and appropriation, as well as pillage.[107] Moreover, the participatory modes of liability in Article 25 of the Rome Statute allow under certain circumstances for prosecutions for the supply of the means to commit a crime, such as arms and ammunition.[108] However, prosecutions based on these provisions focus on the end use of the trafficked goods, not on the illicit trade itself, requiring a corresponding *mens rea*.

In general, regarding all types of illicit trade, establishing a crime definition requires a clear distinction between legal and illegal activities, posing a complex challenge especially in under-regulated markets with weak State institutions or conflict.[109] When introducing new crimes regarding illicit trade to the

105 Vogler and Fouladvand 2016, 121; Garcia Sanchez 2017.
106 E.g., in the DRC: Arimatsu and Mistry 2012.
107 See sections 3.2.3.2.2.1.-2.
108 See section 3.3.2.
109 E.g., Arimatsu and Mistry 2012.

Rome Statute, it may be instructive to include an objective definition of illegal activities in this context.

The Panel of Experts on Illegal Exploitation of Natural Resources in the DRC identified four elements for determining the illegality of an activity, namely the violation of sovereignty, disrespect of the existing regulatory framework in the country or territory of operation, discrepancies with widely accepted practices in trade and business, and the violation of international law including soft law.[110] However, the last two elements lack specificity to be applied in criminal law. The second element disregards the issue of under-regulation. Regarding sovereignty, the identification of the legitimate government, especially in conflicts involving groups claiming their right to self-determination, can pose significant problems and touch upon crucial political questions. Thus, a general definition of illegality that is usable in international criminal law and broadly based on the Panel's proposal could resemble the following:

> «Without prejudice to product-specific requirements laid out in the following articles, activities are defined as illegal if
> – they are conducted in violation of the sovereignty of the State without the consent of the legitimate government; or
> – they are conducted in violation of the regulatory framework applicable in the country or territory where the activities take place; or
> – they violate international law, including but not limited to general principles of commercial law, international humanitarian law, human rights law and resolutions by the UN Security Council acting under Chapter VII of the UN Charter.»

The illicit trade in arms and ammunition, cultural goods, and wildlife and other natural resources such as minerals, oil, and gas has major, long-term detrimental effects for the cultural, societal, and economic development of affected populations. The size and growth of these markets illustrate both the gravity and persisting impunity of illicit trade. Regarding weapons, it is estimated that every year, a minimum of 7.5 million units of small arms and light weapons are manufactured and traded globally at a value of $4 to $7 billion, of which one-quarter is illicit and supplies organized criminals.[111] These arms are used to suppress rival criminal groups, intimidate law enforcement and

110 DRC Panel of Experts 2001, para 15.

111 Fellmeth 2016, 197.

the civil population, protect income sources and leadership, and often fuel conflict.

Regarding natural resources, a 2016 report co-authored by INTERPOL and the UN Environment Program (UNEP) observed:

> Environmental crime is vastly expanding and increasingly endangering not only wildlife populations but entire ecosystems, sustainable livelihoods and revenue streams to governments. [...] Environmental crimes are no longer restricted to iconic wildlife and rare wood species alone—they have become part and parcel of the larger global network of transnational organized environmental crimes. Environmental crime also includes corporate crime in the forestry sector, illegal exploitation and sale of gold and minerals, illegal fisheries/fishing, trafficking in hazardous waste and chemicals [...].[112]

Concerning wildlife only, a 2013 report by the International Fund for Animal Welfare estimated that trade revenues in this market are comparable to revenues from drug trafficking and arms trade and continually growing.[113] Revenues from environmental crime more broadly are estimated at a value of between $91 and $258 billion annually.[114] The illicit exploitation and trade in natural resources not only threaten biodiversity and the livelihood of local populations but also contribute to corruption, undermine the rule of law, and lead to the increasing militarization of vulnerable habitats because of the interrelation between illicit trade and self-funding of non-State armed groups acting in conjunction with organized criminal groups.[115] The illicit trade in nonrenewable natural resources, especially minerals, is valued in the DRC alone at $1.25 billion *per annum*. It is estimated that 98% of net profits in the market go to organized criminal groups, but the remaining 2% still allows 25 to 49 armed groups to finance themselves and continuously resurface after defeat or disarmament, significantly destabilizing the region.[116]

Regarding cultural property, the extent of illegal trade is largely unclear because of a lack of reliable data on the black market. However, recent reports on illicit excavations by armed organized criminal groups in Syria have highlighted the relevance of the issue as well as its interconnectedness with conflict

112 UNEP and INTERPOL 2016, 7.
113 Ratchford, Allgood and Todd 2013.
114 UNEP and INTERPOL 2016, 7.
115 Strydom 2016, 266–267.
116 UNEP, MONUSCO and OSESG 2015.

and development, and furthermore, have demonstrated the tendency of significant growth of the market.[117] For example, the value of declared antiquities from Syria sold in the USA grew by 134% to $11 million in 2013; the total volume of the illicit trade is estimated by US officials at more than $100 million *per annum.*[118]

Consequently, the illicit trade in arms, natural resources, and cultural goods meets the criteria for the inclusion of new crimes in the Rome Statute in terms of gravity and a persisting impunity gap. However, the status of each type of illicit trade in international law differs, which is now examined.

First, illicit trade in arms and ammunition is defined in the Arms Trafficking Protocol of 2001 supplementing the Convention against Transnational Organized Crime as well as in the ATT. The Palermo Convention established the *aut dedere aut iudicare* rule in its Article 15(4). The Protocol contains the definition of acts constituting the crime of illicit trade in arms and ammunitions as well as definitions of key terms. While the definition of a firearm in the Arms Trafficking Protocol is limited and excludes (among others) artillery, air rifles, and BB guns, the ATT of 2013 is wider in scope but mainly concerned with the State Parties' import and export regimes.[119] The crime is thus clearly defined and subject to universal jurisdiction, and hence, meets the criteria for its inclusion in the Rome Statute.

Article 7 of the ATT requires an export assessment that considers the potential that the arms or items could be used to commit or facilitate a serious violation of international humanitarian or human rights law, or an act constituting an offense under relevant treaties regarding terrorism and transnational organized crime. In line with recognized rules of State responsibility,[120] Article 6(3) of the ATT explicitly states that

> [a] State Party shall not authorize any transfer of conventional arms [...] or items [...], if it has knowledge at the time of authorization that the arms or items would be used in the commission of genocide, crimes against humanity, grave breaches of the Geneva Conventions of 1949, attacks directed against civilian objects or civilians protected as such, or other war crimes as defined by international agreements to which it is a Party.

117 von Schorlemer 2016, 72 *et seq.*

118 Parkinson, Albayrak and Mavin 2015, 2.

119 For a detailed discussion, including the ATT and organized crime, see Casey-Maslen, Giacca and Vestner 2013.

120 Responsibility of States for Internationally Wrongful Acts 2001, Articles 16, 41(2).

Under the Rome Statute, such conduct might entail individual criminal responsibility of the acting State official as an accomplice to genocide, crimes against humanity, or war crimes.[121] The distinction between participation in these crimes and the crime of arms trafficking is based on the *mens rea*: If the trafficking individual possesses the *mens rea* required for a contribution (e.g., to genocide) under Article 25 of the Rome Statute, then the person is both responsible for the perpetration of arms trafficking and for participation in another crime (e.g., genocide).

A definition of the crime of illicit trade in arms and ammunition could be taken from the Arms Trafficking Protocol, and then potentially expanded to apply to additional types of arms that are included in the ATT to resemble the following:

> «Illicit trade in arms and ammunition encompasses the following acts:
> a) Illicit manufacturing of firearms, their parts and components and ammunition;
> b) Illicit trafficking in firearms, their parts and components and ammunition;
> c) Falsifying or illicitly obliterating, removing or altering the marking(s) on firearms required by article 8 of [the Protocol against the Illicit Manufacturing of and Trafficking in Firearms, Their Parts and Components and Ammunition, supplementing the United Nations Convention against Transnational Organized Crime][122]
>
> Use of terms
> a) 'Firearm' shall mean any portable barreled weapon that expels, is designed to expel or may be readily converted to expel a shot, bullet or projectile by the action of an explosive, excluding antique firearms or their replicas. Antique firearms and their replicas shall be defined in accordance with domestic law. In no case, however, shall antique firearms include firearms manufactured after 1899;
> b) 'Parts and components' shall mean any element or replacement element specifically designed for a firearm and essential to its operation, including a barrel, frame or receiver, slide or cylinder, bolt or

121 In support of arms trafficking prosecutions under Article 25: Rome 2015; Hamilton 2015.

122 Protocol on Arms Trafficking 2001, Article 5(1)(a)-(c).

breech block, and any device designed or adapted to diminish the sound caused by firing a firearm;

c) 'Ammunition' shall mean the complete round or its components, including cartridge cases, primers, propellant powder, bullets or projectiles, that are used in a firearm, provided that those components are themselves subject to authorization in the respective State Party;

d) 'Illicit manufacturing' shall mean the manufacturing or assembly of firearms, their parts and components or ammunition:
   (i) From parts and components illicitly trafficked;
   (ii) Without a license or authorization from a competent authority of the State Party where the manufacture or assembly takes place; or
   (iii) Without marking the firearms at the time of manufacture, in accordance with article 8 of [the Protocol against the Illicit Manufacturing of and Trafficking in Firearms, Their Parts and Components and Ammunition, supplementing the United Nations Convention against Transnational Organized Crime]. Licensing or authorization of the manufacture of parts and components shall be in accordance with domestic law;

e) 'Illicit trafficking' shall mean the import, export, acquisition, sale, delivery, movement or transfer of firearms, their parts and components and ammunition from or across the territory of one State to that of another State if any one of the States concerned does not authorize it in accordance with the terms of [the Protocol against the Illicit Manufacturing of and Trafficking in Firearms, Their Parts and Components and Ammunition, supplementing the United Nations Convention against Transnational Organized Crime] or if the firearms are not marked in accordance with article 8 of [that] Protocol.[123]»

Second, regarding the illicit trade in natural resources, the focus has historically been on iconic wildlife and endangered species. The Convention on International Trade in Endangered Species of Wild Fauna and Flora (CITES), currently with 183 State Parties, contains an obligation on all State Parties to penalize trade and/or possession of species covered by the Convention in its article VIII(1)(a).[124] The species are listed in three annexes, which differentiate

123 Protocol on Arms Trafficking 2001, Articles 3(a)-(e).

124 CITES 2021.

between species threatened with extinction, species that may become threatened with extinction unless their trade is strictly regulated, and species that are subject to regulation within the jurisdiction of any of the State Parties. The Convention contains specific definitions, such as those of the terms species, specimen, and trade.

However, the CITES does not establish universal jurisdiction; rather, it focuses on trade regulations. Although the UNGA acknowledged at the time of its adoption that the Palermo Convention "will constitute an effective tool and the necessary legal framework for international cooperation in combating [...] illicit trafficking in endangered species of wild flora and fauna,"[125] no explicit mention in the Convention or supplementing protocol exists.

Furthermore, no internationally agreed upon definition exists of trade in natural resources beyond endangered species. Trade in hazardous waste is controlled by three interlinked conventions that do not contain any criminal law provisions.[126] Neither does the universally ratified Montreal Protocol controlling ozone-depleting gases.[127] The ILC considered willfully causing or ordering widespread, long-term, and severe damage to the environment for inclusion in the Draft Code of Crimes against the Peace and Security of Mankind, but did not include it in the final text.[128] The UN Convention Concerning the Protection of the World Cultural and Natural Heritage contains a broad definition of natural heritage that encompasses natural features "of outstanding universal value from an aesthetic or scientific point of view; geological and physiographical formations and precisely delineated areas which constitute the habitat of threatened species of animals and plants [...]; [and] natural sites or precisely delineated natural areas of outstanding universal value from the point of view of science, conservation, or natural beauty."[129] However, the definition refers to features, formations, and areas and does not include flora, fauna, and other (re)movable natural resources. By far the most comprehensive legal text relating to environmental crime can be found in the 2008 EU Directive on the protection of the environment through criminal law. Its focus, however, is on the protection of the environment from radiation, hazardous waste, dangerous substances, nuclear material, and ozone-depleting substances.[130] The

125 A/RES/55/25 2000.

126 Basel Waste Convention 1989; Rotterdam Chemicals and Pesticides Convention 1998; Stockholm Pollutants Convention 2001.

127 Montreal Protocol on Substances that Deplete the Ozone Layer 1987.

128 International Law Commission 1995, para 119–121; International Law Commission 1996; see also Robinson (Commentary edited by Cassese, Gaeta and Jones) 2002, 523.

129 World Heritage Convention 1972, Article 2.

130 Directive 2008/99/EC 2008, Article 3.

only reference to trade is, again, made in relation to wildlife. Although a broad range of international efforts has been made in relation with illicit trade in minerals, especially from Sierra Leone and the Great Lake region, they have not primarily been focused on criminal law but included prosecutions, import and export regulations, as well as due diligence obligations for corporations.[131]

Overall, the crime of illicit trade in natural resources lacks a status in international law with regard to its definition and universal jurisdiction, which would satisfy the criteria for inclusion in the Rome Statute. Illicit trade in wildlife and endangered species is defined in international law but not covered by the *aut dedere aut iudicare* principle.

Third, the protection of cultural goods has entered the realm of international law by way of IHL. The Hague Regulations of 1907 attribute special protection to buildings, including museums, churches, and universities, as well as prohibit the seizure, destruction, willful damage, and pillage to such institutions, historic monuments, and works of art and science.[132] The Hague Regulations are today considered part of customary international law.[133] Furthermore, The Hague Convention for the Protection of Cultural Property in the Event of Armed Conflict of 1954 relates to all "movable and immovable property of great importance to the cultural heritage of every people,"[134] and includes provisions prohibiting acts of hostilities against, military use, theft, pillage, and unlawful misappropriation of, as well as vandalism and reprisals against cultural property in international and noninternational armed conflict regardless of the existence of a State of occupation.[135] These rules have also entered into customary international law.[136] The First Protocol to the Convention adds provisions regarding the prevention of the exportation and rules for the treatment of cultural property that is found in the territory of an occupying State.[137] The obligations to prevent the exportation of cultural property, return property that was exported nevertheless, and not keep cultural property as reparations are now also considered customary international law.[138] The Second Protocol, which was added in 1999, prohibits "illicit export, other removal, or transfer of

131 See section 3.2.3.2.2.1.

132 The Hague Regulations 1907, Articles 27, 47, 56.

133 Kretschmer 2016, 322; International Committee of the Red Cross 2019, Rule 40.

134 Convention for the Protection of Cultural Property 1954, Article 1.

135 *ibid.*, Articles 2, 4(3) and (4), 18, 19(1).

136 International Committee of the Red Cross 2019, Rule 38; International Committee of the Red Cross 2019, Rule 39; International Committee of the Red Cross 2019, Rule 40; International Committee of the Red Cross 2019, Rule 52.

137 Additional Protocol I to the Hague Convention 1954, Articles 1–4.

138 International Committee of the Red Cross 2019, Rule 41.

ownership of cultural property, [...] archeological excavation [...] [and] alteration to, or change of use of cultural property intended to conceal or destroy cultural, historical or scientific evidence."[139] Furthermore, the Protocol establishes as offenses the attack and military use of cultural property, its extensive destruction and appropriation, its theft, pillage and misappropriation, as well as vandalism against it.[140] It establishes the general jurisdictional rule of territorial and personal jurisdiction as well as jurisdiction of the custodial State in cases involving an attack or military use of cultural property of enhanced protection as well as extensive destruction and appropriation.[141] The prohibitions of hostilities directed against cultural property, its use for military purposes, and reprisals against it were also included in the first two Additional Protocols to the Geneva Conventions of 1977.[142]

The pillage and destruction of cultural property have been considered war crimes since the Nuremburg and Tokyo tribunals.[143] The Rome Statute prohibits, among others, intentional attacks against cultural property as well as its pillage, seizure, and extensive appropriation.[144] The rules have received significant attention lately because of the extensive destruction and looting of cultural property in the course of armed conflicts in Iraq and Syria. In several resolutions by the UNSC,

> the international community [...] tied those who participate in the illicit trade of these cultural objects with those who facilitate and engage in other illicit means of funding the gross, systematic and widespread abuses of human rights and international humanitarian law.[145]

To counteract the illegal sale of cultural goods, the UNSC called upon its member States to facilitate their return to Iraq or Syria and prohibit their trade, transfer, purchase, and sale.[146]

The 1970 UNESCO Convention on the Means of Prohibiting the Illicit Import, Export and Transfer of Ownership of Cultural Property focuses directly on the protection of cultural property from illegal sale. In its Article 3, it defines

139 Additional Protocol II to the Hague Convention 1999, Article 9(1)(1).
140 *ibid.*, Article 15.
141 *ibid.*, Article 16(1).
142 Protocol I to Geneva Conventions 1977, Article 53; Protocol II to Geneva Convention 1977, Article 16.
143 Kretschmer 2016, 322.
144 See section 3.2.2.2.4, and 3.2.3.2.2.2.
145 Vrdoljak 2016, 18.
146 S/RES/1483 2003; S/RES/2199 2015; see also A/RES/69/281 2015.

illicit trade in cultural goods. The UNESCO Convention was complemented in 1995 by the International Institute for the Unification of Private Law's (UNIDROIT) Convention on Stolen or Illegally Exported Cultural Objects, aimed at harmonizing domestic legislations. Addressing an important shortcoming of the UNESCO Convention that required cultural property to be explicitly designated by the States, it provides an objective definition of cultural objects.[147] Both Conventions also include rare collections and specimens of fauna, flora, minerals, and anatomy in their definition of cultural property.

However, neither the UNIDROIT nor the UNESCO Convention contain *aut dedere aut iudicare* or related provisions. Hence, illicit trade in cultural goods is sufficiently defined in international law but does not satisfy the criterion of universal jurisdiction.[148]

Self-imposed codes of ethics and the principle of due diligence in any transactions play crucial roles in the protection of cultural property, as well as with regard to so-called conflict minerals.[149] Whether such practices can inform international criminal law with regard to *mens rea* remains to be see, such as through establishing knowledge by inference or introducing a "should have known" standard similar to Article 28 of the Rome Statute.

In sum, the illicit trade in arms and ammunitions satisfies the criteria set out above, and thus, could be included as a new crime under the jurisdiction of the ICC. The illicit trade in natural resources and cultural goods, on the other hand, still lack the necessary status in international law regarding the specificity of existing definitions and universal jurisdiction, and hence should not be included in the Rome Statute at this point.

4.2.3.3 The Crime of Migrant Smuggling

Because of loosened border controls since the end of the Cold War, the globalization of markets, advanced communication, technology and travel and persisting global inequalities, international migration—and migrant smuggling in particular—have grown significantly over the last decades.[150] Virtually

---

147 UNIDROIT Convention on Stolen or Illegally Exported Cultural Objects 1995, Article 2 and annex.

148 For a discussion of possible expansions of Articles 6 (with regard to cultural genocide), 7 (e.g. with regard to a more explicit reference to cultural property) and 8 of the Rome Statute (e.g. with regard to a new war crime of "attacking, by whatever means, cultural property, any structure that containscultural property, or their immediate surroundings" see von Schorlemer 2016, 720 *et seq.* However, the author does not base her analysis of the *lex ferenda* on common criteria including universal jurisdiction.

149 Liu 2016.

150 Aronowitz 2001, 169–170; see section 2.1.2.3.

all countries are affected as either origin, transit, or destination countries. Smuggled migrants are vulnerable to abuse and exploitation and many have died as a consequence of the risks taken by smuggling organizations.[151] The profits of migrant smuggling fuel corruption and empower organized crime.[152] The crime of migrant smuggling thus satisfies the criteria of gravity to be covered by international criminal law.

Concerning impunity for migrant smuggling, the UNODC identified trends indicating significant growth of the market, its high profitability, and its low-risk environment for the perpetrators, although data remain scattered.[153] In any case, there have not been any major domestic prosecutions of leaders of smuggling rings thus far, despite the significant numbers of migrants and refugees in recent years. This clearly points to a persisting impunity gap.

With regard to migrant smuggling in international law, relevant issues of sovereignty and security led to efforts to address and clarify the issue of migrant smuggling during the so-called Vienna Process. In this process, the adoption of the Palermo Convention and its Protocols was prepared.[154] The first proposal for an international legal document to deal with migrant smuggling was proposed by Austria in 1997, facing massive migration flows from the countries of the former Yugoslavia, to the Commission of Crime Prevention and Criminal Justice.[155] Italy, which primarily faced migration over sea from Albania, joined forces after a futile attempt to address the issue via the International Maritime Organization (IMO).[156] Their proposals formed the basis for the Protocol against the Smuggling of Migrants by Land, Sea and Air supplementing the Palermo Convention that was subsequently developed under the auspices of an *Ad Hoc* Committee and adopted in November 2000.[157]

Despite this short history of the international crime of migrant smuggling, 149 States are party to the Protocol today.[158] As with trade in arms and ammunitions, the crime of migrant smuggling is subject to the *aut dedere aut iudicare* provision of the Palermo Convention in Article 15(4). Its status in international law is thus sufficient to consider an inclusion in the Rome Statute.

151 For a short collection of case studies, see Gallagher and David 2014, 7 *et seq.*

152 Schloenhardt and Dale 2012, 130.

153 UNODC 2011b, 6.

154 Gallagher 2001.

155 Austrian Permanent Representative to the UN 1997.

156 Gallagher 2001, 983; IMO Legal Committee 1997.

157 Schloenhardt and Dale 2012, 134.

158 United Nations Treaty Collection 2019, Chapter XVIII: Penal Matters.

Overall, the crime of migrant smuggling satisfies the criteria regarding gravity, impunity, specificity of definition, and universal jurisdiction, and can thus be considered for potential inclusion in the Rome Statute.

Regarding the material elements of the crime of migrant smuggling, the Protocol against the Smuggling of Migrants provides a definition in its Article 3(a) that could be adopted for a new crime in the Rome Statute:

> «'Smuggling of migrants' shall mean the procurement, in order to obtain, directly or indirectly, a financial or other material benefit, of the illegal entry of a person into a State […] of which the person is not a national or a permanent resident.[159]»

The production, procurement, provision, and possession of fraudulent travel or identity documents for the purposes of migrant smuggling, which are also criminalized in the Protocol in Article 6(1)(b), would constitute participation in migrant smuggling under Article 25 of the Rome Statute.

The Protocol also criminalizes enabling a migrant to remain illegally present in a territory by illegal means in its Article 6(1)(c). On this basis, the definition above could be complemented as follows:

> «'Smuggling of migrants' shall also encompass "in order to obtain, directly or indirectly, a financial or other material benefit, […] enabling a person who is not a national or a permanent resident to remain in the State concerned without complying with the necessary requirements for legally remaining in the State by […] illegal means."[160]»

Moreover, in its Article 6(3), the Protocol names as aggravating circumstances to be established in the laws of its State Parties circumstances "that endanger, or are likely to endanger, the lives or safety of the migrants concerned," as well as circumstances "that entail inhuman or degrading treatment, including for exploitation, of such migrants." The latter can be charged as a separate offense under the Rome Statute if committed as part of a systematic or widespread attack. Furthermore, it should be considered whether the aggravating factors currently defined in Rule 145 of the ICC Rules of Procedure and Evidence cover these circumstances or in how far an amendment of the Rules might be sensible.

159 Protocol on Migrant Smuggling 2000, Article 3(a).

160 *ibid.*, Article 6(1) chapeau and subparagraph (c); see also Model Law against Migrant Smuggling 2010.

4.2.3.4 Corruption

For decades, corruption has been a major concern as well as the subject of legal and policy efforts on an international scale. Corruption hurts the legitimacy of democratic institutions, hampers economic development, and destabilizes governmental authority.[161] However, the impact of corruption on human lives is less direct than most of the core crimes in Article 5 of the Rome Statute, including murder or sexual violence. What constitutes the gravity of corruption is rather comparable to property-related war crimes, such as the destruction of cultural buildings, which do not directly cause human suffering but have an effect on the social, economic, spiritual, and cultural life of the affected population. Although data are scarce, it is argued that corruption has grown in scope because of the growth of international trade and business, to economic changes, in particular in transition countries, and to more important government involvement.[162] Its gravity is thus considered sufficient for it to be addressed in international criminal prosecutions.

Because one aim of corruption can be the evasion of law enforcement, the crime is especially vulnerable to the issue of impunity for the perpetrators. Moreover, the effectiveness of the international suppression regime against corruption suffers from difficulties in implementation and enforcement as well as in international criminal cooperation.[163] As a consequence, corruption largely goes unpunished.

Concerning its status in international law, the crime of corruption has been defined in numerous international treaties over the past decades. Following the Watergate Affair, the USA Foreign Corrupt Practices Act of 1977 was the first law criminalizing bribes paid to foreign officials. However, it was only after the end of the Cold War, partly due to the increase in international trade, that the costs of corruption were perceived as no longer tolerable and received a political response as a crucial cause of global poverty.[164] Starting in the late 1990s, various regional and international conventions were drafted and signed, such as the Inter-American Convention against Corruption of 1996, the OECD Convention on Combating Bribery of Foreign Public Officials in International Business Transactions of 1997, the Council of Europe's Criminal Law and Civil Law Conventions on Corruption of 1999, and the AU Convention on Preventing and Combating Corruption of 2003.[165] With 182 States Parties,

161 Council of Europe 2014, 49; van Dijk 2007, 54; see section 2.1.5.

162 Tanzi 1998, 6–7.

163 Posadas 2000; Getz 2016; see section 2.2.1.

164 Batchelor *et al.* 1997; Kubiciel and Rink 2016, 220.

165 An overview of over 20 anti-corruption legal instruments can be found at UNODC 2015.

the UN Convention against Corruption of 2003 is "the first truly global anti-corruption treaty."[166] Its scope exceeds previous agreements and it is not solely focused on criminal law. Rather, it adds chapters on prevention, international cooperation, asset recovery, technical support, and exchange of information. Notably, in case of a criminal prosecution of corruption under the ICC, these provisions could facilitate international cooperation beyond the rules of the Rome Statute. Regarding the criminal law provisions, the UN Convention "carries forward an international tendency of expanding the understanding of corrupt practices to be criminalized"[167] and subjects corruption to the *aut dedere aut iudicare* rule.[168] However, as a transnational instrument, it subdivides the offenses into mandatory and nonmandatory provisions. Thus, only the mandatory provisions reflect a broad consensus among States, are subjected to universal jurisdiction, and can inform a provision in the Rome Statute.

In sum, corruption satisfies the criteria for inclusion in the Rome Statute in relation to its definition in international law, universal jurisdiction, and persisting impunity. The gravity of corruption is manifest not in the direct human suffering it causes, unlike for example violence, but in the long-term detrimental effects on societies and their institutions.

Based on article of the UN Convention against Corruption, a new provision could resemble the following and include bribery, embezzlement, misappropriation, and other diversion of property by a public official, as well as obstruction of justice:

> «Corruption under this Statute means
>
> The promise, offering or giving, to a public official, national or foreign or of a public international organization, directly or indirectly, of an undue advantage, for the official himself or herself or another person or entity, in order that the official act or refrain from acting in the exercise of his or her official duties; including in order to obtain or retain business or other undue advantage in relation to the conduct of international business
> The solicitation or acceptance by a public official, national or foreign or of a public international organization, directly or indirectly, of an undue advantage, for the official himself or herself or another person or entity,

166 Kubiciel and Rink 2016, 221; see section 2.2.2.3.

167 *ibid.*, 222.

168 UN Convention against Corruption 2003, Article 42(4). Corruption is also included as a crime in the Palermo Convention 2000, Article 8.

in order that the official act or refrain from acting in the exercise of his or her official duties; including in order to obtain or retain business or other undue advantage in relation to the conduct of international business[169]

The embezzlement, misappropriation or other diversion by a public official for his or her benefit or for the benefit of another person or entity, of any property, public or private funds or securities or any other thing of value entrusted to the public official by virtue of his or her position.[170]

The use of physical force, threats or intimidation or the promise, offering or giving of an undue advantage to induce false testimony or to interfere in the giving of testimony or the production of evidence in a proceeding in relation to the commission of offences established in accordance with this Convention;
The use of physical force, threats or intimidation to interfere with the exercise of official duties by a justice or law enforcement official in relation to the commission of offences established in accordance with this [Statute].[171]»

The definition of obstruction of justice in paragraphs (d) and (e) are distinct from Article 70 of the Rome Statute as the latter only applies to proceedings before the ICC. The definitions of public officials could also be drawn from the UN Convention:

«'Public official' shall mean:

any person holding a legislative, executive, administrative or judicial office of a State Party, whether appointed or elected, whether permanent or temporary, whether paid or unpaid, irrespective of that person's seniority;

any other person who performs a public function, including for a public agency or public enterprise, or provides a public service, as defined in the domestic law of the State Party and as applied in the pertinent area of law of that State Party;

169 UN Convention against Corruption 2003, Article 15 and 16 (merged).
170 *ibid.*, Article 17.
171 UN Convention against Corruption 2003, Article 25(a) and (b).

any other person defined as a 'public official' in the domestic law of a State Party [...].

'Foreign public official' shall mean any person holding a legislative, executive, administrative or judicial office of a foreign country, whether appointed or elected; and any person exercising a public function for a foreign country, including for a public agency or public enterprise;

'Official of a public international organization' shall mean an international civil servant or any person who is authorized by such an organization to act on behalf of that organization.[172]»

It should be noted that corruption, if introduced as a distinct crime, can also constitute participation in other crimes, such as aiding and abetting drug trafficking. Thus, the appropriate legal qualification must be decided by the Prosecutor and Judges based on the facts of a particular case.[173]

4.2.3.5 Money Laundering

As early as 1975, the international community realized that "as far as transnational financial crime is concerned, national legislations will never be sufficient."[174] Money laundering facilitates corruption and organized crime and contributes to terrorism financing. The total sum of laundered money worldwide is estimated at between $400 billion and $2.85 trillion per year despite intensified efforts to detect and punish money laundering on a national and international level.[175] Hence, the existing mechanisms do not provide for an adequate level of law enforcement and money laundering often remains undetected.

In terms of gravity, money laundering is a secondary offense dependent on a primary offense that the laundered proceeds originate from. It can thus be argued that its gravity is dependent on the primary offense and consequently not comparable to current core crimes. However, the criminalization of money laundering has been applied as a mechanism not only against

172 *ibid.*, Article 2(a)-(c).

173 This overlap is already inherent in the Palermo Convention and its Protocols; Gallagher and David 2014, 374.

174 Fifth UN Congress on Prevention of Crime and the Treatment of Offenders 1975, chapter I, para 31.

175 Schneider and Windischbauer 2008, 392; see section 2.1.2.6.

illegal financial activities but also as a means to identify the underlying activity from which proceeds are derived.[176] Moreover, money laundering aims to render the economic loss to a society originally caused by the primary offense irreversible, and thus, plays an essential role in the gravity of the consequences caused. In the Palermo Convention, money laundering is only criminalized if the proceeds were derived from a primary activity, also defined as a crime in the Convention. A similar requirement can be envisaged for the Rome Statute to ensure that only the most serious crimes are prosecuted.

Regarding the status of the crime of money laundering in international law, the UN Anti-Corruption Convention includes money laundering in its mandatory provisions, and thus subjects it to universal jurisdiction. Historically, money laundering is closely connected to organized crime, particularly drug trafficking. Complementing the approach of disrupting the business model of drug supply networks, a strategy focusing on the illegal proceeds aims to strengthen the deterrence and punishment of organized criminals.[177] Money laundering is thus also included as an offense in the 1988 UN Drug Trafficking Convention, the 1999 UN International Convention for the Suppression of the Financing of Terrorism, and the UN Convention against Transnational Organized Crime. The latter also subjects money laundering to universal jurisdiction in Article 8. There is an ongoing debate on whether the rapid developments in this field, including in soft law and standard setting, the breadth of legal regimes concerned, and the wide ratification of treaties including money laundering provisions can be interpreted as an evolution of customary international law.[178] In any case, money laundering is sufficiently defined and subjected to universal jurisdiction by several treaties.

In sum, while money laundering largely remains unpunished, it is clearly defined in international law and subject to universal jurisdiction via treaty. It remains debatable whether its gravity as a secondary offense is comparable to other crimes included in the Rome Statute. Thus, introducing a requirement that the proceeds in question were derived from a crime under the Statute could ensure consistency in terms of gravity.

176 Naylor 2003a, 277.

177 Koker and Turkington 2016, 243.

178 In favor: Koh 2006, 165 and 193 *et seq;* Ambos and Timmermann 2014, 307, on the other hand, do not even include money laundering in their discussion of potential new crimes for the Rome Statute.

A new provision in the Rome Statute could draw from definitions of money laundering in a multitude of international legal documents, such as from the parallel provision in the UN Anti-Corruption Convention and the Palermo Convention:

> «The offense of money laundering includes
> (i) The conversion or transfer of property, knowing that such property is the proceeds of crime, for the purpose of concealing or disguising the illicit origin of the property or of helping any person who is involved in the commission of the predicate offence to evade the legal consequences of his or her action;
> (ii) The concealment or disguise of the true nature, source, location, disposition, movement or ownership of or rights with respect to property, knowing that such property is the proceeds of crime.[179]»

As underlined by the term "knowing that such property is the proceeds of crime," the crime of money laundering requires *dolus directus*, in line with Article 30 of the Rome Statute. The FATF Standards, however, require that the requisite *dolus* can be inferred from the circumstances and does not depend on a confession by the offender.[180] Few countries, such as South Africa and Australia, have enacted legislation that extend the offense to negligent acts, where the offender should reasonably have known that he was dealing with proceeds of crime.[181]

The required definitions could also be drawn from the two Conventions, namely

> «For the purposes of this Statute:
>
> ...
>
> 'Property' shall mean assets of every kind, whether corporeal or incorporeal, movable or immovable, tangible or intangible, and legal documents or instruments evidencing title to, or interest in, such assets;

179 UN Convention against Corruption 2003, Article 23(1)(a) ; Palermo Convention 2000, Article 6(1)(a).

180 Financial Action Task Force 2012, INR 3(7)(a).

181 South Africa Prevention of Organised Crime Act 1998; Australia Criminal Code Act 1995, Div. 400.

> 'Proceeds of crime' shall mean any property derived from or obtained, directly or indirectly, through the commission of an offence.[182]»

As for corruption, money laundering can also constitute participation in other crimes under the Rome Statute, such as aiding and abetting pillage.[183]

4.2.4 *Summary*

An expansion of the jurisdiction *ratione materiae* of the ICC has been established as an integral part of the Rome Statute to allow for the system to evolve and to reflect social, technological, and other changes as well as increasing international integration. However, new crimes to be introduced should be in line with the purpose of international criminal law, complementary to domestic prosecutions, and respectful of State sovereignty and the *nullum crimen sine lege* principle. Thus, this section proposes objective criteria for assessing a potential inclusion of a crime in the Rome Statute, namely the gravity of a crime, a persisting impunity gap, the existence of specific definitions in international law, and universal jurisdiction over a crime. To establish an additional threshold that ensures only the worst crimes are prosecuted before the ICC, contextual elements are proposed that require a widespread or systematic commission of the crime in question. Based on an assessment of each criterion, drug trafficking, illicit trade in arms and ammunition, migrant smuggling, corruption, and money laundering are identified as potential new crimes to be included in the Rome Statute. By contrast, illicit trade in natural resources and in cultural goods lack the necessary specificity and status in international law, and hence should not be subjected to ICC jurisdiction.

4.3 An International Tribunal Focused on Organized Crime

While international law can play a greater role in the prosecution of organized crime within the framework of the ICC, namely through (re-)interpretation of the Rome Statute or by amendments as outlined in the previous subchapters. Another option is the emergence of an independent international criminal law regime regarding organized crime based on a new Statute founding a new international tribunal. From a criminal law perspective, using existing

182 Based on UN Convention against Corruption 2003, Article 2(d) and (e); Palermo Convention 2000, Article 2(d) and (e).

183 This overlap is already inherent in the Palermo Convention and its Protocols; Gallagher and David 2014, 374.

structures generally increases legal certainty because of established jurisprudence. New regimes specifically tailored to certain crimes or situations can nevertheless be advantageous in terms of expertise and legitimacy. The weighting between the use of existing structures and the creation of a new regime, however, often depend on the political process, and thus shall not be part of this chapter. Current examples of similar processes include the ongoing discussions regarding the establishment of an Anti-Corruption Court, which will be subject of a special session of the UN General Assembly in April 2021, as well as an International Piracy Tribunal.[184] Options for the latter were explored in a report by the UN Secretary-General to the UNSC in 2010.[185] The establishment of specialized anti-piracy courts with international participation in Somalia have since been subject of debates within the Contact Group on Piracy off the Coast of Somalia, an international governance mechanism established in 2009.[186]

This subchapter represents a thought experiment asking the following question: *De lege ferenda*, if there was a new tribunal to be established in order to prosecute individuals for the commission of organized crime, what considerations would be relevant and what options in terms of jurisdiction, relation to domestic courts, mechanisms to trigger jurisdiction, as well as organizational setup should exist? For each of these areas, the distinction from or interaction with the ICC and other international bodies must also be considered. The discussion is meant to form the basis for a debate and does not claim completeness.

4.3.1 *Procedural Requirements for Jurisdiction*

A crucial feature of any international tribunal is its relationship with national jurisdictions. Historically, two concepts have been applied: complementarity, as enshrined in Article 17 of the Rome Statute, and primacy, as enshrined in Articles 9(2) and 8(2) the Statutes of the ICTY and ICTR, respectively. While under the complementarity regime a case is only admissible before the international tribunal if the national courts are "unwilling or unable genuinely to carry out investigation or prosecution,"[187] the regime of primacy allows the tribunal to request national courts to defer a case to its competence. The relationship with national jurisdictions is a determinant factor for the overall design of an international tribunal, with critical repercussions on jurisdictional

184 A/RES/74/276 2020.

185 S/2010/394 2010.

186 S/RES/2554 2020, para 18.

187 Rome Statute 1998, Article 17(1)(a).

limitations, mechanisms to trigger jurisdiction, as well as organizational setup. Thus, complementarity and primacy are examined in relation to prosecutions of organized crime. Furthermore, the implications on possible trigger mechanisms and preconditions to the exercise of jurisdiction are also discussed.

The primacy of the *ad hoc* tribunals was based on UNSC resolutions acting under Chapter VII of the UN Charter, and identifying the situations in the former Yugoslavia and Rwanda as concrete threats to international peace and security. This "shortcut"[188] making the Statutes binding upon all UN members without negotiation and ratification of any treaty was acceptable because of the limited mandates and jurisdiction of the *ad hoc* tribunals. Generally, however, primacy of international jurisdiction is seen to seriously compromise State sovereignty, and thus, the success at the Rome Conference is often attributed "in no small measure to the delicate balance developed for the complementarity regime."[189] For courts with a broad jurisdiction like the ICC, the complementarity principle also ensures an adequate "division of labor between national and international jurisdictions."[190] Primacy is therefore only preferable to complementarity in case of strictly limited jurisdiction and serious impediments of the national legal systems, such as in terms of infrastructure and expertise or regarding due process.[191] Furthermore, complementarity as applied by the ICC is not only an instrument to monitor State action but also provides for managerial interaction between the Court and States. This so-called "positive complementarity" approach allows the Court to encourage national proceedings or a State to refer a case to the ICC based on comparative advantage of international jurisdiction.[192]

Given the significant number of cases against members of organized criminal groups that have been prosecuted in national courts over the last decades (despite persisting impunity in many cases), primacy of an international tribunal for organized crime prosecutions does not seem feasible in terms of workload, political will, or even necessity. Therefore, adopting a provision of complementarity similar to Article 17 of the Rome Statute seems advisable. It should be noted, in addition, that Article 17 of the Rome Statute deems cases inadmissible that are not of sufficient gravity to justify further action by the Court.

188 Brown 1998, 387.

189 El Zeidy 2002, 969; see section 3.1.3.

190 El Zeidy 2008, 405.

191 Interestingly, there is a debate as to the adequacy of complementarity vis-à-vis the crime of aggression. See Trahan 2012.

192 Stahn 2008, 88.

Complementarity of an international tribunal, more than primacy, requires rules regarding mechanisms to trigger the jurisdiction of the Court. Whereas in the *ad hoc* tribunals the Prosecutor initiated investigations *ex officio*, Article 13 of the Rome Statute allows for States Parties to refer a situation or for the Prosecutor to initiate investigations *proprio motu* in case a jurisdictional nexus required by Article 12 exists, as well as for the UNSC to refer any situation to the Court.[193] All three mechanisms also seem reasonable for the envisaged new tribunal. However, situations such as the civil war in Syria have also revealed the limitations of these mechanisms. Syria is not a State Party to the Rome Statute and the UNSC has not referred the situation because of Russia's veto power despite the prevalence of international crimes. In a new tribunal, the dilemma posed by possible vetoes in the UNSC could be solved by a provision introducing an additional mechanism to refer a situation to the new tribunal, such as by a 2/3 or 4/5 majority in the UNGA, possibly coupled with the requirement of the supporting countries representing a certain percentage of the world or other population. The involvement of regional organizations in a similar way concerning situations in that region could also be considered.

Directly linked to the discussion of trigger mechanisms is the question of preconditions to the exercise of jurisdiction. Except for UNSC referrals, Article 12 of the Rome Statute establishes territorial and personal jurisdiction regarding the perpetrator.[194] Due to the transnational nature of organized crime, however, several international conventions have applied broader rules regarding jurisdiction. For example, the 1988 Drug Trafficking Convention in its Article 4 provides for territorial jurisdiction of a State based on the effects doctrine if the perpetrators conspired outside of its territory to commit a crime within its territory, as well as for jurisdiction of the custodial State unless the perpetrator is extradited. Furthermore, Article 15 of the Palermo Convention establishes jurisdiction based on the nationality of the victim, as well as on the effects doctrine regarding conspiracy to commit a crime and money laundering. Of course, these conventions do not establish international but national jurisdiction. However, it can be argued that granting jurisdiction over a crime to another nation State does not infringe more or less on State sovereignty than does granting jurisdiction to an international body. Therefore, the broader jurisdictional rules should inform the negotiations for a new international criminal law statute.

193 See section 3.1.1.

194 See section 3.1.2.

4.3.2 *Jurisdiction* Ratione Materiae

The jurisdiction *ratione materiae* of a new international criminal tribunal for the prosecution of organized crime would have to reflect its specific mission, as well as simultaneously be allowed to cover the entirety of the worst crimes of members of organized criminal groups while minimizing conflict with other institutions, namely the ICC. Thus, the new tribunal's jurisdiction *ratione materiae* should first include contextual elements constituting a certain gravity threshold and focusing the tribunal solely on organized crime; second, definitions of crimes that capture the core of the business of organized criminal groups; and third, definitions of crimes that are committed as a byproduct of the core criminal business, such as widespread or systematic violence against the civilian population, and which can be prosecuted before the tribunal only if there is a certain nexus to another crime in the Statute that forms the core business of organized crime. These three components are analyzed in detail in the following paragraphs.

First, the contextual elements must ensure that the crimes prosecuted before the new tribunal are committed by organized criminal groups or in the context of organized crime. Its Statute should therefore include a definition of an organized criminal group or of organized crime and require that the crimes be committed within the context of organized crime, or that the perpetrator be a member of such a group. A corresponding definition could be borrowed from the Palermo Convention that stipulates in Article 2:

> «"Organized criminal group" shall mean a structured group of three or more persons, existing for a period of time and acting in concert with the aim of committing one or more serious crimes or offences established in accordance with this Convention, in order to obtain, directly or indirectly, a financial or other material benefit;
>
> [...]
>
> "Structured group" shall mean a group that is not randomly formed for the immediate commission of an offence and that does not need to have formally defined roles for its members, continuity of its membership or a developed structure.[195]»

Moreover, to not overburden the new tribunal and to justify the interest of the international community in the crimes prosecuted, an element of required

195 Palermo Convention 2000, Article 2.

gravity or scope and possibly of transnationality could be considered. The latter is defined in the Palermo Convention in Article 3(2). Following this definition, the new tribunal could require that an offense be transnational, meaning

> «(a) It is committed in more than one State;
> (b) It is committed in one State but a substantial part of its preparation, planning, direction or control takes place in another State;
> (c) It is committed in one State but involves an organized criminal group that engages in criminal activities in more than one State; or
> (d) It is committed in one State but has substantial effects in another State.[196]»

Arguably, the requirement that a crime be committed by an organized criminal group implicitly includes the element of a systematic commission of the crime, as long as that crime constitutes the core business of the group. However, a gravity threshold that requires the commission of a crime "on a large scale"[197] as advanced by the ILC with regard to its Draft Code, would introduce an additional threshold, including for crimes accompanying the core business of organized criminal groups, such as violence and corruption.

Second, the crimes over which the new tribunal has jurisdiction should target the core business of organized crime; that is, the profit-generating activities. The scope will depend on the political consensus that can be reached, but could include: human trafficking, drug trafficking, illicit trade in arms and ammunition, illicit trade in wildlife and endangered species and other natural resources, illicit trade in cultural property, and migrant smuggling.[198] However, illicit trade in natural resources and cultural goods currently lack specificity in their definitions and universal jurisdiction, and thus might complicate the treaty negotiations.[199]

Third, for the new tribunal to be able to prosecute organized criminals for the entirety of their worst crimes, the new Statute should also include crimes that typically accompany organized criminal activities. Candidates for definitions based on existing international law are: corruption, money laundering, and crimes against humanity.[200] With regard to the latter, however, the new Statute could also adopt the enumerated acts of Article 7 of the Rome Statute,

196 *ibid.*, Article 3(2).
197 International Law Commission 1995.
198 See sections 4.2.3.1.–3. for more details on the legal status and definitions of these crimes.
199 See section 4.2.3.2.
200 See sections 4.2.3.4–5. and 3.2.2.2.5.

but replace the contextual elements with requirements as discussed above, creating a new category of crimes. In either case, adaptations, such as the deletion of the crime of apartheid and the adaptation of the groups named under the crime of persecution, would need to be discussed.

In part, the jurisdiction *ratione materiae* outlined above would create overlaps with the jurisdiction of the ICC, such as concerning human trafficking. Therefore, including a *ne bis in idem* provision regarding national courts as well as the ICC is crucial. Furthermore, a cooperation agreement should be sought at least between the Offices of the Prosecutor of the new tribunal and of the ICC to exchange information and avoid parallel investigations and prosecutions. Jurisdiction in a case in which no agreement on the *forum conveniens* can be reached and both tribunals are competent can either be based on the "first-come-first-served" principle (i.e., the first referral of a situation prevails), or a mechanism for conflict resolution could be established (e.g., a joint chamber of judges of both courts), or—to account for the partly political nature of such a decision—the Registrars, possibly together with judges of the Court, could determine which tribunal is best suited to consider the entirety of a certain situation.

4.3.3 *Organizational Setup*

In terms of organizational setup, the organs, seat, and relationship of the new tribunal with other international bodies, among others, must be regulated by its Statute. Regarding its organs, the tribunal will require a Presidency, Appeals, Trial and Pre-Trial Division, OTP, and a Registry as outlined in Article 34 of the Rome Statute. The new tribunal can also adopt a Victims and Witness Unit as well as the concept of the Trust Fund for Victims of the ICC.

Its relationships with the UN and the ICC will largely be determined by the jurisdiction *ratione materiae* of the tribunal as well as the mechanisms triggering its jurisdiction as outlined above.[201] A relationship agreement should be sought in addition to rules set out directly in the Statute and can be informed by previous agreements, such as between the ICC and other international tribunals and the UN.

Moreover, the negotiating parties will be required to choose between a permanent tribunal and one that convenes *ad hoc*, as well as between a centralized institution such as the ICC and a decentralized model. As is evident in the relationship between the ICC and the AU and certain African States in particular, a centralized court is easily conceived as biased, hampering

201 See sections 4.3.1.–2.

its perceived legitimacy and popular and political support.[202] Furthermore, criminal law is an especially sensitive legal area that is difficult to harmonize, interpret, and apply in a globally uniform manner. "States that have closer cultural and political affinity would probably be sooner inclined to establish a court that transcends the rigid division between international and transnational crimes."[203] However, establishing numerous regional tribunals to prosecute the globally prevalent and intercontinental phenomenon of organized crime does not seem advisable from a standpoint of expertise and efficiency. Nevertheless, a new Statute for an international tribunal could provide for a permanent Presidency, Registry, and OTP to ensure the continual and efficient work of the tribunal. Simultaneously, the Chambers, or only the Trial Chambers, could be established on an *ad hoc* basis with a regional composition of judges. Moreover, the place of the trials could be varied according to the countries involved.

4.4 Assessment

Shifting the focus to the *lex ferenda*, this chapter examined a range of legal developments that could facilitate an increased application of international criminal law to fill the impunity gap that remains regarding organized crime. The analysis considered three realms of development: the current framework of the core crimes of the Rome Statute, the framework of the Rome Statute more generally, and beyond. Three main observations can be made, which are elaborated as follows.

First, the legal regime of the Rome Statute as it stands is underexploited with regard to prosecutions of members of organized criminal groups. This is caused by interpretations conflicting with customary international law as well as international and national precedence and a lack of clarity of certain provisions. Among the most striking examples is pillage, where a restrictive reading of its elements contrary to customary understanding and precedence possibly shelters the exploitation of natural resources by consortia of militia and organized criminal groups from ICC jurisdiction. The exclusion of *dolus eventualis* from the mental element of any of the crimes under the Rome Statute frees perpetrators reconciling themselves with the highly likely commission of a crime from the threat of punishment. Moreover, the lack of guidance regarding the

202 Maasho 2017.

203 van der Wilt 2016, 9.

necessary elements to establish the crime of enslavement in cases of human trafficking precludes their prosecution.

Second, the Rome Statute bears significant potential for expansion in terms of jurisdiction *ratione materiae.* Article 121(5) of the Rome Statute provides for the creation of subregimes to the Rome Statute, expanding the ICC's jurisdiction *ratione materiae* only for those States Parties that have accepted the amendment. The provision could be applied to crimes not currently part of ICC jurisdiction *ratione materiae* that first cause major long-term harm to individuals and societies (i.e., are of comparable gravity to the core crimes); that second the international community still fails to tackle successfully; and that third are well defined in international law and subjected to universal jurisdiction by way of custom or treaty. Drug trafficking, the trade in arms and ammunition, and migrant smuggling fall into this category. The crimes of illicit trade in wildlife and endangered species as well as in cultural goods are not currently subjected to universal jurisdiction but meet the other criteria. The crime of illicit trade in natural resources beyond wildlife lacks a clear definition in international law. Corruption and money laundering are clearly defined, subject to universal jurisdiction by treaty, and largely go unpunished. However, the nature of their detrimental impact on individuals differs from other crimes. The negative consequences of corruption affect society as a whole more critically than individual victims, such as in the case of a small bribe. Money laundering is a secondary offense whose gravity is connected to both the primary offense as well as the laundering of its proceeds. In the Palermo Convention, for example, money laundering is only criminalized in connection with another crime under the Convention. This concept could be replicated in the Rome Statute. Furthermore, contextual elements can ensure that only crimes that are committed in a widespread or systematic manner fall under ICC jurisdiction.

Third, international criminal law provides the basis for the creation of suitable venues to address organized crime more successfully beyond the current framework set by the Rome Statute. A regime tailored to organized crime prosecutions was sketched *de lege ferenda* in terms of its relationship to national jurisdictions, mechanisms to trigger and preconditions to the exercise of jurisdiction, jurisdiction *ratione materiae,* and organizational setup. Apart from bundling the expertise required for the prosecution of organized crime through limited crime definitions as well as contextual elements specific to organized crime, the current shortcomings of the ICC system could be overcome. For example, involving other representative international bodies such as the UNGA or regional organizations in triggering the tribunal's jurisdiction in specific circumstances could remediate blockades of the UNSC. Positive complementarity coupled with a decentralized system of Chambers could decrease the perceived remoteness of international justice.

CHAPTER 5

Conclusion

In addition to longstanding historical links between organized crime and international criminal law *stricto sensu,* the subjection of organized crime to international justice has strong legal and empirical underpinnings. The possibilities of prosecutions of organized crime under international jurisdiction *de lege lata* are substantial and remain underexploited. *De lege ferenda,* international criminal law could play more crucial roles of various natures in international efforts to combat organized crime.

The purpose of international criminal law *stricto sensu* is stated in the Preamble of the Rome Statute as ensuring that "the most serious crimes of concern to the international community as a whole [do] [...] not go unpunished" and as "put[ting] an end to impunity for the perpetrators of these crimes."[1] Organized crime has serious detrimental effects on basic human rights, namely life, liberty, and security, and constitutes a threat to State sovereignty, such as by sparking extreme violence or undermining the legitimacy of State institutions because of its corruptive power. Over the last decades, many illicit markets have been flourishing and growing, and despite successful national prosecutions of members of organized criminal groups, organized crime still operates in a relatively low-risk environment; this is also because of a strategy to move operations to areas lacking State control. Thus, an impunity gap regarding organized crime persists that represents a concern for the international community as a whole.

According to this logic, a coalition led by Trinidad and Tobago in 1989 requested the UN to establish a permanent international criminal court with jurisdiction over illicit trafficking in narcotic drugs, marking the starting point of discussions that resulted in the establishment of the ICC. Various crimes perpetrated by organized criminal groups were discussed and preliminarily included in drafts throughout the processes leading up to the adoption of the Rome Statute in 1998. Therefore, their exclusion from the jurisdiction *ratione materiae* of the ICC as it stands was by no means automatic. The lack of a consensus in 1998 was rather caused by a lack of previous practice, the complexity of open questions, and severe time constraints regardless of the relevance

1 Rome Statute 1998, Preamble, para 4–5.

 | DOI:10.1163/9789004462588_006

of international criminal law *stricto sensu* for the containment of organized crime in general.

Furthermore, the changing nature of the crimes currently included in ICC jurisdiction, namely genocide, crimes against humanity, and war crimes, as well as organized crime has created new empirical links that complicate the fight of impunity for one without addressing the other. The increase in noninternational armed conflict, in asymmetric warfare, and in numbers of non-State armed groups as well as the internationalization of organized crime have led to growing interdependencies. While organized crime benefits from weak State institutions and a malfunctioning legal economy, non-State armed groups derive their financing from trade in illicit markets.

As a consequence, the relevance of international criminal law *stricto sensu* to organized crime is based on historical, legal, and empirical observations.

Furthermore, the analyses in this book have demonstrated that specific activities of organized criminal groups can satisfy the elements of genocide, crimes against humanity, and war crimes as well as be subjected to international justice *de lege lata*, although organized crime is not explicitly included in the jurisdiction *ratione materiae* of the ICC.

From a procedural perspective, the principle of complementarity—particularly the concept of positive complementarity—provides an effective mechanism to fill the current impunity gap vis-à-vis organized crime, as well as in the face of judicial and other corruption. Situations concerning organized crime can be referred both by the UNSC acting under Chapter VII of the UN Charter and qualifying organized crime as a threat to peace, or by a State Party to the Rome Statute based on a personal or territorial nexus. Especially if a crime has been perpetrated in several jurisdictions, the ICC can provide a solution to questions regarding the *forum conveniens*. Moreover, the ICC can try crimes in their entirety if one part has been consummated on the territory of a State Party.

With regards to jurisdiction *ratione materiae*, specific business activities as well as related conduct by organized criminal groups satisfy the elements of crimes in the Rome Statute. Human trafficking is explicitly included in the definition of enslavement as a crime against humanity. Moreover, the act of recruiting and removing trafficking victims from their homes can constitute other crimes under the Rome Statute, namely the forcible transfer of children and causing serious mental harm as acts of genocide, or deportation or forcible transfer as a crime against humanity or a war crime. Different types of exploitation of trafficked individuals, such as forced prostitution or organ trafficking, also satisfy the elements of individual acts of crimes against humanity and war crimes. Moreover, illicit exploitation and trade in natural resources and cultural goods constitute the war crime of pillage as well as possibly war crimes prohibiting the appropriation, seizure, destruction, and damage of specific goods and sites. Illicit trade in cultural goods can also amount to the crime of humanity of persecution. Although migrant smuggling does not fall under ICC jurisdiction in and of itself, migrant-related crimes such as their internment, inhumane living conditions, cruel treatment, or enslavement (such as reported from Libya) satisfy the elements of individual acts constituting both crimes against humanity and war crimes.[2] Organized crime-related violence, which is violence perpetrated by organized criminal groups not representing their core business activities and applied—for example—to intimidate the local population or put pressure on the government, can also constitute individual acts of genocide, crimes against humanity, or war crimes, such as murder/killing, extermination, rape, sexual violence, or causing serious bodily or mental harm.

Critically, these activities not only need to satisfy the elements of a specific criminal act included in the Rome Statute but also the contextual elements of the respective crime. Regarding genocide, the *dolus specialis* or intent to destroy a certain group, in whole or in part, is hardly compatible with the profit-focused rationality of organized crime, unless the targeted group constitutes competition. However, according to Article 6 of the Rome Statute, genocide cannot be committed against an economically or socially defined group. With regard to crimes against humanity under Article 7, a crime must be part of a widespread or systematic attack against a civilian population and be based on an organizational policy. While these elements may be met if the crime constitutes the core business of an organized criminal group, such as human trafficking, random acts of violence, for example, even if committed against a substantial number of individuals, do not satisfy the policy element, and thus do not fall under ICC jurisdiction *ratione materiae*. War crimes under Article 8 require that a specific crime is committed in the context of and is associated with an armed conflict. Again, organized criminal groups normally do not hold an interest in participating in conflicts. However, the crimes must be shaped by or be dependent on the armed conflict to fall under ICC jurisdiction.

Although the contextual elements impose important limitations on the applicability of the Rome Statute to organized crime, it must be noted that for members of organized criminal groups to incur criminal responsibility for a crime, the organized criminal group must not necessarily be the driving force behind it and its contextual elements. For example, an organized criminal group can commit a crime against humanity without being otherwise involved

2 Bensouda 2017; Office of the Prosecutor of the International Criminal Court 2019b, para 31.

in the attack it is part of if its members have knowledge of the attack. This is especially relevant in settings where armed groups and organized criminal groups converge.

In addition, members of organized criminal groups can incur individual criminal responsibility as a direct perpetrator of a crime, as well as for the commission of a crime jointly with or through another person. Furthermore, they can participate in the commission of a crime, such as by ordering it, aiding, abetting, and assisting its commission, or contributing in any other way to a group acting with a common purpose. Through participatory modes of liability, members of organized criminal groups can be held accountable; for example, for the provision of arms to a militia commonly known to commit war crimes. Moreover, according to rules regarding superior responsibility, leaders of organized criminal groups are criminally responsible for crimes committed by their subordinates if they knew of or consciously disregarded information indicating the commission of crimes. Crucially, for an individual to be held criminally responsible based on superior responsibility or for a contribution to a group acting with a common purpose, he or she is not required to have the requisite *mens rea* of the crime. In this case, for example, members of an organized criminal group can be convicted for genocide without proving the *dolus specialis*.

Thus, substantial aspects of organized crime satisfy the required procedural and material elements of ICC jurisdiction *de lege lata* and could be tried before the ICC.

Furthermore, based on the legal and empirical considerations discussed above, international criminal law *de lege ferenda* can further contribute to the prosecution of organized criminals. Within the current framework *ratione materiae*, adapting and specifying current interpretations based on customary international law and precedence can facilitate the application of the Rome Statute to organized crime as it stands. In particular, a specification of the crime of enslavement would add legal certainty, particularly the element of the exercise of the right of ownership to clearly encompass the legal definition of human trafficking. Similarly, a (re-)interpretation or abandonment of the mental element of pillage "for personal or private use" would clarify the scope of the provision, especially in hybrid settings where proceeds may be shared between individuals and armed groups. Re-interpreting the *mens rea* requirements of Article 30 of the Rome Statute to allow for *dolus eventualis* for certain crimes, in the sense of a perpetrator reconciling himself with a high probability that a crime will be committed, would conform to previous practice and enable the ICC to hold individuals responsible for acts short of virtual certainty to occur but where a volitional element is present.

In addition, the jurisdiction *ratione materiae* of the Rome Statute *de lege ferenda* can be extended to include crimes that are of comparable gravity to the three crimes discussed in Chapter 3, that currently remain unpunished, and that are clearly defined and subjected to universal jurisdiction in international law, by treaty or by custom. The crimes of drug trafficking, the illicit trade in arms and ammunitions, and migrant smuggling meet these criteria. The illicit trade in cultural goods as well as wildlife and endangered species are currently not subjected to universal jurisdiction. The crimes of corruption and money laundering differ from the three established crimes in the nature of their consequences, which affect a society collectively rather than causing individual suffering, but still meet the criteria.

Finally, the creation of a separate international criminal law regime tailored to organized crime could cluster the necessary expertise and overcome current shortcomings of the ICC. For example, substantial majorities of international bodies other than the UNSC could be allowed to refer situations to the tribunal, breaking possible blockades of the latter. Trials could be held in a decentralized manner reducing the remoteness of the proceedings vis-à-vis the affected populations.

Overall, international criminal law *stricto sensu* provides a pertinent mechanism to combat organized crime. While substantial activities of organized criminal groups already satisfy the jurisdictional requirements *de lege lata*, the *lex ferenda* holds vital additional potential.

References

Abadinsky, Howard. 2016. *Organized Crime.* Cambridge MA: Cengage Learning US.

Ad Hoc Committee on the Establishment of an ICC. 1995. *Report of the Ad Hoc Committee on the Establishment of an International Criminal Court*: General Assembly, Official Record, Fiftieth Session, Supplement No. 22, A/50/22: United Nations.

African Union. 2021. *List of countries which have signed, ratified/acceded to the African Union Convention on Preventing and Combating Corruption.* Available from <https://au.int/sites/default/files/treaties/36382-sl-AFRICAN%20UNION%20CONVENTION%20ON%20PREVENTING%20AND%20COMBATING%20CORRUPTION.pdf >. Accessed 14 April 2021.

Akande, Dapo. 2003. The Jurisdiction of the International Criminal Court over Nationals of Non-Parties: Legal Basis and Limits. *Journal of International Criminal Justice* 1:618–650.

Albanese, Jay S. 2011. *Organized crime in our times.* Oxfordshire, New York: Routledge.

Allain, Jean and John R.W.D. Jones. 1997. A Patchwork of Norms: A Commentary on the 1996 Draft Code of Crimes against the Peace and Security of Mankind. *European Journal of International Law* 8 (1):100–117.

Ambos, Kai. 1996. Observations from an International Criminal Law Viewpoint. *European Journal of International Law* 7 (4):519–544.

Ambos, Kai. 2001. "Verbrechenselemente" sowie Verfahrens-und Beweisregeln des Internationalen Strafgerichtshofs. *Neue Juristische Wochenschrift* 6:405–410.

Ambos, Kai. 2002. Superior responsibility. In *The Rome Statute of the International Criminal Court: A commentary*, edited by Antonio Cassese, Paola Gaeta and John R. W. D. Jones, 823–872. Oxford: Oxford University Press.

Ambos, Kai. 2009. Critical Issues in the Bemba Confirmation Decision. *Leiden Journal of International Law* 22 (04):715.

Ambos, Kai. 2014. *Treatise on International Criminal Law. Volume II: The Crimes and Sentencing*. Oxford: Oxford University Press.

Ambos, Kai. 2016. Article 25: Individual criminal responsibility. In *Rome Statute of the International Criminal Court: A commentary*, edited by Otto Triffterer and Kai Ambos, 979–1029. München: C.H. Beck.

Ambos, Kai and Anina Timmermann. 2014. Neue transnationale Verbrechen für das VStGB? In *Völkerstrafrechtspolitik: Praxis des Völkerstrafrechts*, edited by Christoph Safferling and Stefan Kirsch, 305–338. Berlin, Heidelberg: Springer.

Arimatsu, Louise and Hemi Mistry. 2012. Conflict Minerals: The Search for a Normative Framework. *Chatham House International Law Programme Papers* 01.

Arnold, Roberta and Stefan Wehrenberg. 2016. Article 8. Paragraph 2(b)(xxi). In *Rome Statute of the International Criminal Court: A commentary*, edited by Otto Triffterer and Kai Ambos, 469–476. München: C.H. Beck.

Aronowitz, Alexis A. 2001. Smuggling and Trafficking in Human Beings: The Phenomenon, the Markets that Drive it and the Organisations that Promote it. *European Journal on Criminal Policy and Research* 9:163–195.

Arvidsson, Amélie and Emelie Folkesson. 2010. *Corruption in the Judiciary: Balancing Accountability and Judicial Independence:* Örebro University, Örebro.

ASEAN. 2012. *ASEAN Plan of action to combat transnational crime.* Available from <https://asean.org/?static_post=asean-plan-of-action-to-combat-transnational-crime>. Accessed 26 June 2019.

Askin, Kelly D. 2003. Prosecuting Wartime Rape and Other Gender-Related Crimes under International Law: Extraordinary Advances, Enduring Obstacles. *Berkeley Journal of International Law* 21 (2):288–349.

Associated Press. 2007. Report: Mexican army used rape, torture in drug wars. *USA Today.*

Athanassopoulou, Ekavi. 2005. *Fighting organized crime in southeast Europe.* London: Routledge.

Austrian Permanent Representative to the United Nations. 1997. *Letter from the Austrian Permanent Representative to the United Nations to the United Nations Secretary-General accompanying the Draft International Convention against the Smuggling of Illegal Migrants*, A/52/357, 16 September 1997.

Badar, Mohamed Elewa. 2008. The mental element in the Rome Statute of the International Criminal Court: A commentary from a comparative criminal law perspective. *Criminal Law Forum* 19 (3–4):473–518.

Badar, Mohamed Elewa. 2009. Dolus eventualis and the Rome Statute without it? *New Criminal Law Review* 12 (3):433–467.

Badar, Mohamed Elewa. 2012. *The concept of Mens Rea in international criminal law: The case for a unified approach.* Oxford: Hart.

Bakowski, Piotr. 2013. *The EU response to organized crime. Library Briefing: Library of the European Parliament.* Available from <http://www.europarl.europa.eu/RegData/bibliotheque/briefing/2013/130625/LDM_BRI(2013)130625_REV1_EN.pdf>. Accessed 3 July 2019.

Ballentine, Karen and Heiko Nietzschke. 2003. *Beyond Greed and Grievance: Policy Lessons from Studies in the Political Economy of Armed Conflict.* Policy Report: International Peace Academy.

Balzer, Anthony J. 1996. *International Police Cooperation: Opportunities and Obstacles*: College of Police and Security Studies, Slovenia.

Bank for International Settlements. 2021. *BCBS Publications.* Available from <https://www.bis.org/bcbs/publications.htm?a=1&set=8&mp=any&pi=title&bv=list>. Accessed 14 April 2021.

Barbados, Dominica, Jamaica and Trinidad and Tobago. 1998. *Proposal regarding article 5. Crimes involving the illicit traffic in narcotic drugs and psychortropic substances.* A/

CONF.183/C.1/L.48, 3 July 1998. In: United Nations. 2002. United Nations Diplomatic Conference of Plenipotentiaries on the Establishment of an International Criminal Court, Rome, 15 June—17 July 1998: Official Records, Vol. III, Reports and other documents, A/CONF.183/13(Vol. Ill).

Bargent, James. 2017. *FARC Demobilization Faces Challenges Separating Narcos from Guerrillas*. InSight Crime: Analysis. Available from <http://www.insightcrime.org/news-analysis/farc-demobilization-faces-challenges-separating-narcos-from-guerrillas>. Accessed 3 July 2019.

Bassiouni, M. Cherif. 1988. A Policy-oriented Inquiry of "International Terrorism". In *Legal Responses to International Terrorism: U.S. Procedural Aspects,* edited by M. Cherif Bassiouni, xv–xvi. Dordrecht, Boston and London: Martinus Nijhoff Publishers.

Bassiouni, M. Cherif. 1993. The History of the Draft Code of Crimes Against the Peace and Security of Mankind. *Israel Law Review* 27 (1–2):247–267.

Bassiouni, M. Cherif. 1999. Negotiating the Treaty of Rome on the Establishment of an International Criminal Court. *Cornell International Law Journal* 32 (3):443–470.

Bassiouni, M. Cherif. 2002. A Global Perspective on Trafficking. In *In modern bondage: Sex trafficking in the Americas Central America and the Caribbean,* edited by International Human Rights Law Institute DePaul University College of Law, 92–97. Chicago Ill.

Bassiouni, M. Cherif. 2005. *The legislative history of the International Criminal Court.* Ardsley, N.Y.: Transnational Publishers.

Bassiouni, M. Cherif. 2013. *Introduction to international criminal law.* Leiden, Boston: Martinus Nijhoff Publishers.

Bassiouni, M. Cherif *et al.* 2010. Addressing International Human Trafficking in Women and Children for Commercial Sexual Exploitation in the 21st century. *Revue international de droit pénal* 81 (3):417–491.

Batchelor, Paul *et al.* 1997. *Open letter from European business leaders to OECD Economic Ministers.* Available from <https://www.transparency.org/news/pressrelease/business_leaders_call_on_oecd_ministers_to_act_against_international_corrup>. Accessed 3 July 2019.

Beauvallet, Olivier. 2012. Article 6: Crime de Génocide. In *Statut de Rome de la Cour Pénale Internationale: Commentaire article par article,* edited by Julian Fernandez, Xavier Pacreau and Lola Maze, 389–416. Paris: A. Pedone.

Bedner, Adriaan. 2002. Judicial corruption: Some consequences, causes and remedies. *Centre for International Legal Cooperation,* CILC Seminar in Tribute to Jan van Olden:14–21.

Beittel, June S. 2018. *Mexico: Organized Crime and Drug Trafficking Organizations.* Congressional Research Service Report, US Congress.

Benson, Jana S. and Scott H. Decker. 2010. The organizational structure of international drug smuggling. *Journal of Criminal Justice* 38 (2):130–138.

Bensouda, Fatou. 2017. *Statement of ICC Prosecutor to the UNSC on the Situation in Libya*: Office of the Prosecutor of the International Criminal Court. Available from <https://www.icc-cpi.int/Pages/item.aspx?name=170509-otp-stat-lib>. Accessed 3 July 2019.

Berg, Bradley E. 1996. The 1994 I.L.C. Draft Statute for an International Criminal Court: Principled Appraisal of Jurisdictional Structure. *Case Western Reserve Journal of International Law* 28 (2):221–264.

Bergal, Carina. 2011. The Mexican Drug War: The case for a non-international armed conflict classification. *Fordham International Law Journal* 24:1042–1088.

Berster, Lars. 2014. Article II. In *Convention on the prevention and punishment of the crime of Genocide: A commentary*, edited by Christian J. Tams, Lars Berster and Björn Schiffbauer, 79–156. München, Germany: C.H. Beck.

Bewley-Taylor, Dave and Mike Trace. 2006. *The International Narcotics Control Board: Watchdog or Guardian of the UN Drug Control Conventions?*. Report 7: The Beckley Foundation Drug Policy Programme.

Blakesley, C. L. 2008. Extraterritorial Jurisdiction. In *International Criminal Law*. Volume 2, edited by M. Cherif Bassiouni, 85–152: Transnational Publishers.

Boer, John de and Louise Bosetti. 2015a. *The Crime-Conflict "Nexus": State of the Evidence*. Occasional Paper 5. United Nations University Centre for Policy Research.

Boer, John de and Louise Bosetti. 2015b. *The Crime-Conflict Nexus: Identifying Gaps and Opportunities for Policy Research*. United Nations University Centre for Policy Research. Available from <https://cpr.unu.edu/the-crime-conflict-nexus-identifying-gaps-and-opportunities-for-policy-research.html>. Accessed 3 July 2019.

Boister, Neil. 1998. The Exclusion of Treaty Crimes from the Jurisdiction of the Proposed International Criminal Court: Law, Pragmatism, Politics. *Journal of Armed Conflict* 3:27–44.

Boister, Neil. 2003. 'Transnational Criminal Law'? *European Journal of International Law* 14 (5):953–976.

Bossuyt, Marc J. 1987. *Guide to the "Travaux préparatoires" of the International Covenant on Civil and Political Rights*. Dordrecht, Lancaster: Nijhoff.

Bothe, Michael. 2002. War Crimes. In *The Rome Statute of the International Criminal Court: A commentary*, edited by Antonio Cassese, Paola Gaeta and John R. W. D. Jones, 379–426. Oxford: Oxford University Press.

Bourgon, Stéphane. 2002. Jurisdiction Ratione Loci. In *The Rome Statute of the International Criminal Court: A commentary*, edited by Antonio Cassese, Paola Gaeta and John R. W. D. Jones, 559–569. Oxford: Oxford University Press.

Bovenkerk, Frank. 2003. Organized Crime in Former Yugoslavia. In *Global organized crime: Trends and developments*, edited by Dina Siegel, H. G. van de Bunt and Damián Zaitch, 45–50. Dordrecht, London: Kluwer Academic.

Brady, Sheelagh. 2012. *Organised Crime in Bosnia and Herzegovina: A silent war fought by an ambush of toothless tigers or a war not yet fought?*. Report. Organized Crime and Corruption Reporting Project.

Brown, Bartram. 1998. Primacy or Complementarity: Reconciling the Jurisdiction of National Courts and International Criminal Tribunals. *Yale Journal of International Law* 23:383–436.

Bukit, Mathew. 31 October 2016. Asean and Organized Crime. *Khmer Times*.

Bunch, Charlotte. 1995. Transforming Human Rights from a Feminist Perspective. In *Women's rights, human rights: International feminist perspectives*, edited by Julie Peters and Andrea Wolper, 11–17. New York, London: Routledge.

Bundeskriminalamt. 2009. *Organized Crime—National Situation Report*. Press-Release Summary.

Buscaglia, Edgardo and Jan van Dijk. 2003. Controlling organized crime and corruption in the public sector. *Forum on Crime and Society*. 3 (1/2).

Calderoni, Francesco. 2010. *Organized crime legislation in the European Union: Harmonization and approximation of criminal law, national legislations and the EU Framework Decision on the fight against organized crime*. Heidelberg, New York, N.Y.: Springer.

Cambridge Dictionary. 2019a. *Mutilate*. Available from <http://dictionary.cambridge.org/dictionary/english/mutilate>. Accessed 3 July 2019.

Cambridge Dictionary. 2019b. *Natural resources*. Available from <https://dictionary.cambridge.org/dictionary/english/natural-resources>. Accessed 3 July 2019.

Cambridge Dictionary. 2019c. *Organization*. Available from <https://dictionary.cambridge.org/dictionary/english/organization>. Accessed 3 July 2019.

Casey-Maslen, Stuart, Gilles Giacca, and Tobias Vestner. 2013. *The Arms Trade Treaty (2013)*. Geneva: Geneva Academy of International Humanitarian Law and Human Rights.

Cassese, Antonio. 1999. The Statute of the International Criminal Court: Some preliminary reflections. *European Journal of International Law* 10 (1):144–171.

Cassese, Antonio. 2002a. Crimes against Humanity. In *The Rome Statute of the International Criminal Court: A commentary*, edited by Antonio Cassese, Paola Gaeta and John R. W. D. Jones, 353–378. Oxford: Oxford University Press.

Cassese, Antonio. 2002b. Genocide. In *The Rome Statute of the International Criminal Court: A commentary*, edited by Antonio Cassese, Paola Gaeta and John R. W. D. Jones, 335–351. Oxford: Oxford University Press.

Cassese, Antonio. 2003. *International criminal law*. Oxford: Oxford University Press.

Cassese, Antonio. 2005. *International law.* Oxford: Oxford University Press.

Cassese, Antonio, Paola Gaeta and John R. W. D. Jones (eds.). *The Rome Statute of the International Criminal Court: A commentary*. Oxford: Oxford University Press.

Chossudovsky, Michel. 1999. Kosovo "Freedom Fighters" financed by organized crime. *Peace Research* 31 (2):29–42.

CITES. 2021. *List of Parties to the Convention.* Available from <https://www.cites.org/eng/disc/parties/index.php>. Accessed 14 April 2021.

Clark, David D. and Susan Landau. 2011. Untangling attribution. *Harvard National Security Journal* 2 (323).

Clark, Roger S. 2004. The United Nations Convention Against Transnational Organized Crime. *The Wayne Law Review* 50:161–184.

Commission on Human Rights. 1992. *Programme of Action for the Prevention of the Sale of Children, Child Prostitution and Child Pornography*: Annex Res. 1992/74, E/CN.4/Sub.2/1992/41.

Committee on Foreign Relations, United States Senate. 2009. *Afghanistan's Narco War: Breaking the link between drug traffickers and insurgents*: Report to the Committee.

Condorelli, Luigi and Santiago Villalpando. 2002. Referral and Deferral by the Security Council. In *The Rome Statute of the International Criminal Court: A commentary*, edited by Antonio Cassese, Paola Gaeta and John R. W. D. Jones, 627–655. Oxford: Oxford University Press.

Cormier, Paul *et al.* 2011. "The Problem from Hell": Examing the Role of Peace and Conflict Studies for Genocide Intervention and Prevention. In *Critical issues in peace and conflict studies: Theory, practice, and pedagogy*, edited by Thomas Matyók, Jessica Senehi and Sean Byrne, 271–289. Lanham, Md.: Lexington Books.

Cornell, Svante E. 2005. The Interaction of Narcotics and Conflict. *Journal of Peace Research* 42 (6):751–760.

Cottier, Michael. 2016. Article 8. War crimes. Part I: Introduction/General remarks. In *Rome Statute of the International Criminal Court: A commentary*, edited by Otto Triffterer and Kai Ambos, 304–321. München: C.H. Beck.

Cottier, Michael and Elisabeth Baumgartner. 2016. Article 8. Paragraph 2(b)(viii). In *Rome Statute of the International Criminal Court: A commentary*, edited by Otto Triffterer and Kai Ambos, 404–416. München: C.H. Beck.

Cottier, Michael and Sabine Mzee. 2016. Article 8. Paragraph 2(b)(xii). In *Rome Statute of the International Criminal Court: A commentary*, edited by Otto Triffterer and Kai Ambos, 476–503. München: C.H. Beck.

Council of Europe. 2014. *White paper on transnational organized crime.* Available from <https://edoc.coe.int/en/organised-crime/6837-white-paper-on-transnational-organised-crime.html>. Accessed 25 June 2019.

Council on Foreign Relations. 2013. *The Global Regime for Transnational Crime.* Available from <https://www.cfr.org/report/global-regime-transnational-crime>. Accessed 14 April 2021.

Crawford, James. 1994. The ilc's Draft Statute for an International Criminal Tribunal. *The American Journal of International Law* 88 (1):140–152.

Curtis, Glenn E. and Tara Karacan. 2002. *The nexus among terrorists, narcotics traffickers, weapons proliferators, and organized crime networks in Western Europe*. A Study Prepared by the Federal Research Division, Library of Congress under an Interagency Agreement with the United States Government. US Library of Congress, Federal Research Division.

de Wet, Erika. 2004. *The chapter VII powers of the United Nations Security Council*. Oxford: Hart.

Danileţ, Cristi. 2010. *Corruption and anti-corruption in the justice system*. Bucharest: Editura C. H. Beck.

Decker, Scott H. and Tim Bynum, Deborah Weisel. 1998. A tale of two cities: Gangs as organized crime groups. *Justice Quarterly* 15 (3):395–425.

del Ponte, Carla. 2005. *The dividents of international criminal justice: Address at Goldman Sachs*. Available from <http://www.icty.org/x/file/Press/PR_attachments/cdp-goldmansachs-050610-e.htm>. Accessed 3 July 2019.

Dennis, Morisol. 2006. National Identity and Violence: The Case of Colombia. In *Political Violence and the Construction of National Identity in Latin America*, edited by Will Fowler and Peter Lambert, 91–109: Palgrave Macmillan US.

Desmond Arias, Enrique. 2006. The Dynamics of Criminal Governance: Networks and Social Order in Rio de Janeiro. *Journal of Latin American Studies* 38 (2):293–325.

Dinan, Kinsey Alden. 2002. Trafficking in Women from Thailand to Japan: The Role of Organized Crime and Governmental Response. *Harvard Asia Quarterly* 6 (3):4–13.

Dishman, Chris. 2005. The Leaderless Nexus: When Crime and Terror Converge. *Studies in Conflict & Terrorism* 28 (3):237–252.

Dörmann, Knut. 2003. War Crimes under the Rome Statute of the International Criminal Court, with a Special Focus on the Negotiations on the Elements of Crimes. *Max Planck Yearbook of United Nations Law* 7:341–407.

Dörmann, Knut. 2016. Article 8. War Crimes: Article 8 para. 2: Meaning of 'war crimes'. In *Rome Statute of the International Criminal Court: A commentary*, edited by Otto Triffterer and Kai Ambos, 322–365. München: C.H. Beck.

DRC Panel of Experts. 2001. *Report of the Panel of Experts on the Illegal Explitation of Natural Resources and Other Forms of Wealth of the Democratic Republic of the Congo*, S/2001/357: UN Security Council.

Edman, Angela J. 2008. Crimes of Sexual Violence in the War Crimes Chamber of the State Court of Bosnia and Herzegovina: Successes and Challenges. *Human Rights Brief* 16 (1):21–28.

El Zeidy, Mohamed M. 2008. From Primacy to Complementarity and Backwards: (Re-)Visiting Rule 11bis of the ad hoc Tribunals. *International and Comparative Law Quarterly* 57 (02):403–415.

El Zeidy, Mohammed M. 2002. The Principle of Complementarity: A new Machinery to Implement International Criminal Law. *Michigan Journal of International Law* 23 (4):869–975.

Emmers, Ralf. 2002. The Securitization of Transnational Crime in ASEAN. *Institute of Defence and Strategic Studies Working Paper Series* (39).

Enck, Jennifer L. 2003. The United Nations Convention against Transnational Organized Crime: Is It All That It Is Cracked up to Be—Problems Posed by the Russian Mafia in the Trafficking of Humans. *Syracuse Journal of International Law and Commerce* 30:369–394.

Eser, Albin. 2002. Individual criminal responsibility. In *The Rome Statute of the International Criminal Court: A commentary*, edited by Antonio Cassese, Paola Gaeta and John R. W. D. Jones, 767–822. Oxford: Oxford University Press.

Eudes, Marina. 2012. Article 8: Crimes de Guerre. In *Statut de Rome de la Cour Pénale Internationale: Commentaire article par article*, edited by Julian Fernandez, Xavier Pacreau and Lola Maze, 481–535. Paris: A. Pedone.

Farrior, Stephanie. 1997. The International Law on Trafficking in Women and Children for Prostitution: Making it Live up to its Potential. *Harvard Human Rights Journal* 10:213–256.

Fearon, James D. 2004. Why Do Some Civil Wars Last so Much Longer than Others?. *Journal of Peace Research* 41 (3):275–301.

Feingold, David A. 2005. Human Trafficking. *Foreign Policy* 150:26–32.

Felbab-Brown, Vanda. 2009. Peacekeepers Among Poppies: Afghanistan, Illicit Economies and Intervention. *International Peacekeeping* 16 (1):100–114.

Fellmeth, Aaron X. 2016. The UN Protocol against the Illicit Manufacturing and Trafficking in Firearms, Their Parts and Components, and Ammunition 2001. In *International law and transnational organized crime*, edited by Pierre Hauck and Sven Peterke, 197–218. Oxford: Oxford University Press.

Ferencz, Benjamin B. 1992. International Criminal Code and Court: Where They Stand and Where They're Going. *Columbia Journal of Transnational Law* 30:375–400.

Fernandez, Julian, Xavier Pacreau and Lola Maze (eds.). 2012. *Statut de Rome de la Cour Pénale Internationale: Commentaire article par article*. Paris: A. Pedone.

Fifth UN Congress on Prevention of Crime and the Treatment of Offenders. 1975. *Report prepared by the Secreteriat*: Toronto, Canada.

Financial Action Task Force. 2012. *International Standards on Combating Money Laundering and the Financing of Terrorism and Proliferation: The FATF Recommendations.*

Finckenauer, James O. 2005. Problems of definition: What is organized crime? *Trends in Organized Crime* 8 (3):63–83.

Finckenauer, James O. and Yuri A. Voronin. 2001. *The threat of Russian Organized Crime*: National Institute of Justice.

Fletcher, George P. and Jens David Ohlin. 2005. Reclaiming Fundamental Principles of Criminal Law in the Darfur Case. *Journal of International Criminal Justice* 3 (3):539–561.

Ford, Stuard K. 2006. Crimes against Humanity at the Extraordinary Chambers in the Courts of Cambodia: Is a Connection with Armed Conflict Required. *UCLA Pacific Basin Law Journal* 24:125–200.

Funke, Andreas. 2014. Erga omnes-Pflichten. In: *Völkerrecht. Lexikon zentraler Begriffe und Themen*, edited by Burkhard Schöbener, 83–84. Heidelberg: C.F. Müller.

Gabor, Thomas. 2003. *Assessing the Effectiveness of Organized Crime Control Strategies: A Review of the Literature.* Report by the Research and Statistics Division, Department of Criminology of the Department of Justice, Canada.

Gallagher, Anne. 2001. Human Rights and the New UN Protocols on Trafficking and Migrant Smuggling: A Preliminary Analysis. *Human Rights Quarterly* 23:975–1004.

Gallagher, Anne. 2008. Using international human rights law to better protect victims of human trafficking: the prohibitions on slavery, servitude, forced labor and debt bondage. In *The theory and practice of international criminal law: Essays in honor of M. Cherif Bassiouni*, edited by Leila Nadya Sadat and Michael P. Scharf, 397–430. Leiden: Martinus Nijhoff.

Gallagher, Anne and Fiona David. 2014. *The international law of migrant smuggling.* New York, NY: Cambridge University Press.

Gallahue, Patrick. 2010. Targeted killing of drug lords: traffickers as members of armed opposition groups and/or direct participants in hostilities. *International Journal on Human Rights and Drug Policy* 1:15–34.

Gallahue, Patrick. 2011. Mexico's "War on Drugs"—Real or rethorical armed conflict?. *Journal of International Law of Peace and Armed Conflict* 24/1.

Gallant, Kenneth S. 2012. *Charles Taylor, Arms Dealers and Reparations.* Legal Studies Research Paper, University of Arkansas, William H. Bowen School of Law (12–08).

Gallimore, Tim. 2014. A Closer Look at Where Rwanda's Lethal Weapons Came From. *The Huffington Post.*

Garcia Sanchez, Guillermo J. 2017. A New International Legal Regime for a New Reality in the War Against Drugs. *Harvard International Law Journal Online.*

Gberie, Lansana. 2002. *War and Peace in Sierra Leone.* Diamonds, Corruption and the Lebanese Connection: The Diamonds and Human Security Project. Occasional Paper No. 6: Partnership Africa Canada.

Geraghty, Anne H. 2004. Universal Jurisdiction & Drug Trafficking: A Tool for Fighting One of the World's Most Pervasive Problems. *Florida Journal of International Law* 16:371.

Getz, Kathleen A. 2016. The Effectiveness of Global Prohibition Regimes. *Business & Society* 45 (3):254–281.

Gilsinan, Kathy. 2014. Interpol at 100: Does the World's Police Force Work? *The Atlantic.*

Global Initiative against Transnational Organized Crime. 2014. *Illicit Trafficking and Instability in Mali: Past, Present and Future.* Research Paper: Global Initiative against Transnational Organized Crime series on Governance, Democracy and State Fragility, January 2014.

Goy, Barbara. 2012. Individual Criminal Responsibility before the International Criminal Court. *International Criminal Law Review* 12 (1):1–70.

Guillén, Alejandra and Mago Torres, Marcela Turati. 2018. 2,000 clandestine graves: How a decade of the drug war turned Mexico into a burial ground. *The Intercept.*

Guymon, CarrieLyn Donigan. 2000. International Legal Mechanisms for Combating Transnational Organized Crime: The Need for a Multilateral Convention. *Berkeley Journal of International Law* 18 (1):53–101.

Hagan, Frank E. 1983. The Organized Crime Continuum: A Further Specification of a New Conceptual Model. *Criminal Justice Review* 8 (2):52–57.

Hagan, Frank E. 2006. "Organized Crime" and "Organized Crime": Indeterminate Problems of Definition. *Trends in Organized Crime* 9 (4):127–137.

Hall, Christopher K. 2016. Article 7. Crimes against humanity: ß) Trafficking. In *Rome Statute of the International Criminal Court: A commentary*, edited by Otto Triffterer and Kai Ambos, 246–247. München: C.H. Beck.

Hall, Christopher K. and Kai Ambos. 2016. Article 7. Crimes against humanity: Chapeau. In *Rome Statute of the International Criminal Court: A commentary*, edited by Otto Triffterer and Kai Ambos, 155–178. München: C.H. Beck.

Hall, Christopher K. and Joseph Powderly. 2016. Article 7. Crimes against Humanity: Persecution. In *Rome Statute of the International Criminal Court: A commentary*, edited by Otto Triffterer and Kai Ambos, 275–282. München: C.H. Beck.

Hall, Christopher K., Joseph Powderly, and Niamh Hayes. 2016a. Article 7. Crimes against Humanity: Subparagraphs (g) to (h). In *Rome Statute of the International Criminal Court: A commentary*, edited by Otto Triffterer and Kai Ambos, 206–226. München: C.H. Beck.

Hall, Christopher K., Joseph Powderly, and Niamh Hayes. 2016b. Article 7. Crimes against Humanity: Paragraph 3: Definition of gender. In *Rome Statute of the International Criminal Court: A commentary*, edited by Otto Triffterer and Kai Ambos, 292–294. München: C.H. Beck.

Hall, Christopher K. and Carsten Stahn. 2016. Article 7. Crimes against humanity: Subparagraphs (a)-(f). In *Rome Statute of the International Criminal Court: A commentary*, edited by Otto Triffterer and Kai Ambos, 178–206. München: C.H. Beck.

Hall, Christopher K. and Larissa van den Herik. 2016. Article 7. Crimes against humanity: Subparagraphs (i)-(j). In *Rome Statute of the International Criminal Court: A commentary*, edited by Otto Triffterer and Kai Ambos, 226–235. München: C.H. Beck.

Hamilton, Tomas. 2015. Regulating the arms trade: The potential of international criminal law. *International Crimes Database* (ICD Brief 17).

Harvard Research in International Law. 1935. Draft Convention on Jurisdiction with Respect to Crime. *The American Journal of International Law* 29:439–635.

Hauck, Pierre. 2016. Transnational Organised Crime and International Criminal Law. In *International law and transnational organized crime*, edited by Pierre Hauck and Sven Peterke, 448–469. Oxford: Oxford University Press.

Hauck, Pierre and Sven Peterke. 2010. Organized crime and gang violence in national and international law. *International Review of the Red Cross* 92 (878):407–436.

Hauck, Pierre and Sven Peterke. 2016. *International law and transnational organized crime*. Oxford: Oxford University Press.

Heintze, Hans-Joachim and Charlotte Lülf. 2016. The UN Protocol to Prevent, Suppress, and Punish Trafficking in Persons. In *International law and transnational organized crime*, edited by Pierre Hauck and Sven Peterke, 150–168. Oxford: Oxford University Press.

Higdon, Paul. 2001. Interpol's Role in International Police Cooperation. In *International police cooperation: A world perspective*, edited by Daniel J. Koenig and Dilip K. Das, 29–42. Lanham, MD: Lexington Books.

Holmes, John T. 2002. Complementarity: National Courts versus the ICC. In *The Rome Statute of the International Criminal Court: A commentary*, edited by Antonio Cassese, Paola Gaeta and John R. W. D. Jones, 667–686. Oxford: Oxford University Press.

Holvoet, Mathias. 2017. The Continuing Relevance of the Hybrid or Internationalized Justice Model: The Example of the Kosovo Specialist Chambers. *Criminal Law Forum* 28 (1):35–73.

Hosang, Hans Boddens. 1999. Article 8(2)(b)(xvi)—Pillaging. In *The International Criminal Court: The making of the Rome Statute: issues, negotiations, results*, edited by Roy S. Lee, 176–177. The Hague, London: Kluwer Law International.

Human Rights Committee of the UN General Assembly. 1998. *Report of the Human Rights Committee*. Volume I, A/53/40.

Human Rights Watch. 2017. *Events of 2016*. World Report 2017.

Human Rights Watch. 2019. *Events of 2018*. World Report 2019.

Hutchinson, Steven and Pat O'Malley. 2007. A Crime–Terror Nexus?: Thinking on Some of the Links between Terrorism and Criminality. *Studies in Conflict & Terrorism* 30 (12):1095–1107.

Inglis, Shelley Case. 2001. Expanding International and National Protections Against Trafficking for Forced Labour Using a Human Rights Framework. *Buffalo Human Rights Law Review* 7 (55).

International Atomic Energy Agency. 2020. *Convention on the Physical Protection of Nuclear Material: Status*. Available from <https://www-legacy.iaea.org/Publications/Documents/Conventions/cppnm_status.pdf>. Accessed 14 April 2021.

International Committee of the Red Cross. 2019. *Rule 4. Definition of Armed Forces*. IHL Database: Customary IHL. Available from <https://ihl-databases.icrc.org/customary-ihl/eng/docs/v1_rul_rule4#Fn_2751A911_00001>. Accessed 23 June 2019.

International Committee of the Red Cross. 2019. *Rule 38. Attacks Against Cultural Property*. IHL Database: Customary IHL. Available from <https://ihl-databases.icrc.org/customary-ihl/eng/docs/v1_rul_rule38>. Accessed 3 July 2019.

International Committee of the Red Cross. 2019. *Rule 39. Use of Cultural Property for Military Purposes*. IHL Database: Customary IHL. Available from <https://ihl-databases.icrc.org/customary-ihl/eng/docs/v1_rul_rule39>. Accessed 3 July 2019.

International Committee of the Red Cross. 2019. *Rule 40. Respect for Cultural Property*. IHL Database: Customary IHL. Available from <https://ihl-databases.icrc.org/customary-ihl/eng/docs/v1_rul_rule40>. Accessed 3 July 2019.

International Committee of the Red Cross. 2019. *Rule 41. Export and Return of Cultural Property in Occupied Territory*. IHL Database: Customary IHL. Available from <https://ihl-databases.icrc.org/customary-ihl/eng/docs/v1_rul_rule41>. Accessed 3 July 2019.

International Committee of the Red Cross. 2019. *Rule 52. Pillage*. IHL Database: Customary IHL. Available from <https://ihl-databases.icrc.org/customary-ihl/eng/docs/v1_rul_rule52#Fn_63_6>. Accessed 3 July 2019.

International Committee of the Red Cross. 2019. *Rule 94. Slavery and slave trade*. IHL Database: Customary IHL. Available from <https://ihl-databases.icrc.org/customary-ihl/eng/docs/v1_rul_rule94>. Accessed 3 July 2019.

International Labour Organization. 2005. *A global alliance against forced labour*. Global Report under the Follow-up to the ILO Declaration on Fundamental Principles and Rights at Work. Report of the Director-General. Report I (B).

International Law Commission. 1954. *Yearbook: Documents of the sixth session including the report of the Commission to the General Assembly*, A/CN.4/SER.A/1954/Add.l: United Nations.

International Law Commission. 1991. *Draft Code of Crimes against the Peace and Security of Mankind*. Titles and texts of articles adopted by the Drafting Committee: Parts One and Two; articles 1–26: Extract from the Yearbook of the International Law Commission 1991 Vol. I., A/CN.4/L.459 [and corr.1] and Add.1: United Nations.

International Law Commission. 1993. *Yearbook of the International Law Commission 1993 Vol. II(2): Report of the Commission to the General Assembly on the work of its forty-fifth session*, A/CN.4/SER.A/1993/Add.l (Part 2): United Nations.

International Law Commission. 1994a. *Draft Statute for an International Criminal Court with commentaries*: Extract of the Commission's report covering the work of its forty-sixth session, Yearbook of the International Law Commission, 1994, Vol. II Part 2, A/CN.4/SER.A/1994/Add.l (Part 2): United Nations.

International Law Commission. 1994b. *Report of the International Law Commission on the work of its forty-sixth session*: GAOR Supp. No. 10, A/49/10.

International Law Commission. 1995. *Report of the International Law Commission on the work of its forty-seventh session*, 2 May—21 July 1995, Official Records of the General Assembly, Fiftieth session, Supplement No.10, A/50/10: United Nations.

International Law Commission. 1996. *Report of the International Law Commission on the work of its forty-eighth session*, 6 May -26 July 1996, Official Records of the General Assembly, Fifty-first session, Supplement No.10, A/51/10: United Nations.

International Law Commission. 1997. *Report of the International Law Commission on the work of its forty-eighth session (1996)*: Topical summary of the discussion held in the Sixth Committee of the General Assembly during its fifty-first session prepared by the Secretariat, A/CN.4/479: United Nations.

International Narcotics Control Board. 2019. *Report 2018*, E/INCB/2018/1. United Nations Publication, Sales No. E.19.XI.2.

International Peace Institute. 2013. *A Dangerous Nexus: Crime, Conflict, and Terrorism in Failing States.* Vienna Seminar, November 2013.

INTERPOL. 2021. *Member countries.* Available from <https://www.interpol.int/en/Who-we-are/Member-countries>. Accessed 14 April 2021.

Jiménez de Aréchaga, Eduardo. 1978. International law in the past third of a century. *Hague Recueil* 159 (1):64–67.

Johnson, D. H. N. 1955. The Draft Code of Offenses against the Peace and Security of Mankind. *International and Comparative Law Quarterly* 4 (3):445–468.

Jordan, Jon B. 2000. Universal Jurisdiction in a Dangerous World: A Weapon for All Nations against International Crime. *Michigan State University-DCL Journal of International Law* 9:1.

Jurovics, Yann. 2012. Crimes contre l'humanité. In *Statut de Rome de la Cour Pénale Internationale: Commentaire article par article*, edited by Julian Fernandez, Xavier Pacreau and Lola Maze, 417–480. Paris: A. Pedone.

Kaul, Hans-Peter. 2002. Preconditions to the exercise of jurisdiction. In *The Rome Statute of the International Criminal Court: A commentary*, edited by Antonio Cassese, Paola Gaeta and John R. W. D. Jones, 583–616. Oxford: Oxford University Press.

Keenan, Patrick. 2015. The Problem of Purpose in International Criminal Law. *Michigan Journal of International Law* 37 (3):421–474.

Kemp, Walter. 2009. *Organized crime: a growing threat to security.* Commentary/Essays: Stockholm International Peace Research Institute. Available from <https://www.sipri.org/commentary/essay/2009/organized-crime-growing-threat-security>. Accessed 3 July 2019.

Kemp, Walter, Mark Shaw, and Arthur Boutellis. 2013. *The Elephant in the Room: How Can Peace Operations Deal with Organized Crime?:* International Peace Institute.

Kirsch, Philippe QC and Darryl Robinson. 2002. Reaching Agreement at the Rome Conference. In *The Rome Statute of the International Criminal Court: A commentary*, edited by Antonio Cassese, Paola Gaeta and John R. W. D. Jones, 67–91. Oxford: Oxford University Press.

Ki-moon, Ban. 2010. *Remarks to Security Council Debate on Organized Crime as a Threat to International Peace and Security.* Available from <https://www.un.org/sg/en/content/sg/speeches/2010-02-24/remarks-security-council-debate-organized-crime-threat-international>. Accessed 3 July 2019.

Kleemans, Edward R. 2014. Theoretical Perspectives on Organized Crime. In *The Oxford handbook of organized crime*, edited by Letizia Paoli, 32–52. Oxford: Oxford University Press.

Koh, Jae-myong. 2006. *Suppressing terrorist financing and money laundering.* New York: Springer.

Koker, Louis de and Mark Turkington. 2016. Transnational Organised Crime and the Anti-Money Laundering Regime. In *International law and transnational organized crime*, edited by Pierre Hauck and Sven Peterke, 241–263. Oxford: Oxford University Press.

Kreß, Claus. 2006. The Crime of Genocide under International Law. *International Criminal Law Review* 6 (4):461–502.

Kretschmer, Bernhard. 2016. Transnational Organized Crime and Cultural Property. In *International law and transnational organized crime*, edited by Pierre Hauck and Sven Peterke, 308–333. Oxford: Oxford University Press.

Krisch, Nico. 2012. Article 39. In *The Charter of the United Nations: A commentary*, edited by Bruno Simma, Hermann Mosler, Andreas Paulus and Eleni Chaitidou, 1272–1296. Oxford: Oxford University Press.

Kržalić, Armin (ed.). 2014. Study of Organised Crime in Bosnia and Herzegovina. Sarajevo: Centre for Security Studies BH.

Kubiciel, Michael and Anna Cornelia Rink. 2016. The UN Convention against Corruption. In *International law and transnational organized crime*, edited by Pierre Hauck and Sven Peterke, 219–237. Oxford: Oxford University Press.

Lacher, Wolfram. 2012. *Organized crime and conflict in the Sahel-Sahara region*: Carnegie Endowment for International Peace.

Lakhani, Nina. 8 December 2016. 'Impunity has consequences': the women lost to Mexico's drug war. *The Guardian.*

Laucci, Cyril. 2012. Article 28: Responsabilité des chefs militaires et autres supérieurs hierarchiques. In *Statut de Rome de la Cour Pénale Internationale: Commentaire article par article*, edited by Julian Fernandez, Xavier Pacreau and Lola Maze, 863–886. Paris: A. Pedone.

Levine, Harry G. 2003. Global drug prohibition: its uses and crises. *International Journal of Drug Policy* 14:145–153.

Lilley, Peter. 2006. *Dirty dealing: The untold truth about global money laundering, international crime and terrorism.* London: Kogan Page.

Liu, Zuozhen. 2016. Law and Ethics Protecting Cultural Objects. In *The Case for Repatriating China's Cultural Objects*, edited by Zuozhen Liu, 23–54. Singapore: Springer Singapore.

Louth, John and Lauren Twort. 2012. *Corruption, Cohesion and New Thinking. A Doctrinal Imperative for Sovereign Wealth Recovery Capabilities*. Royal United Services Institute for Defense and Security Studies.

Lundberg, Michael A. 2008. The plunder of natural resources during war: A war crime? *Georgetown Journal of International Law* 39 (3):495–525.

Maasho, Aaron. 1 February 2017. African Union leaders back mass exodus from International Criminal Court. *The Independent*.

MacGibbon, I.C. 1954. The Scope of Acquiescence in International Law. *British Yearbook on International Law* 143: 145–146.

Madsen, Frank G. 2016. The Historical Evolution of the International Coorperation against Transnational Organized Crime: An Overview. In *International law and transnational organized crime*, edited by Pierre Hauck and Sven Peterke, 3–23. Oxford: Oxford University Press.

Malone, Linda A. 2001. Economic Hardship as Coercion Under the Protocol on International Trafficking in Persons by Organized Crime Elements. *Fordham International Law Journal* 25 (54).

Marauhn, Thilo and Konstantin Meljnik. 2007. Völkerrechtliche Maßnahmen zur Bekämpfung von organisierter Kriminalität und Terrorismus. In *Organisierte Kriminalität und kriminelle Organisationen: Präventive und repressive Maßnahmen vor dem Hintergrund des 11. September 2001*, edited by Walter Gropp and Arndt Sinn, 479–502. Baden Baden: Nomos.

Marchuk, Irina. 2009. Confronting Blood Diamonds in Sierra Leone: The Trial of Charles Taylor. *Yale Journal of International Affairs* 4:87–99.

Marcus, Paul. 1998. The Challenge of Prosecuting Organized Crime in the United States: Procedural Issues. *The Wayne Law Review* 44:1379–1400.

Martin, Fanny. 2009. The notion of 'protected group' in the Genocide Convention and its application. In *The UN Genocide Convention: A commentary*, edited by Paola Gaeta, 112–127. Oxford: Oxford University Press.

Marty, Dick. 2011. *Inhuman treatment of people and illicit trafficking in human organs in Kosovo*, Doc. 12462: Council of Europe.

Matthews, Chris. 14 September 2014. *Fortune 5: The biggest organized crime groups in the world*. Fortune. Available from <http://fortune.com/2014/09/14/biggest-organized-crime-groups-in-the-world/>. Accessed 3 July 2019.

McAuley, Finbarr and J. Paul McCutcheon. 2000. *Criminal liability: A grammar*. Dublin: Round Hall Sweet & Maxwell.

McClean, David. 2007. *Transnational Organized Crime. A Commentary on the UN Convention and its Protocols*. Oxford: Oxford University Press.

McConville, Molly. 2000. A Global War on Drugs: Why the United States Should Support the Prosecution of Drug Traffickers in the International Criminal Court. *American Criminal Law Review* 37:75.

McCormack, Timothy L. H. and Gerry J. Simpson. 1994. The International Law Commission's Draft Code of Crimes against the Peace and Security of Mankind: An Appraisal of the Substantive Provisions. *Criminal Law Forum* 5 (1):1–55.

McDougall, Gay J. 1998. *Final Report of the Special Rapporteur on the Working Group on Contemporary Forms of Slavery: Systematic rape, sexual slavery and slavery-like practices during armed conflict*, E/CN.4/Sub.2/1998/13: UN Economic and Social Council.

McGregor, Michael A. 2009. Ending Corporate Impunity: How to Really Curb the Pillaging of Natural Resources. *Case Western Reserve Journal of International Law* 42:469–497.

McIllwain, Jeffrey Scott. 1999. Organized crime: A social network approach. *Crime, Law and Social Change* 32 (4):301–323.

Melzer, Nils. 2009. *Interpretative guidance on the notion of direct participation in hostilities under international humanitarian law*: International Committee of the Red Cross.

Milanovic, Marko. 2011. *How to Qualify the Armed Conflict in Libya?*. EJIL: Talk!, Blog of the European Journal of International Law. Available from: https://www.ejiltalk.org/how-to-qualify-the-armed-conflict-in-libya/. Accessed 3 July 2019.

Mitsilegas, Valsamis. 2011. *The Council Framework Decision on the Fight against Organised Crime: What can be done to strengthen EU legislation in the field?*. Note. PE 453.195: European Parliament, Directorate-General for Internal PoliciesPolicy Department C: Citizens' Rights and Constitutional Affairs.

Moreno Ocampo, Luis. 2006. *OTP response to communications received concerning Iraq*. Office of the Prosecutor of the International Criminal Court. Available from <https://www.legal-tools.org/doc/5b8996/pdf/>. Accessed 3 July 2019.

Nagle, Luz Estella. 2002. The Challenges of Fighting Global Organized Crime in Latin America. *Fordham International Law Journal* 26 (6):1649–1715.

Natarajan, Mangai. 2000. Understanding the structure of a drug trafficking organization: A conversational analysis. *Crime Prevention Studies* 11:273–298.

Naylor, R. T. 2003a. Predators, Parasites, or Free-Market Pioneers: Reflections on the Nature and Analysis of Prodit-Driven Crime. In *Critical reflections on transnational organized crime, money laundering, and corruption*, edited by Margaret E. Beare, 35–54. Toronto, London: University of Toronto Press.

Naylor, R. T. 2003b. Towards a General Theory of Profit-Driven Crimes. *British Journal of Criminology* 43 (1):81–101.

Nebehay, Stephanie. 23 December 2016. Mediterranean death toll is record 5,000 migrants this year. *Reuters*.

Nielsen, Christian Axboe. 2012. The Symbiosis of War Crimes and Organized Crime in the Former Yugoslavia. *Südosteuropa Mitteilungen* (3):6–17.

Obokata, Tom. 2010. *Transnational organised crime in international law.* Oxford: Hart.

OECD. 2006. *Recommendation of the Council on bribery and officially supported export credits.* OECD Council, 14 December 2006.

OECD. 2009a. *Recommendation of the Council for further combating bribery of foreign public officials in international business transactions.* OECD Council, 26 November 2009.

OECD.2009b. *Recommendation of the Council on tax measures for further combating bribery of foreign public officials in international business transactions.* OECD Council, 25 May 2009.

OECD. 2011. *OECD Guidelines for multinational enterprises.*

OECD. 2016. *Recommendation of the Council for development cooperation actors on managing the risk of corruption.* OECD Council, 16 November 2016.

OECD. 2019a. *Country reports on the implementation of the OECD Anti-Bribery Convention.* Available from <https://www.oecd.org/corruption/countryreportsontheimplementationoftheoecdanti-briberyconvention.htm>. Accessed 26 June 2019.

OECD. 2019b. *OECD Convention on Combating Bribery of Foreign Public Officials in International Business Transactions.* Available from <http://www.oecd.org/corruption/oecdantibriberyconvention.htm>. Accessed 26 June 2019.

Office of the Prosecutor of the International Criminal Court. 2007. *Prosecutor opens investigations in the Central African Republic.* Available from <https://www.icc-cpi.int/Pages/item.aspx?name=prosecutor+opens+investigation+in+the+central+african+republic>. Accessed 3 July 2019.

Office of the Prosecutor of the International Criminal Court. 2012. *Situation in Colombia: Interim Report.* Available from <https://www.icc-cpi.int/NR/rdonlyres/3D3055BD-16E2-4C83-BA85-35BCFD2A7922/285102/OTPCOLOMBIAPublicInterimReportNovember2012.pdf>. Accessed 3 July 2019.

Office of the Prosecutor of the International Criminal Court. 2013. *Report on Preliminary Examination Activities.* Available from <https://www.legal-tools.org/doc/dbf75e/pdf/>. Accessed 3 July 2019.

Office of the Prosecutor of the International Criminal Court. 2014a. *Prosecutor of the International Criminal Court, Fatou Bensouda, re-opens the preliminary investigations of the situation in Iraq.* Available from <https://www.icc-cpi.int//Pages/item.aspx?name=otp-Statement-iraq-13-05-2014>. Accessed 3 July 2019.

Office of the Prosecutor of the International Criminal Court. 2014b. *Policy Paper on Sexual and Gender-Based Crimes.* Available from <https://www.icc-cpi.int/iccdocs/otp/OTP-Policy-Paper-on-Sexual-and-Gender-Based-Crimes--June-2014.pdf>. Accessed 3 July 2019.

Office of the Prosecutor of the International Criminal Court. 2014c. *Situation on Registered Vessels of Comoros, Greece and Cambodia: Article 53(1) Report.* Available from <https://www.icc-cpi.int/iccdocs/otp/otp-COM-Article_53(1)-Report-06Nov2014Eng.pdf>. Accessed 3 July 2019.

Office of the Prosecutor of the International Criminal Court. 2015. *OTP Strategic Plan 2016–2018.* Available from <https://www.icc-cpi.int/iccdocs/otp/EN-OTP_Strategic_Plan_2016-2018.pdf>. Accessed 3 July 2019.

Office of the Prosecutor of the International Criminal Court. 2018. *Report on Preliminary Examination Activities.* Available from <https://www.icc-cpi.int/itemsDocuments/181205-rep-otp-PE-ENG.pdf>. Accessed 3 July 2019.

Office of the Prosecutor of the International Criminal Court. 2019a. *OTP Strategic Plan 2019–2021.* Available from <https://www.icc-cpi.int/Pages/item.aspx?name=otp-sp-2019>. Accessed 26 January 2021.

Office of the Prosecutor of the International Criminal Court. 2019b. *Seventeenth report of the Prosecutor of the International Criminal Court to the United Nations Security Council pursuant to UN Security Council Resolution 1970 (2011).* Available from <https://www.icc-cpi.int/itemsDocuments/190508-rep-otp-UNSC-libya-ENG.pdf>. Accessed 3 July 2019.

Orlova, Alexandra V. and James W. Moore. 2005. "Umbrellas" or "Building Blocks"?: Defining International Terrorism and Transnational Organized Crime in International Law. *Houston Journal of International Law* 27 (2):267–311.

Overseas Security Advisory Council of the US Department of State. 2012. *Rwanda Crime and Safety Report.* Available from <https://www.osac.gov/Content/Report/c956eafc-f90e-4ae0-aca7-15f4ad1c51c1>. Accessed 3 July 2019.

Paoli, Letizia. 2002. The Paradoxes of Organized Crime. *Crime, Law and Social Change* 37 (1):51–97.

Paoli, Letizia and Tom Vander Beken. 2014. Organized Crime: A Contested Concept. In *The Oxford handbook of organized crime*, edited by Letizia Paoli, 13–31. Oxford: Oxford University Press.

Papachristos, Andrew V. and Sandy Y. Zhao. 2015. Crime: Organized. In *International encyclopedia of the social & behavioural sciences*, edited by James D. Wright, 170–175: Elsevier Ltd.

Parashiv, Gavril. 2013. Conceptualizing Transnational Organized Crime. *Economics, Management and Financial Markets* 8 (2):173–178.

Parkinson, Joe and Ayla Albayrak, Duncan Mavin. 10 February 2015. Syrian "Monuments Men" Race to Protect Antiquities as Looting Bankrolls Terror. Culture Brigade, *The Wall Street Journal.*

Permanent Representatives of Argentina, Bolivia, Brazil, Colombia, Ecuador, Peru and Venezuela. *New York Declaration against Drug Trafficking and the Illicit Use of Drugs*, A/39/551.

Peterke, Sven and Joachim Wolf. 2016. International Humanitarian Law and Transnational Organised Crime. In *International law and transnational organized crime*, edited by Pierre Hauck and Sven Peterke, 381–405. Oxford: Oxford University Press.

Picarelli, John T. 2007. The Turbulent Nexus of Transnational Organised Crime and Terrorism: A Theory of Malevolent International Relations. *Global Crime* 7 (1):1–24.

Pictet, Jean S. 1958. *Commentary. IV Geneva Convention relative to the protection of civilian persons in time of war.* Geneva: International Committee of the Red Cross.

Piragoff, Donald K. and Derryl Robinson. 2016. Article 30. Mental element. In *Rome Statute of the International Criminal Court: A commentary*, edited by Otto Triffterer and Kai Ambos, 849–861. München: C.H. Beck.

Posadas, Alejandro. 2000. Combating Corruption under International Law. *Duke Journal of Comparative and International Law* 10:345–414.

Preparatory Committee on the Establishment of an ICC. 1996. *Report of the Preparatory Committee on the Establishment of an International Criminal Court*, Vol. I., UN General Assembly, Official Records, Fifty-first Session, Supplement No. 22, A/51/22.

Preparatory Committee on the Establishment of an ICC. 1998a. *Report of the intersessional meeting from 19 to 30 January 1998 in Zutphen, Netherlands*, A/AC.249/1998/L.13: UN General Assembly.

Preparatory Committee on the Establishment of an ICC. 1998b. *Report of the Preparatory Committee on the Establishment of an International Criminal Court*, Addendum, A/CONF.183/2/ADD.1: UN General Assembly.

Princeton Project on Universal Jurisdiction. 2001. *The Princeton principles on universal jurisdiction.* Princeton, NJ: Program in Law and Public Affairs, Princeton University.

Rapp, Stephen J. 2008. The compact model in international criminal justice: The Special Court for Sierra Leone. *Drake Law Review* 57:11–49.

Ratchford, Marina and Beth Allgood, Paul Todd. 2013. *Criminal Nature: The Global Security Implications of the Illegal Wildlife Trade*: International Fund for Animal Welfare.

Rauf, Tariq. 2016. *The entry into force of the Amendment to Convention on the Physical Protection of Nuclear Material.* Commentary: Stockholm International Peace Research Institute. Available from <https://www.sipri.org/commentary/2016/entry-force-amendment-convention-physical-protection-nuclear-material>. Accessed 26 June 2019.

Rayfuse, Rosemary. 1997. The Draft Code of Crimes against the Peace and Security of Mankind: Eating Disorders at the International Law Commission. *Criminal Law Forum* 8 (1):43–86.

Reiger, Caitlin. 2012. Hybrid and Internationalized Tribunals. In *The rules, practice, and jurisprudence of international courts and tribunals*, edited by Chiara Giorgetti, 283–322. Leiden, Boston: Martinus Nijhoff Publishers.

Reuter, Peter and Edwin M. Truman. 2004. *Chasing dirty money: The fight against money laundering*. Washington, DC, Great Britain: Institute for International Economics.

Robinson, Patrick. 2002. The missing crimes. In *The Rome Statute of the International Criminal Court: A commentary*, edited by Antonio Cassese, Paola Gaeta and John R. W. D. Jones, 497–526. Oxford: Oxford University Press.

Rome, Leigh. 2015. The Case for Prosecuting Arms Traffickers in the International Criminal Court. *Cordozo Law Review* 36:1149–1189.

Room, Robin and Peter Reuter. 2012. How well do international drug conventions protect public health? *The Lancet* 379:84–91.

Rosenne, Shabtai. 2000. Antecedents of the Rome Statute of the International Criminal Court Revisited. *International Law Studies* 75:387–420.

Ross, M. L. 2003. Oil, Drugs, and Diamonds: The Varying Roles of Natural Resources in Civil War. In *The political economy of armed conflict: Beyond greed and grievance*, edited by Karen Ballentine and Jake Sherman, 47–72. Boulder, London: Lynne Rienner Publishers.

Roxin, Claus. 1997. *Strafrecht: Allgemeiner Teil*. München: C. H. Beck.

Sainz-Borgo, Juan Carlos. 2012. The International Criminal Court, Drug Trafficking and Crimes against Humanity: A local Interpretation of the Rome Statute. *The Journal Jurisprudence*:373–388.

Saul, Ben. 2008. *Defining 'terrorism' to protect human rights*. Sydney Law School Legal Studies Research Paper, No. 08-125.

Schabas, William. 2016. *The International Criminal Court: A commentary on the Rome Statute*. Second edition. Oxford: Oxford University Press.

Schabas, William A. 2016. Article 6: Genocide. In *Rome Statute of the International Criminal Court: A commentary*, edited by Otto Triffterer and Kai Ambos, 127–143. München: C.H. Beck.

Schabas, William A. and Mohammed M. El Zeidy. 2016. Article 17: Issues of admissibility. In *Rome Statute of the International Criminal Court: A commentary*, edited by Otto Triffterer and Kai Ambos, 781–831. München: C.H. Beck.

Schabas, William A. and Giulia Pecorella. 2016. Article 12: Preconditions to the exercise of jurisdiction. In *Rome Statute of the International Criminal Court: A commentary*, edited by Otto Triffterer and Kai Ambos, 672–689. München: C.H. Beck.

Schloenhardt, Andreas. 2004. *Transnational organized crime and the International Criminal Court: Towards global criminal justice*. Speaking Notes: Australian Institute of Criminology Conference.

Schloenhardt, Andreas and Jessica E. Dale. 2012. Twelve years on: Revisiting the UN Protocol Against the Smuggling of Migrants by Land, Sea and Air. *Zeitschrift für öffentliches Recht* 67 (1):129–156.

Schneider, Friedrich and Ursula Windischbauer. 2008. Money laundering: Some facts. *European Journal of Law and Economics* 26 (3):387–404.

Serrano, Mónica. 2002. Transnational Organized Crime and International Security: Business as Usual? In *Transnational organized crime and international security: Business as usual?*, edited by Mats R. Berdal and Mónica Serrano, 13–36. Boulder, London: Lynne Rienner.

Shaw, Malcolm N. 2008. *International law*. Cambridge: Cambridge University Press.

Shelley, Louise. 2006. Organized Crime Groups: "Uncivil Society". In *Russian civil society: A critical assessment*, edited by Alfred B. Evans, Laura A. Henry and Lisa McIntosh Sundstrom, 95–109. Armonk, N.Y., London: M.E. Sharpe.

Shelley, Louise I. 1995. Transnational Organized Crime: An Imminent Threat to the Nation-State? *Journal of International Affairs* 48 (2):463–489.

Simma, Bruno, and Daniel-Erasmus Khan, Georg Nolte, Andreas Paulus (eds.). 2012. *The Charter of the United Nations. A commentary*. Oxford: Oxford University Press.

Sinha, Jay. 2001. *The history and development of the leading international drug control conventions*. Prepared for the Senate Special Committee on Illegal Drugs: Canada Parliamentary Research Branch, Law and Government Division.

Smillie, Ian, Lansana Gberie, and Ralph Hazleton. 2000. The Heart of the Matter. Sierra Leone, Diamonds and Human Security: Partnership Africa Canada.

Smith, Jennifer M. 2009. An International Hit Job: Prosecuting Organized Crime Acts as Crimes Against Humanity. *The Georgetown Law Journal* 97:1111–1154.

Snider, Thomas R. and Won Kidane. 2007. Combating Corruption through International Law in Africa: A Comparative Analysis. *Cornell International Law Journal* 40 (3):697–748.

Stahn, Carsten. 2008. Complementarity: A Tale of Two Notions. *Criminal Law Forum* 19 (1):87–113.

State Prosecutor of the Republic of Kosovo. 2016. *SPRK files two indictments related to Ogranised Crime and Money Laundering. Press release.* Available from <http://www.psh-ks.net/en/news/sprk-files-two-indictments-related-to-ogranised-crime-and-money-laundering>. Accessed 3 July 2019.

Stessens, Guy. 2000. *Money laundering: A new international law enforcement model.* Cambridge: Cambridge University Press.

Steward, David P. 1990. Internationalizing the War on Drugs: The UN Convention against Illicit Traffic in Narcotic Drugs and Psychotropic Substances. *Denver Journal of International Law and Policy* 18 (3):387–404.

Steward, James G. 2010. Atrocity, Commerce and Accountability. The International Criminal Accountability of Corporate Actors. *Journal of International Criminal Justice* 8 (1):313–326.

Stojarová, Vera. 2007. Organized Crime in the Western Balkans. *HUMSEC Journal* 1 (1):91–114.

Strydom, Hennie. 2016. Transnational Organized Crime and the Illegal Trade in Endangered Species of Wild Fauna and Flora. In *International law and transnational organized crime*, edited by Pierre Hauck and Sven Peterke, 264–286. Oxford: Oxford University Press.

Tanzi, Vito. 1998. *Corruption around the World: Causes, Consequences, Scope and Cures.* IMF Working Paper (63).

The Court of Bosnia and Herzegovina. 2021. *Statistics on judgements of the Court of Bosnia and Herzegovina for the period of 2004–2020.* Available from < http://www.sudbih.gov.ba/stranica/102/pregled>. Accessed 14 April 2021.

Tine, Abdoulaye. 2012. Article 13: Exercice de la compétence. In *Statut de Rome de la Cour Pénale Internationale: Commentaire article par article*, edited by Julian Fernandez, Xavier Pacreau and Lola Maze, 607–618. Paris: A. Pedone.

Tomuschat, Christian. 2006. The Legacy of Nuremberg. *Journal of International Criminal Justice* 4 (4):830–844.

Trahan, Jennifer. 2012. Is Complementarity the Right Approach for the International Criminal Court's Crime of Aggression—Considering the Problem of Overzealous National Court Prosecutions. *Cornell International Law Journal* 45 (3):569–601.

Triffterer, Otto, and Kai Ambos (eds.). 2016. *Rome Statute of the International Criminal Court: A commentary.* München: C.H. Beck.

Triffterer, Otto, and Morten Bergsmo, Kai Ambos. 2016. Preamble. In *Rome Statute of the International Criminal Court: A commentary*, edited by Otto Triffterer and Kai Ambos, 1–13. München: C.H. Beck.

Triffterer, Otto and Roberta Arnold. 2016. Article 28: B. Analysis and interpretation of elements. In *Rome Statute of the International Criminal Court: A commentary*, edited by Otto Triffterer and Kai Ambos, 1084–1103. München: C.H. Beck.

Tucci, Sabrina. 2012. Libya and International Refugee and Asylum Law: Addressing the Protection of Refugees and Migrants Displaced by the 2011 Conflict. *Oxford Monitor of Forced Migration* 2 (2):49–55.

UN Diplomatic Conference of Plenipotentiaries on the Establishment of an ICC. 1998. *Final Act of the UN Diplomatic Conference of Plenipotentiaries on the Establishment of an International Criminal Court*, A/CONF.183/10*.

UN General Assembly. 1948. *Genocide: draft Convention (E/794) and report of the Economic and Social Council*: amendment to Article 2 / Syria, A/C6/234.

UN General Assembly. 2000. *Report of the Ad Hoc Committee on the Elaboration of a Convention against Transnational Organized Crime on the work of its first to eleventh sessions*, Addendum: Interpretative notes for the official records (*travaux préparatoires*) of the negotiation of the United Nations Convention against Transnational Organized Crime and the Protocols thereto: UNGA 55th Session, A/55/383/Add.1.

UN General Assembly Ad Hoc Committee on the Elaboration of a Convention against Transnational Organized Crime. 1998. *Proposals and contributions received from governments.* A/AC.254/5.

UN General Assembly Sixth Committee. 1989. *Summary Record of the 38th Meeting*: UNGA 44th Session, A/C.6/44/SR.38.

UN General Assembly Third Committee. 1996. *Question of the elaboration of an international Convention against organized transantional crime*. Letter dated 24 September 1996 from the Minister for Foreign Affairs of the Republic of Poland addressed to the Secretary-General: UNGA 51st Session, A/C.3/51/7.

UN Office of Counter-Terrorism. 2019. *International Legal Instruments*. Available from <http://www.un.org/en/counterterrorism/legal-instruments.shtml>. Accessed 3 July 2019.

UN Security Council. 1992. *Note by the President of the Security Council*, S/23500.

UN Security Council. 2006. *Reports of the Secretary-General on the Sudan*. Meeting record, S/PV.5589.

UN Security Council. 2010. *Report of the Secretary-General on possible options to further the aim of prosecuting and imprisoning persons responsible for acts of piracy and armed robbery at sea off the coast of Somalia, including, in particular, options for creating special domestic chambers possibly with international components, a regional tribunal or an international tribunal and corresponding imprisonment arrangements, taking into account the work of the Contact Group on Piracy off the Coast of Somalia, the existing practice in establishing international and mixed tribunals, and the time and resources necessary to achieve and sustain substantive results*, S/2010/394.

UN Security Council. 2011. *Maintenance of international peace and security*. Meeting record, S/PV.6668.

UN Security Council. 2012. *Threats to international peace and security*. Meeting record, S/PV.6760.

UN Security Council Panel of Experts. 2000. *Report of the Panel of Experts appointed pursuant to Security Council resolution 1306 (2000), paragraph 19, in relation to Sierra Leone*, S/2000/1195: United Nations.

UN Support Mission in Libya. 2016. *"Detained and dehumanized": Report on human rights abuses against migrants in Libya*: UN High Commissioner for Human Rights.

UNEP and INTERPOL. 2016. *The Rise of Environmental Crime: A Growing Threat to Natural Resources, Peace, Development and Security*.

UNEP, MONUSCO, and OSESG. 2015. *Experts' background report on illegal exploitation and trade in natural resources benefitting organized criminal groups and recommendations on MONUSCO's role in fostering stability and peace in eastern DR Congo*: Final report.

UNESCO. 2021. *The 1970 Convention. States Parties*. Available from <https://en.unesco.org/fighttrafficking/1970>. Accessed 14 April 2021.

Üngör, Uğur Ümit and Mehmet Polatel. 2011. *Confiscation and destruction: The Young Turk seizure of Armenian property*. London: Continuum.

United Nations. 2015. *Combating Transnational Organized Crime Through Better International Cooperation.* 13th UN Congress on Crime Prevention and Criminal Justice. Available from <http://www.un.org/en/events/crimecongress2015/pdf/Factsheet_4_International_cooperation_EN.pdf>. Accessed 3 July 2019.

United Nations Economic and Social Council. 1953. *Slavery, the Slave Trade and Other Forms of Servitude*: Report of the Secretary-General, E/2357.

United Nations Meetings Coverage and Press Releases. 1996. *Terrorism should be 'core crime' of proposed international court, India tells Preparatory Committee.* Press Release L/2766, 27 March 1996.

United Nations Treaty Collection. 2019. Multilateral Treaties Deposited with the Secretary-General. Status of Treaties. Available from <https://treaties.un.org/Pages/ParticipationStatus.aspx?clang=_en>. Accessed 19 June 2019.

UNODC. 2005. *World Drug Report 2005*. Volume I. United Nations Publication, Sales No. E.05.XI.10.

UNODC. 2010. *The Globalization of Crime: A Transnational Organized Crime Threat Assessment.* United Nations Publication, Sales No. E.10.IV.6.

UNODC. 2011a. *Organized Crime and Instability in Central Africa: A threat assessment.* Vienna: United Nations Office on Drugs and Crime.

UNODC. 2011b. *The role of organized crime in the smuggling of migrants from West Africa to the European Union.* Vienna: United Nations Office on Drugs and Crime.

UNODC. 2012. *Global report on trafficking in persons.* Vienna: United Nations Office on Drugs and Crime.

UNODC. 2015. *Compendium of international legal instruments on corruption.* Vienna: United Nations Office on Drugs and Crime.

UNODC. 2018a. *Global report on trafficking in persons.* Vienna: United Nations Office on Drugs and Crime.

UNODC. 2018b. *Global report on trafficking in persons—in the context of armed conflict.* Vienna: United Nations Office on Drugs and Crime.

UNODC. 2018c. *World Drug Report 2018.* United Nations Publication, Sales No. E.18.XI.9.

UNODC. 2019. *UN Convention against Corruption Country Profiles.* Available from <https://www.unodc.org/unodc/en/treaties/CAC/country-profile/index.html>. Accessed 26 June 2019.

UNODC. 2021. *Drug-related resolutions and decisions 2010 to 2019.* Available from <https://www.unodc.org/unodc/en/commissions/CND/Resolutions_Decisions/Resolutions-Decisions_2010-2019.html>. Accessed 14 April 2021.

UNODC and League of Arab States. 2016. *Regional Programme for the Arab States (2016–2021) to prevent and combat crime terrorism and health threats and strengthen criminal justice systems in line with human rights standards.* Programme Report.

UNODC and League of Arab States. 2018. *2018 Progress Report.* Regional Programme for the Arab States (2016–2021) to prevent and combat crime terrorism and health threats and strengthen criminal justice systems in line with human rights standards.

U.S. Attorney's Office Eastern District of New York. 2019. *Joaquin "El Chapo" Guzman, Sinaloa Cartel Leader, Convicted of Running a Continuing Criminal Enterprise and Other Drug-Related Charges.* 12 February 2019. Available from <https://www.justice.gov/usao-edny/pr/joaquin-el-chapo-guzman-sinaloa-cartel-leader-convicted-running-continuing-criminal>. Accessed 24 June 2019.

van den Herik, Larissa and Daniëlla Dam-de Jong. 2011. Revitalizing the antique war crime of pillage: The potential and pitfalls of using international criminal law to address illegal resource exploitation during armed conflict. *Criminal Law Forum* 15:237–273.

van der Wilt, Harmen. 2014. Trafficking in Human Beings, Enslavement, Crimes Against Humanity: Unravelling the Concepts. *Chinese Journal of International Law* 13 (2):297–334.

van der Wilt, Harmen. 2016. Expanding Criminal Responsibility in Transnational and International Organised Crime. *Groningen Journal of International Law* 4 (1):1–9.

van Dijk, Jan. 2007. Mafia markers: Assessing organized crime and its impact upon societies. *Trends in Organized Crime* 10 (4):39–56.

van Duyne, Petrus C. 1996. The phantom and threat of organized crime. *Crime, Law and Social Change* 24:341–377.

van Schaack, Beth and Ron Slye. 2007. A concise history of International Criminal Law. *Santa Clara Law Digital Commons Faculty Publications*:7–47.

von Hebel, Herman and Derryl Robinson. 1999. Crimes within the jurisdiction of the Court. In *The International Criminal Court: The making of the Rome Statute: issues, negotiations, results*, edited by Roy S. Lee, 79–126. The Hague, London: Kluwer Law International.

von Lampe, Klaus. 2002. Afterword: Organized Crime Research in Perspective. In *Upperworld and underworld in cross-border crime*, edited by Petrus C. van Duyne, Klaus von Lampe and Nokos Passas, 189–198.

von Lampe, Klaus. 2016. *Organized crime: Analyzing illegal activities, criminal structures, and extra-legal governance*: SAGE Publications.

von Schorlemer, Sabine. 2016. *Kulturgutzerstörung. Die Auslöschung von Kulturerbe in Krisenländern als Herausforderung für die Vereinten Nationen.* Baden-Baden: Nomos.

Verwimp, Philip. 2005. An economic profile of peasant perpetrators of genocide: Micro-level evidence from Rwanda. *Journal of Development Economics* 77 (2):297–323.

Violante, Luciano. 2000. Foreword. In *The antimafia: Italy's fight against organized crime*, edited by Alison Jamieson, ix–xi. Basingstoke: Macmillan.

Vogler, Richard and Shahrzad Fouladvand. 2016. The Convention against Illict Traffic in Narcotic Drugs and Psychotropic Substances 1988 and the Global War on Drugs. In *International law and transnational organized crime*, edited by Pierre Hauck and Sven Peterke, 107–125. Oxford: Oxford University Press.

Vorrath, Judith. 2014. From War to Illicit Economies. Organized Crime and State-building in Liberia and Sierra Leone. *SWP Reserach Paper* (13).

Vrdoljak, Ana Filipa. 2016. The Criminalisation of the Illicit Trade in Cultural Property. *Selected Works*:1–25.

Washburn, John. 1999. The negotiation of the Rome Statute for the International Criminal Court and international lawmaking in the 21st century. *Pace International Law Review* 11 (2):361–377.

Wenger, Claude F. 1987. Article 53. In *Commentary on the additional protocols of 8 June 1977*, edited by Yves Sandoz, Christophe Swinarski and Bruno Zimmermann, 639–650. Geneva: Martinus Nijhoff Publishers.

Wennmann, Achim. 2014. Negotiated Exits from Organized Crime?: Building Peace in Conflict and Crime-affected Contexts. *Negotiation Journal* 30 (3):255–273.

Werle, Gerhard and Florian Jessberger. 2005. 'Unless otherwise provided': Article 30 of the ICC Statute and the Mental Element of Crimes under International Criminal Law. *Journal of International Criminal Justice* 3:35–55.

Werle, Gerhard and Florian Jessberger. 2014. *Principles of International Criminal Law.* Third edition. Oxford: Oxford University Press.

West, Jessica. 2006. The political economy of organized crime and State failure: The nexus of greed, need and grievances. *Innovations: A Journal of Politics* 6:1–17.

West Sands Advisory LLP. 2012. *Europe's Crime-Terror Nexus: Links between terrorist and organised crime groups in the European Union*, PE 462.503: European Parliament Committee on Civil Liberties, Justice and Home Affairs.

Winter, Renate. 2010. The Special Court for Sierra Leone. In *International criminal justice: Law and practice from the Rome Statute to its review*, edited by Roberto Bellelli, 101–121. Farnham: Ashgate.

Wise, Edward M. 1999. Aut dedere aut iudicare: The duty to extradite or prosecute. In *International criminal law*, edited by M. Cherif Bassiouni, 15. Ardsley, N.Y.: Transnational Publishers.

Wolfrum, Rüdiger. 2012. Chapter I Purposes and Priciples. Article 1. In: *The Charter of the United Nations. A commentary*, edited by Bruno Simma Daniel-Erasmus Khan, Georg Nolte, Andreas Paulus, 107–120. Oxford: Oxford University Press.

Working Group on Arbitrary Detention. 1993. *Report of the Working Group on Arbitrary Detention*, E/CN.4/1993/24: United Nations.

Working Group on Contemporary Forms of Slavery. 1998. Report of the Working Group on Contemporary Forms of Slavery on its twenty-first session, E, CN.4/Sub.2/1998/14: United Nations Economic and Social Council.

Yacoubian, George S. 2007. The most international of international crimes: Toward the incorporation of drug trafficking into the subject matter jurisdiction of the International Criminal Court. In *Criminology research focus*, edited by Karen T. Froeling, 277–294. New York: Nova Science Publishers.

Zimmermann, Andreas. 2016. Article 5. Crimes within the jurisdiction of the Court. In *Rome Statute of the International Criminal Court: A commentary*, edited by Otto Triffterer and Kai Ambos, 111–126. München: C.H. Beck.

Zimmermann, Andreas and Robin Geiß. 2016a. Article 8. War Crimes: Paragraphs (2) (b)(xiii)—(xvi). In *Rome Statute of the International Criminal Court: A commentary*, edited by Otto Triffterer and Kai Ambos, 436–454. München: C.H. Beck.

Zimmermann, Andreas and Robin Geiß. 2016b. Article 8. War Crimes: Paragraphs 2 (c)-(f) and para. 3: War crimes committed in an armed conflict not of an international character. In *Rome Statute of the International Criminal Court: A commentary*, edited by Otto Triffterer and Kai Ambos, 528–579. München: C.H. Beck.

Index

a. Tribunals, courts and international institutions

b. Key international conventions

c. International legal norms and concepts

d. Elements of organized crime

e. Case studies and examples

Printed in the United States
by Baker & Taylor Publisher Services